TREATY PROFILES

By Peter H. Rohn
WORLD TREATY INDEX, *5 volumes*

WITHDRAWN
University of
Illinois Library
at Urbana-Champaign

NOT TO BE TAKEN FROM LIBRARY...
FOR ROOM USE ONLY

TREATY PROFILES

Peter H. Rohn

CLIO BOOKS

Santa Barbara, California • Oxford, England

© 1976 by The University of Washington

All rights reserved.
This book or any part thereof may not be reproduced in any form without written permission of the publishers.

Library of Congress Card Number 73-83352
ISBN Clothbound 5-Volume Set 0-87436-125-7
ISBN Clothbound 6-Volume Set 0-87436-132-X
ISBN Clothbound Volume 6 — 0-87436-131-1

American Bibliographical Center — Clio Press, Inc.
2040 Alameda Padre Serra
Santa Barbara, California

European Bibliographical Center — Clio Press, Inc.
Woodside House
Hinskey House Hill
Oxford OX1 5BE, England

Manufactured in the United States of America

Contents

Introduction   1
1. Acknowledgements   3
2. Purpose   4
   a. Research   4
   b. Teaching   4
   c. Reference   5
3. Context   5
   a. Magnitudes in Law   5
   b. Quantification in International Law   5
   c. Law in International Politics   8
4. Data Base   10
   a. Coverage   10
   b. Definitions   11
5. Format   12
   a. Overall Design   12
   b. Columns   13
   c. Lines   16
6. Use   18
   a. Partners   18
   b. Time Trends   20
   c. Topics   22
   d. Institutions   22
   e. Registration   23
   f. Combinations   24
7. Problems   27
   a. Overall Structure   27
   b. Data Choices   28
   c. Data Permutations   29
8. Reference   30
   a. WORLD TREATY INDEX   30
   b. Individual Printouts   31
9. Thesaurus   32
   a. Parties and Treaties   32
   b. State Groups   37
   c. Treaty-Active Institutions   38
   d. Treaty-Passive Institutions   39
   e. National Treaty Collections   42
   f. Topics   43
   g. Abbreviations   45

Treaty Profiles   49

Introduction

1. Acknowledgements

Both the WORLD TREATY INDEX and the present TREATY PROFILES rely on the same computerized data bank, and everybody who has contributed in some way to that data bank has thereby also contributed to the PROFILES. I need not repeat here the names of the many helpful people identified in the introduction to the INDEX, and I am repeating only the institutions through which their help materialized: National Science Foundation, University of Washington, American Society of International Law, International Studies Association, American Political Science Association and numerous foreign universities and governments in the following countries: Argentina, Australia, Austria, Brazil, Canada, France, Great Britain, Greece, Guatemala, Iran, Israel, Italy, Japan, Malta, Mexico, Morocco, Netherlands, New Zealand, Philippines, Poland, Portugal, South Africa, Spain, Switzerland, Taiwan, Turkey and West Germany.

While the people named in the above institutions have contributed to the common data base, and thus to both INDEX and PROFILES, there are some individuals and institutions that should be singled out for their help toward PROFILES. In 1959 the Rockefeller Foundation gave me a post-doctoral grant at Columbia University and thus subsidized my first large-scale attempt at a quantitative taxonomy of international law and organization. Kenneth Thompson at the Rockefeller Foundation as well as Leland Goodrich and Philip Jessup, both then at Columbia University, helped me greatly with their advice and also with the patience they displayed toward my many false starts. For similar patience and encouragement, and for many hours of dependable research assistance, I am grateful to Ellen Colburn Rohn. Neither I nor any of them knew it at the time, and even today it may not be obvious, but some seemingly futile work I did at Columbia was a necessary detour on the way to the present PROFILES. Some years later, when PROFILES was in nearly publishable shape, the Rockefeller Foundation again gave me a chance to lean back from the daily hassles of academic life and spend a month at the Bellagio Center to tie the remaining loose ends together. The most helpful person in Bellagio was William Olson, both as Director of the Center and as one of the earliest contemporary theoreticians of international relations.

Chapter 3, which puts the whole effort into a theoretical perspective, is a radically revised version of a guest lecture I gave at the University of Madrid, and I am grateful to Manuel Medina Ortega and Manuel Diez de Velasco for their thoughtful and stimulating comments and to the Fulbright program for providing the opportunity. A later version of the same chapter has been read by James Easterling, Dana Fischer, John Gamble, Gunther Hartmann and Gary Scott, and has benefited from their comments.

At the University of Washington, the first prototype of a computer program to generate the various national treaty profiles from our data bank was designed by Elton Hay in 1964-65. Subsequently, Charlene Haug took over all programming tasks related to PROFILES and radically redesigned Elton Hay's original program. She has also made dozens of major and hundreds of minor revisions over the years. The only research assistant on the Treaty Project closely associated with PROFILES has been John Panattoni. His quiet efficiency has helped in many ways throughout the final phase. Laura Braendlein, with an exemplary combination of cheer and thoroughness, has typed and re-typed numerous drafts and has helped with proofreading and double-checking facts and figures.

The publisher, Lloyd Garrison of ABC-Clio Press, has been as patient with my delays and as cooperative with my idiosyncrasies as any publisher can be, and the associate editor, Barbara Phillips, has made many valuable suggestions regarding form and style. The publisher's team has done what only those can appreciate who have been involved in a similar effort to translate a computer program of expert-baffling complexity into a different print format on a different machine over a thousand miles away.

Finally, there is one basic distinction which needs to be made between the working modes of WORLD TREATY INDEX and TREATY PROFILES. While of course I alone am responsible for the end result in both cases, the extent of my personal involvement has varied greatly among different tasks at different times. In particular, I delegated to others many operational responsibilities for the INDEX in several confluent assembly lines, but I have tried to come as close as possible to doing everything myself for the PROFILES.

TREATY PROFILES

2. Purpose

This book has several purposes for research, teaching and reference—all regarding the international aspects of law and politics.

a. Research

(1) International Law

Few quantitative studies have as yet been published in international law, and none has made a general claim to the effect that magnitudes are relevant to a comprehension of the field as a whole. To make and to substantiate that claim is the primary purpose of TREATY PROFILES. A former Judge on the Permanent Court of International Justice and Professor at Harvard Law School, Manley Hudson, once said about quantification in international law (as related by Julius Stone):

"Count, by all means count, but count the things that count."

TREATY PROFILES is an attempt to take that quip seriously, as it deserves, and to work it out in systematic detail. The book tries to achieve that purpose not by argument but by experiment. It does not polemicize against traditional scholarship. It simply offers a new approach—to be blended with conventional approaches where appropriate and to be ignored where irrelevant.

(2) Political Science/International Studies

Both fields, where they overlap and where they diverge, devote only a small and shrinking portion of their total activity to international law. The second major purpose of this book is to help reverse that trend—not by trying to revive the Grotian tradition, but by showing a new way to use international law as a resource in political science research.

There are two main reasons why interest in international law has declined among political scientists, one having to do with method and the other with substance. In method, international law has fallen behind the post-war trend toward quantification. In substance, political scientists have re-discovered the fact that international law is not terribly effective as a restraint on governmental behavior.

This book should weaken the methodological argument and bypass the substantive argument against international law. The methodological point is obvious. If unquantifiability is what has prevented international law from being studied by contemporary political scientists, that barrier has now fallen. The substantive point is more complicated. International law can be viewed not only in the traditional-normative way as a body of rules, but it can also be seen as a set of clues about the reality of world politics. The two views can co-exist and indeed do co-exist in this book. Whatever international law is to international lawyers, political scientists can use it as an epistemological gold mine. The real world of international politics is outside our Platonic cave, and we cannot observe it directly. We have to choose among various shadows of reality, such as newspaper reports, statesmen's memoirs, foreign office bulletins, military budgets and UN votes. Among the shadows that give us clues about the real world, international law is remarkably useful because it optimizes three crucial conditions: universality, meticulosity and parsimony, as will be shown in detail in Chapter 3.

b. Teaching

This is only a subsidiary purpose of TREATY PROFILES but pre-print copies have been used in political science courses and seminars. Aside from the obvious uses in courses in international law and international organization, selected treaty profiles have been used in general survey courses in international relations, in regional studies (e.g., Latin America, Middle East, Eastern and Western Europe, etc.) and in methodology courses. Students learn to combine treaty data with other information they find about foreign areas and world affairs. Students in fields outside political science can learn how to compare treaty data to similarly structured data with which they are familiar, e.g., international trade patterns in economics, multinational corporate ties in business administration, various events in diplomatic history, treaty maps in geography (analogous to air traffic maps and other thematic maps) and cross-cultural affinities in sociology and the humanities.

c. Reference

The profiles have not been designed for documentary reference but they can be and have been used for that purpose, especially in combination with the WORLD TREATY INDEX. Librarians and other reference users will develop their own methods, but some guidelines are suggested in Chapter 8.

3. Context

Law in general and international law in particular have experienced hardly a ripple from the wave of quantification and computer application that has swept through the other social sciences in recent decades. Yet it is obvious that quantity does matter in law as elsewhere. Law, indeed, is saturated with quantitative notions throughout, and without them it is difficult to see how any part of the legal process could function properly—from the first moment in legislation to the ultimate effect of law on people.

a. Magnitudes in Law

Quantitative notions begin their long-range effect even before law can be created. Legislators cannot be elected without counting votes and computing the required majorities. Once elected, they cannot make laws without an analogous process of vote counting. Important legislative actions require special majorities. This is a quantitative way of defining non-routine circumstances, e.g., overriding a presidential veto, impeaching a president or amending the Constitution. It is obviously more difficult to obtain special majorities of 67% or 75% than the simple 50% plus one vote, and the increment in difficulty is a measure of how important the matter appeared to the framers of the Constitution—again, a quantitative concept.

The laws themselves are replete with quantitative notions, e.g., speed limits for vehicular traffic, purity standards for food and drugs, proportion of pollutants in industrial effluents, stress limits for bridges, occupancy limits for buildings, age limits for drinking and voting, minimum wages and maximum work hours and on and on—the list of examples can be extended through any set of statutes.

Adjudication, too, has quantitative aspects. The goddess of justice in ancient Rome was depicted as holding a scale to weigh the evidence, and the symbol has been adopted and endorsed by many later legal systems all over the world. But we need not resort to folklore for evidence of quantification in the adjudicative phase of the legal process. In procedure, there are such quantitative concepts as majority or unanimity of jurors, preponderance of evidence, number of precedents and many more. As Chief Justice Marshall developed the basic idea of unconstitutionality in *Marbury v. Madison*, he used a quantitative distinction in a hypothetical example. It would be unconstitutional, he wrote, for a court to convict a person of treason on the testimony of *one* witness rather than *two* as required by the Constitution. As we go from procedure to substance in adjudication we find a wide range of examples—comparative negligence, substantial performance, habitual domicile, irreparable damage—all turning on questions of degree, quantity or relative weight in the interplay of several factors.

Finally, the result of a court's decision may appear in yes/no form (guilty/innocent, win/lose), but the impact often depends heavily on quantitative notions. In civil cases, the amount of money awarded by a court is an obvious example; in criminal cases, the amount of the fine or the length of the prison term. Quantitative notions linger on even beyond the courthouse in the aftermath of the legal process. Prison discipline and probation rely on tests expressed in quantitative terms, and even clemency and pardon stem from an awareness of the ultimate relativity of crime and punishment.

b. Quantification in International Law

If magnitudes are relevant to domestic law, we should expect the same for international law. Its primary sources are treaties and custom accepted as law. Evidence for custom requires that a practice be long and continuous as well as shared by an overwhelming majority of countries—both quantitative concepts. Substantive rules of customary international law, likewise, abound with quantitative notions in critical places, e.g., effective and continuous occupation subsequent to discovery, the width of the territorial sea, compensation for expropriation, proportionality of reprisals, unreasonable delay as denial of justice, substantial territory controlled by insurgents claiming recognition and a

TREATY PROFILES

revolutionary government's effective control of a country.

Treaties contain quantitative concepts as often as statutes. The 1969 Vienna Convention on the Law of Treaties includes a wide variety of quantitative and quasi-quantitative notions in the procedures for the making and applying of treaties, for instance: "two-thirds" vote on a treaty text at an international conference (Article 9); conditions "similar" to ratification (Art. 18); "number" of parties in acceptance of reservations (Art. 20); "extent" of application of earlier treaty (Art. 30); general rule and "supplementary" means of interpretation (Art. 31 and 32); meaning which "best" reconciles texts in different languages (Art. 33); "essential" basis of consent (Art. 44 and 48); "manifest" violation and "fundamental" importance of a rule of internal law (Art. 46); "number" of remaining parties falling below number necessary for entry into force (Art. 55); "material" breach and "radical" change in terminating a treaty (Art. 60); "number" of conciliators and "length" of time periods in settlement procedures (Art. 66 and Annex) and "extent" of conflict with peremptory norm of general international law (Art. 71).

Quantitative concepts abound also in substantive provisions, e.g., most-favored nation clause, import and export quotas, expense sharing formulas, claims settlements, fair and reasonable avoidance of double taxation, military or civilian preponderance in use of atomic energy, definitions of dangerous goods, formulas for sharing multiple uses of international rivers and other resources and innumerable lists of goods with quantitative limits in trade agreements and customs conventions.

International arbitration and adjudication also rely heavily on quantitative notions. Let us take some examples from one of the most often cited arbitrations, the *Island of Palmas* case (1928). Arbitrator Huber of the Permanent Court of Arbitration, who had just previously been President of the Permanent Court of International Justice (1925-1927) and was clearly one of the world's leading international lawyers in the inter-war period, used the following quantitative concepts in decisive parts of his award:

> The acts of . . . display of Netherlands sovereignty . . . are not numerous, and there are considerable gaps in . . . continuous display.
>
> . . . manifestations of sovereignty over a small and distant island . . . cannot be expected to be frequent [or going] back to a very far distant period.
>
> . . . sovereignty may be the outcome . . . of a progressive intensification of state control.
>
> . . . no evidence . . . of display of sovereignty over the island by Spain . . . such as might counterbalance . . . the manifestations of Netherlands sovereignty.
>
> . . . absence . . . of conflict . . . during more than two centuries.
>
> It remains now to be seen whether the United States [can] bring forward an equivalent or stronger title.
>
> An inchoate title however cannot prevail over a definite title.

Another well-known arbitration is that of the Tinoco claims between Great Britain and Costa Rica (1923), in which the arbitrator was Chief Justice Taft of the United States Supreme Court. He used the following terms in decisive passages:

> Some 61,000 votes were cast for Tinoco and 259 for another candidate.
>
> For a full two years Tinoco . . . administered . . . Costa Rica.
>
> Undoubtedly recognition . . . is an important evidential factor. [List of 20 recognizing countries follows.]
>
> . . . non-recognition loses something of evidential weight [if determined not by factual inquiry but by policy].
>
> Such non-recognition cannot outweigh the evidence.
>
> Their action under the treaty could not be of more weight . . . than the policy of the United States, already considered.
>
> Moreover . . . all the signatories but Nicaragua. . . .
>
> The evidential weight of such non-recognition. . . .
>
> To sustain this view a great number of decisions in English and American courts are cited.
>
> . . . indicating a general acquiescence of nations in such a rule.

Similar examples come from adjudication proper, namely, from the International Court of Justice. In the *Reparation for Injuries* case (1949), the ICJ referred to the United Nations as the "supreme" type of international organization, implying the relevance of a gradation among IGO's and leaving undecided the question of whether an IGO of a lesser grade would have "international personality" under otherwise similar circumstances. The ICJ reasoned in that case that the UN could not function if it had to involve "the concurrent action . . . of 58 or more Foreign Offices." Would it have affected the ICJ's conclusion if only 20 or 10 or 3 foreign offices had been involved? Presumably so, or why else would the Court specify 58, which at that time represented most of the world's countries? We read later in the same case that

> the Court's opinion is that 50 States, representing the vast majority of the international community, had the power [to establish an objective international personality].

We may assume, again, that if the UN had been established by less than 50 States (how many less?), or if 50 (or later 58) had been less than the overwhelming majority of all the States of the world (how much less?), the Court would have concluded differently.

Alternatively, let us assume that the ICJ, as one of the six principal organs of the UN, wanted to come to a pro-UN decision if at all legally possible and to support that decision with the best possible argument. In that case, the example shows that the Court chose a quantitative argument to support a unanimous decision that was institutionally important to the whole UN structure including the Court itself. Both assumptions lead to the notion that magnitudes are relevant to judicial decisions in international law.

Space permits only a few examples from other ICJ cases, merely to show that the *Reparation for Injuries* case is not exceptional in its reliance on quantitative notions.

Corfu Channel case (merits). The volume and multinational composition of traffic in the channel helped the

Court determine that it was an international waterway: "During the period of one year nine months, the total number of ships was 2,884. The flags of the ships are Greek, Italian, Roumanian, Yugoslav, French, Albanian and British. . . . These figures . . . do not include the large number of vessels which went through the Strait without calling at Corfu at all." (ICJ Reports, 1949, p. 29.)

Asylum case. The existence of regional international customary law for the Americas depended in part on quantitative evidence as to its uniformity within the Western Hemisphere: "The Convention of 1933 has . . . been ratified by not more than 11 States and the Convention of 1939 by 2 States only." (ICJ Reports, 1950, p. 277.)

Rights of U.S. Nationals in Morocco case. The intention of France and the practice of other States to abolish foreign extraterritorial rights were found by the Court to be evident from: ". . . agreements negotiated by France with some 20 foreign States . . . [and] . . . eleven of the (12) Powers have abandoned their capitulatory privileges." Also, in US-French correspondence the Court contrasted "isolated expressions" with the "general tenor." (ICJ Reports, 1952, pp. 195, 197, 200.)

Voting Procedure case (Advisory Opinion, Judge Lauterpacht's Dissenting Opinion). The Court considered "degree of supervision" a substantive question unrelated to the voting procedure by which the UN General Assembly could exercise that supervision, for instance, by unanimity, two-thirds majority or simple majority. Judge Lauterpacht disagreed: ". . . the less exacting method of voting adds to the stringency and the degree of supervision. . . . The procedure of voting determines the degree of supervision." (ICJ Reports, 1955, pp. 94-95.)

Temple case (merits). One major issue was the notoriety of certain maps which could have prompted Siam (Thailand) to protest against the boundary as shown on those maps relied on by Cambodia: "The full original distribution consisted of about 160 sets of 11 maps each. Fifty sets . . . were allocated to the Siamese Government." (ICJ Reports, 1962, p. 23.)

South West Africa case (second phase, 1966). In reviving a jurisdictional issue from the preliminary phase to bar consideration of the merits, the Court relied on the frequency and normalcy of League practice to solve Mandate-related questions politically rather than judicially: ". . . in the 27 years of the League, all questions were . . . resolved by the Council . . . and no cases were referred to the Permanent Court." (ICJ Reports, 1966, p. 45.) Judge Jessup's much cited dissent argued for an evaluation on the merits and was concerned with "measuring" the degree of performance by South Africa of its obligations as Mandatory: "In my opinion, such a standard exists and could have been . . . utilized by the Court in . . . measuring . . . the Mandatory's obligation." (ICJ Reports, 1966, p. 433.)

Continental Shelf case. As in the *Asylum* case, the Court had to decide at what point treaty law mirrors a practice so uniform as to constitute customary international law and said in reference to the Geneva Convention on the Law of the Sea: ". . . the number of ratifications and accessions . . . is, though respectable, hardly sufficient" to convert a conventional rule into a general rule of international law. Quantitative notions abound also in the numerous references of the Court to "just and equitable shares" of the continental shelf. (ICJ Reports, 1969, p. 42 et passim.)

Barcelona Traction case. The Court relied on frequency to show that non-Belgian diplomatic protection for Barcelona Traction was available: ". . . the Canadian government made numerous representations . . ." and to contrast the lack of Belgian treaty rights in this case with normal contemporary practice: "States ever more frequently provide for such protection [of foreign investment] . . . in the form of multilateral or bilateral treaties." (ICJ Reports, 1970, pp. 44, 47.)

In spite of all the cited examples in domestic and international law, it can be argued that quantitative notions are relevant only to the *content* of law, not to its *existence*. It is one thing, for instance, to see the relevance of quantity in a claims settlement, but it is quite another to count the number of claims settlement treaties and to impute to that number some significance for our understanding of international law. And yet, that precisely is one claim on which the merit of the treaty profiles depends.

Let us call the two kinds of quantification "exegetical" and "existential." Where non-legal facts are counted (e.g., ships in the Corfu Channel), quantification is exegetical. Where elemental particles of law themselves are being counted (e.g., treaties, court cases), quantification is existential. Both types of quantification occur in the cited examples, and there are some hybrids. The extent of UN membership, as used by the ICJ in the *Reparation for Injuries* case, shows existential quantification for exegetical purposes. So is the number of ratifications of the Havana Convention in the *Asylum* case, and of the Geneva Convention in the *Continental Shelf* case, but we need not limit ourselves to court cases.

Quantification goes beyond jurisdiction. International law is more than a set of tools with which to win (or lose) a case in court. There is existential quantification in much of our thinking and writing about international law, and always has been from the pre-Grotians to the present. Numbers play a key role in any theory of relevance. Academic and governmental discussions of international legal topics ebb and flow with the number of external events that prompt the discussions—expropriation, hijacking, terrorism, oil embargo, war crimes, micro-statehood, space satellites. The list is endless and the correlation of discussion with external events is nearly perfect. Large numbers translate into importance, small numbers into triviality. Andorra and San Marino were once mere footnotes in international law texts, but the advent of dozens of very small States, with the prospect of more to come, has turned a quaint legal fossil into a live issue on UNITAR's agenda. The small number of cases at the International Court of Justice is widely considered as a sign of its political irrelevance. The growth in numbers and functions of international organizations is widely viewed as one of the key features of modern (as distinct from classical) international law. The number of reservations, and objections to reservations, in multilateral conventions is a measure of the cumbersomeness of the international law-making process, and of the importance of the problem. That list, too, can be extended over the whole range of international law.

The curious fact remains that the relevance of magni-

TREATY PROFILES

tudes in international law has often been given its due in concrete cases, but it has not been recognized as having theoretical significance for our understanding of international law as a whole. Therefore, there is no general inventory of quantifiable data in international law, comparable in dependability and sophistication to international trade statistics, international gold flow figures, foreign aid accounts, production and consumption indices, population growth rates and many other statistical data which allow us to measure and hence better understand other aspects of public life on our planet. In international law we have not even reached the point where we take it for granted that a basic inventory of facts and magnitudes is both necessary and available. TREATY PROFILES is offered as a step toward reaching that point.

c. *Law in International Politics*

The linkage between law and politics in world affairs is usually treated in terms of the effectiveness (or ineffectiveness) of law in controlling governmental behavior. From the popularized interest in whether international law "works" to the various civic and scholarly efforts at achieving "world peace through law" and policy analyses in terms of "world public order" and "relevant utopias"—they all have in common the use of international law as an instrument of policy.

The law/politics linkage is seen in TREATY PROFILES in a radically different way. International law is seen here not as a means of social control but as a means to learn more about the real world of international politics. International law serves here as a mirror of international society, just as domestic law can serve as a mirror of domestic society. If all books and all human memories about American history were suddenly lost, we could still reconstruct a reasonably accurate image of American history with nothing but a complete record of all cases decided by the Supreme Court of the United States. There is more than law in the records of the Supreme Court, from *Marbury v. Madison* to *United States v. Nixon*. What emerges from the cases is a "constitution" in a very broad sense. It is a constitution as a framework for social behavior, a description of the rules of the game, a definition of normalcy and aberration—in short, a general theory of American government and society.

What is the international analog for that image? Is it the World Court (ICJ)? Both courts make legally unreviewable decisions for their respective realms—the Supreme Court for America and the ICJ for the world. But, intuitively, the analogy seems weak. Why? Technical reasons immediately come to mind. The ICJ has no comparable enforcement mechanism, and consequently it has neither the effect on world politics nor the standing in world society that the Supreme Court has in American life. The ICJ has no appellate jurisdiction and hence no indirect effect on adjudicatory processes world-wide. The ICJ has no jurisdiction over individuals, and therefore its judgments lack the down-to-earth quality of Supreme Court decisions. Many more examples—all true—could be cited, yet they too would fail to give an instant image of the overwhelming difference between the two courts as mirrors of their realms.

The starkest statement of the difference is quantitative. During the first two post-war decades the ICJ decided 22 contentious cases and gave 12 advisory opinions, which averages less than 2 decisions per year. During the same time the US Supreme Court decided an average of about 200 cases per year. The decisional activity of the Supreme Court thus relates to that of the International Court as 100:1. No wonder, then, that Supreme Court jurisdiction renders a fine-screen image, while the International Court shows only a few gross strokes.

If not the International Court, what else? Let us try treaties. Again, we can find all sorts of good qualitative reasons why treaties are better than ICJ cases in mirroring world politics. Most textbooks list treaties first and judicial decisions last among sources of international law. Article 38 of the ICJ Statute goes so far as to relegate judicial decisions to "subsidiary means for the determination of rules of law." Treaties always prevail over custom, even among those countries which have no quarrel with the notion of custom itself. Revolutionary governments and ex-colonial countries challenge custom as a source of international law but they always agree to be bound by treaties they made themselves and often also by treaties made by their predecessors.

All this is true, but the really telling point is again quantitative. One unmistakable sign of political reality is hectic activity. The 34 ICJ decisions in 20 years are anything but hectic. During the same time the States of the world made more than 12,000 treaties, over 600 per year; compared to ICJ decisions, this is a rate of 300:1. Here we may find a fine-screen image of world politics comparable to the Supreme Court image of American life and politics.

Quantitative analysis is more than crude magnitudes. What matters is not only the gross total but also its various components and how they relate to each other. The 12,000 treaties might be perceived symbolically as so many bricks of the temple of international law. Lest laymen be too impressed with the simile, let us hasten to add that the 12,000 treaties do not fit together in any neat pattern. They resemble much less a systematic framework than a random patchwork. But that, precisely, is what mirrors reality. Let us imagine a world map with as many lines drawn between capital cities as there are bilateral treaty links between them. That map would show wildly uneven densities. Washington, Moscow, Paris, London, Bonn and Peking would be covered by a jungle of lines coming and going in all directions. Some newer and smaller countries would show only a few lines. Similar unevenness would appear in lines between *pairs* of capital cities. Washington-Ottawa, Moscow-Peking, Bonn-Paris, London-Rome and various permutations among leading treaty-makers would be thick with dozens of overlapping lines. On the other hand, about three-quarters of all possible country pairs in the world would show a total of *zero* mutual bilateral treaties, and not merely such contrived mis-matches as Nepal and Paraguay or Iceland and Mauritius, but even such plausible pairs as Argentina and Jamaica or Japan and Portugal.

This patchwork pattern of treaties represents international law and world affairs much better than the artificial, ineffective neatness of the International Court. The patchwork is global in scope but riddled with gaps, vivid in contrasts and yet repetitive within any one pattern, confusing in its appearance and yet undeniable in its existence — all in all a truly multidimensional image of world politics.

Of course, treaties are not the only formal interactions among States which scholars can quantify to construct a theoretical model of the international system. David Singer has reviewed and partly reproduced some of the other efforts in *Quantitative International Politics* (1968). The common purpose of these efforts has been to improve upon the truisms about world affairs which professionals share with college-educated laymen. Such improvement is easier said than done. There are only two areas of relevant knowledge in which professionals clearly surpass the lay population:

(1) Knowledge of diplomatic history and factual details about whatever case studies of international events and institutions and foreign areas we happen to have made.

(2) Bibliographical and methodological knowledge in the context of the total effort of our profession, i.e., knowing who has tried to do what and when, how far they have gone, what problems they have encountered and at what point they have changed their approaches, or given up or are still persisting.

This is not negligible knowledge, to be sure, and it is worth preserving through archives, worth enlarging through research and worth transmitting through teaching to future generations. But one thing it clearly is not — it is not a body of theory as that term is understood in the natural sciences or as theory building was understood among internationalists during the optimistic 1960's. It is theory only in the etymological sense of the Greek root of the word — observation and contemplation.

Our theoretical models of the international system, likewise, are not "models" in the sense of the natural sciences; they do not isolate effective causes or predict future behavior. And yet our models are not idle games. They fulfill one important function quite well. They reduce the size and chaos of the real world to human scale, and to some minimal orderliness, so that we can in fact observe and contemplate the international system. In constructing such models the builder has to decide what data to use as building blocks and, in this particular case, to answer the question: Why treaties? It might be enough to answer: Why *not* treaties? After all, there is no exclusiveness about the various international data that can be used and have been used for model building, e.g., UN votes, diplomatic visits, mail flow, trading patterns, press coverage, and so forth. Each data user is, in a much cited simile, like one of the blind men touching a different part of the elephant and assuming that the part represents the shape and nature of the whole animal (i.e., the international system). So, why *not* treaties?

There is, however, a more affirmative answer. International data users have to overcome the blind-men-and-elephant problem by one of two strategies. Either they have to affirm that their chosen data set is indeed a balanced microcosm of the whole system or they have to achieve the balance by merging several data sets into a model. Both strategies have encountered serious problems. The single-microcosm strategy tends to run head-on into problems of sense-distorting magnitude. For example, how can we build a model out of UN votes if China, West Germany, East Germany and Switzerland are missing for most or all of the UN period to date? The multidata approach provides a solution but only at the cost of creating new problems. There is as yet no widely accepted way in which the fantastic variety of cross-national data can be standardized and meaningfully compared. Compendia such as Banks and Textor, *A Cross-Polity Survey* (1963), and Taylor and Hudson, *World Handbook of Political and Social Indicators* (1972), have helped provide a basis for future work, and Rudolph Rummel has pioneered some ingenious techniques in *The Dimensions of Nations* (1972), but the basic problem remains unsolved.

If there were an easy solution, it would probably have been found a long time ago, and we must therefore live with a choice among various lesser evils. It is in this very limited sense that treaties may prove to be as useful as any data set with which to build a model of the international system. As suggested in the statement of purpose, treaties optimize three crucial conditions if we use them as "shadows" of the not directly observable reality outside our Platonic cave: (1) universality, (2) meticulosity and (3) parsimony.

Universality applies in two ways — as comprehensiveness and as standardization. All countries make treaties, and treaty formats and procedures are remarkably similar all over the world. Hence the products are standardized, easily comparable and globally quantifiable within a single consistent system.

Meticulosity is ensured by the lawyers who draft the treaties and by the importance attributed by all participants to the treaty-making process. Unlike UN votes, press coverage, private trade, tourism and many other factors, little or nothing is left to chance in the making of treaties. Every treaty is a deliberate governmental act, slowly and carefully prepared, and self-consciously put into the space/time framework of all other relations with the treaty partner. This is not to deny that random negligence pervades governmental actions, including treaties, and indeed human activities in general, but the treaty-making process is about as far on the meticulous end of the scale as any set of events that is relevant to the international system.

Finally, there is parsimony. The treaty-making process itself is a filtering device. It represents all the relevant forces in government, and each is careful to avoid unnecessary commitments and indeed to question the need for the treaty itself. Thereby, the trivia and the petty impulses which abound in other events between nations (ceremonial matters, verbal praise and blame, etc.) tend to get filtered out of the treaty-making process. State Department Circular 175 of 22 December 1955 (as revised by Public Notice 396, *Federal Register*, 15 August 1973) shows in abundant detail how many different units of government must cooperate in developing an institutional consensus for a treaty. Then the process still needs the endorsement of the chief executive, and that brings in all the familiar opportunities for lateral

TREATY PROFILES

inputs at the White House level. And even that may not be the end. Foreign relations is the only political game where the buck does not stop at the President's desk. If the foreign partner objects to any non-trivial part of the draft treaty, the whole process must be re-iterated throughout the domestic constituencies and the foreign negotiation.

Admittedly, the American example may be an extreme case, due to the sheer size and the fiercely competitive subcultures of our pluralistic establishment, but most of the other major treaty-makers are also large countries with complex governments. Even non-democratic governments have to reconcile the interests of various established fiefdoms in their internal treaty-making processes, and of course they all face the same complexities in their external negotiations as do democratic governments. Ultimately, then, any treaty which emerges from these political wind tunnels has been buffeted by so many different influences that it represents, most parsimoniously, the *total* policy output with which the treaty-making country addresses its treaty partner, and vice versa.

The major argument against treaties as data is that they are fragile. True, treaties can be and have been broken. In fact, governments over the centuries have devised and perfected many clever ways of extricating themselves from uncomfortable treaty obligations, usually without resorting to the crudeness of breakage. Treaties can be re-interpreted. They can be partially or fully suspended and of course formally terminated. Moreover, any country can ask at any time to negotiate for an amendment to a treaty. And, finally, treaties can be quietly ignored — a trick which governments use with consummate skill in many fields. So, breakage is by no means the only cause of ineffectiveness of a treaty, and all these causes together appear to make a strong argument against the use of treaties as data.

The anti-treaty argument may apply to any one treaty but not to the aggregate pattern of all treaties. There is safety in numbers. Something happens as we change focus from a single datum to a massive data bank. Any one treaty can be ignored or violated, and by itself that would tend to distort the image, but the distortions cancel out in the aggregate. The reason is that, in our modern bureaucratic world, nothing happens without paperwork, and in the international arena paperwork takes the form of treaties. Immortal like government itself, despite the human mortality of those who govern, treaties *as a class* survive their own deaths. What replaces an *old* treaty, invariably, is a *new* treaty. Even a partial change of an old treaty involves the machinery of treaty making and often takes the form of a separate treaty amending the prior one, and thus enters the data bank and reflects the reality of post-treaty politics between the two countries. Even treaty silence becomes conspicuous in the aggregate. A single non-treaty is of course invisible, but if a country's total treaty profile has lows or gaps where normal treaty activity would be expected, those gaps are clues to some unusual political situations.

All in all, then, treaties can tell us a lot about the international system but we must learn to repress the conditioned reflexes of international lawyers in ourselves. We must not take treaties as contracts between States and bury ourselves in fine print for exegeses of legal subtleties. A treaty profile, as an instrument of observation, is more like a telescope than a microscope — bringing broader vistas of international law into our range of perception. It tells us little or nothing about specific rights and duties, but it helps the user map out broader contexts for particular inquiries in international law and politics. PROFILES uses treaties as pieces in the global mosaic of the international system, and it views each treaty as a unit — infinitely combinable and re-combinable on the ever-changing chessboard where the game of world politics is being played by real people with real power.

Whether TREATY PROFILES is (or has) a "theory" of international politics is a question of terminology, not substance. But whether it is competitive among other academic "blind man's" images of the "elephant" of world politics — that is a question which can be answered, and the best way to answer it is to test the usefulness of the profiles by working with them as suggested in the next chapters.

4. Data Base

a. *Coverage*

The data base for TREATY PROFILES is a subset of the data base for the WORLD TREATY INDEX. The PROFILES subset consists of selected data from every bilateral INDEX treaty signed between 1 January 1946 and 31 December 1965. It covers 12,732 bilateral treaties, of which 7,980 are from the United Nations Treaty Series (UNTS) and 4,752 from various national treaty collections (see Thesaurus, 9/e). Due to the time frame, the League of Nations Treaty Series is excluded.

Two types of unilateral declarations are assimilable to the bilateral format of PROFILES and are included in the data base and in the above count of 12,732. The first type consists of 68 acceptances of the obligations of the UN Charter; the second comprises 62 acceptances of the jurisdiction of the International Court of Justice under the optional clause. These 130 declarations have been bilateralized in PROFILES by creating two fictitious parties called "Accept UN Charter" and "ICJ Option Clause." The other party in each case is of course the party making the unilateral declaration.

For each of these 12,732 treaties, a certain set of information has been selected from the common data base of the INDEX. That set includes the following items:
(1) First Party.
(2) Second Party.
(3) Year of Signature.
(4) Topic.

For UNTS treaties (but not for treaties from national collections), there is further information on the following items:

(5) Textual References to IGO's.
(6) UNTS Registrant.

b. Definitions

(1) First Party

There is nothing significant about any party's being "first" or "second." The words "one" and "other" could have been used instead without change of meaning. Whether first or second, every party occurs twice for the same treaty, once for each half of a "dyad" as defined below. For instance, a Belgian-French treaty occurs once in the Belgian profile under France and once in the French profile under Belgium. (A dyad, for our purposes, is the basic building block of any bilateral treaty profile and is defined here as two parties connected by a treaty.)

(2) Second Party

This is merely the other side of the same coin. For definition, see "First Party" above.

(3) Year of Signature

Day and month of the date of signature are omitted as unnecessary details in a macroscopic survey. Even the year is needed only to let the computer determine into which of the four 5-year periods any given treaty should fall.

(4) Topic

One single topic has been assigned to every treaty even though, of course, many treaties cover more than one subject. Trade agreements sometimes include provisions about payments and exchange rates; status of forces agreements usually refer also to privileges and immunities; friendship treaties often cover a wide range of subjects. And yet, almost any treaty has a single *dominant* theme, usually though not always identified in the title of the treaty. That theme is the sole basis for the topical category of every treaty here. The coverage of secondary topical themes has been deliberately sacrificed in these profiles in order to achieve their primary purpose, namely, macroscopic comparability. The artificial simplicity—one topic per treaty—does not prevent the complexity of the real world from coming through as the building blocks of party/time/topic begin to accumulate in multiple combinations. Those, however, who need details and who use TREATY PROFILES as a reference tool rather than as a data set for quantitative analyses will find topical sub-categories in the Thesaurus, 9/f, and further topical refinements in the WORLD TREATY INDEX, Volume 1, pages xxxv-xl, and throughout Volume 5.

(5) Textual References to IGO's

For this item as well as for the last one (UNTS Registrant), the data base is limited to UNTS treaties. The rules for counting treaties with IGO references are complicated but need to be understood by the user in order to avoid misinterpretations of data. To be counted the treaty's IGO reference must be more than nominal and must involve some actual or potential *function* on the part of the IGO. For instance, it is not enough if a treaty has a commitment that the parties will act in the spirit of the UN Charter. That commitment by itself does not give the UN any function it would not have without the treaty. But the condition is fulfilled if, for example, a treaty provides for the UN Secretary General to appoint a mediator. The appointive act is a small but *new* function for the UN which it would not have without that particular treaty. It makes no difference whether the function is big or small, whether it is actual or potential—the treaty will count. If, however, the IGO itself is a party to the treaty, no reference to that IGO counts—regardless of whether a function is involved or not.

The IGO may but need not be one of the well-known institutions, e.g., UN, Specialized Agencies or major regional organizations. It may also be any of the minor agencies like the International Halibut Commission or the South Pacific Health Service, and it may even be any one of the hundreds of nameless ad hoc agencies, usually bilateral, whose function is limited to a single treaty, such as boundary commissions or cultural exchange committees. For a list of all IGO's referred to in treaty texts, see Thesaurus, 9/d.

TREATY PROFILES

Only one reference per IGO is counted in any one treaty but if several IGO's are referenced, each counts once. Suppose a treaty has 15 functional references to the UN, 5 to the ILO, 4 to the FAO and 3 to the ICJ. That treaty would count *once* for each IGO regardless of the number of actual references.

The purpose of this complex system is to measure the *net* role given IGO's in conventional international law. What is significant about IGO references is the legal act of giving an IGO some concrete function under the terms of a treaty; but the incidental repetition of the same IGO function within the same treaty is not significant and neither is the automatic reference to an IGO when it is a party to the treaty. Information on IGO's as treaty partners is available elsewhere, in IGO profiles and in the Thesaurus, 9/c.

(6) UNTS Registrant

By definition, the data base for this item is limited to UNTS treaties because any treaty becomes a UNTS treaty by being registered, and no treaty can be in the UNTS without having first been registered. One peculiarity of this process is important for a proper interpretation of registration data, particularly for percentages. It is logical but may not be obvious at first glance that, from the viewpoint of the registering party, normalcy in treaty registration is only 50%, not 100%. Every treaty can be registered by either of the two parties but normally not by both, and so the world average per registrant is near 50% even though the world total for all treaties is of course 100%. The world average is not even exactly 50% but actually 45%. The main reason for this distortion is the practice by which an IGO may register a treaty to which it is not a party but which was concluded under its auspices. These treaties are "lost" from the registration count (but not from the data base) because they are not "self-registered" by any party. The opposite kind of distortion could theoretically come from those rare cases where a treaty is registered by more than one party, but only the first registrant has been counted in those cases and the other registrants have been disregarded for the sake of simplicity. This distortion occurs in less than a tenth of one percent of all treaties and is therefore statistically negligible.

5. Format

Before starting to read this description of the format, users will find it helpful to make a photocopy of a sample profile and have it handy while reading this chapter. Without that visual aid new users will find it practically impossible to follow the details concerning 20 columns and 44 lines of tabular material; with it, however, the task is surprisingly easy. Since the profiles are standardized, users can choose *any* profile as a sample, but there is some advantage in choosing one of the major countries—they have more treaties and hence more illustrative details.

a. Overall Design

The profiles are designed to present a maximum of information in a minimum of space, and thereby to facilitate comparisons among countries and regions in every detail within any one table and between tables. Therefore, all tables have the same data base and also the same standard format. Only the content varies from one table to the next.

Every page tabulates the treaty pattern of the country or region or other treaty-making entity identified in the top center of each page as "Treaty Profile of . . . ." The following three types of figures are in each profile:

(1) Absolute numbers of treaties: everywhere except as noted below.
(2) Percentages of numbers of treaties: in shaded areas, i.e., Columns 4 and 5, and Lines 42-44.
(3) Number of parties over 30: in one place only, Column 1, Line 31, in parentheses following the words "All Others."

The only exception to full comparability has already been mentioned in the description of the data base. The sections on institutions and registration (Columns 15-20) are limited to UNTS treaties.

Columns and lines are numbered only to make it convenient to refer to them here in these explanations and in actual use for research and teaching. The numbering system has no hierarchy or purpose other than convenience. Some of the sequences have an intrinsic and obvious logic of their own. For instance, the time section goes from the earliest to the latest period, and the partners go from the highest to the lowest number of mutual treaties. Others have been put next to each other simply because of the likelihood of mutual comparisons, e.g., the United Nations and the Specialized Agencies. Other sequences are purely arbitrary. Under Topics, for instance, the military might have been put next to administrative-diplomatic matters instead of where it is, next to Aid, and it would not make any difference either way. Some other choices have been very difficult. For instance, the party groups are alphabetized rather than ordered by mutual treaties. The numerical order would have

12

been consistent with the individual party pattern but the alphabetized order provides the habit-forming convenience of standardization.

In short, the rationale for the design will be quickly apparent to professional users, and even to student users, but the detailed definitions of columns and lines are *not* obvious and, therefore, all users should read the following definitions before interpreting any part of the statistical information.

b. Columns

The systematic overview below is followed by detailed definitions for every column.

Columns	Headings	Definitions
1	Partners	The various co-signatories of the treaties of each profiled party.
2	Partner's World Total	Each partner's total number of treaties with the rest of the world.
3-5	Dyads	Mutual treaties between pairs of parties.
6-9	Time	Treaty trends in four 5-year blocks between 1946 and 1965.
10-14	Topics	Subject matter of treaties in five topical clusters.
15-19	Institutions	Textual references to selected international organizations.
20	Self-Registered	Treaties registered by the profiled party.

(1) Partners

This column identifies the partners of the profiled party. (The "profiled party" itself is identified in the top line of each table heading.) The partners are listed in the following order. First come up to 30 top partners in descending order of frequency of mutual treaties, as per Column 3. If there are more than 30 individual treaty partners, all others are combined into Line 31. Then come regional groups of partners, in alphabetical order, and a special group for international organizations. Below the groups are the totals, both absolute and percentage.

(2) Partner's World Total

This column shows the total number of treaties which each listed partner has with the rest of the world. These figures remain constant throughout all tables and are repeated for convenience so that the user need not flip pages back and forth to look for the same information in the profiles of various treaty partners.

(3) Absolutes

This column is the backbone of each profile. It shows the total number of dyadic (mutual) treaties between the profiled party and any one of its listed partners. The first 30 lines are ordered by this column, which also serves as a general reference for all other information in each profile. Two of the three major column groups (Time and Topics) add up horizontally on each line to Column 3. The remaining columns (15-20) are non-exhaustive breakdowns of the single total in Column 3, Line 41.

TREATY PROFILES

(4) - (5) Ratios — Self/Other

These two columns are two sides of the same coin. Column 4 (Self) shows the percentage of the mutual treaties of each pair in the total treaties of the *profiled* party, and Column 5 (Other) does the same for the *other* party. The two figures give us a measure of how important each party is to the other.

(6) - (9) Time

These four columns break the dyadic total in Column 3 into four 5-year periods as defined in each column heading. This information allows us to analyze trends over time for each profiled party as a whole (Line 40) and for each party pair, line for line.

(10) - (14) Topics

These columns break the dyadic total in Column 3 into five major treaty topics or combinations of topics, each being the dominant theme of the entire treaty. For an overview of the whole range of topics as well as a detailed frequency count of each topic, see Thesaurus, 9/f; but the following definitions may suffice to convey the key points.

(10) Admin & Dipl

This column covers the greatest variety among the five topical columns. It includes all the typical treaties of friendship, recognition, boundaries, visas, extradition, judicial assistance, diplomatic and consular relations, privileges and immunities and dispute settlement. This column covers also agreements establishing an international organization or relating primarily to its function and operation, such as basic charters and constitutional documents as well as headquarters agreements. Also included in this column are all agreements on particular items rather than classes of items, e.g., operation of a lighthouse, construction of a bridge or sale of a vessel or building. Finally, this column includes any other agreement that does not clearly fall within any of the other four categories.

(11) Social Coop

Social cooperation is here defined as all those treaties which correspond to the substantive concerns of national ministries of health, education, welfare, labor and transportation. They comprise, for instance, such typical agreements as health inspection, vaccination, sanitation, academic degrees and diplomas, student and teacher exchange, vocational training, protection of cultural objects, research projects, migratory labor, social security, labor safety standards, transport on land and water and in the air, postal matters, telecommunications, newspapers, radio and television.

(12) Econ Coop

This column includes all economic agreements except those which are of a non-commercial nature, mainly foreign aid and technical assistance. Typical instruments in this column include agreements on trade and payments, tariffs, customs, export and import quotas, banking, indemnities, investments and investment guarantees, exchange rates, claims, debts, assets, liens, lump sum settlements, most-favored nation treatment, taxation, patents and any other financial or commercial matter that is not part of foreign aid and technical assistance.

(13) Aid

This column comprises all agreements related primarily to foreign aid and technical assistance, even in cases where the name of the agreement does not necessarily suggest a donor-recipient relationship, e.g., in a "joint development agreement," but where it is clear from the contents of the treaty, and from the disparity in wealth between the parties, that it is indeed a matter of foreign aid.

(14) Milit

This column includes all agreements related to military matters, with doubts resolved in favor of inclusion. For instance, military missions and status of forces agreements, which might legitimately come under administrative and diplomatic matters, are included under military matters; so are peace treaties and agreements on citizenship in the military service, war graves and occupation regimes. Similarly, doubts between the military and economic or aid categories have also been resolved in favor of the military, as, for instance, in war claims, reparations, military assistance missions, lend-lease and military training and equipment. In all these matters the assumption has been, given national sensitivities in military matters, that in any intra-governmental consensus on a treaty combining military and non-military elements, the military segment of the government will be likely to have the decisive influence and will thus reflect the dominant theme of the entire treaty.

(15) – (19) Institutions

These five columns show the number of treaties containing at least one textual reference to an international organization (IGO), and they identify the references by IGO's or groups of IGO's. All figures in these five columns are limited to UNTS treaties. Allowance must be made for this difference when Columns 15-19 are compared to any preceding columns because Columns 2-14 cover the combined totals of UNTS treaties and national treaty collections.

Proper perspective can always be gained by looking at the percentage figures in Line 42. The percentages relate the IGO references to the *net* total of UNTS treaties only, rather than to the sum of all treaties. The difference between net and gross totals varies from country to country (it is usually at or near zero for IGO's) and can be found in every profile by comparing Lines 40 and 41 in Column 3. It also appears in the list of parties in the Thesaurus, 9/a.

There is another reason why IGO references are more numerous than might appear at first sight. Each percentage has been calculated *separately* against the UNTS total, and therefore the five percentages must be added together (rather than averaged) to arrive at the correct proportion of all IGO references in all UNTS treaties.

The Thesaurus, 9/d, has a detailed list of all referenced IGO's, broken down by columns (15-19) and giving a frequency count for each IGO and each column; but the following brief definitions will suffice for many purposes.

(15) UN

The United Nations is defined for this column as only the main institution itself including five of its six principal organs. The sixth organ, the International Court of Justice, is separately treated in Column 17, and the Specialized Agencies and all other UN-related bodies (often collectively called the "UN Family") are lumped together in Column 16.

(16) Spec Ag's

This column covers all UN-related institutions excluding the UN itself (Column 15) and the International Court of Justice (Column 17). Included are the major Specialized Agencies (e.g., ILO, UNESCO, FAO, etc.), the special-status IAEA and numerous other bodies (e.g., UNICEF, UNTAB, UNKRA, etc.) which are not Specialized Agencies but which are similarly part of the UN Family. Also included here are predecessor agencies under the League of Nations system and the League itself.

(17) Intl Court

This column covers only the International Court of Justice and its predecessor, the Permanent Court of International Justice. An earlier version of TREATY PROFILES included in this column other international courts, i.e., the European Court of Human Rights and the Court of Justice of the European Communities. That had the advantage of producing a single category for all judicial bodies. However, the number of treaties referring to these other courts turned out to be insignificant, and it seemed therefore preferable to have a pure statistic for ICJ/PCIJ and to put the other courts into the residual category in Column 19.

(18) Arbitration

This column covers the Permanent Court of Arbitration as well as several hundred ad hoc commissions created by bilateral treaties to serve some arbitrational function under the terms of those treaties. The information is exclusive in

TREATY PROFILES

the sense that all institutions in this column are formally and solely arbitrational in character. It does not mean, on the other hand, that no other IGO can occasionally perform an arbitrational function in addition to whatever may be its primary function. For instance, some Specialized Agencies include among their functions some quasi-arbitrational tasks, but their primary functions are elsewhere.

(19) Other

This column comprises the full remainder of any and all IGO's not included in any of the four previous columns. Thus included here are all of the so-called commodity agencies (e.g., international bodies for cotton, wheat, oil, tin, coffee, fisheries, and so forth), the various regional institutions (e.g., Council of Europe, Organization of American States, Arab League and others) and hundreds of nameless ad hoc bodies created by bilateral treaties for any functions other than arbitration (Column 18) to be performed under the terms of those treaties. Anyone interested in using Column 19 will be well advised to check the Thesaurus, 9/d, because the large number and variety of IGO's in this residual category may otherwise cause misinterpretations.

(20) Self-Registered

This column shows how many UNTS treaties were registered by the profiled party. Here, as in Columns 15-19, it is important to remember that the information is limited to UNTS treaties. Users should always check Line 42 before drawing conclusions from any other figure in Column 20. The percentage in Line 42 shows the proportion of UNTS treaties registered by the profiled party and is calculated on the basis of the net UNTS total (Column 3, Line 41) rather than the All Data total (Column 3, Line 40). The need for special attention to this problem obviously varies from country to country and increases with the difference between these two totals. For a quick overview of the differences from party to party, see the list of parties in the Thesaurus, 9/a.

c. Lines

The lines are much more likely than the columns to be self-explanatory to the user. Most of the lines identify easily recognizable parties or groups of parties, but a few words of explanation may nevertheless be useful.

(1) - (30) Top Thirty

The first 30 lines show those parties with which the profiled party has the most mutual treaties. They are listed in descending order of the total number of mutual treaties as shown in Column 3. Where the same total of mutual treaties applies to more than one partner, the partners are listed in reverse alphabetical order within the same numerical block. This is purely a matter of convenience in the computer program and has no substantive significance. If a profiled party has less than 30 treaty partners altogether, of course, there are blank lines between the last treaty partner and Line 31.

(31) All Others

This line combines the treaty information of all those partners of the profiled party which rank 31 or below in the total number of mutual treaties. The number of excess partners over 30 is shown in parentheses immediately following the words "All Others" on Line 31, Column 1. This is the only place in a profile where a figure does not refer to the number or percentage of treaties, but to the number of parties. Profiles with less than 31 partners show a zero in that particular location and show no numerical information anywhere else on Line 31.

(32) - (39) Groups

Each of these eight lines shows an aggregation of treaty partners into the most frequently used groups. The first seven groups consist of countries with some geographical, historical or ideological affinities. The eighth group comprises all treaty-making international organizations. The eight groups are mutually exclusive but not exhaustive. No party is represented in more than one group, and four countries are not represented in any group, i.e., Israel, Japan, USA and Yugoslavia. The seven country groups are listed in alphabetical order, and the IGO group comes last. All group members are identified in the Thesaurus, 9/b (States) and 9/c (IGO's).

(32) African Group

This group is defined as Black Africa and consists of the 30 African countries which made treaties during the 1946–1965 period. Included is the Malagasy Republic but excluded are the Arab countries of North Africa and the two white-governed countries of South Africa.

(33) Arab Group

This group is defined as the 13 countries that were members of the League of Arab States during 1946–1965. This definition excludes the Sultanate of Muscat and Oman, which is included in the Asian Group below.

(34) Asian Group

This group consists of 21 countries of Asia and Oceania. The Asian Group excludes the non-group countries of Israel and Japan as well as those Asian countries which belong to more clearly definable groups, i.e., Arab Group, Commonwealth and Communist Group. Since the Commonwealth is defined as the "old" Commonwealth (see below), countries like India and Pakistan are included in the Asian Group rather than in the Commonwealth. Also included is the Sultanate of Muscat and Oman.

(35) Commonwealth

This group is defined as the "old" Commonwealth prior to the recent independence of British possessions in Africa and Asia. It is the smallest group, consisting of only 7 countries. In addition to the obvious core group—United Kingdom, Canada, Australia and New Zealand—it includes South Africa and Rhodesia (Federation of Rhodesia and Nyasaland), which for most of the 1946–1965 period either belonged to the Commonwealth or fit there better than in any other group. The last country is Newfoundland. Although independent only briefly and having only one treaty (with Canada), Newfoundland appears in the data bank and has been grouped with the Commonwealth. Ireland is not part of the Commonwealth and has been included in Western Europe.

(36) Communist Group

This group is narrowly defined as 12 of the 13 contiguous countries in Europe and Asia with governing Communist parties. The excluded 13th country, of course, is Yugoslavia, which is not in any group. Doubtful cases like Cuba (and even more doubtful ones like Guinea and Indonesia) have been resolved by exclusion from the Communist Group and inclusion in the appropriate geographical group.

(37) Latin America

This group consists of 22 countries, comprising all 20 Latin American republics as well as Jamaica and Trinidad/Tobago. The only somewhat doubtful case, Cuba, has been included here rather than with the Communist Group because Latin America was Cuba's dominant affiliation during most of 1946–1965.

(38) Western Europe

This group consists of 25 countries. Treaty-making mini-states have been included, i.e., Liechtenstein, Monaco, San Marino, Trieste and Vatican/Holy See. Also included are Turkey and the Eastern Mediterranean island countries of Malta and Cyprus. The only two exclusions of doubtful cases are the United Kingdom, which is included in the Commonwealth, and Yugoslavia, which is a non-group country.

(39) Intl Organs

This group includes every international governmental organization (IGO) of whatever kind—large or small, global or regional, political or technical—that occurs in the data bank as a treaty maker for the 1946–1965 period, see Thesaurus, 9/c. This definition involves no doubts or special decisions.

(40) – (41) Totals

Line 40 (All Data) shows in each column the total of Lines 1–31, *regardless* of the figures in the partner groups, Lines 32–39. The reason is that (because of the four non-group countries) the partner groups do not necessarily add

TREATY PROFILES

up to the totals, and yet they would be similar enough in many cases to be potentially misleading. Therefore, the sum of the partner groups is not shown at all. Each group stands alone for whatever comparisons a user may wish to make.

Another peculiarity of the totals is not visible in Line 40 but is logically related. A treaty between two members of the same group is counted once for the group totals in Column 2 but twice in Column 3. The Commonwealth, for instance, shows 1,641 and 1,725 treaties in these two columns. The difference (5%) results from the double count of those 84 treaties where *both* parties are members of the Commonwealth. The discrepancy is quite small in most groups. The only two exceptions are Western Europe and the Communist Group, both of which have an unusually high in-group/out-group ratio of treaty activity. Details can be seen from the World Total profile, where Columns 2, 3 and 5 specify the difference for each group in absolute terms and in percentages. Users should be aware of the differences not only to guard against distortion but also to take advantage of information on in-group/out-group ratios that would otherwise involve considerable extra work to compile.

Another peculiarity is the absence of a total in Column 5. It would have been more misleading than meaningful to add up or to average all the percentages which express the ratio of the treaties of the profiled party in the world total of each of its partners.

Next, the totals in the four Time columns (6-9) and in the five Topics columns (10-14) add up *horizontally* to the dyadic total in Column 3, but the totals in the five Institutions columns (15-19) do not follow this pattern. As has been mentioned earlier in the section on data coverage and in the definition of the various columns, the Institutions columns represent a smaller universe than the other columns. First, they are limited to UNTS treaties, and second, they show only those UNTS treaties which contain a textual reference to an international organization. To remind users of this limitation, the totals of Institutions are printed in Line 41 (UNTS Only) rather than with the other totals in Line 40 (All Data). IGO references vary from country to country and from treaty to treaty and usually add up to less than the dyadic total. Their horizontal totals are not shown anywhere in the profiles (for no other reason than lack of space), but they can easily be calculated by adding up the five figures in Line 41. Since the five categories exhaust the IGO universe, the sum of the five figures represents a true total.

Finally, the total in Column 20, like those of Columns 15-19, is only a vertical total of Lines 1-31 but does not match horizontally with any of the other totals. Being the number of treaties registered by the profiled party in the UNTS, it is limited by definition to UNTS treaties and should therefore be compared primarily to the UNTS Only total in Line 41 rather than to the All Data total in Line 40.

(42) - (44) Comparisons

All figures in these three lines are percentages. They serve to make comparisons easy by normalizing the absolute figures. Any profile can be compared to any other profile on Line 42 (Party Total). Line 43 automatically reproduces the corresponding percentages for any party's group profile, except of course for the non-group countries—Israel, Japan, USA and Yugoslavia—where Line 43 remains blank. Line 44 reproduces the percentages of the World Total as a set of constants for the sake of visual convenience.

The figures are computed as follows. Line 42 expresses each total in Columns 6-14 as a percentage of the All Data total in Column 3. The process is the same for Columns 15-20 except that the reference point in Column 3 is the UNTS Only total. Line 43 uses analogous totals from the corresponding group profile rather than from any figures in the party profile itself, and Line 44 is computed analogously from the World Total profile. Some apparent inconsistencies in the group profiles result from the in-group/out-group problem as explained above under (40)-(41) Totals.

6. Use

The use of PROFILES in research and teaching depends largely on the interests and preferences of different users. PROFILES falls between two categories. It is more focused than a reference work but less so than a monograph that develops a single thesis and marshals evidence for that one purpose. Potential uses of PROFILES are so manifold that space permits only a few illustrative examples. Most of the examples are taken from actual practice at the Treaty Research Center, both from in-house projects and from responses to requests for treaty information from academicians elsewhere.

a. Partners

The most basic question about a country's treaty pattern usually concerns the ranking and grouping of its treaty partners. If someone wants to get a general sense of the political status and alignments of a country, it is useful to ask for a list of its major treaty partners, rank-ordered by number of treaties and grouped by the usual regional and ideological criteria. Suppose, for instance, we asked for these points of general orientation with regard to Sri Lanka (Ceylon). We would find that the first four partners are, in this order, China, USA, USSR and the United Kingdom. The next eight partners are WHO, India, West Germany, Sweden, ILO, IBRD, Pakistan and Canada. Some preliminary conclusions will be already obvious at this early point. Sri Lanka is oriented toward the Great Powers, and there appears to be a delicate balance not only between East and West but also between the two power centers within each group. In the case of the next eight partners, there is a special emphasis on industrialized countries and Specialized Agencies. That combination often reveals a need for foreign aid, and a quick glance at Column 13, Lines 42-44, shows at least a partial confirmation. Sri Lanka's proportion of aid treaties is higher than the world average (25% against 20%) but it is lower than the regional average for Asia (25% against 30%). So, some further research is needed to clarify this point. A tentative hypothesis might be that Sri Lanka has a relatively high treaty volume (123 treaties, Column 3, Line 40) compared to typical aid recipients (e.g., Nigeria, 27 treaties, 44% in aid), and if that holds true in further checks it would explain the earlier ambiguity. Also among the top twelve partners are India and Pakistan, whose historical affinities with Sri Lanka are well known. The empirical question remains whether such historical affinities tend to show in other treaty profiles in otherwise similar circumstances. A quick check in the profiles of Burma, India and Pakistan shows that, indeed, there is a similar pattern in most of the dyads between these countries, e.g., India and Pakistan ranking 10 and 11 in Burma's profile, and 4 and 5 in each other's profiles.

Let us next look at groups of partners, even though some of what we will find here was already implicit in the review of individual partners. The Communist Group is by far the largest partner group for Sri Lanka. With 45 treaties it is almost three times as large as the next largest group, which is Western Europe with 17, followed by IGO's with 15 (where the non-group USA would tie for third place with 15), the Commonwealth with 13 and Asia with 10. Treaty making between Sri Lanka and non-neighboring groups of Third World countries is near or at zero. The individual dyads are evidently typical of their respective group patterns. This might have been expected but we could not know it for sure, and in the absence of group totals it would have taken substantial time and effort to pull the figures together from among 200 other profiles, let alone from raw data.

So far the discussion of partners has either assumed that all dyads are symmetrical or has disregarded the question of dyadic symmetry altogether. Asymmetry, in this sense, is any difference in how important the same treaties are to one or the other of the two parties. Importance is measured as percentage of mutual treaties in total treaties, as shown in Columns 4 and 5. Most dyads are in fact asymmetrical, and in many cases the asymmetry is quite dramatic. For instance, the 28 treaties between China and Sri Lanka remain of course 28 regardless of whether we count them as part of the Chinese profile or as part of that of Sri Lanka. But the percentages vary widely. The same 28 treaties account for 23% of Sri Lanka's total treaties but for only 4% of China's total treaties. This is a ratio of approximately 6 to 1. It suggests that their mutual treaties are about six times more important to Sri Lanka than to China. The very next line shows an even greater discrepancy, and through it a similar political asymmetry. The percentages for Sri Lanka and USA are 12% and 1%. The decimals (not shown in the printed version) enlarge the difference further, since the actual figures are 12.20% and 0.58%, thus creating a ratio of 21 to 1. And the ratio between Sri Lanka and the Soviet Union is approximately 9 to 1. Thus, while the absolute rank order of Sri Lanka's first three partners is China/USA/USSR, the relative importance of Sri Lanka's treaties to her three major partners re-ranks them as China/USSR/USA with ratios of 1:6, 1:9 and 1:21. These ratios may serve as a rough measure of the bargaining power of Sri Lanka with each of the three major countries.

Equally interesting is the reverse question. Which parties are less important to Sri Lanka than Sri Lanka is to them? Whom does Sri Lanka "dominate" according to the mutual/total ratio of their treaties? There is only one party in Sri Lanka's profile that fulfills this condition, and it is not a country but an IGO, namely, the International Labor Organization. The ratio is 2 to 5 in favor of Sri Lanka. The World Health Organization is near symmetry with a ratio of 4 to 3, but it is in WHO's favor. All other dyads are asymmetrical in favor of the other party, not Sri Lanka; or they are so small in total number as to make percentages nearly meaningless.

Is this pattern typical of medium-sized Third World countries? Let us take a few comparable cases. The profile of Burma does not show a single dyad with a treaty ratio in Burma's favor, and the two parties nearest symmetry are Thailand and (as in Sri Lanka's case) the World Health Organization. The rest of Burma's pattern is similarly lopsided as is Sri Lanka's. Thailand's profile is more assertive. True, on balance the ratio favors most of Thailand's partners, but there are several notable exceptions—IGO's as well as a few nearby countries. They are, in order of Thai "dominance," Laos 7:2, Cambodia 7:3 and Burma 3:2. Taiwan is a draw at 2:2. The Thai ratio with IGO's is even more favorable, UNESCO 5:1, ICAO 9:2 and ILO 3:2. Changing the perspective in yet another way, we can also look at the profile of a Specialized Agency, e.g., WHO, to see which countries it "dominates" in its treaty ratio. Those countries are, in this order, Malawi, Rwanda, Sierra Leone, Saudi Arabia, Somalia, Sudan and over two dozen other Third World countries.

A more extreme version of these relatively minor variations in treaty dominance is represented by a satellite relationship which, in quantitative terms, can be defined as an extremely steep downward slope from the first to the second and third treaty partners. In Sri Lanka's case, the slope is steep but not precipitous—from 23% for China to 12% for USA and 9% for the USSR. The corresponding figures for Burma are similar—22%, 16% and 9%, except that the third partner is not the USSR but WHO. The USSR is in fifth place, with 7% of Burma's treaties. For other countries in the same general area, the slopes among their first three partners are even less steep, e.g., India 13/10/10, Indonesia 20/17/13, Malaysia 15/15/12, Pakistan 15/9/7 and Thailand 17/11/8.

TREATY PROFILES

Despite their differences these countries fall into one recognizable pattern. None of them is clearly "dominated" in its treaties by a single country or one group of countries, and we must look elsewhere to find examples of a distinct satellite pattern. If we look first at the Communist Group, analogous figures for Mongolia, for instance, are 51/24/13 — for USSR, China and East Germany. The slope is steeper; the share of the first one in the total profile is over twice as large as in the case of Sri Lanka (51% against 23%) and over three times as large as in most other Asian examples. Even more dramatic is the share of the whole Communist Group in Mongolia's profile — 96%. This is high even for a Communist country. Analogous rates for China, Czechoslovakia and Poland are 57%, 58% and 58%. Mongolia is exceeded only by North Korea's 98% and North Vietnam's flat 100%. North Vietnam is also similar to Mongolia in having the same first three partners, but switching the order of the first two: China 47%, USSR 32% and East Germany 12%. North Korea, incidentally, holds a middle position between the Vietnamese and the Mongolian patterns: USSR 38%, China 36% and East Germany 13%. These figures can be interpreted, of course, in many different ways but they show some reasonable image of how the Sino-Soviet conflict affects neighboring Communist countries, and it also documents the rise of East Germany to a position approaching that of a triarchy in Communist international affairs.

In the West, there is no comparable dominance by a single group but there are similar preponderances of single countries. France tends to dominate the treaty profiles of former French colonies, and the slope from France to the second partner is even steeper than in the Communist Group, but the second and third partners show much more variety especially by criss-crossing group lines. Here are a few examples for the percentage slope between France as first partner and various second partners in the following former French possessions: Algeria 48/15, Chad 54/13, Mauritania 56/6, Senegal 33/13 and Togo 36/14. Morocco and Tunisia, having been protectorates rather than colonies and having maintained at least a modicum of international legal personality during the protectorate, show a characteristically flatter curve, and a glimpse of their recent history appears in their top treaty partners: Morocco has France and Spain at 15% each, and Tunisia has France and USA at 14% and 11%.

American preponderance in the Western Hemisphere is reflected in such first-partner percentages as Haiti 71, Panama 60 and Bolivia 59. Most other Western Hemisphere countries are in the 50% and 40% range, and among the lowest percentages (least "dominated") are those of Canada 36, Mexico 34, Brazil 27, Cuba 17, Argentina 13. All except Cuba have the USA as their first treaty partner, even Argentina, where the USA is closely followed by Italy with 10%. As in the case of France, second-ranking partners vary greatly and include here mainly Western European countries, other Latin American countries and Specialized Agencies.

On the other end of the scale of satellite patterns are the traditional neutrals, e.g., Austria, Sweden and Switzerland. Their profiles are extremely even, and they tend to show geographical neighbors more prominently than the Great Powers. Austria's first four partners are West Germany/Switzerland/Yugoslavia/USA and their percentages are 9/7/7/7. Analogous information for Sweden is Norway/France/Great Britain/Denmark at 8/5/5/5, and for Switzerland it is France/Italy/West Germany/Austria at 12/10/8/8.

It may seem that these illustrations and comparisons have carried us some distance away from the original example of Sri Lanka. True, but this precisely is the best way to use the profiles. They are not made for the country expert, or would-be expert, who looks for detail and depth. The profiles give breadth, not depth. They are comparative rather than immersive. While most of the individual profiles are national, their optimal use is cross-national, regional and global. Thus, it is quite typical in the use of the profiles that an inquiry into the treaties of Sri Lanka leads the user to a whole kaleidoscope of treaty patterns elsewhere. Of course, Sri Lanka should not get lost in the process. Each comparison refines or adds some new perspective on the *relative* significance of any one detail in Sri Lanka's profile. Otherwise, a detail is nothing but a piece of raw data — meaningless until put into a broader perspective of comparable cases. Then, expected results will confirm prior hypotheses, and surprises may generate new ideas. The image can be refined almost indefinitely by adding further details as well as new dimensions in multiple perspectives — for countries and groups of countries and, as we shall see presently, for trends over time, for topics and for textual references to international institutions and for any combinations of any subsets of these data.

b. *Time Trends*

The best way to start any trend analysis of treaty profiles is to look at Lines 42-44. That information normalizes the trend and puts it into regional and global perspective. Suppose we are interested in Belgium, but we want to start with a broader perspective. The world trend, of course, is the basic benchmark, and therefore it is repeated as a constant on the bottom line of every profile. The world trend goes up slightly during the first three 5-year periods and then levels off: 18/23/29/29. (The figures are percentages of the 20-year total.) Belgium's regional group, Western Europe, behaves similarly but the rise is even slighter and it actually drops by one percentage point instead of leveling off in the last period: 22/25/27/26. In terms of these two trends it is significant that Belgium's treaty frequency goes down slowly but consistently throughout the 20-year period with a sharp drop-off in the last segment: 29/28/26/17. Could it have anything to do with Belgian membership in the European Community? Have regional institutional processes replaced part of the traditional treaty-making? A quick glance at France and West Germany disproves the idea — both go up sharply, especially West Germany. Italy goes up, too, but drops off again in the last period. Then, finally, there is a similar case. Netherlands goes down, very much like Belgium: 28/30/24/17. Could it be a Benelux phenomenon? No, Luxembourg goes down and up again, and on balance more up than down: 25/24/22/29. In the absence of an obvious explanation that isolates Belgium from neighboring and similar countries we must go through the entire Belgian profile to look for clues. Are there other time clusters, counter-trends or special situations? No, strangely, there is really nothing of the sort. The trend appears evenly distributed over all major partners and even most of the minor ones. Hence, it must be something that is peculiar to Belgium alone, and it may confirm or refute whatever hypothesis prompted the suppositional interest in Belgian treaties in the first place.

Similarly puzzling is the steady decline of British treaties with Western Europe. British treaties remain fairly constant over the whole 20-year period, world-wide, and show only minor and inconclusive variations. Great Britain has an upward trend, or at worst a mildly erratic trend, with all other groups, but the British-European pattern is unequivocally waning: 127-102-94-82. This decline has strange implications for the simultaneous efforts by Great Britain to move closer to the countries of Western Europe, as symbolized by the long process of joining the European Community. Even stranger, the British decline is closely paralleled and indeed exceeded by some of the countries which shared Great Britain's move toward Europe or at least gave serious thought to it. The figures are as follows: Ireland 29-21-13-6, Denmark 60-38-38-31, Norway 75-58-58-31 and—most spectacular of all—Sweden 110-90-56-18. It is unlikely that this trend has much to do with British leadership in the European Free Trade Association. The timing of EFTA overlaps with only a small part of the decline, and other EFTA members do not share the British decline of treaties with Europe. Austria, Portugal and Switzerland show various ups and downs but fail to fit into the pattern of the above examples. The same is true for a non-EFTA control group of such peripheral European countries as Greece, Iceland, Finland, Spain and Yugoslavia. None of them follows the British-Irish-Scandinavian pattern of a consistent decline of treaties with Western Europe. A final complication is the fact that Denmark, Ireland and Sweden show a *general* decline of treaty activity, world-wide, and this helps explain the decline of their European treaties, but that explanation does not hold true for Norway and evidently not for Great Britain itself. The Norwegian and British figures for all treaties with the rest of the world are 132-106-134-89 and 282-234-221-244. What do these inconsistencies mean? Only further research can tell, but the profiles may help put the researcher on a high-yield track.

Other examples have clearer messages—and obvious reasons. The Cuban trend clearly reverses Western and Communist group affinities. If we combine USA and Western Europe and contrast it with the Communist Group, Cuba's treaties distribute as follows over the four 5-year periods: West 6-22-6-2, and East 0-0-23-42. The Albanian trend is perhaps the stormiest of all. Albania's primary partner is Yugoslavia, but the treaties between them oscillate between high and zero: 23-0-7-0. Albania has also had some ups and downs in its treaties with the Soviet Union and East Germany. They are similar to each other but different and less spectacular than those with Yugoslavia. Finally, there is a consistent rise of Albania's treaties with China, which differs from all three other patterns: 0-5-9-14. Erratic as these trends may appear by themselves, they correlate quite nicely with what is generally known about the changes in Albanian foreign policy during those periods.

Africa poses a special problem for analysis because the treaties of the entire group go up at the uniquely steep rate of 1/5/18/75. It is not necessarily meaningful, therefore, to find that any country's treaties with Africa are going up over time. That is true for nearly all countries. It depends on how rapidly they go up, and especially if they exceed or lag behind the African average. Taking only the second half of the 20-year period, when most African countries achieved independence, we find that the rate of increase among Africa's treaty partners ranks approximately as follows: China 1:12, Israel 1:11, West Germany 1:9, USA 1:6. Now we cross the African average at 1:4, and find among the sub-average partners France at 1:3 and the Soviet Union at 1:2. On the other hand, the ranking changes if we take the total amounts rather than the trend of merely the last decade. Now the top three are USA, France and West Germany (140, 129 and 110), while the USSR and China are trailing at some distance with 87 and 51. Finally, if we multiply the total treaties by the rate of increase to obtain a weighted dual indicator, West Germany moves to the top with 990 followed by USA (840) and China (612).

Another possible use of time trends is to correlate them with some outstanding political personalities who presumably have had an influence on the treaty behavior of their countries. For instance, the Khrushchev years show almost twice the rate of Soviet treaty-making as compared with the late Stalin years. The early Dulles era marks the highest rate of treaty making by the United States compared to any other period before or after. De Gaulle's years nearly doubled the previous treaty volume of France. The early Nasser era raised Egypt's treaty volume by almost 50% but it went back to pre-Nasser levels after 1960. The troubled last years of Perón in the early 1950's show by far the lowest rate of Argentinian treaties in post-war history. South Korea's treaty rate more than doubled after Syngman Rhee left the presidency in 1960. Many more examples can be found not only for major political personalities but also for major impersonal events which affect the whole political life of a given country, including its treaty behavior. The shift, for instance, in South Vietnam's treaties from France to USA as its major partner correlates perfectly with the timing of the Vietnam War and the changing roles of these two outside countries, and of course the earlier examples of Albania, Cuba and Yugoslavia fit equally well into the present perspective.

All trend analyses, finally, should take advantage of the regional profiles for an intermediate perspective that is broader than national and yet not as all-inclusive as the global data. The clearly upward trends of the African and Arab groups and IGO's (in this order) contrast with only one clearly downward trend of any group (Commonwealth) and with mixed trends in all other groups.

TREATY PROFILES

c. Topics

In working with profile topics, users should remember two caveats. First, profile topics are aggregates or clusters of topics, rather than individual treaty topics, and the component parts are identified and quantified in the Thesaurus, 9/f. Second, all topics are relatively "soft" data, at least when compared to such hard facts as treaty partners and dates of signature. Users should therefore refrain from fine distinctions and overly subtle interpretations. Only the grossest contrasts are safe where each piece of quantitative information is surrounded by an arguable fringe. But some contrasts are indeed stark enough to convey a clear message.

The party groups, for example, offer some extreme cases. The global average proportion of aid treaties in all treaties is 20%. The highest proportion of aid treaties within any group is in IGO's, 68%, and the lowest is in Western Europe, 8%. Military treaties also offer some strong contrasts. The global average is 7%, but Commonwealth and USA have twice and three times the world-wide rate, 14% and 22%. Some of the neutral countries have as little as one-seventh or one-third the global rate, e.g., Switzerland at 1%, Austria and Sweden at 2%. The Communist Group is at the same level as the neutrals, 2% for the group as a whole, with variations between the USSR at 3% and China at 1%. In economic treaties (defined as non-aid commercial and financial matters) there is little variation among country groups, from a high for Western Europe at 34% to a low for Africa at 18%. And yet two major countries stand out with extreme scores, and in reverse order of their stereotyped images of commercial and proletarian values. The American rate of commercial treaties is lower than that of the lowest country group, and the Chinese is higher than that of the highest country group. There are good reasons, of course. The figures are relative, not absolute, and the American profile leans more heavily toward foreign aid and military matters than any group of countries in the world, thus leaving fewer percentage points for other topics. Part of the reason for the preponderance of Chinese commercial treaties is the "limbo" status of the Chinese Government during most of that period, when commercial and other non-political agreements were often the only kind that some Western countries would make with China. Nevertheless, it remains as a curious contrast between stereotype and reality.

The biggest single deviation from the global average among topical group profiles is the proportion of aid treaties in the IGO group. Aid accounts for more than two-thirds (68%) of all IGO treaties, about twice the rate of the next group (Africa, 35%) and USA (34%). There is no other figure above 41% in the entire matrix of party groups and topical percentages. The preponderance of IGO's in aid is most dramatic in percentages but it is still noticeable even in absolute figures. The two leading national aid donors, USA at 873 and USSR at 283, trail behind the all-IGO total of 1,003, but if we break the IGO total into individual donors the figure of 1,003 disappears and the first three donors are USA at 873, IBRD at 445 and USSR at 283, followed by WHO, UNICEF, UNSF and West Germany.

The extreme rate of aid in all IGO treaties raises a question of international law that has received much attention in recent years, especially in connection with the drafting history of the 1969 Vienna Convention on the Law of Treaties and the even broader question of the legal personality of IGO's. In both contexts it has been argued that IGO's play a large role in international law (and the profiles show that they do), but that IGO's are nevertheless somehow limited in their legal activities and categorically different from nation states in their treaty-making behavior. The difference has been more often asserted than documented because it is indeed difficult to document in hundreds of details, but the profiles aggregate the differences into a clear quantitative statement. The proportion of 68% aid treaties differentiates IGO's from States in precisely the categorical manner which non-quantitative research has found so difficult to prove. It shows that IGO's are indeed only limited-purpose associations compared to nation states which spread their formal interactions over the whole spectrum of human activities.

d. Institutions

Here we are looking again at hard data, unlike the soft topical categories, but it is a species of data that is not within the mainstream of professional habits and expectations in international law. Even professional researchers in international law and international organization may not find these references intuitively obvious or relevant to any concepts with which they are familiar. It is well known that IGO's play an *active* role as treaty makers, but not much attention has been paid to their *passive* role as objects of treaties. Only the passive role is used here under IGO references to measure the degree to which international law relies upon and involves IGO's. For a complete list of IGO's found in this passive mode, see Thesaurus, 9/d.

With this understanding in mind a user can find all sorts of interesting differences in the treaty behavior of various countries and groups of countries and can correlate them with other legal and political facts. For example, any academic or governmental effort to rank the effectiveness of various IGO's may find it useful to compare other rank orders with a ranked list of IGO references in treaties. The profiles identify only two individual IGO's (UN and ICJ) and cluster others together by types (Specialized Agencies, arbitration courts and commissions and all others). One look at the World Total profile shows the dominant position of the UN with 656 treaty references, followed by the ICJ/PCIJ with 464. (The World Total profile shows double counts.) The other columns are sums of several IGO's and must therefore be broken down into their component parts or averaged out. Details are available in the Thesaurus, 9/d, and can be further refined in the WORLD TREATY IN-

DEX, Volume 4, pp. 677-716. There are only about a dozen IGO's with non-trivial numbers of treaty references. In addition to UN and ICJ they are the following Specialized Agencies: ICAO, ILO, IMF, IBRD, IAEA, GATT and FAO; the following regional agencies: OECD/EPU, NATO and Council of Europe; and hundreds of arbitration and special commissions grouped together under these two headings. None of the individual IGO's can compete with the UN. The ICAO is the second largest single IGO with 498 treaty references, followed closely by the ICJ with 462 references.

Equally significant is the negative evidence. Which IGO's usually figure prominently on other lists but do not rank high in IGO references? The European Economic Community, for instance, appears grossly underrepresented as compared with common professional perceptions of its importance. It has only 8 bilateral treaty references as compared with 116 for the similar but less significant OECD, not to speak of the Specialized Agencies and the United Nations. Why? One obvious reason is the difference in membership, and hence the smaller universe of total treaties in the case of the Community. But the rate is so low that it remains below professional expectations even after we allow for it by expressing treaties as a percentage of membership. So there must be some other explanation. We might hypothesize a non-linear correlation between IGO references in treaties and the effectiveness of an IGO. It may be that up to a point the correlation is positive, but beyond that point it turns negative. The European Community may already have developed beyond that turning point. By now there are so many internal Community procedures for dealing with issues that used to be regulated by treaties (and within treaties by IGO references) that the treaty route is obsolescing for those intra-group relations which fall under Community jurisdiction.

How can we test this hypothesis? If true, intra-group commercial treaties should taper off after 1958. This is not directly testable in the profiles because topics are not permutated against country pairs and time. A fair approximation, however, can be worked out with the data on hand in the profiles. We can compare for Community countries the ratio of economic treaties in total treaties, and then check if the ratio differs between in-group treaties and out-group treaties. The post-1958 period cannot be isolated but it should have some effect on the total, and hence even a slight but consistent deviation in the expected direction would confirm the hypothesis. This is indeed the case. In-group economic treaties run at about 20% of total in-group treaties, and a sample of out-group treaties with Community countries shows a 25% rate under otherwise identical circumstances. The test can be further refined, of course, by enlarging the sample and differentiating between time periods. Even this rough first measure, however, serves as a reasonable corroboration of the hypothesis. The hypothesis itself had the limited purpose of explaining the low rate of Community references compared with other IGO references, and only as an illustration of how to use the institutional section of the profiles.

The above example shows also that not every answer is immediately visible in any one profile. Some questions need more complicated responses. Data may have to be pieced together from different profiles and rearranged to suit a particular research context. In the process of working out complex answers a user will create derivative data sets from the figures given in the profiles themselves. This is a perfectly normal and indeed highly desirable type of use, and further examples are given under "Combinations" (6/f) below, but first we must complete the description of the relatively simple and straightforward uses to be made of the data as they appear in the profiles.

e. *Registration*

Registration figures have little substantive use in broader questions of international law and politics, but they have some practical value in the use of the profiles and some indirect long-range effect on government behavior.

The only substantive use of registration figures is to serve as a rough measure of a country's compliance with Article 102 of the UN Charter and hence, arguably, its general cooperativeness in international legal processes. Article 102 provides for the registration of treaties of UN Member States. The obligation, however, is oddly phrased. Article 102 only says that treaties must be registered as soon as possible but not by whom. Since treaties obviously cannot register themselves, the passive voice in Article 102 obscures the crucial point as to which of two or more signatories has the obligation to register the treaty. In UN practice, either party to a bilateral treaty (or any party to a multilateral treaty) can register the treaty, and all other parties are thereby relieved of their obligation. Thus the question often reduces itself to such non-political and uninteresting matters as speed of internal administrative processes and length of the mail run. The United States, for instance, has the highest rate of treaty registration of any country in the world but this high rate may reflect in part at least the relative efficiency of the paperwork assembly line in the State Department and the short mail run from Washington to New York rather than any deliberate policy on the part of the United States Government. On the other hand, other factors are not quite irrelevant because the mail run argument should hold also for Canada and Mexico, and yet Canada ranks only 16th on the world list and Mexico is in the unranked bottom category of countries which have registered zero percent of their treaties.

The world list starts with USA at 93% and drops quite rapidly below the 60% level. Besides USA, only the following countries are above 60%: Belgium 77, United Kingdom 74, USSR 65, Israel and Netherlands 62 each. Then there are four more countries above 50%: Denmark 58, Australia 55, New Zealand 54 and Greece 53. All the rest are below 50%, again leaving out countries with a treaty volume below statistical significance. Countries with non-trivial numbers of UNTS treaties and a zero self-registration rate are Chile, Colombia, Mexico, Portugal, Spain, Switzerland

TREATY PROFILES

and West Germany. The last two have an obvious explanation—non-membership in the UN. If, however, the others suggest an Iberian cultural factor, a quick glance at Argentina (33%) and Brazil (18%) will partly refute that hypothesis.

The practical side of registration figures is that they give the user a clue about the completeness of a country's treaties in the profiles. Very generally speaking, the higher the rate of self-registration, the more complete are the country's treaties. This is broadly true for whole countries as well as for particular dyads but there are some special circumstances where the rough measure of self-registration may need refinement. A user can check the rate of UNTS to non-UNTS treaties in the Thesaurus, 9/a. A low proportion of non-UNTS treaties tends to confirm whatever the self-registration rate suggested earlier. A high proportion of non-UNTS treaties, however, needs a further check in another section of the Thesaurus, 9/e. If that country's national treaty sources have been used for the data bank, the rate of completeness is high, regardless of the UNTS/non-UNTS ratio. If not, completeness relates inversely to the non-UNTS ratio. Most of these differences are quite subtle and will not affect normal use of the profiles. If, however, a high degree of precision is needed, users should feel free to consult with the Treaty Research Center at the University of Washington.

Finally, there is an indirect effect of registration figures on the real world of government behavior in treaty registration. Governments try to optimize their images as good registrants, and the publication of treaty statistics serves as an incentive.

f. Combinations

By now the reader is presumably familiar with the various methods of looking for answers to research questions that are directly answerable on the basis of any one profile. In some of the earlier examples there has already been a hint at more complicated situations. Sometimes the information is not available exactly as sought but must first be pieced together from several profiles and transformed into a derivative data set. This should not be viewed as a burden but as an additional option in using the profiles. This capacity is precisely what distinguishes TREATY PROFILES from an index or other reference work. The profiles allow for a wide variety of increasingly sophisticated responses to highly complicated questions. Users can exploit the strength of this resource by expanding a question from a simple factual inquiry to a self-enlarging game of testing all kinds of hypotheses by combining partial answers from different profiles. Then, in the hands of an experienced user, the profiles can grow from information almanac to research laboratory.

Suppose a scholar wants to quantify what President Kennedy called the effort to enlarge the area in which the writ of law may run in world affairs. He will first need to operationalize Kennedy's rhetoric by defining several quantifiable concepts. Suppose the "area" to be enlarged can be defined as the number of countries in which the "writ of law" may run; the "writ of law" as treaties; the act of "running" as the functional involvement of international institutions in the implementation of treaties. This is not to claim, of course, that there are no other, or better, ways to do empirical research on Kennedy's policy pronouncement and its implications for the development of international law. It is only an example for the use of treaty profiles in a complex issue which relates academic research to the real world, and where the response depends on a derivative data set.

The World Total profile gives a useful overview of the absolute amounts of IGO involvement in the treaties of the various regions of the world, see Columns 15-19 and Lines 32-39. The absolute amounts, however, do not lend themselves easily to comparisons, and the percentage comparisons are scattered over the various regional profiles. They need to be assembled into an analogous table. The information is in the same place in every regional profile, Columns 15-19 and Line 42. In the process of pulling the information together the user might as well do a few other things that are available in the profiles but not in exactly the needed form. For instance, he can add up the percentages horizontally, make a new column for totals on the right and rank-order the lines according to the totals. This will produce the following table:

Percentage of Treaties with IGO References in All UNTS Treaties

(Arranged by Party Groups and IGO Types)

Party Group	UN	Spec Ag's	Intl Court	Arbitration	Other	Total
Intl Organs	28	12	13	14	4	71
Arab Group	14	21	8	15	9	67
African Group	19	14	10	16	4	63
Western Europe	3	14	5	8	18	48
Asian Group	10	15	8	8	6	47
Commonwealth	4	14	4	5	12	39
Latin America	7	9	4	6	7	33
Communist Group	4	3	—	3	18	28
World Average	8	12	6	7	12	45

Here, now, are not merely raw data but a whole set of inter-related propositions, numerical in form but substantive in content. The totals alone convey a distinct message. The ranking prompts questions and suggests answers. Why are the first three so much higher than the rest, and what do they have in common that causes their location on the scale? The answer happens to be simple. IGO's include in their treaties routinely some provisions for IGO-administered dispute settlement and other IGO involvements, and IGO's happen to be among the top treaty partners for African and Arab countries and have a statistical effect on them. The middle ranks are close to the global average and need no special explanation. The bottom ranks have an explanation that is the converse of that of the top ranks. They, too, are under the statistical influence of major treaty partners which, conversely, have unusually low rates of IGO involvement in their treaties. Those partners are one or more of the following three major powers, analogously tabulated below:

Percentage of Treaties with IGO References in All UNTS Treaties

(Arranged by Selected States and IGO Types)

Party	UN	Spec Ag's	Intl Court	Arbitration	Other	Total
USA	5	8	3	2	9	27
USSR	2	2	—	1	15	20
China	5	—	—	—	14	19
Average	5	8	3	1	10	27

Note: USA largely determines group averages because of high absolutes.

The low rating of USA seems ironic in the context of Kennedy's rhetoric. Suppose, however, Kennedy did not know about America's low performance in this field; suppose someone told him; suppose Kennedy wanted to change the facts to fit his purpose. How? A record of decades could not have been changed overnight, but he could certainly have instructed the State Department to translate presidential policy into the drafting of American treaties. If so, we would now look back on the early 1960's as the beginnings of a trend, visible in these treaty profiles, whereby the United States moved away from the company of countries which share the arrogance of power, and toward those for which equality under the law is at least a statistical appearance if not a literal truth. This was not the case but it might have been the case if the message implicit in treaty statistics had been as well researched by scholars and as well internalized by policy makers as are some other international statistics, e.g., trends in international trade and payments, UN votes, state visits, diplomatic representation and many similar patterns.

The global inventory is but a first step. It opens up a macroscopic view but it does not yet suggest specific steps on how to enlarge the area in which the writ of law may run.

Let us exemplify one of various possible next steps by looking at the most obvious symbol of the writ of law in world affairs—the International Court of Justice and its function as a reference point in treaties. Within the whole range of ICJ references let us focus on one problem that has been much discussed in the profession and that has a direct bearing on the overall inquiry, namely, whether the ICJ should be "regionalized" by instituting special chambers for intra-regional disputes.

There may be other ways to operationalize the question so that treaty profiles can help with partial answers, but one possible way is to compare intra-regional and extra-regional treaties for their rates of ICJ references. Here again there is no ready-made answer in any one profile but a user can combine various partial answers from different profiles and work them into a derivative data base. We can make a matrix similar to the first one, showing the seven regional country groups (Column 1, Lines 32–38) both horizontally and vertically. Then we fill in the matrix cells with information taken from the seven group profiles, each from Column 17, Lines 32–38, and the totals of Column 17, Line 41, as a separate line at the bottom. The matrix will now look as follows:

Mutual Treaties with ICJ References

	Afri	Arab	Asia	C'lth	C'ist	Latin	W.Eur
African Group	—	—	2	1	—	—	12
Arab Group	—	2	—	6	—	—	11
Asian Group	2	—	14	4	—	—	22
Commonwealth	1	6	4	4	—	1	21
Communist Group	—	—	—	—	—	—	—
Latin America	—	—	—	1	—	2	6
Western Europe	12	11	22	21	—	6	44
World Total	58	47	114	60	2	59	217

Note: Most world totals are much greater than sums of entries because totals include but entries exclude treaties with non-group parties, IGO's and unilateral declarations. Differences do not affect in-group/out-group ratio.

TREATY PROFILES

Next we construct an identical table and fill in analogous information from Column 3 of the same profiles, same lines, and an analogous total line:

All Mutual Treaties

	Afri	Arab	Asia	C'lth	C'ist	Latin	W.Eur
African Group	14	4	5	42	203	—	330
Arab Group	4	32	33	70	221	6	288
Asian Group	5	33	250	146	322	27	390
Commonwealth	42	70	146	168	77	81	675
Communist Group	203	221	322	77	2,910	86	579
Latin America	—	6	27	81	86	114	442
Western Europe	330	288	390	675	579	442	3,866
World Total	975	953	2,062	1,725	4,765	1,731	7,839

Note: Most world totals are much greater than sums of entries because totals include but entries exclude treaties with non-group parties, IGO's and unilateral declarations. Differences do not affect in-group/out-group ratio.

Now we take from each matrix every cell along the diagonal and express it as a percentage of the corresponding total in the bottom line. We will get two percentage lines as follows:

Percentages of Intra-Regional Treaty Activity

	Afri	Arab	Asia	C'lth	C'ist	Latin	W.Eur	World Average
ICJ References	—	4%	12%	7%	—	3%	20%	7%
All Treaties	1%	3%	12%	10%	61%	7%	49%	31%

Both lines show intra-regional activity as a percentage of world-wide activity—the first line for ICJ references, and the second line for all treaties. The world averages (right-hand column) are computed separately against the All States total.

What do the figures mean? If we look only at the world averages, it seems that the advocates of regional chambers have a good case. The rate of intra-regional ICJ references is less than a quarter of the rate of intra-regional treaties (7:31), both normalized as percentages of the world total. Thus there seems to be a genuine potential for increasing the role of the ICJ in intra-regional treaties and dispute settlement. The standard argument runs as follows. National governments consider the ICJ too remote, too global and too cumbersome to really understand local disputes between neighboring countries, and local disputes should be handled by small panels of ICJ judges with expertise in the particular region and its traditions and problems.

The two global averages support this view, but the regional details suggest a different interpretation. The averages do not spread evenly over the regions. In fact, there are only two regions that show a promising discrepancy between ICJ references and regional treaties, the Communist Group and the West European Group. These two groups seem to have a "genuine potential" for increasing ICJ references in intra-regional treaties, but *only* these two groups, not the others. A closer look throws doubts even on these two groups. The Communist Group has the lowest possible rate of ICJ use. Its world-wide ICJ score for any and all countries has remained zero throughout the 20-year period under review, whether in-group or out-group, and so there does not appear to be a great potential for change in any direction, regional or otherwise. Western Europe, by contrast, has a good statistical case, but there are powerful extra-statistical reasons to question its suitability as an example. The Court happens to be located in The Hague, Netherlands, near the geographical center of Western Europe, and it is also European in origin and design. Thus the Court is not "remote" from either the scene or the legal traditions of European treaty-making and dispute settlement. In fact, a frequent argument of non-European lawyers and politicians is the exact opposite, namely, that the ICJ is too European and hence too remote from the interests and traditions of non-European countries and lawyers.

And so we find a paradox in almost every one of the major regions when we try to operationalize the research questions which arise from Kennedy's pronouncement about the writ of law in world affairs. The United States has the greatest discrepancy between favorable rhetoric and laggard use. The Communist countries are consistent—they have no favorable rhetoric for the Court; neither do they have any use for it in their treaties, whether in-group or out-group. Western Europe has the best case for referring to the Court, historically as well as statistically, and it has an unused potential as defined, but Western Europe also happens to be the one region where the existence of regional chambers would probably make no difference. Latin America is in a somewhat similar situation, but less clearly so. Third World countries, finally, have considerable variety in their statistics and in their responses, and in some cases the numbers are insignificant. The discrepancy, however, tends to be the reverse of that of the West—unfavorable rhetoric and yet favorable action, but the favorable action is not so much the result of so many individual policy decisions as it is a matter of automatic inclusion of ICJ references in the aid agreements with Specialized Agencies, and these agreements in turn constitute a high percentage of Third World treaties.

Let us remember, though, that this is only an illustration of the use of the profiles, and not a "real" treatment of the substantive issue. The illustration need not stop here. The same matrix method can be used to break regional groups into sub-groups—for instance, Western Europe into Scandinavia/Benelux/Other or into EFTA/Common Market/Other. We can also break any region into individual countries, and we can go from countries to topics. ICJ chambers may be topical rather than geographical, and in fact the ICJ Statute refers primarily to topical specialization as the rationale for Court chambers. The more combinations and complexity and inter-relatedness, the better will the user optimize the potential of the profiles. They have been designed to make it easy to aggregate, to compare, to analyze, to hypothesize and in many other ways to "play" with concepts and hunches. Users can thus combine the advantages of looking at the forest and looking at the trees, and can concretize and refine whatever ideas about international law and world politics may be floating through their awareness.

7. Problems

The main problem in designing the profiles has been an overabundance of interesting data competing for limited space. Any part of the standard profile could have been designed differently. Any change would have made some comparisons possible or easy that are now difficult or impossible, and of course some of those which are now available would have been lost. There are three reasons for discussing the aborted alternatives: (1) in the presentation of such a large array of material to a wide and varied audience, it seems necessary and proper to explain why certain choices have been made, especially since any one choice is likely to please some users and displease others; (2) the alternatives discussed here will give users an opportunity to make suggestions for future editions of TREATY PROFILES, and to do so on the basis of concrete and realistic options; (3) the alternatives also serve to illustrate what kinds of additional services are available at the Treaty Research Center of the University of Washington, through individual computer printouts custom-made for particular research purposes, as will be further explained below under "Reference," 8/b. The following alternatives have been seriously considered but rejected for a variety of reasons.

a. Overall Structure

One conspicuous problem in the general layout is the large amount of empty space in the profiles of low-volume treaty-makers. Much of that space could have been saved by omitting treaty makers below some arbitrary cut-off point, say, 50 treaties or 10 partners, and the space could have been used for additional information on high-volume treaty-makers. Such a switch, however, would have had serious drawbacks. There is neatness and rigor in the flat statement that every treaty-making party in the world is represented in the profiles, and every profile has exactly the same standard format. These two criteria outweigh the others in a work that emphasizes quantification and comparability.

Similar arguments apply for and against the exclusion of IGO's as treaty makers. IGO's tend to have few treaties and little variety among them. A minimum requirement of 50 treaties would have eliminated all but about a dozen of the IGO's, and a categorical exclusion of IGO's would have eliminated all of them, of course. In either case, the profiles would have gained space but lost coverage of one of the most interesting and novel features of contemporary international law, namely, the appearance and active participation of legal entities other than the traditional nation states.

The opposite argument can be made for the inclusion of multilateral treaties. The profiles exclude multilaterals, and much of the empty space could have been filled by including them. Costs, however, would have been incommensurate. It would have involved sacrificial efforts in computer programming not only financially out of line with the rest of the work but actually beyond the physical limit of available machinery. Even the present program nearly exhausts the memory capacity of the computer, and the inclusion of multilaterals would have meant transferring the whole computation to another machine at some other location—theoretically possible but impracticable within the time-money frame of the whole production. Besides, the inclusion of multilaterals, even if possible, would raise a serious question of data validity. Participation in multilaterals is less representative of national policy and purpose than is the individual negotiation of a bilateral treaty. It is almost like the difference in involvement between a vote in a corporate body (multilateral) and the personal commitment of an individual contract (bilateral). Finally, there is a statistical reason. Only one out of ten treaties in the world, roughly speaking, is multilateral, but each involves a variable number of parties, from three to over a hundred. It would have been difficult to standardize the multilaterals among themselves and to make them comparable to the bilaterals, and it would have strained not only the design and production of the profiles but also their usability. For many potential users, the profiles would have become so complex as to be obscure, and thus useless.

TREATY PROFILES

A case has been made for including the League of Nations Treaty Series. It can be done. The material is in the data bank, and if merged into the profiles it would extend the time span from 20 years to 45 years, and would enlarge the volume of treaties from about 13,000 to about 17,000. The enlargement would solidify trend projections or other conclusions that can now be assailed on grounds of inadequacy of number of treaties or shortness of time span or both. The arguments are good, but they do not overcome the problem of various discontinuities in parties and IGO's. There are not many countries with serious discontinuity problems but they happen to be among the largest treaty-makers, and would therefore affect the statistics quite severely. Typical problem cases would be the British Empire, China and Germany, whose successor States account together for about a third of all the treaties in the present profiles. IGO successions would create similar problems. Besides, IGO involvement in treaties, both active and passive, was much smaller in the inter-war period than it is now, and thus the League-time IGO's would add little in substance at a great cost in complexity.

b. *Data Choices*

(1) Partners

The basic threefold division into individual partners, partner groups and totals has held up against all suggestions for alternatives, such as eliminating the groups and extending the individual partners from 30 to 40. Some alternatives have been considered among the group partners, especially whether to split larger groups (like Western Europe and Asia) into sub-groups, but the present format has remained the best compromise between maximizing the number of individual partners and covering the major regions of the world. The UNTS total could have been extended across the entire line but it might create more confusion than additional information. As it is, the single reference total is the basis for the percentages in the institutional and registration columns, and that figure is unambiguous in its isolation. The comparisons, finally, cannot be changed without changing the rest of the profile structure, and no alternative appears necessary or possible.

The only major alternative that has been seriously considered and reluctantly rejected in the partner column is to extend the World Total and the group profiles beyond the standard 30 partners to cover *all* partners individually rather than to lump them together in Line 31. This is a most attractive proposition, and there is no substantive counter-argument, especially if it can be done in addition to rather than in lieu of the standard format. The only reason it has not been done is that it cannot be handled within the computer hardware-software limits of this particular effort. If possible, it will be included in future editions.

(2) Partner's World Total

This column can be eliminated without loss of information but at a substantial cost in convenience. Users would have to switch pages back and forth every time they wanted to see the dyadic total in the perspective of the partner's total.

(3) Dyads

The dyadic total is necessary as the backbone of each profile, and no alternative has even been contemplated. The other two dyadic columns give the percentage rates of the dyadic total in the world total of the profiled party and each of its partners. These two columns could be eliminated without loss of information because every entry is the result of a calculation with data available elsewhere in the profiles. Nevertheless, the inconvenience would be even greater than in the case of the partner's world total because the figures cannot be found merely by turning pages but must be calculated for each case when the need arises. In-house use of pre-print versions of the profiles has rated these two columns among the most useful ones, and no change is presently contemplated.

(4) Time

Several alternatives have been considered in addition to the ultimate choice of four 5-year periods. New users normally ask for finer subdivisions, 2-year periods, single years or even half years. A quick look at the dyadic totals for the whole 20-year period usually disposes of these suggestions. The totals are too small for meaningful sub-division into such fine time slices. More realistic would be one of the opposite options, having periods of more than five years. Two 10-year periods would still give us a sense of the general trend, up or down, but of course at a loss of detail. Even more radical but still reasonably possible would be a single column showing the net gain or net loss by subtracting the first 10-year period from the second. If a dyad, for instance, had a total of 17 treaties for the whole 20-year period, 10 in the first half and 7 in the second, the single entry would show –3. Combined with the total of 17, the single figure really tells the whole story, but at a substantial cost in clarity. In-house tabulations at the Treaty Research Center have used this method successfully, but it would probably be too obscure for general use. In short, there are reasonable alternatives, preferably for fewer long periods than for many shorter ones, and the present choice of four 5-year periods is conditioned by the total time span. If future editions can cover the 30-year period from 1946 to 1975, there will be three time columns at 10 years each.

(5) Topics

Topics, like time, can be sub-divided almost infinitely. The data bank has nearly 70 mutually exclusive topics, and it is obviously impossible within the book format to have one column for each topic on one page. There has to be some form of grouping and clustering, and the only questions are (a) how far to go in aggregation and (b) which topics to group with which others. The simplest way, it seems, would be to have two columns following the traditional distinction between political and technical treaties. That distinction is easy to make in extreme cases, as between a treaty of alliance and a visa agreement, but it blurs in hundreds of intermediate cases and thus becomes useless as an ordering device. Another way to achieve a reduction to two columns would be to group the first three and the last two columns together. The analytic distinction between the two groups would follow the traditional distinction between equal and unequal treaties. One could argue that administrative, diplomatic, social and commercial treaties create an equal relation among partners at least for the limited purpose of any one treaty of that kind, whatever inequality may exist between the parties in other ways, whereas aid and military treaties usually show an inequality in rights and obligations in the very terms and purpose of the treaty itself. In practice, however, the distinction also tends to blur, although not as badly as the traditional one between political and technical treaties.

Alternatively, it is possible to sub-divide the bulkier columns into their component parts, e.g., social cooperation into sanitation, education, cultural exchange, labor, social security, transportation, communication and any of their logical sub-divisions or sub-groups. The same can be done for administrative and diplomatic and economic matters. A mere list of topics shows the practical problem of where to stop in making the screen progressively finer, see Thesaurus, 9/f. Each step in this direction, of course, reduces the space available for other purposes and also creates new problems of comparing progressively unequal and trivial magnitudes. If future editions have a change in the topic structure it will probably be in the direction of reducing rather than increasing the number of topic columns.

(6) Institutions

This is the section with the biggest problems and the greatest potential for change. A good argument can be made (and has been made in the design phase) to eliminate it altogether because it is not exactly comparable to the information in the other columns. IGO references are available in the data bank for UNTS treaties only, but all other data rely on the combined total of UNTS and national collections. The counter-argument, however, has consistently prevailed. IGO references are such an unusual set of data, collected at such great cost (reading and coding the full text of every treaty), that they must remain available despite some flaws in comparability. Besides, the flaws are all explicit and systemic, and users can make allowance for them as shown in Chapter 6/d above.

Retaining the IGO references in the profiles does not necessarily mean keeping them in exactly the same form. A good case can be made, here as elsewhere, for contraction as well as expansion. To accomplish the former, we should probably combine UN and Specialized Agencies into a single UN Group column, and we might combine ICJ and Arbitration into a single column for dispute settlement agencies. Then we could pull regional courts and various conciliation commissions out of the Other column and merge them with the dispute settlement agencies, where they would logically belong if the definition were to be so broadened. On the other hand, if more details are needed, the Other column could be split into regional and other agencies, which would probably interest many users, and the Specialized Agencies could be divided into smaller groups or individual entities. All these changes are possible, but they would involve losing the single identities of such key agencies as the UN and ICJ. They have been deliberately singled out in the present version of the profiles, as is the separate comparability of ICJ and arbitration agencies. The three major types of formal international dispute settlement—political, arbitrational and judicial—are thus made comparable in whatever combination a user may choose. This format offers a high degree of research flexibility which would be lost under any of the constrictive options.

(7) Registration

This column loses much of its usefulness if the preceding institutional columns are eliminated or if, as may happen in the near future, the institutional columns are brought up to the same level of treaty coverage as the rest of the profiles. Until that happens, however, the Registration column fulfills a small but useful methodological function.

c. Data Permutations

This is the most interesting type of possible changes. It would offer a whole range of new permutations between topics and time, and between institutions and time. This would not be merely a matter of convenience but it would

TREATY PROFILES

actually supply some information not presently available in the profiles. If we contract existing columns and/or enlarge the format, we could add to every matrix cell in each topical and institutional column its own time trend indicator. For instance, the Soviet profile shows that there are 108 Sino-Soviet treaties, and 18 of them concern foreign aid, but it does not show the timing of the aid treaties. It shows the overall trend of *all* Sino-Soviet treaties, and it separates all Soviet treaties into topics, but it does not break any one topic into its own time segments. And yet, this may be crucial information in a given research context, and if widely available for all topics and all institutions it might prompt new research questions presently not even contemplated because of the difficulty of finding the answers. The data bank has the information, and it would take but a policy decision to so adjust the program for future editions of the profiles.

All of this could be done by adding a single trend column after each topical and institutional column, subtracting the treaties of the first half from those of the second and thus indicating whether the trend is up or down and by how much. If, in the above example, the 18 Sino-Soviet aid treaties are distributed 17 and 1 between first and second halves, the Aid column would show 18 as dyadic total and −16 as the trend indicator. Another possibility would be to abolish the dyadic totals in the topical and institutional columns and to show two sub-columns, one for the first half and one for the second, and to let the user compute the combined total where needed.

Analogous arrangements and examples can be imagined for the institutional columns; and some general rearrangement such as this has a good chance for future editions — depending of course on the opinions and suggestions of users. The only reason it has not been adopted for the first edition, despite good arguments and careful consideration, is that it would tend to overcomplicate a presentation which, for many first-timers, will already be near the margin of tolerance for visual complexity.

8. Reference

Experience with pre-print versions of the profiles suggests that there are occasions when a user finds the profiles helpful as a first step but comes to a halt before he finds what he really wants. Most of these frustrations fall into one of two categories. First, something about a treaty in the profiles catches the interest of a user and he wants to get more details about it including the citation so he can read the full treaty text if necessary. That need can be satisfied through the WORLD TREATY INDEX, as will be shown below. Second, the user is looking for some quantitative information that is reasonably within the scope of the profiles but not available in exactly the format or combination in which it is needed. That need can usually be satisfied by writing to the Treaty Research Center at the University of Washington and negotiating a custom-made computer printout for that particular purpose.

a. *WORLD TREATY INDEX*

Suppose a researcher is working with the treaty profile of the Ivory Coast and notices an aid treaty with the UN Special Fund, but the bare fact of the existence of this treaty is not enough for his purpose. He can take any treaty index, of course, but the WORLD TREATY INDEX has a number of advantages for being used together with the treaty profiles. Other indexes may or may not include the particular treaty someone is looking for, but the WORLD TREATY INDEX categorically includes all treaties in TREATY PROFILES. The two works are based on the same computerized data bank, have the same nomenclature and are designed to be used as complementary research tools.

Suppose, then, we decide to use the WORLD TREATY INDEX. What is the best way to make the transition from PROFILES to INDEX? The basic principle is to scan the information given in profiles to determine the *smallest category* under which the treaty can be found in the INDEX, because obviously the smallest category is the easiest in which to find any particular treaty. In our example of an aid treaty between the Ivory Coast and the UN Special Fund concluded during the 1961–1965 period, we can check for the smallest category on the same treaty profile where we found the treaty in the first place. The world total for the Ivory Coast is 32 (Column 3, Line 40), and the world total for UNSF is 113 (Column 2, Line 9). That settles the question, and we can look for the treaty in Volume 4, Party Section, under Ivory Coast, p. 477. If it had been the social cooperation treaty with Mali (Column 11, Line 12), the difference would have been so small that either country could have served as a point of entry to the INDEX.

If the treaty involves two countries with hundreds of treaties, the problem appears to be different but the solution is the same. Dyads (country pairs) have fewer treaties than any of the larger countries. In fact, there are only three country pairs in the entire world with more than 100 dyadic treaties, i.e., Canada-USA 113, China-USSR 108, and UK-USA 104. The average number of treaties for all possible dyads throughout the profiles is as low as two-thirds of one treaty (exactly 0.65), and even if we exclude dyads with zero treaties, the average goes up to only just over two and a half treaties (exactly 2.61). The Party Section of the INDEX (Volume 4) takes account of this statistical fact and is organized within countries by dyads, and within dyads by date of signature. As an extreme example, let us take the 12

British-French economic treaties. They are in the British profile under France, and in the French profile under UK Great Britain. How can we trace them farther? They may seem like 12 needles in the twin haystacks of 981 British and 1,033 French treaties, but the dyadic system of the INDEX reduces the search to a matter of minutes. We need not go through all British or all French treaties but only through the much smaller number of British-French treaties—49 in the profiles and 62 in the INDEX. If we happen to limit the search to treaties within a certain time span, the task is still easier because the 62 British-French treaties are listed in the INDEX in chronological order. Once we have located the treaty in the INDEX, there are three options (for details, see User's Guide in the INDEX):

(1) At the point of encountering the treaty in the INDEX, there is always some additional information about the treaty—more details than in the profiles but less than in the Main Entry Section of the INDEX.

(2) If further details are needed, the user can trace the treaty by means of its serial number to the full entry in the Main Entry Section, and the full entry has all the information the INDEX has to offer on that particular treaty.

(3) If still further details are needed, the user can trace the full text of the treaty through the citation. The citation is also repeated at every point of encounter, not only in the Main Entry Section. The user can thus skip the main entry and go directly to the text if he knows that only the full text will satisfy his inquiry, no matter what details there may be in the Main Entry Section.

There are other types of situations in which the WORLD TREATY INDEX can be used as a complement to the profiles. Suppose a user wishes to extend an analysis of one country back in time through the League of Nations era. Such an effort would take about 20 to 30 man-hours for any of the small or medium-sized countries. The result would be purely longitudinal in one isolated case and it would necessarily lack the comparative perspective of other information in the profiles, such as regional and global averages. Nevertheless, it can be done and may be worthwhile in a given research context. If so, the user would go through the LTS portion of the Party Section of the INDEX (Volume 4, pp. 179-309), count the treaties in every dyad of the chosen country, note separately their topics and time periods and rank-order the several dyadic lines to produce a comparable format. If IGO references are needed, they can be added separately from Volume 4, pp. 673-676.

Thesaurus and INDEX can answer questions about nomenclature and about the various component parts of what appears in the profiles in aggregated form only. The five topic groups of the profiles, for instance, are broken down into 68 particular topics in the Thesaurus, 9/f, and a global count is given for each topic. Any one of these topics is retrievable from the data bank through a custom-made computer program. It works as if it were an analytical magnifying glass—making details visible which the profiles presently submerge in larger aggregations. And beyond simple magnification, there are countless ways in which the data can be re-arranged and re-combined to satisfy particular research needs, but that leads us from the INDEX to individual printouts.

b. *Individual Printouts*

The profiles represent only one of the many possible formats in which the same information can be cast. Furthermore, the data bank on which the profiles are based contains a wide range of additional information that has not been used in the profiles. Users should therefore look beyond the actual format and data limits of the profiles and view the information as a set of modules that can be almost infinitely recombined in alternate ways—expanded or contracted or otherwise modified for individual needs. The Treaty Research Center at the University of Washington is available for consultation as well as design and supply of custom-made printouts for particular research needs which cannot be satisfied by using the present profiles or the WORLD TREATY INDEX.

The user of course decides whether to stay with the printed material on hand or to consult about a custom-made printout. In general, the decision will be similar to any commercial or administrative decision on whether or not to use a computer—the larger the task, the more cost-efficient the computer. If a user of the profiles needs only a minor modification of the printed information, it will usually be most economical and sensible to do it directly, as exemplified above in reference to the WORLD TREATY INDEX and in much more detail in Chapter 6 above.

Even in larger tasks there may well be an idiosyncratic or other non-economic purpose in working with the printed material alone. There is always challenge and sometimes pleasure in going the do-it-yourself route, and of course in colleges and universities there is an educational value, both substantive and methodological, in having students work out things by themselves. The profiles can be used as a quasi-laboratory to teach students how to challenge a given framework and to modify it and put it to new uses. In all these cases it would defeat the purpose of the exercise if the learning experience were short-circuited by writing directly to the Treaty Research Center for the desired information, but there are other cases where that is an appropriate alternative.

Suppose someone is interested in the interplay of trade and aid in the relations between the United States and Latin America. He will almost certainly wish to subdivide Economic Cooperation into some components (e.g., trade, payments, investments) and probably also Aid into its several types (e.g., grants, loans, technical assistance). He will also prefer a finer time scale than the 5-year periods provided in the profiles. Finally, he will wish to cross-relate the topical sub-divisions to the time slices. He will find that none of these subtleties can be extracted from the profiles as they are. The answers are in the INDEX, and if the information happens to be needed for a seminar in Latin American studies, it may be a good idea to divide the task among the students, each student taking one country and tracing all the details in the INDEX, and then to have them all merge their

TREATY PROFILES

data and discuss the results as a cooperative seminar project.

Suppose, however, it is an individual research project. Then the process itself is unimportant and the only important thing is the result. That hypothetical researcher is facing a matrix with 20 countries on the vertical axis, 6 topics on the horizontal axis and 10 permutations of the entire matrix for the 10 biennial periods from 1946 to 1965. That means 1,200 matrix cells, each of which requires an average, say, of 10 minutes of research in the INDEX. We are now at 200 man-hours, and we have not even begun to consider the computation of totals and, if desired, averages and percentages, not to speak of error-proofing, formating, typing, proofreading, correcting, re-typing, and so forth. Under those circumstances it would save substantial amounts of time and money to negotiate a custom-made printout with the Treaty Research Center. Moreover, if any analogous information is needed from other areas (e.g., Africa, Asia, Western Europe), whether for spot checks or for item-by-item comparisons, the task would escalate into the range of thousands of man-hours by manual methods, yet the cost of a computer printout would increase only marginally.

The break-even point will vary from user to user depending on a multitude of factors including cost and dependability of research assistants and typists, need for statistical manipulation and time pressures, among others. Users may take the 20-man-hour limit as a very general rule of thumb. If a project is expected to take less than 20 man-hours of additional search time in the INDEX or in other treaty sources beyond the profiles, it will usually not be worth involving the Treaty Research Center; if more, it will at least be worth an inquiry and a preliminary consultation.

9. Thesaurus

This Thesaurus is limited to the internal reference needs of the profiles. For a more detailed thesaurus and especially for cross-reference to the WORLD TREATY INDEX, please refer to its own thesaurus, Volume 1, Introduction, Section 8

a. Parties and Treaties. This list shows all profiled parties in the same order in which they appear in the book, giving for each the number of UNTS treaties, non-UNTS treaties and total treaties.

b. State Groups. This list identifies the countries grouped together in each of the State Groups (Tables 1-7).

c. Treaty-Active Institutions. Unlike States, the names of international organizations are usually far longer than the 18-character limit of party titles, and the shortened versions may not always be recognizable with certainty even by professionals in the field. Therefore, the list matches the shortened version with the full title of every profiled organization. The short versions are not abbreviations in the usual sense of the term, and they are therefore separated from the abbreviations in 9/g.

d. Treaty-Passive Institutions. This section individuates the IGO's clustered in Columns 15-19 and gives a separate treaty count for each. This will help users decide which passive IGO's they may wish to trace in the International Organization Section in Volume 4 of the INDEX. It will also help users decide when to ask the Treaty Research Center for individually modified profiles singling out one or more of the IGO's presently clustered together in Columns 15-19.

e. National Treaty Collections. This list shows all national treaty collections used for the profiles. Due to variety among sources as to beginning and end of coverage as well as different time lags and overlaps with each other and with the UNTS, it is impossible to make a general statement about non-UNTS coverage. The sources listed below have been used only to *supplement* the UNTS and each other, and only to the extent available. For a quantitative comparison of UNTS and non-UNTS treaties, party by party, see 9/a, list of parties and treaties.

f. Topics. This list sub-divides the topical clusters of Columns 10-14 into individual topics. The individual topics define the contents of the topic clusters both qualitatively and quantitatively. They also illustrate what further refinements of the profiles are available to users either by tracing the topics in the INDEX or by ordering an individually modified version of any profile directly from the Treaty Research Center.

g. Abbreviations. This list shows all abbreviations used in the text or in the tables except for the short titles of international organizations, see 9/c above.

a. *Parties and Treaties*

Table	Party	Treaties UNTS	Non-UNTS	Total
1	African Group	564	411	975
2	Arab Group	593	360	953
3	Asian Group	1,354	708	2,062
4	Commonwealth	1,657	68	1,725
5	Communist Group	1,262	3,503	4,765

THESAURUS

Table	Party	Treaties UNTS	Non-UNTS	Total
6	Latin America	1,316	415	1,731
7	Western Europe	4,303	3,536	7,839
8	Intl Organs	1,431	54	1,485
9	All States	14,399	9,450	23,849
10	World Total	15,960	9,504	25,464
11	Accept UN Charter	68	0	68
12	ICJ Option Clause	62	0	62
13	Afghanistan	37	46	83
14	Afromalagasy Org	1	0	1
15	Albania	47	78	125
16	Algeria	19	33	52
17	Arab League	1	0	1
18	Argentina	115	49	164
19	Asian Productivity	1	0	1
20	Australia	195	6	201
21	Austria	230	215	445
22	Bank Int Settlement	0	1	1
23	Belgium	423	76	499
24	Bel-Lux Econ Union	1	0	1
25	Benelux Econ Union	1	0	1
26	Bolivia	52	6	58
27	Brazil	141	54	195
28	Bulgaria	110	126	236
29	Burma	70	32	102
30	Burundi	6	6	12
31	Cambodia	22	33	55
32	Cameroon	31	21	52
33	Canada	291	19	310
34	Central Afri Rep	8	14	22
35	CERN (Nuc Resrch)	2	1	3
36	Ceylon (Sri Lanka)	83	40	123
37	Chad	10	14	24
38	Chile	92	27	119
39	China People's Rep	22	744	766
40	Colombia	93	19	112
41	COMECON (Econ Aid)	5	0	5
42	Congo (Brazzaville)	7	19	26
43	Congo (Zaire)	21	8	29
44	Costa Rica	40	11	51
45	Council of Europe	3	1	4
46	Cuba	49	62	111
47	Cyprus	40	9	49
48	Czechoslovakia	222	171	393
49	Dahomey	12	13	25
50	Denmark	330	50	380
51	Dominican Republic	39	10	49
52	East Afri Service	2	0	2
53	ECSC (Coal/Steel)	2	1	3
54	Ecuador	70	27	97
55	EEC (Econ Commnty)	4	2	6

TREATY PROFILES

Table	Party	Treaties UNTS	Non-UNTS	Total
56	EFTA (Free Trade)	0	1	1
57	El Salvador	56	14	70
58	Ethiopia	83	15	98
59	Eur Plant Protect	0	1	1
60	Eur Space Research	4	1	5
61	Eur Space Vehicle	1	1	2
62	EURATOM	7	0	7
63	FAO (Food Agri)	13	6	19
64	Fed of Malaya	23	0	23
65	Fed Rhod/Nyasaland	11	0	11
66	Finland	162	83	245
67	France	409	624	1,033
68	Gabon	12	10	22
69	Gambia	4	3	7
70	Germany, East	46	510	556
71	Germany, West	286	604	890
72	Ghana	41	40	81
73	Greece	277	41	318
74	Guatemala	42	8	50
75	Guinea	23	52	75
76	Hague Private IL	1	0	1
77	Haiti	38	3	41
78	Honduras	38	5	43
79	Hungary	150	140	290
80	IAEA (Atom Energy)	44	0	44
81	IBRD (World Bank)	452	0	452
82	ICAO (Civil Aviat)	23	0	23
83	Iceland	73	26	99
84	ICJ (Int Court)	1	0	1
85	IDA (Devel Assoc)	82	0	82
86	ILO (Labor Org)	58	1	59
87	IMCO (Maritime Org)	5	0	5
88	IMF (Fund)	2	0	2
89	India	236	63	299
90	Indonesia	49	77	126
91	Int Bureau Educ	0	1	1
92	Int Exhibit Bureau	0	1	1
93	Int Org Metrology	0	1	1
94	Int Rail Transport	0	1	1
95	Int Wine Office	0	1	1
96	Inter-Am Devel Bnk	1	0	1
97	Inter-Am Nuc Energ	1	0	1
98	Intgov Eur Migrat	0	1	1
99	Iran	62	108	170
100	Iraq	67	29	96
101	Ireland	99	4	103
102	IRO (Refugee Org)	3	0	3
103	Israel	221	11	232
104	Italy	322	433	755
105	ITU (Telecommun)	3	1	4
106	Ivory Coast	24	8	32

THESAURUS

Table	Party	Treaties UNTS	Non-UNTS	Total
107	Jamaica	19	2	21
108	Japan	283	160	443
109	Jordan	58	7	65
110	Kenya	16	10	26
111	Korea, North	15	84	99
112	Korea, South	64	16	80
113	Kuwait	10	0	10
114	LAFTA (Free Trade)	1	0	1
115	Laos	20	8	28
116	League of Nations	9	0	9
117	Lebanon	52	23	75
118	Liberia	40	6	46
119	Libya	37	8	45
120	Liechtenstein	2	14	16
121	Luxembourg	92	44	136
122	Malagasy	13	14	27
123	Malawi	8	3	11
124	Malaysia	21	5	26
125	Maldive Islands	2	0	2
126	Mali	24	30	54
127	Malta	14	1	15
128	Mauritania	9	9	18
129	Mexico	100	38	138
130	Monaco	20	16	36
131	Mongolia	20	99	119
132	Morocco	42	52	94
133	Muscat and Oman	5	0	5
134	NATO (North Atlan)	2	0	2
135	Nepal	14	22	36
136	Netherlands	448	100	548
137	New Zealand	100	1	101
138	Newfoundland	1	0	1
139	Nicaragua	46	4	50
140	Niger	13	12	25
141	Nigeria	20	7	27
142	Norway	270	191	461
143	OAS (Am States)	5	0	5
144	OAU (Afri Unity)	2	0	2
145	OECD (Econ Coop)	1	2	3
146	Org Ctrl Am States	1	0	1
147	Org Rail Collabor	0	1	1
148	Pakistan	206	39	245
149	Pan Am Health Org	1	0	1
150	Panama	48	9	57
151	Paraguay	52	23	75
152	Peru	92	17	109
153	Petrol Export Org	1	0	1
154	Philippines	144	92	236
155	Poland	194	299	493
156	Portugal	94	37	131
157	Romania	124	127	251

TREATY PROFILES

Table	Party	Treaties UNTS	Non-UNTS	Total
158	Rwanda	10	4	14
159	San Marino	8	9	17
160	Saudi Arabia	29	2	31
161	SEATO (SE Asia)	2	0	2
162	Senegal	18	22	40
163	Sierra Leone	19	8	27
164	Singapore	3	0	3
165	Somalia	21	16	37
166	South Africa	113	7	120
167	South Pacific Com	2	0	2
168	Spain	121	316	437
169	Subsahara Tech Com	2	0	2
170	Sudan	24	13	37
171	Sweden	271	212	483
172	Switzerland	160	266	426
173	Syria	47	37	84
174	Taiwan	121	51	172
175	Tanzania	25	20	45
176	Thailand	123	9	132
177	Togo	20	8	28
178	Trieste	3	0	3
179	Trinidad/Tobago	10	1	11
180	Tunisia	49	48	97
181	Turkey	147	151	298
182	Uganda	11	10	21
183	UK Great Britain	946	35	981
184	UN Hi Com Refugees	1	0	1
185	UN Relief Palestin	9	0	9
186	UN Special Fund	111	2	113
187	UNECSO (Educ/Cult)	17	2	19
188	UNICEF (Children)	121	1	122
189	United Arab Rep	145	87	232
190	United Nations	228	5	233
191	UNRRA (Relief)	1	1	2
192	UNTAB (Tech Assis)	0	10	10
193	Upper Volta	8	7	15
194	UPU (Postal Union)	1	1	2
195	Uruguay	43	20	63
196	USA (United States)	2,490	109	2,599
197	USSR (Soviet Union)	305	1,051	1,356
198	Vatican/Holy See	2	14	16
199	Venezuela	41	6	47
200	Vietnam, North	7	74	81
201	Vietnam, South	40	66	106
202	Western Samoa	9	1	10
203	WEU (West Europe)	0	1	1
204	WHO (World Health)	183	4	187
205	WMO (Meteorology)	6	0	6
206	Yemen	14	21	35
207	Yugolsavia	356	169	525
208	Zambia	7	2	9
	Total	7,980	4,752	12,732

b. *State Groups*

Line	Group	States Included in Group
32	African Group (30 States)	Burundi, Cameroon, Central Afri Rep, Chad, Congo (Brazzaville), Congo (Zaire), Dahomey, Ethiopia, Gabon, Gambia, Ghana, Guinea, Ivory Coast, Kenya, Liberia, Malagasy, Malawi, Mali, Mauritania, Niger, Nigeria, Rwanda, Senegal, Sierra Leone, Somalia, Tanzania, Togo, Uganda, Upper Volta, Zambia.
33	Arab Group (13 States)	Algeria, Iraq, Jordan, Kuwait, Lebanon, Libya, Morocco, Saudi Arabia, Sudan, Syria, Tunisia, United Arab Rep, Yemen.
34	Asian Group (21 States)	Afghanistan, Burma, Cambodia, Ceylon (Sri Lanka), Fed of Malaya, India, Indonesia, Iran, Korea South, Laos, Malaysia, Maldive Islands, Muscat and Oman, Nepal, Pakistan, Philippines, Singapore, Taiwan, Thailand, Vietnam South, Western Samoa.
35	Commonwealth (7 States)	Australia, Canada, Fed Rhod/Nyasaland, Newfoundland, New Zealand, South Africa, UK Great Britain.
36	Communist Group (12 States)	Albania, Bulgaria, China People's Rep, Czechoslovakia, Germany East, Hungary, Korea North, Mongolia, Poland, Romania, USSR (Soviet Union), Vietnam North.
37	Latin America (22 States)	Argentina, Bolivia, Brazil, Chile, Colombia, Costa Rica, Cuba, Dominican Republic, Ecuador, El Salvador, Guatemala, Haiti, Honduras, Jamaica, Mexico, Nicaragua, Panama, Paraguay, Peru, Trinidad/Tobago, Uruguay, Venezuela.
38	Western Europe (25 States)	Austria, Belgium, Cyprus, Denmark, Finland, France, Germany West, Greece, Iceland, Ireland, Italy, Liechtenstein, Luxembourg, Malta, Monaco, Netherlands, Norway, Portugal, San Marino, Spain, Sweden, Switzerland, Trieste, Turkey, Vatican/Holy See.
	Not included in any group (4 States)	Israel, Japan, USA (United States), Yugoslavia.

TREATY PROFILES
c. *Treaty-Active Institutions*

Table	IGO Short Title	Full Title
8	Intl Organs	International Organizations (total of all organizations listed below)
11	Accept UN Charter	Unilateral declaration accepting UN Charter obligations
12	ICJ Option Clause	Unilateral declaration accepting ICJ optional clause
14	Afromalagasy Org	Afro-Malagasy Organization
17	Arab League	League of Arab States
19	Asian Productivity	Asian Productivity Organization
23	Bel-Lux Econ Union	Belgium-Luxembourg Economic Union
24	Benelux Econ Union	Benelux Economic Union
25	Bank Int Settlement	Bank for International Settlements
35	CERN (Nuc Resrch)	European Organization for Nuclear Research
41	COMECON (Econ Aid)	Council for Mutual Economic Assistance
45	Council of Europe	Council of Europe
52	East Afri Service	East African Common Services Organization
53	ECSC (Coal/Steel)	European Coal and Steel Community
55	EEC (Econ Commnty)	European Economic Community
56	EFTA (Free Trade)	European Free Trade Association
59	Eur Plant Protect	European and Mediterranean Plant Protection Organization
60	Eur Space Research	European Space Research Organization
61	Eur Space Vehicle	European Space Vehicle Launcher Development Organization
62	EURATOM	European Atomic Energy Community
63	FAO (Food Agri)	Food and Agriculture Organization of the UN
76	Hague Private IL	The Hague Conference on Private International Law
80	IAEA (Atom Energy)	International Atomic Energy Agency
81	IBRD (World Bank)	International Bank for Reconstruction and Development
82	ICAO (Civil Aviat)	International Civil Aviation Organization
84	ICJ (Int Court)	International Court of Justice
85	IDA (Devel Assoc)	International Development Association
86	ILO (Labor Org)	International Labor Organization
87	IMCO (Maritime Org)	Inter-Governmental Maritime Consultative Organization
88	IMF (Fund)	International Monetary Fund
91	Int Bureau Educ	International Bureau of Education
92	Int Exhibit Bureau	International Exhibition Bureau
93	Int Org Metrology	International Organization of Legal Metrology
94	Int Rail Transport	Central Office for International Railway Transport
95	Int Wine Office	International Vine and Wine Office
96	Inter-Am Devel Bnk	Inter-American Development Bank
97	Inter-Am Nuc Energ	Inter-American Nuclear Energy Commission

THESAURUS

Table	IGO Short Title	Full Title
98	Intgov Eur Migrat	Intergovernmental Committee for European Migration
102	IRO (Refugee Org)	International Refugee Organization
105	ITU (Telecommun)	International Telecommunication Union
114	LAFTA (Free Trade)	Latin American Free Trade Association
116	League of Nations	League of Nations
134	NATO (North Atlan)	North Atlantic Treaty Organization
143	OAS (Am States)	Organization of American States
144	OAU (Afri Unity)	Organization of African Unity
145	OECD (Econ Coop)	Organization for Economic Cooperation and Development
146	Org Ctrl Am States	Organization of Central American States
147	Org Rail Collabor	Organization for the Collaboration of Railways
149	Pan Am Health Org	Pan American Health Organization
153	Petrol Export Org	Organization of Petroleum Exporting Countries
161	SEATO (SE Asia)	South-East Asia Treaty Organization
167	South Pacific Com	South Pacific Commission
169	Subsahara Tech Com	Commission for Technical Cooperation in Africa South of the Sahara
184	UN Hi Com Refugees	Office of the UN High Commissioner for Refugees
185	UN Relief Palestin	UN Relief and Works Agency for Palestine Refugees in the Near East
186	UN Special Fund	UN Special Fund
187	UNESCO (Educ/Cult)	UN Educational, Scientific and Cultural Organization
188	UNICEF (Children)	UN Children's Fund
190	United Nations	United Nations
191	UNRRA (Relief)	UN Relief and Rehabilitation Administration
192	UNTAB (Tech Assis)	UN Technical Assistance Board
194	UPU (Postal Union)	Universal Postal Union
203	WEU (West Europe)	Western European Union
204	WHO (World Health)	World Health Organization
205	WMO (Meteorology)	World Meteorological Organization

d. *Treaty-Passive Institutions*

Column	Institution	Number of References Individual	Total
15	United Nations	656	656
16	Food and Agriculture Organization of the United Nations	5	
	General Agreement on Tariffs and Trade	73	
	Inter-Governmental Maritime Consultative Organization	12	
	International Atomic Energy Agency	96	

TREATY PROFILES

Column	Institution	Number of References Individual	Total
	International Bank for Reconstruction and Development	26	
	International Civil Aviation Organization	498	
	International Development Association	5	
	International Finance Corporation	2	
	International Labor Organization	4	
	International Monetary Fund	86	
	International Refugee Organization	9	
	International Telecommunication Union	10	
	League of Nations	3	
	Office of the United Nations High Commissioner for Refugees	1	
	United Nations Children's Fund	17	
	United Nations Commission for the Unification and Rehabilitation of Korea	1	
	United Nations Educational, Scientific and Cultural Organization	9	
	United Nations Relief and Rehabilitation Administration	6	
	United Nations Relief and Works Agency for Palestine Refugees in the Near East	2	
	United Nations Special Fund	4	
	United Nations Technical Assistance Board	3	
	Universal Postal Union	39	
	World Health Organization	13	
	World Meteorological Organization	1	925
17	International Court of Justice	462	
	Permanent Court of International Justice	2	464
18	Permanent Court of Arbitration	55	
	Arbitration Commissions (category)	513	568
19	Allied Military Occupation Agencies (category)	15	
	Inter-Allied Reparations Agency	1	
	League of Arab States	2	
	Asian Crime Prevention Organization	1	
	Asia Economic Development Organization	1	
	Bank for International Settlements	4	
	Benelux Economic Union	4	
	Caribbean Commission	1	
	Central Office of International Railway Transport	1	
	Central Treaty Organization	1	
	Claims Commissions (category)	12	
	Colombo Plan	6	
	Committee of Control of the International Zone of Tangier	1	
	Conciliation Commissions (category)	8	
	Council for Mutual Economic Assistance	3	
	Council of Europe	15	

THESAURUS

Column	Institution	Number of References	
		Individual	Total
	Court of Justice of the European Community	2	
	Danube Commission	1	
	East African Common Services Organization	1	
	Economic Commission for Asia and the Far East	1	
	European Atomic Energy Community	5	
	European Coal and Steel Community	2	
	European Defense Community	2	
	European Economic Community	8	
	European Free Trade Association	7	
	European Nuclear Energy Agency	3	
	European Payments Union	70	
	Inter-American Development Bank	3	
	Intergovernmental Committee on Refugees	1	
	International Emergency Food Organization	3	
	International Fisheries Commission	1	
	International Halibut Commission	1	
	International North Pacific Fisheries Commission	1	
	International Office of Epizootics	2	
	International Union for the Protection of Industrial Property	1	
	Nauru Administrative Authority	1	
	Nordic Council	1	
	North Atlantic Treaty Organization	64	
	Organization for Economic Cooperation and Development	116	
	Organization of American States	9	
	Other United Nations Organizations (category)	1	
	Pan American Health Organization	9	
	Pan American Institute of Geography and History	1	
	South-East Asia Treaty Organization	3	
	South Pacific Health Service	2	
	Special Commissions (category)	520	
	United Nations Administrative Tribunal	1	
	United Nations Economic Commission for Europe	1	
	United Nations Mission to the Congo	1	
	United Nations Refugee Fund	1	
	United Nations Temporary Executive Authority	1	
	United Nations Unified Command in Korea	1	
	United States-Canadian Defense Organizations (category)	6	
	Western European Union	1	931
	World Total		3,544

TREATY PROFILES
e. *National Treaty Collections*

Country	Collection
Austria	*Bundesgesetzblatt*
Canada	*Canada Treaty Series*
China, People's Republic	*Agreements of the People's Republic of China, 1949-1967: A Calendar,* by Chiu and Johnston (Cambridge: Harvard University Press, 1968)
France	*Recueil des Traités et Accords de la France*
France	*Journal Officiel*
France	*Moniteur Officiel,* later *Documentation Française*
Germany, East	*Dokumente zur Aussenpolitik der Deutschen Demokratischen Republik*
Germany, East	*Dokumentation der Zeit*
Germany, West	*Bundesanzeiger*
Germany, West	*Bundesgesetzblatt*
Guatemala	*Diario Centro América*
Iran	*Traités Bilatéraux Conclus Entre L'Iran et les Autres Etats* (Ministry of Foreign Affairs, Legal Department, Status as of 21 March 1972, single volume)
Italy	*Gazzetta Ufficiale*
Italy	*Diritto Internazionale* (during 1949-1953 named *Annali di Diritto Internazionale*)
Italy	*Trattati* (Ministry of Foreign Affairs)
Japan	*Horei Zensho*
Japan	*Japanese Annual of International Law*
Japan	*Genko Joyaku Iken*
Japan	*Joyaku Shu*
Mexico	*Diario Oficial de la Federación*
Netherlands	*Tractatenblad*
Norway	*The Treaties of Norway*
Philippines	*Philippine Treaty Series*
Poland	*Dziennik Ustaw Polskiej Rzeczypospolitej Ludowej*
Poland	*Zbiór Umów Międzynarodwych Polskiej Rzeczypospolitej Ludowej*
Spain	*Boletín Oficial del Estado*
Sweden	*Sveriges Överenskommelser med Främmande Makter*
Switzerland	*Recueil Officiel des Lois et Ordonnances*
Switzerland	*Recueil Systematique des Lois et Ordonnances*
Taiwan	*Treaties Between the Republic of China and Foreign Powers, 1927-1961* (Ministry of Foreign Affairs, Taipei, 1963, single volume)
Taiwan	*Treaties and Agreements Between the Republic of China and Other Powers, 1929-1954,* by Yin Ching Chen (Washington, D.C., 1957, single volume)
Turkey	*Resmi Gazete*
USSR	*A Calendar of Soviet Treaties, 1917-1957,* by Slusser and Triska (Stanford University Press, 1959)
USSR	Continuation of above, by George Ginsburgs in *Osteuropa Recht*
USA	*United States Treaties and Other International Agreements*
USA	*Treaties and Other International Acts Series*
Vietnam, South	*List of Treaties and Conventions, 1945-1970,* and *1971 Supplement* (Ministry of Foreign Affairs, single volume)

f. Topics

Column Number	Column Name/Topic Cluster/Topic	Number of Treaties Column	Cluster	Topic
10	Administration and Diplomacy	2,777		
	General relations and amity		1,862	
	General amity			234
	Frontier formalities			686
	Refugees and stateless persons			17
	Status of state, recognition			50
	Diplomatic and consular relations			280
	Extradition, deportation, repatriation			62
	Administrative cooperation			469
	Privileges and immunities			21
	Dispute settlement			43
				1,862
	International organizations (IGO's)		395	
	IGO establishment and status			33
	IGO operations, privileges, immunities			236
	Adherence to UN Charter			70
	Optional Clause ICJ			56
				395
	Disposition of particulars		520	
	Various particular matters			17
	Specific claims or waivers			34
	Facilities and property			156
	Boundaries of territory			144
	Specific goods and equipment			45
	Conservation of specific resources			124
				520
11	Social Cooperation	3,230		
	General health, education, culture, welfare, labor		1,653	
	Sanitation			219
	Education			203
	Culture			472
	Humanitarian matters			32
	Labor and social security			411
	Research and scientific projects			212
	General and other social cooperation			104
				1,653
	Transportation		1,136	
	General transportation			28
	Air transport			874
	Water transport			114
	Land transport			120
				1,136

TREATY PROFILES

Column Number	Column Name/Topic Cluster/Topic	Number of Treaties — Column	Cluster	Topic
	Communications		441	
	General communications			61
	Postal service			162
	Telecommunications			98
	Mass media			120
				441
12	Economic Cooperation	3,180		
	General economics		3,180	
	General trade			1,056
	Finances and payments			502
	Claims, debts and assets			279
	Commodity trade			157
	Most-favored nation clause			56
	Taxation			396
	Patents, copyrights, trademarks			123
	Customs duties			109
	General and other economic matters			502
				3,180
13	Aid	2,601		
	Aid and development		2,601	
	General aid			133
	Technical assistance			700
	Direct aid			541
	Loans and credits			190
	Agricultural commodities assistance			274
	Atomic energy assistance			160
	World Bank projects			442
	Non-Bank projects			161
				2,601
14	Military	944		
	Military		944	
	General military			64
	Military assistance			333
	Military assistance missions			70
	Status of military forces			93
	Military installations and equipment			106
	Military service and citizenship			32
	Peace and disarmament			30
	War claims and reparations			154
	Occupation regime			16
	War graves and other military matters			46
				944
10-14	All Topics	12,732		

g. *Abbreviations*

Short titles of international organizations, whether or not they include acronyms or abbreviations, are listed above in the section on international organizations and are excluded from this list. However, frequently used parts of short titles are included here as an alternative way of identifying international organizations, e.g., Com, Econ, Eur, Int, Nuc, Org.

Admin & Dipl	Administrative and diplomatic matters as treaty topics. For details, see Chapter 5, Column 10.
Afri	Africa, African
Aid	Foreign aid and technical assistance as treaty topics. For details, see Chapter 5, Column 13.
Am	America, American
Com	Commission, Committee
Coop	Cooperation
Devel	Development
Econ	Economic
Econ Coop	Economic cooperation and related treaty topics. For details, see Chapter 5, Column 12.
Eur	Europe, European
Fed	Federation
ICJ	International Court of Justice
IGO	International governmental organization as a generic term for any treaty-based institution under public international law. The term excludes international non-governmental organizations and private corporations of a multinational character.
IL	International law
Int, Intl	International
LTS	League of Nations Treaty Series
Milit	Military matters as treaty topics. For details, see Chapter 5, Column 14.
Nuc	Nuclear
Org	Organization
PCIJ	Permanent Court of International Justice
Social Coop	Social cooperation and related treaty topics. For details, see Chapter 5, Column 11.
Spec Ag's	Specialized Agencies of the United Nations
Tech	Technical
UN	United Nations
UNTS	United Nations Treaty Series

Treaty Profiles

Table 1 • 49

TREATY PROFILE OF AFRICAN GROUP

Partners (1)	Partner's World Total (2)	Absolutes (3)	Dyads Ratios Self (4)	Other (5)	Time 1946-1950 (6)	1951-1955 (7)	1956-1960 (8)	1961-1965 (9)	Topics Admin & Dipl (10)	Social Coop (11)	Econ Coop (12)	Aid (13)	Milit (14)	Institutions UN (15)	Spec Ag's (16)	Intl Court (17)	Arbitration (18)	Other (19)	Self-Registered (20)
TOP THIRTY																			
1 USA (United States)	2599	140	14%	5%	7	25	15	93	13	18	24	69	16	13	4	9	4	11	
2 France	1033	129	13%	12%			30	99	54	36	27	6	6		4		3	1	
3 Germany, West	890	110	11%	12%			11	99	1	24	34	48	3						
4 USSR (Soviet Union)	1356	87	9%	6%			29	58	25	13	28	21	2	1				2	
5 China People's Rep	766	51	5%	7%			4	47	6	19	11	13	4	1	6	1	2	4	5
6 UK Great Britain	981	39	4%	4%	1	5	13	20	19		7			1	2		1		
7 Israel	232	35	4%	15%			3	32	14	7		15	4	1	2	1	7	4	
8 WHO (World Health)	187	33	3%	18%		2	6	25	4	6		29		14		1			
9 UN Special Fund	113	32	3%	28%			5	27	4			28		22	16	26	14	1	
10 Germany, East	556	31	3%	6%			6	25	4	9	10	8							
11 United Nations	233	30	3%	13%		2	6	22	9	1		19	1	2	3	2	26	2	
12 Accept UN Charter	68	29	3%	43%			15	14	29					29					
13 UNICEF (Children)	122	25	3%	20%		2	4	19	8			17		18					
14 IBRD (World Bank)	452	23	2%	5%	2	1		16				23							
15 Italy	755	21	2%	3%			6	15	4	6	3	7	1			4	3		
16 Poland	493	16	2%	3%				16		8	1	7			4				
17 Netherlands	548	16	2%	3%			3	13	1	8	2	5			6	2	3		
18 Switzerland	426	15	2%	4%			1	14	1	6	8				1		4	1	
19 IDA (Devel Assoc)	82	12	1%	15%				12				12							
20 Norway	461	12	1%	3%		3		9	2	2	6	2			1	2	2		
21 Czechoslovakia	393	12	1%	3%			6	6	1	9		2			3		2		
22 Denmark	380	7	1%	2%				7	1	1	4	1							
23 Japan	443	6	1%	1%			1	5	1	2	4			2					
24 Greece	318	6	1%	2%		2	1	3	1	2	4					2	1		
25 Belgium	499	6	1%	1%			1	5	1	2	3	2			1	2		2	
26 Sweden	483	5	1%	1%		1	2	2		3		2			2	2	2		
27 Mali	54	5	1%	9%				5		5					5		5		
28 ICJ Option Clause	62	5	1%	8%	1	1		4	5	1	1			2	1	4			
29 Spain	437	3	1%	1%		2		1	1			1			1				
30 ILO (Labor Org)	59	3	1%	5%		1		2	2					3		1	1		
31 All Others (19)	2856	31	3%	1%	2	4	3	22	1	23	2	3	2		16	2	11	1	1
GROUPS																			
32 African Group	968	14	1%	1%			1	14		14					14				1
33 Arab Group	937	4	1%			1	1	3	1	4					4		12		
34 Asian Group	1937	5	1%		2			2		4					3		3		
35 Commonwealth	1641	42	4%	3%	1	6	13	22	19	7	8	2	6	1	6	2	1	4	5
36 Communist Group	3310	203	21%	6%			46	157	36	64	50	51	2		3	1	2	2	
37 Latin America	1674																		
38 Western Europe	5906	330	34%	6%	2	8	55	267	66	89	92	73	10	2	20	12	15	3	
39 Intl Organs	1399	160	16%	11%		9	25	124	27	1		131	1	59	21	30	48	4	
TOTALS																			
40 All Data	18337	975	100%		12	51	175	737	211	209	177	343	35	107	77	58	88	24	6
41 UNTS Only		564																	
COMPARISONS																			
42 Party Total					1%	5%	18%	76%	22%	21%	18%	35%	4%	19%	14%	10%	16%	4%	1%
43 Group Total					1%	5%	18%	75%	22%	21%	18%	35%	4%	19%	13%	10%	15%	4%	1%
44 World Total					18%	23%	29%	29%	22%	25%	25%	20%	7%	8%	12%	6%	7%	12%	100%

TREATY PROFILE OF ARAB GROUP

Partners (1)	Partner's World Total (2)	Absolutes (3)	Dyads Ratios Self (4)	Other (5)	Time 1946-1950 (6)	1951-1955 (7)	1956-1960 (8)	1961-1965 (9)	Topics Admin & Dipl (10)	Social Coop (11)	Econ Coop (12)	Aid (13)	Milit (14)	Institutions UN (15)	Spec Ag's (16)	Intl Court (17)	Arbi-tration (18)	Other (19)	Self-Registered (20)
TOP THIRTY																			
1 USA (United States)	2599	149	16%	6%	9	69	35	36	8	25	5	97	14	10	11	4	3	9	1
2 USSR (Soviet Union)	1356	82	9%	6%	1	11	46	24	18	12	30	21	1	2	10			1	1
3 UK Great Britain	981	68	7%	7%	13	29	11	15	16	13	21	11	7	5	10	6	8	7	5
4 France	1033	63	7%	6%	3	3	13	44	18	26	8	11			4	1	1	1	
5 China People's Rep	766	59	6%	8%		7	20	32	2	17	35	5							
6 Italy	755	43	5%	6%	4	7	14	18	8	11	15	8	1	1	1	1		9	
7 Germany, East	556	41	4%	7%		5	17	19	8	11	19	4							
8 Germany, West	890	33	3%	4%		6	10	17	7	6	14	8	1					2	1
9 WHO (World Health)	187	26	3%	14%	1	10	7	8	4	1		22		16	2	3	2	4	
10 Spain	437	25	3%	6%	3	3	15	1	3	6	6	1							
11 United Nations	233	25	3%	11%		2	12	11	12	1		12			9		15	2	6
12 Turkey	298	20	2%	7%	12	4	4		10	7	4		2	1	4	1	1	1	
13 Switzerland	426	18	2%	4%	2	4	5	7	8	9	8	1	1		9		7		
14 Netherlands	548	16	2%	3%	3	4	4	5		11					5	3	4		
15 Japan	443	16	2%	4%		2	2	12	2	7	4	2	1	1	4	2	4	1	1
16 Belgium	499	16	2%	3%	4	2	6	4	4	6	4				3	3	4	1	
17 Greece	318	14	1%	4%	7	3	2	2	2	5	5	1	1	1	10	1	1	8	1
18 UN Special Fund	113	13	1%	12%		5	9	4	1		1	13		12	3		6		
19 UNICEF (Children)	122	13	1%	11%		1	4	8			1	12		12					
20 IBRD (World Bank)	452	13	1%	3%	1		3	9				12			1		2		
21 Poland	493	13	1%	3%		5	4		7	7	1	5		1	3			1	1
22 Pakistan	245	13	1%	5%	5	7	1		2	5	1				5				1
23 Norway	461	12	1%	3%	2		8	2		8	2				3		4		
24 Czechoslovakia	393	11	1%	3%			6	5		9	1	1			3		2		1
25 Sweden	483	10	1%	2%	1	2	5	2		6	4				5		5		
26 Denmark	380	10	1%	3%		3	3	3		8	1	1		1	7		3		
27 United Arab Rep	232	8	1%	3%	1	4	2	1	1	5	1		1		4	1	3	1	3
28 Accept UN Charter	68	8	1%	12%	1	2	2	3	8					8					
29 Syria	84	7	1%	8%		4		3	2	2	2		1		1	1	1	1	
30 IDA (Devel Assoc)	82	7	1%	9%				7				7			1				
31 All Others (36)	5187	101	11%	2%	12	26	23	40	26	40	15	16	4	15	18	7	11	10	9
GROUPS																			
32 African Group	968	4	3%	3%	4		1	3		4									
33 Arab Group	937	32	3%	2%	8	12	4	12	10	14	6		2	1	4	2	3	4	10
34 Asian Group	1937	33	3%	2%	8	13	7	5	15	13	5				12		8		
35 Commonwealth	1641	70	7%	4%	13	31	11	15	16	14	22	11	7	1	5	6	1	8	5
36 Communist Group	3310	221	23%	7%	1	23	99	98	30	67	87	36	1	5	11		8	7	4
37 Latin America	1674	6	1%		1		1	4		3	3			2	4		2	4	
38 Western Europe	5906	288	30%	5%	42	44	91	111	60	112	77	35	4	3	52	11	33	20	8
39 Intl Organs	1399	117	12%	8%	3	30	36	48	17	3	2	93	2	49	23	19	28	3	1
TOTALS																			
40 All Data	21120	953	100%		86	228	293	346	169	264	211	274	35	84	124	47	90	52	32
41 UNTS Only		593																	
COMPARISONS																			
42 Party Total					9%	24%	31%	36%	18%	28%	22%	29%	4%	14%	21%	8%	15%	9%	5%
43 Group Total					9%	24%	31%	36%	18%	27%	22%	29%	4%	15%	20%	8%	15%	9%	5%
44 World Total					18%	23%	29%	29%	22%	25%	25%	20%	7%	8%	12%	6%	7%	12%	100%

TREATY PROFILE OF ASIAN GROUP

Table 3 • 51

	Part- ner's World Total	Dyads Abso- lutes	Dyads Ratios Self	Dyads Ratios Other	Time 1946 1950	Time 1951 1955	Time 1956 1960	Time 1961 1965	Topics Admin & Dipl	Topics Social Coop	Topics Econ Coop	Topics Aid	Topics Milit	Institutions UN	Institutions Spec Ag's	Institutions Intl Court	Institutions Arbi- tration	Institutions Other	Self- Regis- tered
Part- ners (1)	(2)	(3)	(4)	(5)	(6)	(7)	(8)	(9)	(10)	(11)	(12)	(13)	(14)	(15)	(16)	(17)	(18)	(19)	(20)
TOP THIRTY																			
1 USA (United States)	2599	439	21%	17%	105	92	122	120	52	75	45	174	93	29	27	15	5	16	25
2 USSR (Soviet Union)	1356	152	7%	11%	12	16	85	39	38	24	37	52	1					6	3
3 China People's Rep	766	122	6%	16%		23	42	57	29	22	48	23							4
4 Japan	443	98	5%	22%	1	26	39	32	19	32	25	10	12	2	10	8	8	8	12
5 IBRD (World Bank)	452	96	5%	21%	6	12	33	45				96		2	2	1	3	1	
6 UK Great Britain	981	87	4%	9%	30	16	21	20	19	23	32	5	8		17	2	7	5	9
7 France	1033	80	4%	8%	17	28	18	17	27	27	15	4	7	1	5	1	1	1	5
8 Germany, West	890	67	3%	8%	1	8	19	39	6	15	22	22	2		4	2	3	2	12
9 WHO (World Health)	187	58	3%	31%	5	42	9	2	3	22		33		19	5	13	6	1	
10 IDA (Devel Assoc)	82	41	2%	50%				41				41							
11 Pakistan	245	40	2%	16%	14	9	12	5	17	14	8	5	1	4	8	3	3	4	9
12 India	299	40	2%	13%	17	13	8	2	15	10	14	22	1	2	7	2	5	3	16
13 Netherlands	548	39	2%	7%	8	14	9	8	10	15	6	5	3	3	10	5	7	2	1
14 United Nations	233	37	2%	16%	2	14	11	10	8	5		22	2		1	4	17	3	
15 Philippines	236	31	2%	13%	5	5	7	14	14	8	5	2	2	1	3	3	2		3
16 Italy	755	29	1%	4%	6	4	14	5	9	5	12	1	2		3	3	1	3	6
17 Australia	201	26	1%	13%	5	7	7	7	6	11	8		1	2	10	3	3	3	5
18 Denmark	380	25	1%	7%	4	4	6	11	4	9	5	6			9	2	6	1	4
19 Iran	170	24	1%	14%	3	2	11	8	9	9	6					1	1	1	3
20 Turkey	298	23	1%	8%	5	11	6	1	8	10	5						1	1	7
21 UNICEF (Children)	122	23	1%	19%	11	4	4	4	12			10		3	3				3
22 Norway	461	23	1%	5%	5	6	6	6	4	9	10			18	1	2	3	2	
23 Sweden	483	22	1%	5%	7	6	8	1		8	12	2			6	3	5		3
24 Canada	310	22	1%	7%	3	7	8	4	5	1	5	11		1	7		1	5	1
25 Thailand	132	20	1%	15%	3	4	9	4	12	7	1				3		2	1	3
26 UN Special Fund	113	20	1%	18%			13	7	1			19		5	4	3			3
27 Germany, East	556	19	1%	3%		2	7	10	1	6	10	2		15	14	15	8	1	
28 Belgium	499	18	1%	4%	1	4	9	4	7	5	4				3	2	1		1
29 Switzerland	426	17	1%	4%	4	4	7	2	3	7	7		2	1	6	1			3
30 Spain	437	17	1%	4%	5	4	7	1	8	7	2				1		4	1	5
31 All Others (63)	7454	307	15%	4%	50	77	88	92	106	88	67	40	6	33	31	22	11	9	95
GROUPS																			
32 African Group	968	5		1%	2	1		2	1	4	5	4		1	3	2	1		2
33 Arab Group	937	33	2%	4%	8	13	7	5	15	13	5	18	8	18	5		1		15
34 Asian Group	1937	250	12%	13%	60	54	74	62	106	76	56	4	9		34	14	18	10	63
35 Commonwealth	1641	146	7%	9%	40	30	38	38	32	40	47	18	1	2	31	4	11	13	21
36 Communist Group	3310	322	16%	10%	12	42	150	118	71	66	104	80		18	2			12	13
37 Latin America	1674	27	1%	2%	4	3	5	15	8	10	9			1	1				21
38 Western Europe	5906	390	19%	7%	68	96	122	104	93	125	112	41	19	8	60	22	36	13	58
39 Intl Organs	1399	308	15%	22%	25	94	73	116	27	30	2	247	2	65	28	35	35	8	3
TOTALS																			
40 All Data	23147	2062	100%		335	464	645	618	452	474	412	580	144	140	202	114	115	82	238
41 UNTS Only		1354																	
COMPARISONS																			
42 Party Total					16%	23%	31%	30%	22%	23%	20%	28%	7%	10%	15%	8%	8%	6%	18%
43 Group Total					16%	23%	31%	30%	21%	23%	20%	30%	7%	10%	15%	8%	8%	6%	16%
44 World Total					18%	23%	29%	29%	22%	25%	25%	20%	7%	8%	12%	6%	7%	12%	100%

52 • Table 4

TREATY PROFILE OF COMMONWEALTH

	Partners	Partner's World Total	Dyads Absolutes	Dyads Ratios Self	Dyads Ratios Other	Time 1946-1950	Time 1951-1955	Time 1956-1960	Time 1961-1965	Topics Admin & Dipl	Topics Social Coop	Topics Econ Coop	Topics Aid	Topics Milit	Institutions UN	Institutions Spec Ag's	Institutions Intl Court	Institutions Arbitration	Other	Self-Registered
	(1)	(2)	(3)	(4)	(5)	(6)	(7)	(8)	(9)	(10)	(11)	(12)	(13)	(14)	(15)	(16)	(17)	(18)	(19)	(20)
	TOP THIRTY																			
1	USA (United States)	2599	281	16%	11%	76	71	58	76	57	77	39	29	79	8	27	3	1	42	61
2	France	1033	82	5%	8%	34	20	7	21	18	30	19		15	1	9	4	2	10	66
3	Italy	755	67	4%	9%	21	25	12	21	19	19	16	2	11	10	3	1	3	6	54
4	Netherlands	548	61	4%	11%	29	15	11	6	13	18	16	1	14		4	1	1	8	30
5	Germany, West	890	56	3%	6%	1	14	27	14	15	12	13	1	15	1	7	4	5	19	51
6	UK Great Britain	981	55	3%	6%	18	5	18	14	13	20	22	1	9		12	1	3	4	21
7	Belgium	499	45	3%	9%	17	18	7	3	3	10	9	2	11			3	1	12	19
8	Japan	443	43	2%	10%		15	9	19	13	9	14	3	4		13	3	2	1	25
9	Denmark	380	43	2%	11%	19	7	10	7	9	11	14	1	8		8		2	8	28
10	Sweden	483	39	2%	8%	11	13	9	6	9	9	19	2			10	1	1	7	29
11	IBRD (World Bank)	452	38	2%	8%	1	11	11	15				38							
12	Norway	461	38	2%	8%	15	9	10	4	14	7	9	1	7	1	6	1	3	8	28
13	Greece	318	36	2%	11%	13	12	5	6	14	4	11	1	6		2	2	2	5	30
14	Yugoslavia	525	33	2%	6%	9	8	7	9	4	9	11	5	4		3	2	1		33
15	USSR (Soviet Union)	1356	31	2%	2%	5	2	12	12	10	12	8				1				15
16	Canada	310	30	2%	10%	10	4	13	3		10	13	2	5		8		3	2	16
17	Austria	445	30	2%	7%	4	12	11	3	12	5	8	2	3		4	2		7	29
18	Switzerland	426	29	2%	7%	6	8	10	5	6	8	12	3			4	1		5	22
19	Australia	201	29	2%	14%	6	3	10	10	4	15	9	1	1	3	5	2	2	1	10
20	South Africa	120	26	2%	22%	7	6	10	3	2	6	17		1		3			1	10
21	Finland	245	25	1%	10%	6	4	5	10	13	5	6		1		2	1			19
22	Turkey	298	22	1%	7%	4	4	11	3	8	3	6	3	2		4	1	3	5	21
23	Portugal	131	22	1%	17%	4	10	3	5	7	5	6		2				2	8	18
24	India	299	22	1%	7%	4	6	3	9	2	4	8	5	3		6	1	1	2	19
25	Spain	437	21	1%	5%	4	5	6	6	6	2	11	2			1		1	2	16
26	Israel	232	21	1%	9%	4	7	6	4	6	6	9				3				13
27	United Arab Rep	232	20	1%	9%	7	10	1	2	6	3	9	1	2		5	1	1	2	17
28	New Zealand	101	19	1%	19%	6	2	6	5	5	6	8		3		5		2	2	6
29	Pakistan	245	18	1%	7%	5	8	3	2	1	8	5	4			8		3	1	9
30	Thailand	132	15	1%	11%	6	2	5	2	2	3	8	1	1		2			3	8
31	All Others (92)	8090	428	25%	5%	115	90	103	120	127	92	120	56	33	37	60	25	30	30	315
	GROUPS																			
32	African Group	968	42	2%	4%	1	6	13	22	19	7	8	2	6	1	6	1	2	4	36
33	Arab Group	937	70	4%	7%	13	31	11	15	16	14	22	11	7	5	11	6	8	7	59
34	Asian Group	1937	146	8%	8%	40	30	38	38	32	40	47	18	9	2	31	4	11	13	98
35	Commonwealth	1641	168	10%	10%	48	22	62	36	12	60	74	4	18		34	4	10	10	70
36	Communist Group	3310	77	4%	2%	31	10	21	15	19	21	29	3	5	7	7		1	3	56
37	Latin America	1674	81	5%	5%	31	15	10	25	16	19	33	5	8		12	1	4	5	72
38	Western Europe	5906	675	39%	11%	202	186	161	126	204	160	189	24	98	17	76	21	31	114	505
39	Intl Organs	1399	80	5%	6%	11	21	21	27	8	6		65	1	20	4	7	5	2	10
	TOTALS																			
40	All Data	23667	1725	100%		467	426	419	413	414	428	475	169	239	61	226	60	77	201	1038
41	UNTS Only		1657																	
	COMPARISONS																			
42	Party Total					27%	25%	24%	24%	24%	25%	28%	10%	14%	4%	14%	4%	5%	12%	63%
43	Group Total					27%	25%	24%	24%	25%	24%	27%	10%	14%	4%	13%	4%	5%	12%	63%
44	World Total					18%	23%	29%	29%	22%	25%	25%	20%	7%	8%	12%	6%	7%	12%	100%

TREATY PROFILE OF COMMUNIST GROUP

Table 5 • 53

	Partners (1)	Partner's World Total (2)	Dyads Absolutes (3)	Dyads Ratios Self (4)	Dyads Ratios Other (5)	Time 1946 1950 (6)	Time 1951 1955 (7)	Time 1956 1960 (8)	Time 1961 1965 (9)	Topics Admin & Dipl (10)	Topics Social Coop (11)	Topics Econ Coop (12)	Topics Aid (13)	Topics Milit (14)	Institutions UN (15)	Institutions Spec Ag's (16)	Institutions Intl Court (17)	Institutions Arbitration (18)	Institutions Other (19)	Self-Registered (20)
	TOP THIRTY																			
1	USSR (Soviet Union)	1356	651	14%	48%	147	127	292	85	151	168	141	162	29	3				23	23
2	China People's Rep	766	439	9%	57%	33	140	144	122	50	195	161	29	4	1			3	3	14
3	Germany, East	556	429	9%	77%	37	145	173	74	82	190	123	26	8	1				8	45
4	Poland	493	288	6%	58%	58	59	112	59	69	129	53	28	9	5	2		2	28	16
5	Czechoslovakia	393	229	5%	58%	45	44	95	45	62	92	61	11	3	1	2		2	14	38
6	Yugoslavia	525	226	5%	43%	79	24	87	36	44	86	68	20	8	3	1		7	47	42
7	Hungary	290	183	4%	63%	36	32	76	39	44	74	49	9	7	1			1	8	34
8	Romania	251	169	4%	67%	37	37	64	31	42	66	41	15	5	1				9	21
9	Bulgaria	236	147	3%	62%	25	32	60	30	25	54	46	19	3	1				6	38
10	Mongolia	119	114	2%	96%	9	25	56	24	27	37	21	28	1					2	14
11	Korea, North	99	97	2%	98%	8	20	49	20	13	46	21	16	1					1	13
12	Albania	125	83	2%	66%	6	17	41	19	12	28	25	18					1	4	12
13	Vietnam, North	81	81	2%	100%	1	14	44	22	5	35	24	17						2	7
14	United Arab Rep	232	75	2%	32%	1	10	42	22	7	23	31	14			3		1	1	13
15	USA (United States)	2599	70	1%	3%	22	8	20	20	22	21	7	11	9	2	6			1	3
16	Finland	245	69	1%	28%	22	11	20	16	19	12	31	4	3	1	1		2	5	12
17	Austria	445	67	1%	15%	3	15	15	34	20	25	20	1	1		1		3	5	21
18	Cuba	111	65	1%	59%			23	42	6	26	17	16						2	8
19	Sweden	483	64	1%	13%	40	10	12	2	6	12	45	1			1			1	3
20	Italy	755	61	1%	8%	12		25	24	10	11	34	3	3					2	7
21	France	1033	60	1%	6%	15	6	16	23	4	24	27	2	3						8
22	Indonesia	126	55	1%	44%	2	6	18	29	9	11	15	19	1				1	2	4
23	Norway	461	54	1%	12%	15	4	19	16	18	13	22				1			10	4
24	India	299	51	1%	17%	1	14	25	11	8	15	15	13			1			3	8
25	UK Great Britain	981	50	1%	5%	20	6	14	10	9	16	19	1	5		2			2	3
26	Denmark	380	45	1%	12%	15	10	14	6	5	10	30				1			6	3
27	Ceylon (Sri Lanka)	123	45	1%	37%		3	23	19	2	4	30	9		3				6	3
28	Ghana	81	44	1%	54%			8	36	5	15	14	8	2		1		1		2
29	Guinea	75	38	1%	51%			21	17	4	14	10	10		1	1				11
30	Syria	84	37	1%	44%		6	11	20	4	17	12	4							2
31	All Others (67)	8045	679	14%	8%	76	74	228	301	176	152	244	104	3	24	18	2	7	24	82
	GROUPS																			
32	African Group	968	203	4%	21%	1	23	46	157	36	64	50	51	2	2	3		2	2	40
33	Arab Group	937	221	5%	24%	12	42	99	98	30	67	87	36	1		4		2	4	38
34	Asian Group	1937	322	7%	17%	12	42	150	118	71	66	104	80	1	2	4			12	28
35	Commonwealth	1641	77	2%	5%	31	10	21	15	19	21	29	3	5	7	7		1	3	5
36	Communist Group	3310	2910	61%	88%	442	692	1206	570	582	1114	766	378	70	14	4		10	108	275
37	Latin America	1674	86	2%	5%	1	6	28	51	10	28	29	19		1	1			3	12
38	Western Europe	5906	579	12%	10%	164	84	167	164	102	149	302	13	13	2	12	2	8	42	71
39	Intl Organs	1399	24	1%	2%	7		3	14	15	1	1	7		8	2		2	1	
	TOTALS																			
40	All Data	21848	4765	100%		765	899	1847	1254	960	1621	1457	618	109	48	42	2	32	223	518
41	UNTS Only		1262																	
	COMPARISONS																			
42	Party Total					16%	19%	39%	26%	20%	34%	31%	13%	2%	4%	3%		3%	18%	41%
43	Group Total					16%	17%	38%	29%	20%	32%	32%	13%	2%	4%	4%		3%	17%	33%
44	World Total					18%	23%	29%	29%	22%	25%	25%	20%	7%	8%	12%	6%	7%	12%	100%

54 • Table 6

TREATY PROFILE OF LATIN AMERICA

Partners (1)	Partner's World Total (2)	Abso- lutes (3)	Dyads Ratios Self (4)	Other (5)	Time 1946 1950 (6)	1951 1955 (7)	1956 1960 (8)	1961 1965 (9)	Topics Admin & Dipl (10)	Social Coop (11)	Econ Coop (12)	Aid (13)	Milit (14)	Institutions UN (15)	Spec Ag's (16)	Intl Court (17)	Arbi- tration (18)	Other (19)	Self- Regis- tered (20)
TOP THIRTY																			
1 USA (United States)	2599	627	36%	24%	145	200	135	147	60	162	57	221	127	16	29	11	12	45	4
2 IBRD (World Bank)	452	149	9%	33%	13	42	41	53				149			3		7	3	
3 Spain	437	78	5%	18%	9	30	26	13	19	32	26		1		2		3		7
4 Italy	755	77	4%	10%	22	12	23	20	22	20	20	7	8		1	2	1		3
5 Germany, West	890	73	4%	8%	1	23	18	31	12	15	34	12			10		1	3	7
6 UK Great Britain	981	64	4%	7%	25	13	8	18	15	11	26	5	7		2	1	3	5	4
7 France	1033	44	3%	4%	6	11	9	18	6	17	16	5					2		3
8 USSR (Soviet Union)	1356	43	2%	3%	1	4	16	22	7	7	18	11			2			1	
9 Norway	461	40	2%	9%	4	8	15	13	7	5	8							9	
10 WHO (World Health)	187	37	2%	20%	8	27		2	26	21		16	1	16	4	8	2	1	8
11 Argentina	164	32	2%	20%	3		12	17	10	14	6	2			10		3	1	
12 Netherlands	548	29	2%	5%	7	8	4	10	10	13	5	1			2	2	5	1	
13 United Nations	233	28	2%	12%		13	6	9	10	2		15	1	1	7	1	15	2	1
14 Japan	443	27	2%	6%		1	8	18	7	9	10	1			3			2	
15 Belgium	499	27	2%	5%	5	4	9	9	16	4	5	1	1		7	1		2	2
16 UNICEF (Children)	122	23	1%	19%	12	5	3	3	7	1		15		20	1				
17 UN Special Fund	113	22	1%	19%			10	12				22		19	15	21	12	1	4
18 Brazil	195	21	1%	11%	3	1	9	8	8	6	5	2		1	1			4	
19 Denmark	380	20	1%	5%	5	6	7	2		4	13	1	2		4		2		
20 Israel	232	18	1%	8%		1	5	12	6	9	7	3		1					
21 Taiwan	172	18	1%	10%	3	6	3	11	3	8	7		1		1		1		
22 Canada	310	17	1%	5%		2	2	7	1	8	7				2		2	1	1
23 Switzerland	426	16	1%	4%	6	6	6	1		3	11	1	1		3				
24 China People's Rep	766	14	1%	2%	3		4	10		6	5	3							
25 Austria	445	14	1%	3%		1	10	3			4							1	1
26 ILO (Labor Org)	59	13	1%	22%			1	13	10			11		10					
27 IDA (Devel Assoc)	82	13	1%	16%		12	1		2			13		1	5		2	1	
28 Mexico	138	12	1%	9%	5		5	2		10	2						1		1
29 Germany, East	556	12	1%	2%			2	10	1	5	2	4							
30 Sweden	483	11	1%	2%	4	4	3		1	4	5		1		3		1		1
31 All Others (37)	5480	112	6%	2%	22	13	30	47	30	45	29	7	1	7	10	10	7	12	44
GROUPS																			
32 African Group	968	6		1%	1		1	4		3	3			1	1				
33 Arab Group	937	27	2%	1%	4	3	5	15	8	10	9	5	8		12	1	4	5	3
34 Asian Group	1937	81	5%	3%	31	15	10	25	16	19	33	19		1				3	5
35 Commonwealth	1641	86	5%	5%	1	6	28	51	10	28	29	6		1					
36 Communist Group	3310	86	5%	3%	1	6	28	51	10	28	29	6	8		6	2	22	16	7
37 Latin America	1674	114	7%	7%	20	6	42	46	30	52	26	28	16	2	33	6	40	5	45
38 Western Europe	5906	442	26%	7%	70	116	133	123	124	124	150	245	1	68	37	34	40	16	25
39 Intl Organs	1399	291	17%	21%	34	100	62	95	21	24									
TOTALS																			
40 All Data	20997	1731	100%		312	448	430	541	289	441	321	528	152	92	125	59	82	92	91
41 UNTS Only		1316																	
COMPARISONS																			
42 Party Total					18%	26%	25%	31%	17%	25%	19%	31%	9%	7%	9%	4%	6%	7%	7%
43 Group Total					18%	27%	24%	31%	16%	25%	18%	31%	9%	7%	10%	5%	6%	7%	6%
44 World Total					18%	23%	29%	29%	22%	25%	25%	20%	7%	8%	12%	6%	7%	12%	100%

Table 7 • 55

TREATY PROFILE OF WESTERN EUROPE

Partners (1)	Partner's World Total (2)	Dyads Absolutes (3)	Ratios Self (4)	Ratios Other (5)	Time 1946-1950 (6)	Time 1951-1955 (7)	Time 1956-1960 (8)	Time 1961-1965 (9)	Admin & Dipl (10)	Social Coop (11)	Econ Coop (12)	Aid (13)	Milit (14)	UN (15)	Spec Ag's (16)	Intl Court (17)	Arbi-tration (18)	Other (19)	Self-Registered (20)
TOP THIRTY																			
1 USA (United States)	2599	686	9%	26%	194	203	169	120	76	97	138	181	194	41	81	30	9	98	59
2 Germany, West	890	431	5%	48%	27	132	151	121	157	128	111	7	28		14	4	12	23	113
3 France	1033	430	5%	42%	102	98	114	116	118	157	124	5	26		9	4	10	37	105
4 UK Great Britain	981	405	5%	41%	127	102	94	82	122	85	121	18	59	10	46	19	20	104	52
5 Italy	755	325	4%	43%	68	105	96	56	68	126	106	6	19	1	10	4	6	62	60
6 Belgium	499	292	4%	59%	92	86	74	40	108	89	73	6	16		10	5	6	38	25
7 Sweden	483	274	3%	57%	110	90	56	18	45	58	168	1	2	1	13	7	9	14	52
8 Netherlands	548	274	3%	50%	72	95	74	33	79	83	88	2	22	2	14	3	11	70	43
9 Switzerland	426	260	3%	61%	53	78	79	50	71	87	96	3	3		14	4	9	14	55
10 Spain	437	247	3%	57%	26	44	112	65	27	109	110	1			5		7	9	37
11 Austria	445	232	3%	52%	36	81	65	50	92	70	67	2	1	1	10		8	20	62
12 Norway	461	222	3%	48%	75	58	58	31	53	42	111	6	10		14	1	13	31	46
13 USSR (Soviet Union)	1356	211	3%	16%	63	38	76	34	70	44	84	7	6	1	1		1	10	29
14 Denmark	380	167	2%	44%	60	38	38	31	28	37	95	1	6	2	13	2	8	39	37
15 Yugoslavia	525	163	2%	31%	29	36	57	41	53	48	55	2	5	2	11	7	11	23	33
16 Greece	318	134	2%	42%	35	58	19	22	17	29	81	3	4	1	15	1	8	57	20
17 Turkey	298	126	2%	42%	41	31	34	20	22	26	58	20			9	1	3	13	26
18 Finland	245	101	1%	41%	25	32	25	19	26	23	50	1	1	1	8	4	7	6	37
19 Canada	310	101	1%	33%	37	23	25	16	29	22	23	3	24		13	1	7	7	14
20 Luxembourg	136	94	1%	69%	23	20	20	31	28	44	16	2	4		12		4	5	42
21 Poland	493	89	1%	18%	29	10	18	32	4	29	53	2	1		1			11	26
22 IBRD (World Bank)	452	86	1%	19%	17	23	27	19	1			85							
23 Japan	443	85	1%	19%	4	32	34	15	29	15	36	1	4	2	12	2	11	3	17
24 Czechoslovakia	393	80	1%	20%	43	10	9	18	8	20	47	2	3		8	5	4	9	27
25 Israel	232	78	1%	34%	2	39	19	18	36	14	25	1	2		7		6	9	11
26 Brazil	195	74	1%	38%	16	12	30	16	20	25	22	4	3	1	7	4	4	3	16
27 Australia	201	72	1%	36%	16	27	17	12	25	20	16	3	8	4	9	2	9	2	7
28 Portugal	131	70	1%	53%	22	14	19	15	11	28	30	1			11	1	4	2	26
29 Ireland	103	69	1%	67%	29	21	13	6	18	21	29		1		12		7	9	12
30 Argentina	164	63	1%	38%	22	4	20	17	6	27	22	2	6		4	6	9	2	15
31 All Others (135)	9216	1898	24%	21%	259	378	491	770	503	538	577	221	59	70	189	103	129	65	375
GROUPS																			
32 African Group	968	330		34%	42	8	55	267	66	89	92	73	10	2	20	12	15	3	62
33 Arab Group	937	288	4%	31%		44	91	111	60	112	77	35	4	3	52	11	33	20	77
34 Asian Group	1937	390	5%	20%	68	96	122	104	93	125	112	41	19	8	60	22	36	13	75
35 Commonwealth	1641	675	9%	41%	202	186	161	126	204	160	189	24	98	17	76	21	31	114	90
36 Communist Group	3310	579	7%	17%	164	84	167	164	102	149	302	13	13	2	12		8	42	136
37 Latin America	1674	442	6%	26%	70	116	133	123	124	124	150	28	16	2	33	6	22	5	83
38 Western Europe	5906	3866	49%	65%	922	1114	1066	764	1016	1184	1452	68	146	8	204	44	146	462	825
39 Intl Organs	1399	227	3%	16%	44	55	49	79	61	24	4	132	6	37	15	34	33	9	10
TOTALS																			
40 All Data	25148	7839	100%		1754	2018	2133	1934	1950	2141	2632	599	517	137	583	217	352	795	1479
41 UNTS Only		4303																	
COMPARISONS																			
42 Party Total					22%	26%	27%	25%	25%	27%	34%	8%	7%	3%	14%	5%	8%	18%	34%
43 Group Total					22%	25%	27%	26%	24%	26%	32%	10%	8%	4%	14%	6%	8%	17%	32%
44 World Total					18%	23%	29%	29%	22%	25%	25%	20%	7%	8%	12%	6%	7%	12%	100%

Table 8

TREATY PROFILE OF INTL ORGANS

	Partners	Partner's World Total	Dyads Absolutes	Ratios Self	Ratios Other	Time 1946-1950	Time 1951-1955	Time 1956-1960	Time 1961-1965	Topics Admin & Dipl	Topics Social Coop	Topics Econ Coop	Topics Aid	Topics Milit	Institutions UN	Institutions Spec Ag's	Institutions Intl Court	Institutions Arbitration	Institutions Other	Self-Registered
	(1)	(2)	(3)	(4)	(5)	(6)	(7)	(8)	(9)	(10)	(11)	(12)	(13)	(14)	(15)	(16)	(17)	(18)	(19)	(20)
	TOP THIRTY																			
1	India	299	74	5%	25%	5	23	17	29	2	8		63	1	11	3	7	8	3	70
2	Pakistan	245	51	3%	21%	2	11	10	28	2	2		47		6	5	3	2	3	49
3	UK Great Britain	981	45	3%	5%	9	10	11	15	6	1		38		15	3	1	1	1	23
4	United Nations	233	43	3%	18%	25	4	7	7	40	1		2		7	10	8	2	2	
5	Japan	443	43	3%	10%		12	18	13	5	1	1	34	2	2	2	2	2	1	37
6	Colombia	112	33	3%	29%	4	11	8	10		2		31		3	4	3	1	2	31
7	Mexico	138	31	2%	22%	4	10	5	12		2		24		7		2	3	1	29
8	Philippines	236	29	2%	12%	2	15	3	9	5			27		3	1	3	1		11
9	France	1033	29	2%	3%	5	8	7	9	2	6		10		6	1	3			15
10	Thailand	132	28	2%	21%	6	7	4	11	13	5		19		5	1		1		24
11	Peru	109	27	2%	25%	4	8	7	8	4	1		24		3	2	3	1	1	25
12	USA (United States)	2599	26	2%	1%	3	5	5	13	2	3	4	11		3	5	1	2	2	9
13	ILO (Labor Org)	59	24	2%	41%	8	3	7	6	23			1		9					4
14	Chile	119	23	2%	19%	3	8	5	7	6	3		18		6	3	1	3		20
15	Netherlands	548	22	1%	4%	10	4	3	5	6	1		14	1	5	2	2	3	4	12
16	Ethiopia	98	22	1%	22%	2	5	5	10	4			18		5	1	2	3		19
17	Yugoslavia	525	21	1%	4%	2	6	5	11	2	2		16	1	4	1	4	4		18
18	United Arab Rep	232	20	1%	9%	2	6	6	6	7	1		11	1	8	5	5	8	3	14
19	Brazil	195	20	1%	10%	3	10	5	2	1	1		17		4		1	2		18
20	Austria	445	20	1%	4%	2	3	8	7	6	1		13		3	2	2	2		15
21	Turkey	298	19	1%	6%	4	5	1	9		2	1	17		1	2	2	3		14
22	Finland	245	19	1%	8%	4	3	4	8	1	2		15		2	2	2	4		18
23	Italy	755	18	1%	2%	1	4	6	7	6	1		11	1	4	3	3		1	15
24	Iran	170	18	1%	11%		3	6	9	3		1	14		4	1	1	1	1	11
25	Switzerland	426	17	1%	4%	8	4	3	2	14	1		2	1	1	1	7	5	1	9
26	Nicaragua	50	17	1%	34%	2	9	2	4	1	1		15	2	2	2	2	2	2	15
27	Jordan	65	16	1%	25%		8	4	4	2			14	1	4	7	2	2		11
28	Taiwan	172	16	1%	9%	2	5	1	8	2	2	1	12		5	3	1	1		12
29	Israel	232	15	1%	6%	1	4	4	6				14		5	1	1	3		11
30	Ceylon (Sri Lanka)	123	15	1%	12%	2	7	2	4	2	2	1	11		6	3	1	2		13
31	All Others (132)	12368	684	46%	6%	77	131	174	302	178	51	7	440	8	245	94	110	137	27	484
	GROUPS																			
32	African Group	968	160	11%	17%	2	9	25	124	27	1		131	1	59	21	30	48	4	104
33	Arab Group	937	117	8%	12%	3	30	36	48	17	3	2	93	2	49	23	19	28	3	82
34	Asian Group	1937	308	21%	16%	25	94	73	116	27	30	2	247	2	65	28	35	35	8	240
35	Commonwealth	1641	80	5%	5%	11	21	21	27	8	6	1	65	1	20	4	7	5	2	52
36	Communist Group	3310	24	2%	1%	7		3	14	15	1		7		8	2	2	2	1	12
37	Latin America	1674	291	20%	17%	34	100	62	95	21	24		245	1	68	37	34	40	16	246
38	Western Europe	5906	227	15%	4%	44	55	49	79	61	24	4	132	6	37	15	34	33	9	167
39	Intl Organs	1399	172	12%	12%	70	16	52	34	158	6		8		74	30	16	4	8	77
	TOTALS																			
40	All Data	23685	1485	100%		202	352	350	581	350	101	15	1003	16	394	169	186	206	54	1056
41	UNTS Only		1431																	
	COMPARISONS																			
42	Party Total					14%	24%	24%	39%	24%	7%	1%	68%	1%	28%	12%	13%	14%	4%	74%
43	Group Total					12%	25%	23%	40%	19%	7%	1%	71%	1%	27%	11%	13%	15%	4%	74%
44	World Total					18%	23%	29%	29%	22%	25%	25%	20%	7%	8%	12%	6%	7%	12%	100%

TREATY PROFILE OF ALL STATES

Table 9 • 57

	Partners (1)	Partner's World Total (2)	Dyads Absolutes (3)	Dyads Ratios Self (4)	Dyads Ratios Other (5)	Time 1946 1950 (6)	Time 1951 1955 (7)	Time 1956 1960 (8)	Time 1961 1965 (9)	Topics Admin & Dipl (10)	Topics Social Coop (11)	Topics Econ Coop (12)	Topics Aid (13)	Topics Milit (14)	Institutions UN (15)	Institutions Spec Ag's (16)	Institutions Intl Court (17)	Institutions Arbitration (18)	Institutions Other (19)	Self-Registered (20)
	TOP THIRTY																			
1	USA (United States)	2599	2572	11%	99%	571	738	594	669	315	494	338	862	563	124	203	74	36	231	169
2	USSR (Soviet Union)	1356	1354	6%	100%	251	221	595	287	353	309	368	282	42	7	6		4	46	97
3	France	1033	1002	4%	97%	219	190	235	358	262	340	266	48	86	7	43	18	21	59	282
4	UK Great Britain	981	930	4%	95%	272	222	208	228	231	212	283	67	137	23	120	33	46	144	169
5	Germany, West	890	888	4%	100%	32	229	286	341	222	222	263	107	74	5	37	14	28	61	260
6	China People's Rep	766	766	3%	100%	33	186	253	294	104	271	311	73	7	1				3	22
7	Italy	755	736	3%	97%	161	188	219	168	170	215	226	55	70	15	24	13	14	99	203
8	Germany, East	556	556	2%	100%	40	152	214	150	99	227	178	44	8	1				8	46
9	Netherlands	548	524	2%	96%	145	163	128	88	128	162	155	23	56	12	56	23	32	91	106
10	Yugoslavia	525	504	2%	96%	127	94	172	111	109	151	154	65	25	9	17	10	22	74	170
11	Poland	493	485	2%	98%	110	76	165	134	83	198	133	58	13	8	5		2	49	88
12	Belgium	499	483	2%	97%	144	135	124	80	166	137	121	17	42	3	29	20	12	68	70
13	Sweden	483	474	2%	98%	189	142	104	39	70	109	277	10	8	5	47	15	24	23	110
14	Norway	461	449	2%	97%	131	103	129	86	124	96	182	14	33	4	43	11	28	57	113
15	IBRD (World Bank)	452	448	2%	99%	41	97	136	174	1		3	444		2	7	3	24	4	
16	Spain	437	429	2%	98%	51	101	181	96	77	166	162	15	9	1	13	1	15	13	99
17	Austria	445	424	2%	95%	54	126	127	117	165	117	111	20	11	2	22	3	15	38	157
18	Switzerland	426	407	2%	96%	88	112	118	89	87	131	172	12	5		49	11	31	19	100
19	Japan	443	396	2%	89%	7	117	137	135	106	87	119	43	41	10	53	20	18	21	125
20	Czechoslovakia	393	390	2%	99%	115	55	133	87	81	154	127	16	12	3	24		13	35	102
21	Denmark	380	367	2%	97%	114	93	89	71	55	92	177	14	29	7	50	8	22	63	101
22	Greece	318	311	1%	98%	80	108	64	59	48	64	147	23	29	4	31	8	14	94	109
23	Canada	310	305	1%	98%	89	72	77	67	71	79	72	19	64	1	34	3	13	39	143
24	Hungary	290	287	1%	99%	70	41	100	76	61	106	96	11	13	7	3		6	21	79
25	Turkey	298	278	1%	93%	82	72	79	45	51	55	99	57	16	6	23		10	27	105
26	Romania	251	246	1%	98%	50	42	92	62	54	104	64	17	7	5	2	3	2	20	58
27	Bulgaria	236	233	1%	99%	39	48	88	58	41	93	76	20	3	2	17			21	83
28	Finland	245	224	1%	91%	57	55	58	54	64	44	98	12	6	5	17	5	11	13	91
29	India	299	223	1%	75%	40	59	66	58	36	59	66	45	17	4	31	8	12	13	117
30	Israel	232	214	1%	92%	15	69	45	85	76	43	43	43	9	6	20	6	7	9	60
31	All Others (154)	8033	6944	29%	86%	1043	1476	1905	2520	1564	1822	1458	1663	437	548	672	372	448	344	2661
	GROUPS																			
32	African Group	968	781	3%	81%	10	41	135	595	150	208	177	212	34	17	56	24	40	20	318
33	Arab Group	937	825	3%	88%	82	196	251	296	141	261	209	181	33	26	101	25	62	48	355
34	Asian Group	1937	1729	7%	89%	300	363	566	500	400	444	410	333	142	62	174	66	80	74	679
35	Commonwealth	1641	1637	7%	100%	455	401	396	385	398	422	475	104	238	40	222	45	72	199	438
36	Communist Group	3310	4735	20%	143%	755	897	1844	1239	939	1620	1456	611	109	34	40	20	30	222	656
37	Latin America	1674	1433	6%	86%	273	348	368	444	261	417	321	283	151	22	88		42	76	887
38	Western Europe	5906	7582	32%	128%	1697	1958	2074	1853	1859	2117	2628	467	511	86	568	162	319	786	2193
39	Intl Organs	1399	1312	6%	94%	132	336	298	546	191	95	15	995	16	320	139	170	202	46	43
	TOTALS																			
40	All Data	25433	23849	100%		4460	5582	6921	6886	5074	6359	6345	4199	1872	837	1681	682	930	1807	6095
41	UNTS Only		14399																	
	COMPARISONS																			
42	Party Total					19%	23%	29%	29%	21%	27%	27%	18%	8%	6%	12%	5%	6%	13%	42%
43	Group Total					18%	23%	29%	29%	22%	25%	25%	20%	7%	8%	12%	6%	7%	12%	
44	World Total																			100%

TREATY PROFILE OF WORLD TOTAL

Part-ners (1)	Partner's World Total (2)	Dyads Abso-lutes (3)	Ratios Self (4)	Ratios Other (5)	Time 1946 1950 (6)	Time 1951 1955 (7)	Time 1956 1960 (8)	Time 1961 1965 (9)	Topics Admin & Dipl (10)	Topics Social Coop (11)	Topics Econ Coop (12)	Topics Aid (13)	Topics Milit (14)	Institutions UN (15)	Institutions Spec Ag's (16)	Institutions Intl Court (17)	Institutions Arbi-tration (18)	Institutions Other (19)	Self-Regis-tered (20)
TOP THIRTY																			
1 USA (United States)	2599	2599	20%	100%	575	743	599	682	324	497	342	873	563	127	208	76	38	233	2308
2 USSR (Soviet Union)	1356	1356	11%	100%	251	221	596	288	354	309	368	283	42	7	6		4	46	197
3 France	1033	1033	8%	100%	225	198	243	367	277	346	266	58	86	13	44	23	22	59	77
4 UK Great Britain	981	981	8%	100%	282	234	221	244	243	213	283	105	137	39	123	40	47	145	700
5 Germany, West	890	890	7%	100%	32	229	286	343	223	222	264	107	74	5	37	14	28	61	
6 China People's Rep	766	766	6%	100%	33	186	253	294	104	271	311	73	7	1				3	
7 Italy	755	755	6%	100%	162	192	226	175	177	216	226	66	70	20	27	16	14	99	85
8 Germany, East	556	556	4%	100%	40	152	214	150	99	227	178	44	8	1				8	
9 Netherlands	548	548	4%	100%	156	167	132	93	136	163	155	37	57	17	58	27	35	95	277
10 Yugoslavia	525	525	4%	100%	129	100	174	122	111	153	154	81	26	13	18	14	26	74	153
11 Belgium	499	499	4%	100%	146	139	131	83	168	137	123	28	43	4	29	22	13	69	327
12 Poland	493	493	4%	100%	111	76	167	139	86	198	134	62	13	10	6	1	3	50	92
13 Sweden	483	483	4%	100%	191	143	107	42	77	109	277	11	9	7	47	19	26	25	108
14 Norway	461	461	4%	100%	132	106	134	89	127	97	182	21	34	4	43	16	30	57	110
15 IBRD (World Bank)	452	452	4%	100%	42	97	137	176	4		3	445		2	9	3	4	4	449
16 Austria	445	445	3%	100%	56	130	135	124	172	118	111	33	11	6	24	5	17	38	39
17 Japan	443	443	3%	100%	7	132	156	148	115	88	120	77	43	15	55	26	20	22	96
18 Spain	437	437	3%	100%	51	104	182	100	79	166	162	21	9	4	14	2	15	13	
19 Switzerland	426	426	3%	100%	98	116	121	91	103	132	172	14	5	2	50	20	36	20	1
20 Czechoslovakia	393	393	3%	100%	117	55	133	88	82	155	127	17	12	4	24		13	35	95
21 Denmark	380	380	3%	100%	117	98	93	72	58	98	177	17	30	10	50	12	24	64	192
22 Greece	318	318	2%	100%	82	110	65	61	49	66	147	27	29	7	32	9	17	94	147
23 Canada	310	310	2%	100%	90	73	80	67	72	81	72	20	65	2	34	6	15	39	125
24 India	299	299	2%	100%	45	82	85	87	40	67	66	108	18	16	34	17	20	16	26
25 Turkey	298	298	2%	100%	87	77	80	54	53	55	100	74	16	7	25	6	13	27	13
26 Hungary	290	290	2%	100%	72	41	100	77	64	106	96	11	13	9	3		6	21	63
27 Romania	251	251	2%	100%	51	44	92	64	59	104	64	17	7	9	1	1	3	20	58
28 Pakistan	245	245	2%	100%	41	68	72	64	57	62	42	74	10	19	52	23	19	11	55
29 Finland	245	245	2%	100%	61	59	63	62	67	46	98	27	7	8	17	9	15	13	42
30 Philippines	236	236	2%	100%	66	54	47	69	73	50	30	52	31	9	14	12	8	5	41
31 All Others (168)	8051	8051	63%	100%	1150	1732	2188	2981	1901	1908	1510	2319	413	915	766	509	585	396	1275
GROUPS																			
32 African Group	968	975	4%	101%	12	51	175	737	211	209	177	343	35	107	77	58	88	24	6
33 Arab Group	937	953	4%	102%	86	228	293	346	169	264	211	274	35	84	124	47	90	52	32
34 Asian Group	1937	2062	8%	106%	335	464	645	618	452	474	412	580	144	140	202	114	115	82	238
35 Commonwealth	1641	1725	7%	105%	467	426	419	413	414	428	475	169	239	61	226	60	77	201	1038
36 Communist Group	3310	4765	19%	144%	765	899	1847	1254	960	1621	1457	618	109	48	42	2	32	223	518
37 Latin America	1674	1731	7%	103%	312	448	430	541	289	441	321	528	152	92	125	59	82	92	91
38 Western Europe	5906	7839	31%	133%	1754	2018	2133	1934	1950	2141	2632	599	517	137	583	217	352	795	1479
39 Intl Organs	1399	1485	6%	106%	202	352	350	581	350	101	15	1003	16	394	169	186	206	54	1056
TOTALS																			
40 All Data	25464	12732	100%		4698	5958	7312	7496	5554	6460	6360	5202	1888	1312	1850	928	1136	1862	7151
41 UNTS Only		7980																	
COMPARISONS																			
42 Party Total					18%	23%	29%	29%	22%	25%	25%	20%	7%	8%	12%	6%	7%	12%	45%
43 Group Total					18%	23%	29%	29%	22%	25%	25%	20%	7%	8%	12%	6%	7%	12%	
44 World Total																			100%

Table 11 • 59

TREATY PROFILE OF ACCEPT UN CHARTER

Partners (1)	Partner's World Total (2)	Dyads Absolutes (3)	Ratios Self (4)	Ratios Other (5)	Time 1946-1950 (6)	Time 1951-1955 (7)	Time 1956-1960 (8)	Time 1961-1965 (9)	Topics Admin & Dipl (10)	Topics Social Coop (11)	Topics Econ Coop (12)	Topics Aid (13)	Topics Milit (14)	Institutions UN (15)	Institutions Spec Ag's (16)	Institutions Intl Court (17)	Institutions Arbitration (18)	Institutions Other (19)	Self-Registered (20)
TOP THIRTY																			
1 Tanzania	45	2	3%	4%				2	2					2					
2 Romania	251	2	3%	1%		2			2					2					
3 Zambia	9	1	1%	11%				1	1					1					
4 Yemen	35	1	1%	3%	1				1					1					
5 Upper Volta	15	1	1%	7%			1		1					1					
6 Uganda	21	1	1%	5%				1	1					1					
7 Tunisia	97	1	1%	1%			1		1					1					
8 Trinidad/Tobago	11	1	1%	9%				1	1					1					
9 Togo	28	1	1%	4%			1		1					1					
10 Thailand	132	1	1%	1%	1				1					1					
11 Sweden	483	1	1%		1				1					1					
12 Sudan	37	1	1%	3%			1		1					1					
13 Spain	437	1	1%			1			1					1					
14 Somalia	37	1	1%	3%			1		1					1					
15 Singapore	3	1	1%	33%				1	1					1					
16 Sierra Leone	27	1	1%	4%			1		1					1					
17 Senegal	40	1	1%	3%			1		1					1					
18 Rwanda	14	1	1%	7%				1	1					1					
19 Portugal	131	1	1%	1%	1				1					1					
20 Pakistan	245	1	1%					1	1					1					
21 Niger	25	1	1%	4%			1		1					1					
22 Nigeria	27	1	1%	4%		1			1					1					
23 Nepal	36	1	1%	3%			1		1					1					
24 Morocco	94	1	1%	1%				1	1					1					
25 Mongolia	119	1	1%	1%			1		1					1					
26 Mauritania	18	1	1%	6%			1		1					1					
27 Malta	15	1	1%	7%				1	1					1					
28 Mali	54	1	1%	2%			1		1					1					
29 Maldive Islands	2	1	1%	50%				1	1					1					
30 Malawi	11	1	1%	9%				1	1					1					
31 All Others (36)	3970	36	53%	1%	9	6	13	8	36					36					
GROUPS																			
32 African Group	968	29	43%	3%	1	2	15	14	29					29					
33 Arab Group	937	8	12%	1%	1	2	3	2	8					8					
34 Asian Group	1937	12	18%	1%	6	3	1	2	12					12					
35 Commonwealth	1641																		
36 Communist Group	3310	6	9%		3	2		1	6					6					
37 Latin America	1674	2	3%					2	2					2					
38 Western Europe	5906	9	13%		2	2	3	2	9					9					
39 Intl Organs	1399																		
TOTALS																			
40 All Data	6469	68	100%		13	10	22	23	68					68					
41 UNTS Only		68																	
COMPARISONS																			
42 Party Total					19%	15%	32%	34%	100%					100%					
43 Group Total					18%	23%	29%	29%	22%	25%	25%	20%	7%	8%	12%	6%	7%	12%	100%
44 World Total																			100%

60 • Table 12

TREATY PROFILE OF ICJ OPTION CLAUSE

			Dyads			Time				Topics					Institutions				
				Ratios		1946	1951	1956	1961	Admin	Social	Econ				Spec	Intl	Arbi-	Self-Regis-
Partners	Partner's World Total	Abso-lutes	Self	Other		1950	1955	1960	1965	& Dipl	Coop	Coop	Aid	Milit	UN	Ag's	Court	tration	Other	tered
(1)	(2)	(3)	(4)	(5)		(6)	(7)	(8)	(9)	(10)	(11)	(12)	(13)	(14)	(15)	(16)	(17)	(18)	(19)	(20)
TOP THIRTY																				
1 UK Great Britain	981	6	10%	1%		1	2	2	1	6					1		6			
2 Pakistan	245	3	5%	1%		1		2		3							3			
3 Japan	443	3	5%	1%			2	1		3					2		3			
4 United Arab Rep	232	2	3%	1%						2					1		2		1	
5 Switzerland	426	2	3%			2		2		2					1		2			
6 Sweden	483	2	3%			1		1		2							2			
7 Norway	461	2	3%			1		1		2							2			
8 Netherlands	548	2	3%	13%		1		1		2					1		2			
9 Liechtenstein	16	2	3%	1%		2				2					1		2			
10 Israel	232	2	3%	1%		1		1		2							2			
11 India	299	2	3%					2		2							2			
12 France	1033	2	3%			1		1		2					1		2			
13 Finland	245	2	3%	1%			1	1		2							2			
14 Denmark	380	2	3%	1%		1		1		2							2			
15 Cambodia	55	2	3%	4%			1		1	2							2			
16 Belgium	499	2	3%			1	1			2							2			
17 Vietnam, South	106	1	2%	1%		1				1							1			
18 USA (United States)	2599	1	2%						1	1							1			
19 Uganda	21	1	2%	5%						1							1			
20 Turkey	298	1	2%			1				1							1			
21 Thailand	132	1	2%	1%		1				1							1			
22 Sudan	37	1	2%	3%				1		1					1		1			
23 Somalia	37	1	2%	3%			1			1							1			
24 South Africa	120	1	2%	1%			1			1					1		1			
25 San Marino	17	1	2%	6%						1							1			
26 United Nations	233	1	2%						1	1					1					
27 Portugal	131	1	2%	1%		1				1							1			
28 Philippines	236	1	2%				1			1							1			
29 Nigeria	27	1	2%	4%						1										
30 Mexico	138	1	2%	1%		1			1	1							1			
31 All Others (10)	942	10	16%	1%		5	4		1	10					1		10			
GROUPS																				
32 African Group	968	5	8%	1%			1	3	4	5					2		4			
33 Arab Group	937	3	5%				4	5		3					1		3			
34 Asian Group	1937	13	21%	1%		4	4	5		13					1		13			
35 Commonwealth	1641	8	13%			1	4	2	1	8					1		8			
36 Communist Group	3310																			
37 Latin America	1674	5	8%			5				5							5			
38 Western Europe	5906	21	34%			11	3	7		21					5		21			
39 Intl Organs	1399	1	2%						1	1										
TOTALS																				
40 All Data	11652	62	100%			23	14	19	6	62					13		60		1	
41 UNTS Only		62																		
COMPARISONS																				
42 Party Total			100%			37%	23%	31%	10%	100%					21%		97%		2%	
43 Group Total						18%	23%	29%	29%	22%	25%	25%	20%	7%	8%	12%	6%	7%	12%	
44 World Total																				100%

TREATY PROFILE OF AFGHANISTAN

Table 13 • 61

	Partner's World Total	Dyads Absolutes	Ratios Self	Ratios Other	Time 1946-1950	Time 1951-1955	Time 1956-1960	Time 1961-1965	Topics Admin & Dipl	Topics Social Coop	Topics Econ Coop	Topics Aid	Topics Milit	Institutions UN	Institutions Spec Ag's	Institutions Intl Court	Institutions Arbitration	Institutions Other	Self-Registered
Partners (1)	(2)	(3)	(4)	(5)	(6)	(7)	(8)	(9)	(10)	(11)	(12)	(13)	(14)	(15)	(16)	(17)	(18)	(19)	(20)
TOP THIRTY																			
1 USSR (Soviet Union)	1356	24	29%	2%	3	3	14	4	5	6	3	10						1	1
2 USA (United States)	2599	11	13%	4%		4	3	4	1	3	3	7							
3 Iran	170	7	8%	4%	1		1	5	2	2	3	1							
4 China People's Rep	766	7	8%	1%			2	5	2	1	2	1		1	1		1		
5 Germany, West	890	4	5%				3	1	3	2	1				1				
6 India	299	3	4%	1%	3					1	1				1		1		3
7 Turkey	298	2	2%	1%			2		1	2									
8 WHO (World Health)	187	2	2%	1%	1		1	1		1		2		1			1		
9 United Nations	233	2	2%	1%						1		1							
10 Poland	493	2	2%				1	1		1		1							
11 Italy	755	2	2%				2			1		1							
12 France	1033	2	2%				1	1		2									
13 Czechoslovakia	393	2	2%	1%			1	1		1									
14 UK Great Britain	981	1	1%				1			1									
15 Switzerland	426	1	1%				1			1									
16 Spain	437	1	1%				1		1										
17 UN Special Fund	113	1	1%	1%	1			1				1		1	1				
18 UNICEF (Children)	122	1	1%	1%	1				1	1									
19 UNESCO (Educ/Cult)	19	1	1%	5%				1		1									1
20 IDA (Devel Assoc)	82	1	1%	1%				1				1			2	1			
21 IAEA (Atom Energy)	44	1	1%	2%			1			1		1			1	1			
22 Pakistan	245	1	1%					1		1									
23 Japan	443	1	1%					1		1									
24 Bulgaria	236	1	1%					1		1									
25 Austria	445	1	1%				1												
26 Accept UN Charter	68	1	1%	1%	1				1					1					
27																			
28																			
29																			
30																			
31 All Others (0)																			
GROUPS																			
32 African Group	968																		
33 Arab Group	937																		
34 Asian Group	1937	11	13%	1%	4		2	5	3	4	4				2	1			3
35 Commonwealth	1641	1	1%					1		1									
36 Communist Group	3310	36	43%	1%	3	3	18	12	8	11	5	12						1	1
37 Latin America	1674																		
38 Western Europe	5906	13	16%	1%			10	3	1	8	1	3			2		2		1
39 Intl Organs	1399	9	11%		3		3	3	1	2		6		3	3	2	1		
TOTALS																			
40 All Data	13133	83	100%		11	7	36	29	15	30	10	28		5	7	3	3	1	5
41 UNTS Only		37																	
COMPARISONS																			
42 Party Total					13%	8%	43%	35%	18%	36%	12%	34%	7%	14%	19%	8%	8%	3%	14%
43 Group Total					16%	23%	31%	30%	21%	23%	20%	30%	7%	10%	15%	8%	8%	6%	16%
44 World Total					18%	23%	29%	29%	22%	25%	25%	20%		8%	12%	6%	7%	12%	100%

62 • Table 14

TREATY PROFILE OF AFROMALAGASY ORG

Partners (1)	Partner's World Total (2)	Dyads Absolutes (3)	Ratios Self (4)	Ratios Other (5)	Time 1946 1950 (6)	Time 1951 1955 (7)	Time 1956 1960 (8)	Time 1961 1965 (9)	Topics Admin & Dipl (10)	Topics Social Coop (11)	Topics Econ Coop (12)	Topics Aid (13)	Topics Milit (14)	Institutions UN (15)	Institutions Spec Ag's (16)	Institutions Intl Court (17)	Institutions Arbitration (18)	Institutions Other (19)	Self-Registered (20)
TOP THIRTY																			
1 ILO (Labor Org)	59	1	100%	2%				1	1					1					
2																			
3																			
4																			
5																			
6																			
7																			
8																			
9																			
10																			
11																			
12																			
13																			
14																			
15																			
16																			
17																			
18																			
19																			
20																			
21																			
22																			
23																			
24																			
25																			
26																			
27																			
28																			
29																			
30																			
31 All Others (0)																			
GROUPS																			
32 African Group	968																		
33 Arab Group	937																		
34 Asian Group	1937																		
35 Commonwealth	1641																		
36 Communist Group	3310																		
37 Latin America	1674																		
38 Western Europe	5906		100%																
39 Intl Organs	1399	1						1	1					1					
TOTALS																			
40 All Data	59	1	100%																
41 UNTS Only		1																		
COMPARISONS																			
42 Party Total								100%	100%					100%					
43 Group Total					12%	25%	23%	40%	19%	7%	1%	71%	1%	27%	11%	13%	15%	4%	74%
44 World Total					18%	23%	29%	29%	22%	25%	25%	20%	7%	8%	12%	6%	7%	12%	100%

TREATY PROFILE OF ALBANIA

Table 15 • 63

Partners (1)	Partner's World Total (2)	Dyads Absolutes (3)	Ratios Self (4)	Ratios Other (5)	Time 1946-1950 (6)	Time 1951-1955 (7)	Time 1956-1960 (8)	Time 1961-1965 (9)	Topics Admin & Dipl (10)	Topics Social Coop (11)	Topics Econ Coop (12)	Topics Aid (13)	Topics Milit (14)	Institutions UN (15)	Institutions Spec Ag's (16)	Institutions Intl Court (17)	Institutions Arbitration (18)	Institutions Other (19)	Self-Registered (20)
TOP THIRTY																			
1 Yugoslavia	525	30	24%	6%	23	4	7		3	9	7	11						9	
2 USSR (Soviet Union)	1356	28	22%	2%	5	4	18	1	4	6	9	9					1	1	
3 China People's Rep	766	28	22%	4%		5	9	14	1	10	12	5							
4 Germany, East	556	19	15%	3%		6	10	3	4	7	4	4							
5 Italy	755	7	6%	1%			5	2	1	2	2		2						
6 Poland	493	3	2%	1%	1	1	1			2									
7 Romania	251	2	2%	1%		1		1		3								2	
8 Czechoslovakia	393	2	2%	1%			2		2	2								1	
9 UNICEF (Children)	122	1	1%	1%	1				1					1					
10 Hungary	290	1	1%				1		1										
11 France	1033	1	1%					1	1		1								
12 Cuba	111	1	1%	1%				1			1								
13 Austria	445	1	1%																
14 Accept UN Charter	68	1	1%	1%	1				1					1				1	
15																			
...																			
31 All Others (0)																			
GROUPS																			
32 African Group	968																		
33 Arab Group	937																		
34 Asian Group	1937																		
35 Commonwealth	1641																		
36 Communist Group	3310	83	66%	3%	6	17	41	19	12	28	25	18						4	
37 Latin America	1674	1	1%					1			1								
38 Western Europe	5906	9	7%				5	4	2	2	3		2					1	
39 Intl Organs	1399	1	1%		1				1					1					
TOTALS																			
40 All Data	7164	125	100%		31	17	53	24	19	39	36	29	2	2			1	14	
41 UNTS Only		47																	
COMPARISONS																			
42 Party Total					25%	14%	42%	19%	15%	31%	29%	23%	2%	4%	4%		2%	30%	
43 Group Total					16%	17%	38%	29%	20%	32%	32%	13%	2%	4%	4%		3%	17%	33%
44 World Total					18%	23%	29%	29%	22%	25%	25%	20%	7%	8%	12%	6%	7%	12%	100%

64 • Table 16

TREATY PROFILE OF ALGERIA

		Dyads			Time				Topics						Institutions				
Partners	Partner's World Total	Absolutes	Ratios Self	Other	1946 1950	1951 1955	1956 1960	1961 1965	Admin & Dipl	Social Coop	Econ Coop	Aid	Milit	UN	Spec Ag's	Intl Court	Arbitration	Other	Self-Registered
(1)	(2)	(3)	(4)	(5)	(6)	(7)	(8)	(9)	(10)	(11)	(12)	(13)	(14)	(15)	(16)	(17)	(18)	(19)	(20)
TOP THIRTY																			
1 France	1033	25	48%	2%				25	6	8	1	10			1		1	1	
2 China People's Rep	766	8	15%	1%				8		4	3	1							
3 Poland	493	3	6%	1%				3		2		1							
4 Italy	755	2	4%			1		1	1	1									
5 Germany, West	890	2	4%					2			1	1							
6 Czechoslovakia	393	2	4%	1%				2		2									
7 USSR (Soviet Union)	1356	1	2%					1	1										
8 Tunisia	97	1	2%	1%				1		1				1					
9 WHO (World Health)	187	1	2%	1%				1				1		1	1				
10 UN Special Fund	113	1	2%					1	1						1		1		
11 United Nations	233	1	2%					1						1		1	2		
12 UNICEF (Children)	122	1	2%	1%				1				1							
13 IBRD (World Bank)	452	1	2%					1		1					1		1	1	
14 Morocco	94	1	2%	1%				1		1									
15 Mali	54	1	2%	2%				1											
16 Accept UN Charter	68	1	2%	1%				1	1					1					
17																			
18																			
19																			
20																			
21																			
22																			
23																			
24																			
25																			
26																			
27																			
28																			
29																			
30																			
31 All Others (0)																			
GROUPS																			
32 African Group	968	1	2%					1		1					1		1		
33 Arab Group	937	2	4%					2		2					2		1		
34 Asian Group	1937																		
35 Commonwealth	1641																		
36 Communist Group	3310	14	27%					14	1	8	3	2							
37 Latin America	1674																		
38 Western Europe	5906	29	56%			1		28	7	9	2	11			1	1	1		
39 Intl Organs	1399	5	10%					5	1			4		3	1		3		
TOTALS																			
40 All Data	7106	52	100%		1	1		51	10	20	5	17		4	5	1	6		
41 UNTS Only		19																		
COMPARISONS																			
42 Party Total					9%	2%		98%	19%	38%	10%	33%		21%	26%	5%	32%	9%	5%
43 Group Total					18%	24%	31%	36%	18%	27%	22%	29%	4%	15%	20%	8%	15%		
44 World Total					18%	23%	29%	29%	22%	25%	25%	20%	7%	8%	12%	6%	7%	12%	100%

Table 17 • 65

TREATY PROFILE OF ARAB LEAGUE

Partners (1)	Partner's World Total (2)	Dyads Absolutes (3)	Dyads Ratios Self (4)	Dyads Ratios Other (5)	Time 1946 1950 (6)	Time 1951 1955 (7)	Time 1956 1960 (8)	Time 1961 1965 (9)	Topics Admin & Dipl (10)	Topics Social Coop (11)	Topics Econ Coop (12)	Topics Aid (13)	Topics Milit (14)	Institutions UN (15)	Institutions Spec Ag's (16)	Institutions Intl Court (17)	Institutions Arbitration (18)	Institutions Other (19)	Self-Registered (20)
TOP THIRTY																			
1 ILO (Labor Org)	59	1	100%	2%			1		1					1					
2																			
3																			
4																			
5																			
6																			
7																			
8																			
9																			
10																			
11																			
12																			
13																			
14																			
15																			
16																			
17																			
18																			
19																			
20																			
21																			
22																			
23																			
24																			
25																			
26																			
27																			
28																			
29																			
30																			
31 All Others (0)																			
GROUPS																			
32 African Group	968																		
33 Arab Group	937																		
34 Asian Group	1937																		
35 Commonwealth	1641																		
36 Communist Group	3310																		
37 Latin America	1674																		
38 Western Europe	5906																		
39 Intl Organs	1399	1	100%				1		1					1					
TOTALS																			
40 All Data		1	100%																
41 UNTS Only	59	1					1		1										
COMPARISONS																			
42 Party Total									100%					100%					
43 Group Total					12%	25%	23%	40%	19%	7%	1%	71%	1%	27%	11%	13%	15%	4%	74%
44 World Total					18%	23%	29%	29%	22%	25%	25%	20%	7%	8%	12%	6%	7%	12%	100%

66 • Table 18

TREATY PROFILE OF ARGENTINA

Part-ners (1)	Partner's World Total (2)	Dyads Abso-lutes (3)	Dyads Ratios Self (4)	Dyads Ratios Other (5)	Time 1946 1950 (6)	Time 1951 1955 (7)	Time 1956 1960 (8)	Time 1961 1965 (9)	Topics Admin & Dipl (10)	Topics Social Coop (11)	Topics Econ Coop (12)	Topics Aid (13)	Topics Milit (14)	Institutions UN (15)	Institutions Spec Ag's (16)	Institutions Intl Court (17)	Institutions Arbi-tration (18)	Institutions Other (19)	Self-Regis-tered (20)
TOP THIRTY																			
1 USA (United States)	2599	22	13%	1%	3	4	9	6	1	4	4	6	7		1			4	1
2 Italy	755	17	10%	2%	4	2	7	4	1	9	5	2						1	1
3 UK Great Britain	981	14	9%	1%	5	1	3	5		3	9	1	1		3			2	3
4 Brazil	195	11	7%	6%	1		6	4	4	3	3							1	
5 Japan	443	10	6%	2%				10	3	4	3				2				
6 Spain	437	9	5%	2%	5		2	2	1	7			1						2
7 USSR (Soviet Union)	1356	6	4%	8%	1	3	2		1	1	2	2						1	5
8 Uruguay	63	5	3%		2		2	2	2	1	1	1			1				
9 Norway	461	5	3%	1%				3	1	1	2								2
10 France	1033	5	3%		3		2	1		3	2				1				
11 Denmark	380	5	3%	1%	3		1		2	1	3		1		1				
12 Sweden	483	4	2%	1%	2		2		1	2	2				1				4
13 Paraguay	75	4	2%	5%	1		1	3	2	2	1		1						2
14 Belgium	499	4	2%	1%	1	1	1	2	1	1	2								
15 Switzerland	426	3	2%	1%	1		2			1	1				1				3
16 Netherlands	548	3	2%	1%	2	1				1	2								1
17 Germany, West	890	3	2%	5%			2	1		1	2								2
18 Bolivia	58	3	2%	1%			2	1		1	2								
19 Yugoslavia	525	2	1%	1%				2			2								2
20 United Arab Rep	232	2	1%	2%				2		1	2								1
21 IBRD (World Bank)	452	2	1%	2%		1		1				2			1				
22 Chile	119	2	1%		1			1	1		1								
23 Turkey	298	1	1%				1			1									
24 Thailand	132	1	1%	1%				1				1		1	1	1	1		
25 UN Special Fund	113	1	1%	1%			1					1		1					
26 UNICEF (Children)	122	1	1%	2%			1					1							
27 IAEA (Atom Energy)	44	1	1%	2%				1			1					1			
28 Poland	493	1	1%																
29 Philippines	236	1	1%	2%			1		1										1
30 Panama	57	1	1%	1%				1		1									
31 All Others (15)	2533	15	9%		3		3	9	4	8	2		1	2	1	2	1		8
GROUPS																			
32 African Group	968	3	2%		1		1	3	2	1	2	1						2	3
33 Arab Group	937	4	2%					2		1	1	2	1		3			1	
34 Asian Group	1937	15	9%	1%	6	4	3	5	2	3	10	2			3			1	1
35 Commonwealth	1641	7	4%		1		1	2	1	1	3	2						1	
36 Communist Group	3310	32	20%	2%	3	2	12	17	10	14	6	2			2	1		1	24
37 Latin America	1674	63	38%	1%	22	4	20	17	6	27	22	2	6		4	2	1	2	9
38 Western Europe	5906	5	3%				2	3				5		2	1				
39 Intl Organs	1399																		
TOTALS																			
40 All Data	17038	164	100%		36	13	50	65	23	56	53	18	14	2	13	2	1	10	38
41 UNTS Only		115																		
COMPARISONS																			
42 Party Total					22%	8%	30%	40%	14%	34%	32%	11%	9%	2%	11%	2%	1%	9%	33%
43 Group Total					18%	27%	24%	31%	16%	25%	18%	31%	9%	7%	10%	5%	6%	7%	6%
44 World Total					18%	23%	29%	29%	22%	25%	25%	20%	7%	8%	12%	6%	7%	12%	100%

Table 19

TREATY PROFILE OF ASIAN PRODUCTIVITY

Partners	Partner's World Total	Dyads Absolutes	Ratios Self	Ratios Other	Time 1946-1950	Time 1951-1955	Time 1956-1960	Time 1961-1965	Topics Admin & Dipl	Topics Social Coop	Topics Econ Coop	Topics Aid	Topics Milit	Institutions UN	Institutions Spec Ag's	Institutions Intl Court	Institutions Arbitration	Institutions Other	Self-Registered
(1)	(2)	(3)	(4)	(5)	(6)	(7)	(8)	(9)	(10)	(11)	(12)	(13)	(14)	(15)	(16)	(17)	(18)	(19)	(20)
TOP THIRTY																			
1 ILO (Labor Org)	59	1	100%	2%				1	1										
2																			
3																			
4																			
5																			
6																			
7																			
8																			
9																			
10																			
11																			
12																			
13																			
14																			
15																			
16																			
17																			
18																			
19																			
20																			
21																			
22																			
23																			
24																			
25																			
26																			
27																			
28																			
29																			
30																			
31 All Others (0)																			
GROUPS																			
32 African Group	968																		
33 Arab Group	937																		
34 Asian Group	1937																		
35 Commonwealth	1641																		
36 Communist Group	3310																		
37 Latin America	1674																		
38 Western Europe	5906																		
39 Intl Organs	1399	1	100%																
TOTALS																			
40 All Data	59	1	100%																
41 UNTS Only		1																		
COMPARISONS																			
42 Party Total									100%										
43 Group Total					12%	25%	23%	40%	19%	7%	1%	71%	1%	27%	11%	13%	15%	4%	74%
44 World Total					18%	23%	29%	29%	22%	25%	25%	20%	7%	8%	12%	6%	7%	12%	100%

TREATY PROFILE OF AUSTRALIA

(1) Partners	(2) Partner's World Total	(3) Abso-lutes	Dyads Ratios (4) Self	(5) Other	Time (6) 1946 1950	(7) 1951 1955	(8) 1956 1960	(9) 1961 1965	Topics (10) Admin & Dipl	(11) Social Coop	(12) Econ Coop	(13) Aid	(14) Milit	Institutions (15) UN	(16) Spec Ag's	(17) Intl Court	(18) Arbi-tration	(19) Other	(20) Self-Regis-tered
TOP THIRTY																			
1 USA (United States)	2599	34	17%	1%	6	7	10	11	4	12	6	3	9		5			3	9
2 UK Great Britain	981	15	7%	2%	3	1	4	7	2	10	3				2	1			6
3 Netherlands	548	12	6%	2%	3	4	4	1	3	6	3		1		2			1	6
4 Italy	755	11	5%	1%	3	5	2	1	2	4	4	1	3	3	1	1	2		9
5 Germany, West	890	10	5%	1%		2	4	4	2	5	2		1		1	1	1		9
6 IBRD (World Bank)	452	7	3%	2%	1	3	2	1				7							
7 New Zealand	101	7	3%	7%	2		2	3	2	2	3	1			1			1	4
8 Japan	443	7	3%	2%		2	2	3	2	3	3				3	2	1		2
9 Greece	318	6	3%	2%		3	1		3	1	1	1			1				5
10 Austria	445	5	2%	1%	2	2		1	2	1	1	1	1		1				5
11 Yugoslavia	525	4	2%	1%	1	1	2		2	1	1	1			1				4
12 USSR (Soviet Union)	1356	4	2%		2		2		1	1	1				1				
13 Thailand	132	4	2%	3%		1	3		1	2	1				1			1	1
14 Sweden	483	4	2%	1%	2	2			1		3					1			2
15 Philippines	236	4	2%	2%	2		1	1	1	1	1		2	1	1				1
16 France	1033	4	2%	2%	1	2		1	1		1		2	1					3
17 Finland	245	4	2%	2%	1	1	1	2	3		2								4
18 Canada	310	4	2%	1%			3	1		1		1			2		1		2
19 Poland	493	3	1%	1%	1	1	1		1	1	1	1			2				2
20 Israel	232	3	1%	1%	1	2			1	1	1				1				2
21 India	299	3	1%	1%	1			2	1	1	1		1		1	1			2
22 Hungary	290	3	1%	1%	2	1			1	1	1				1				3
23 Fed of Malaya	23	3	1%	13%			2	1	1	1	2	1		1	1				1
24 Belgium	499	3	1%	1%	1	2			1		1							1	2
25 Vietnam, South	106	2	1%	2%		2			2		2								1
26 South Africa	120	2	1%	2%		1	1			2									
27 FAO (Food Agri)	19	2	1%	11%			1	1				2		1	2			1	2
28 Pakistan	245	2	1%	1%	1	1				2						1			
29 Norway	461	2	1%		1	1			1		1								2
30 Denmark	380	2	1%	1%	1	1			1		1								2
31 All Others (23)	3533	25	12%	1%	2	9	5	9	9	9	7			3	8	4	3	2	17
GROUPS																			
32 African Group	968																		
33 Arab Group	937	1				1				1					1				
34 Asian Group	1937	26	13%	1%	5	7	7	7	6	11	8		1	2	10	3	3	3	13
35 Commonwealth	1641	29	14%	2%	6	3	10	10	4	15	9	1			5	1	2	1	13
36 Communist Group	3310	12	6%		5	3	3	1	5	4	1	2		2	5				7
37 Latin America	1674																		
38 Western Europe	5906	72	36%	1%	16	27	17	12	25	20	16	3	8	4	9	1	4	2	56
39 Intl Organs	1399	12	6%	1%	1	4	3	4	1	2		9		2		2	1	1	2
TOTALS																			
40 All Data	18552	201	100%		41	58	53	49	50	70	43	20	18	10	40	10	11	10	108
41 UNTS Only		195																	
COMPARISONS																			
42 Party Total					20%	29%	26%	24%	25%	35%	21%	10%	9%	5%	21%	5%	6%	5%	55%
43 Group Total					27%	25%	24%	24%	25%	24%	27%	10%	14%	4%	13%	4%	5%	12%	63%
44 World Total					18%	23%	29%	29%	22%	25%	25%	20%	7%	8%	12%	6%	7%	12%	100%

TREATY PROFILE OF AUSTRIA

Table 21 • 69

Partners (1)	Partner's World Total (2)	Dyads Absolutes (3)	Ratios Self (4)	Ratios Other (5)	Time 1946 1950 (6)	Time 1951 1955 (7)	Time 1956 1960 (8)	Time 1961 1965 (9)	Topics Admin & Dipl (10)	Topics Social Coop (11)	Topics Econ Coop (12)	Topics Aid (13)	Topics Milit (14)	Institutions UN (15)	Institutions Spec Ag's (16)	Institutions Intl Court (17)	Institutions Arbitration (18)	Other (19)	Self-Registered (20)
TOP THIRTY																			
1 Germany, West	890	41	9%	5%		23	10	8	25	11	5								1
2 Switzerland	426	32	7%	8%	10	8	9	5	11	13	8				1				1
3 Yugoslavia	525	31	7%	6%		10	7	14	20	9	2			2	1	1	1	3	7
4 USA (United States)	2599	31	7%	1%	11	5	12	3	3	4	4	14	6		5	1	2	3	
5 Italy	755	28	7%	4%	7	13	5	3	10	10	7		1		2		1	3	1
6 Sweden	483	21	5%	4%	3	10	7	1	4	5	12				1		1	1	
7 USSR (Soviet Union)	1356	18	4%	1%	1	12	5		7	4	5	1	1						
8 UK Great Britain	981	18	4%	2%	3	8	5	2	4	3	8	1	2		3	1		7	1
9 Netherlands	548	17	4%	3%	1	6	8	2	9	5	3							2	6
10 Hungary	290	16	4%	6%		1	3	12	7	5	4				1			1	
11 Belgium	499	14	3%	3%	2	4	5	3	8	5	1				1	1		1	
13 Spain	437	12	3%	3%			7	5	2	6	4						1	2	2
13 Norway	461	12	3%	3%	5	2	4	1	3	1	8						1	2	
14 Czechoslovakia	393	11	2%	3%	2		3	6	2	6	3				1		2	2	1
15 France	1033	10	2%	1%	1	1	3	5	2	5	3						1	2	
16 Denmark	380	10	2%	3%	4	2	1	3	3	2	5				1		1	4	1
17 IBRD (World Bank)	452	9	2%	2%		2	6	1				9							3
18 Romania	251	8	2%	3%	1	1	2	6	2	4	2								
19 Turkey	298	7	2%	2%	1	2	2	2	3	1	1	2			1			1	1
20 Greece	318	6	1%	2%		3	1	2	2	1	3				1		1	4	
21 Finland	245	6	1%	2%			1	5	2	2	2								
22 Bulgaria	236	6	1%	3%		1	1	4	1	3	2						2	1	4
23 Liechtenstein	16	5	1%	31%		3		2	4		1						1		
24 Israel	232	5	1%	2%		1	2	2	2	3					1				
25 Australia	201	5	1%	2%	1	2		2	2	1		1	1		1		1		
26 Vatican/Holy See	16	4	1%	25%					2	1									
27 Poland	493	4	1%	1%			2	2	1	3									
28 Luxembourg	136	4	1%	3%		1	1	2		2	2							1	1
29 Japan	443	4	1%	1%			1	3	2		2								
30 Brazil	195	4	1%	2%			3	1	2		2								1
31 All Others (33)	4519	46	10%	1%	3	7	18	18	27	3	11	5		4	2	2	2	1	6
GROUPS																			
32 African Group	968	4		1%				4	2		1	1							2
33 Arab Group	937	6		1%			4	2	2		3								1
34 Asian Group	1937	30		7%	4	12	11	3	12	1	8	2	3		4	1		7	
35 Commonwealth	1641	67		15%	3	15	15	34	20	5	20	1	1		1	1	3	5	16
36 Communist Group	3310	14		3%		1	10	3	10	25	4								2
37 Latin America	1674	232		52%	36	81	65	50	92	70	67	2	1	3	10	2	8	20	10
38 Western Europe	5906	20		4%	2	3	8	7	6	1		13			2		2		1
39 Intl Organs	1399			1%															
TOTALS																			
40 All Data	20107	445	100%		56	130	135	124	172	118	111	33	11	6	24	5	17	38	39
41 UNTS Only		230																		
COMPARISONS																			
42 Party Total					13%	29%	30%	28%	39%	27%	25%	7%	2%	3%	10%	2%	7%	17%	17%
43 Group Total					22%	25%	27%	26%	24%	26%	32%	10%	8%	4%	14%	6%	8%	17%	32%
44 World Total					18%	23%	29%	29%	22%	25%	25%	20%	7%	8%	12%	6%	7%	12%	100%

70 • Table 22

TREATY PROFILE OF BANK INT SETTLEMENT

Partners	Partner's World Total	Dyads Ratios				Time				Topics						Institutions				Self-Registered
		Abso-lutes	Self	Other		1946 1950	1951 1955	1956 1960	1961 1965	Admin & Dipl	Social Coop	Econ Coop	Aid	Milit	UN	Spec Ag's	Intl Court	Arbi-tration	Other	
(1)	(2)	(3)	(4)	(5)		(6)	(7)	(8)	(9)	(10)	(11)	(12)	(13)	(14)	(15)	(16)	(17)	(18)	(19)	(20)
TOP THIRTY																				
1 Germany, West	890	1	100%						1			1								
2																				
3																				
4																				
5																				
6																				
7																				
8																				
9																				
10																				
11																				
12																				
13																				
14																				
15																				
16																				
17																				
18																				
19																				
20																				
21																				
22																				
23																				
24																				
25																				
26																				
27																				
28																				
29																				
30																				
31 All Others (0)																				
GROUPS																				
32 African Group	968																			
33 Arab Group	937																			
34 Asian Group	1937																			
35 Commonwealth	1641																			
36 Communist Group	3310																			
37 Latin America	1674																			
38 Western Europe	5906	1	100%						1			1								
39 Intl Organs	1399																			
TOTALS																				
40 All Data	890	1	100%						1			1								
41 UNTS Only		0																		
COMPARISONS																				
42 Party Total						12%	25%	23%	100%	19%	7%	100%	71%	1%	27%	11%	13%	15%	4%	74%
43 Group Total						18%	23%	29%	40%	22%	25%	1%	20%	7%	8%	12%	6%	7%	12%	100%
44 World Total								29%	29%		25%	25%									

Table 23

TREATY PROFILE OF BELGIUM

	Partners (1)	Partner's World Total (2)	Abso-lutes (3)	Dyads Ratios Self (4)	Dyads Ratios Other (5)	Time 1946 1950 (6)	Time 1951 1955 (7)	Time 1956 1960 (8)	Time 1961 1965 (9)	Topics Admin & Dipl (10)	Topics Social Coop (11)	Topics Econ Coop (12)	Topics Aid (13)	Topics Milit (14)	Institutions UN (15)	Institutions Spec Ag's (16)	Institutions Intl Court (17)	Institutions Arbi-tration (18)	Institutions Other (19)	Self-Regis-tered (20)
	TOP THIRTY																			
1	Netherlands	548	44	9%	8%	16	13	10	5	18	12	9	1	4			1		8	26
2	Germany, West	890	43	9%	5%		20	14	9	24	11	4		4		1	1	2	4	25
3	France	1033	42	8%	4%	15	11	10	6	16	13	7	1	5			2	1	5	32
4	USA (United States)	2599	36	7%	1%	12	13	4	7	6	5	10	3	12	2	4	2		7	15
5	UK Great Britain	981	28	6%	3%	11	11	4	2	9	6	5	2	8		2	2	1	11	15
6	Italy	755	24	5%	3%	8	9	3	4	6	15	2		1					4	11
7	Luxembourg	136	22	4%	16%	11	3	1	7	8	3	8	2			1			4	22
8	Spain	437	19	4%	4%	1	4	14		4	8	7							1	8
9	Sweden	483	17	3%	4%	7	4	4	2	3	5	9				1			1	11
10	Austria	445	14	3%	3%	2	4	5	3	8	2	4				1		1	1	14
11	Turkey	298	13	3%	4%	6	2	4	1	3	2	6	2			1	1		2	9
12	Switzerland	426	10	2%	2%	4	1	5		5	2	2		1						9
13	IBRD (World Bank)	452	10	2%	2%	1	3	6					10							
14	Greece	318	9	2%	3%	3	5	1		1	3	5				1		1	4	5
15	USSR (Soviet Union)	1356	8	2%	1%	6		2		1	1	6								
16	Norway	461	8	2%	2%	5	2	1		1	2	5				1			3	6
17	Denmark	380	8	2%	2%	5		3		4	1	3				1			1	4
18	South Africa	120	7	1%	6%	1	2		2		4	2				2				5
19	Israel	232	7	1%	3%		6	1		6	2	3								5
20	Czechoslovakia	393	7	1%	2%		1	2	4	2	2	1	1	3		1	1		1	6
21	Poland	493	6	1%	1%	4		1			4	3							1	4
22	Japan	443	6	1%	1%	1		4	4	2	1	1	2			2	1			6
23	Tunisia	97	5	1%	5%	2		1	1	1	2	3						1		5
24	Portugal	131	5	1%	4%	3	2			1	2	2				1	1			5
25	Pakistan	245	5	1%	2%		2	2	1	2	1	1	1			2	1			4
26	Ireland	103	5	1%	5%	2	2	1		2	2								1	3
27	Canada	310	5	1%	2%	4	1			1		1					1			2
28	Brazil	195	5	1%	3%		3	2		4	1				1			1		5
29	United Arab Rep	232	4	1%	2%	3		1		1	2	2		1		1		1	1	4
30	Iran	170	4	1%	2%		1	2	1	1	1	1				1	1	1		2
31	All Others (38)	4972	73	15%	1%	13	15	22	23	28	20	17	4	4	2	7	7	2	9	57
	GROUPS																			
32	African Group	968	6	1%	1%	4	2	1	5	1	6	3	2		1	1	2		2	6
33	Arab Group	937	16	3%	2%	4	2	6	4	4	5	4	2			4	3	4	1	16
34	Asian Group	1937	18	4%	1%	1	4	9	4	7	4	5		2		3	2	1	1	13
35	Commonwealth	1641	45	9%	3%	17	18	7	3	13	10	9	2	11		3	3	1	12	23
36	Communist Group	3310	27	5%	1%	11	1	8	7	3	13	10	1						4	17
37	Latin America	1674	27	5%	2%	5	4	9	9	16	4	5	1	1		1	1			25
38	Western Europe	5906	292	59%	5%	92	86	74	40	108	89	73	6	16		10	5	6	38	198
39	Intl Organs	1399	14	3%	1%	1	4	6	3			2	11	1	1			1	1	
	TOTALS																			
40	All Data	20134	499	100%		146	139	131	83	168	137	123	28	43	4	29	22	13	69	327
41	UNTS Only		423																	
	COMPARISONS																			
42	Party Total					29%	28%	26%	17%	34%	27%	25%	6%	9%	1%	7%	5%	3%	16%	77%
43	Group Total					22%	25%	27%	26%	24%	26%	32%	10%	8%	4%	14%	6%	8%	17%	32%
44	World Total					18%	23%	29%	29%	22%	25%	25%	20%	7%	8%	12%	6%	7%	12%	100%

72 • Table 24

TREATY PROFILE OF BEL-LUX ECON UNION

Partners (1)	Partner's World Total (2)	Dyads Absolutes (3)	Ratios Self (4)	Ratios Other (5)	Time 1946-1950 (6)	Time 1951-1955 (7)	Time 1956-1960 (8)	Time 1961-1965 (9)	Admin & Dipl (10)	Social Coop (11)	Econ Coop (12)	Aid (13)	Milit (14)	UN (15)	Spec Ag's (16)	Intl Court (17)	Arbitration (18)	Other (19)	Self-Registered (20)
TOP THIRTY																			
1 Morocco	94	1	100%	1%				1			1								
2																			
3																			
...																			
30																			
31 All Others (0)																			
GROUPS																			
32 African Group	968																		
33 Arab Group	937	1	100%																
34 Asian Group	1937																		
35 Commonwealth	1641																		
36 Communist Group	3310																		
37 Latin America	1674																		
38 Western Europe	5906																		
39 Intl Organs	1399																		
TOTALS																			
40 All Data	94	1	100%					1			1								
41 UNTS Only		1																	
COMPARISONS																			
42 Party Total					12%	25%	23%	100%	19%	7%	100%	71%	1%	27%	11%	13%	15%	4%	74%
43 Group Total					18%	23%	29%	40%	22%	25%	1%	20%	7%	8%	12%	6%	7%	12%	100%
44 World Total							29%	29%		25%	25%								

Table 25 • 73

TREATY PROFILE OF BENELUX ECON UNION

	Partners (1)	Partner's World Total (2)	Dyads Absolutes (3)	Dyads Ratios Self (4)	Dyads Ratios Other (5)	Time 1946-1950 (6)	Time 1951-1955 (7)	Time 1956-1960 (8)	Time 1961-1965 (9)	Topics Admin & Dipl (10)	Topics Social Coop (11)	Topics Econ Coop (12)	Topics Aid (13)	Topics Milit (14)	Institutions UN (15)	Institutions Spec Ag's (16)	Institutions Intl Court (17)	Institutions Arbitration (18)	Institutions Other (19)	Self-Registered (20)
	TOP THIRTY																			
1	Poland	493	1	100%					1			1							1	
2																				
3																				
4																				
5																				
6																				
7																				
8																				
9																				
10																				
11																				
12																				
13																				
14																				
15																				
16																				
17																				
18																				
19																				
20																				
21																				
22																				
23																				
24																				
25																				
26																				
27																				
28																				
29																				
30																				
31	All Others (0)																			
	GROUPS																			
32	African Group	968																		
33	Arab Group	937																		
34	Asian Group	1937																		
35	Commonwealth	1641																		
36	Communist Group	3310	1	100%					1			1							1	
37	Latin America	1674																		
38	Western Europe	5906																		
39	Intl Organs	1399																		
	TOTALS																			
40	All Data	493	1	100%					1			1							1	
41	UNTS Only		1																	
	COMPARISONS																			
42	Party Total					12%	25%	23%	100% 40%	19%	7%	100% 1%	71%	1%	27%	11%	13%	15%	100% 4%	100% 74%
43	Group Total					18%	23%	29%	29%	22%	25%	25%	20%	7%	8%	12%	6%	7%	12%	100%
44	World Total																			

74 • Table 26

TREATY PROFILE OF BOLIVIA

	Partner's World Total	Dyads Absolutes	Ratios Self	Ratios Other	Time 1946-1950	Time 1951-1955	Time 1956-1960	Time 1961-1965	Topics Admin & Dipl	Topics Social Coop	Topics Econ Coop	Topics Aid	Topics Milit	Institutions UN	Institutions Spec Ag's	Institutions Intl Court	Institutions Arbitration	Institutions Other	Self-Registered
Partners (1)	(2)	(3)	(4)	(5)	(6)	(7)	(8)	(9)	(10)	(11)	(12)	(13)	(14)	(15)	(16)	(17)	(18)	(19)	(20)
TOP THIRTY																			
1 USA (United States)	2599	34	59%	1%	8	8	5	13		8	2	17	7		1		1	1	
2 Argentina	164	3	5%	2%			2	1		1	2					1	1		
3 United Nations	233	2	3%	1%		1						2			3				
4 IDA (Devel Assoc)	82	2	3%	2%			1	2				2						1	
5 Italy	755	2	3%		1	1	1		1	1	1								
6 Belgium	499	2	3%				1	1	1						1				
7 UK Great Britain	981	1	2%			1			1										
8 Spain	437	1	2%					1	1	1								1	
9 WHO (World Health)	187	1	2%	1%						1					1				
10 UN Special Fund	113	1	2%	1%	1		1					1		1	1				
11 UNICEF (Children)	122	1	2%	1%								1		1					
12 Philippines	236	1	2%					1	1										
13 Norway	461	1	2%					1	1										
14 Netherlands	548	1	2%	1%			1	1	1	1									
15 Mexico	138	1	2%							1									
16 Japan	443	1	2%																
17 Canada	310	1	2%				1		1										
18 Austria	445	1	2%													1			
19 ICJ Option Clause	62	1	2%	2%	1														
20																			
21-30																			
31 All Others (0)																			
GROUPS																			
32 African Group	968																		
33 Arab Group	937																		
34 Asian Group	1937	1	2%				1	1	1	1									
35 Commonwealth	1641	2	3%					1											
36 Communist Group	3310																		
37 Latin America	1674	4	7%		1	1	2	2		2	2				1				
38 Western Europe	5906	8	14%		1	2	2	4		1	1				5	2	1	1	
39 Intl Organs	1399	7	12%	1%			2	2	6			6		2				2	
TOTALS																			
40 All Data	8815	58	100%		11	11	13	23	9	14	5	23	7	2	7	3	2	4	
41 UNTS Only		52																	
COMPARISONS																			
42 Party Total					19%	19%	22%	40%	16%	24%	9%	40%	12%	4%	13%	6%	4%	8%	6%
43 Group Total					18%	27%	24%	31%	16%	25%	18%	31%	9%	7%	10%	5%	6%	7%	6%
44 World Total					18%	23%	29%	29%	22%	25%	25%	20%	7%	8%	12%	6%	7%	12%	100%

Table 27 • 75

TREATY PROFILE OF BRAZIL

Partners (1)	Partner's World Total (2)	Dyads Absolutes (3)	Dyads Ratios Self (4)	Dyads Ratios Other (5)	Time 1946 1950 (6)	Time 1951 1955 (7)	Time 1956 1960 (8)	Time 1961 1965 (9)	Topics Admin & Dipl (10)	Topics Social Coop (11)	Topics Econ Coop (12)	Topics Aid (13)	Topics Milit (14)	Institutions UN (15)	Institutions Spec Ag's (16)	Institutions Intl Court (17)	Institutions Arbi- tration (18)	Institutions Other (19)	Self- Regis- tered (20)
TOP THIRTY																			
1 USA (United States)	2599	52	27%	2%	16	14	7	15	3	13	5	20	11	2	2			8	
2 Italy	755	16	8%	2%	4	2	8	2	4	4	4	1	3				1	1	
3 IBRD (World Bank)	452	14	7%	3%	2	7	3	2				14				1	1		5
4 Spain	437	12	6%	3%	1	1	8	2	3	7	2						1		4
5 Germany, West	890	12	6%	1%	1	3	2	6	3	2	5	2							
6 Argentina	164	11	6%	7%	1		6	4	4	3	3	1							8
7 UK Great Britain	981	8	4%	1%	4	2	2			1	4	2	1		2		1	1	
8 France	1033	8	4%	1%	2		2	4	1	3	3	1				1		1	
9 USSR (Soviet Union)	1356	7	4%	1%			1	6	1		5	1							
10 Japan	443	6	3%	1%			2	4	1	3	2							1	
11 Norway	461	5	3%	1%	1	1	2	1	2	3					1		1		
12 Belgium	499	5	3%	1%		3	2		4	1	2								
13 Netherlands	548	4	2%	1%	2	1	1		1	2	2				1		1	1	
14 Ecuador	97	4	2%	4%	1	1	1	1	2		1							2	3
15 Austria	445	4	2%	1%			3	1	2		2								
16 Switzerland	426	2	1%		1		1			1	1				1				
17 Sweden	483	2	1%			1		1		1	1				1		1		
18 WHO (World Health)	187	2	1%	1%		2								2					
19 United Nations	233	2	1%	1%		1	1						1	1					
20 Poland	493	2	1%					1 1	1		1	1						1	2
21 Colombia	112	2	1%	2%			1	1	1										
22 Taiwan	172	2	1%								1								1
23 Venezuela	47	1	1%	2%						1					1				
24 Turkey	298	1	1%				1					1		1	1	1			
25 UN Special Fund	113	1	1%	1%										1					
26 UNICEF (Children)	122	1	1%	1%						1									
27 Portugal	131	1	1%	1%			1		1										
28 Mexico	138	1	1%	1%			1			1									
29 Israel	232	1	1%							1									
30 Iran	170	1	1%				1			1									
31 All Others (5)	881	5	3%	1%	2		1	2	1	3	1				1		1		2
GROUPS																			
32 African Group	968	3	2%		1			1		2	1	2							
33 Arab Group	937	8	4%		4	2	1	1		1	4	1			2			1	
34 Asian Group	1937	9	5%			1	1	7		1	6		1	1					
35 Commonwealth	3310	21	11%	1%		2	9	8	1	6	5	2				1			
36 Communist Group	1641	9	5%	1%	3	1		2	8	25	22	17			7	2	9	4	16
37 Latin America	1674	74	38%	1%	16	12	30	16	20	1		4	3		1	1	2	2	9
38 Western Europe	5906	20	10%	1%	3	10	5	2	1	1		17	1	4					
39 Intl Organs	1399																		
TOTALS																			
40 All Data	15398	195	100%		44	40	56	55	35	53	45	46	16	7	12	4	12	16	25
41 UNTS Only		141																		
COMPARISONS																			
42 Party Total					23%	21%	29%	28%	18%	27%	23%	24%	8%	5%	9%	3%	9%	11%	18%
43 Group Total					18%	27%	24%	31%	16%	25%	18%	31%	9%	7%	10%	5%	6%	7%	6%
44 World Total					18%	23%	29%	29%	22%	25%	25%	20%	7%	8%	12%	6%	7%	12%	100%

76 • Table 28

TREATY PROFILE OF BULGARIA

Partners (1)	Partner's World Total (2)	Dyads Absolutes (3)	Dyads Ratios Self (4)	Dyads Ratios Other (5)	Time 1946-1950 (6)	Time 1951-1955 (7)	Time 1956-1960 (8)	Time 1961-1965 (9)	Topics Admin & Dipl (10)	Topics Social Coop (11)	Topics Econ Coop (12)	Topics Aid (13)	Topics Milit (14)	Institutions UN (15)	Institutions Spec Ag's (16)	Institutions Intl Court (17)	Institutions Arbitration (18)	Other (19)	Self-Registered (20)
TOP THIRTY																			
1 USSR (Soviet Union)	1356	48	20%	4%	12	4	26	6	6	10	12	18	2					1	
2 Germany, East	556	39	17%	7%	3	16	13	7	4	17	17	1							
3 Yugoslavia	525	25	11%	5%	1	9	15		8	13	4				1			9	
4 China People's Rep	766	23	10%	3%		9	5			9	14								
5 Poland	493	15	6%	3%	6	1	7	7	5	6	3		1					3	1
6 Czechoslovakia	393	9	4%	2%	2	1	2	6	4	5								1	
7 Hungary	290	7	3%	2%	1		4	2	2	5								1	
8 Greece	318	7	3%	2%		2	1	4	1	4	2	1						1	
9 Romania	251	6	3%	2%	1	1	4		4	2								1	
10 Italy	755	6	3%	1%	1		2	3		1	4								
11 Austria	445	6	3%	1%	1	2	1	4	1	3	2								2
12 Turkey	298	4	2%	1%							4								1
13 Sweden	483	4	2%	1%	3		1			1	3								3
14 Germany, West	890	4	2%	2%	1	1		2	1	2	2								
15 France	1033	4	2%	1%	1		1	2	1	1	1								
16 Syria	84	3	1%	4%				3		3									
17 Denmark	380	3	1%	1%	2		1			1	2							1	
18 Yemen	35	2	1%	6%				2		1									
19 USA (United States)	2599	2	1%	1%	1	1				1	1			1					1
20 UK Great Britain	981	2	1%	1%			1	1		1	1								
21 United Arab Rep	232	2	1%	1%			1	1	1	1	1				1				
22 Netherlands	548	2	1%	1%			1	1		1	1								
23 Cuba	111	2	1%	2%				2		1								2	
24 Ceylon (Sri Lanka)	123	2	1%	2%		1	2		1	1	2								
25 Switzerland	426	1						1	1		1								
26 COMECON (Econ Aid)	5	1		20%	1									1					
27 UNICEF (Children)	122	1		1%				1	1	1									1
28 Norway	461	1					1				1								
29 India	299	1						1		1								1	
30 Cyprus	49	1		2%				1		1				1					1
31 All Others (3)	650	3	1%		1		1	1	1	2									
GROUPS																			
32 African Group	968																		
33 Arab Group	937	7	3%	1%		1	1	6	2	5	2				1			2	4
34 Asian Group	1937	4	2%				2	2		2	1								2
35 Commonwealth	1641	2	1%		1	1				1									
36 Communist Group	3310	147	62%	4%	25	32	60	30	25	54	46	19	3	1	1			6	1
37 Latin America	1674	2	1%					2	1	1	1								
38 Western Europe	5906	44	19%	1%	11	6	10	17	4	17	22	1		1				4	4
39 Intl Organs	1399	2	1%		1			1	2	2									
TOTALS																			
40 All Data	15957	236	100%		41	48	88	59	44	93	76	20	3	4	2			21	11
41 UNTS Only		110																	
COMPARISONS																			
42 Party Total					17%	20%	37%	25%	19%	39%	32%	8%	1%	4%	2%		3%	19%	10%
43 Group Total					16%	17%	38%	29%	20%	32%	32%	13%	2%	4%	4%	6%	7%	17%	33%
44 World Total					18%	23%	29%	29%	22%	25%	25%	20%	7%	8%	12%			12%	100%

TREATY PROFILE OF BURMA

Table 29

Partners (1)	Partner's World Total (2)	Absolutes (3)	Dyads Ratios Self (4)	Dyads Ratios Other (5)	Time 1946 1950 (6)	Time 1951 1955 (7)	Time 1956 1960 (8)	Time 1961 1965 (9)	Topics Admin & Dipl (10)	Topics Social Coop (11)	Topics Econ Coop (12)	Topics Aid (13)	Topics Milit (14)	Institutions UN (15)	Institutions Spec Ag's (16)	Institutions Intl Court (17)	Institutions Arbitration (18)	Institutions Other (19)	Self-Registered (20)
TOP THIRTY																			
1 China People's Rep	766	22	22%	3%		8	8	6	7	6	8	1		4	1		1		1
2 USA (United States)	2599	16	16%	1%	5	2	8	1	1	2	1	9		2	2	3	2	1	1
3 WHO (World Health)	187	9	9%	5%		8	8			7		2	3		1	1	1		
4 UK Great Britain	981	8	8%	1%	3	1	3	1	1	1	6								
5 USSR (Soviet Union)	1356	7	7%	1%	1	1	3	2	2		2	3							
6 Yugoslavia	525	5	5%	1%		2	3			1	2	3		1					
7 Japan	443	5	5%	1%		3	2					1					1		
8 Thailand	132	3	3%	2%			2	1	2				2			2	1	1	3
9 IBRD (World Bank)	452	3	3%	1%			2	1	3			3						1	
10 Pakistan	245	3	3%	1%	2			1	1										
11 India	299	3	3%			1	1	1	1	2					1				
12 Sweden	483	2	2%		1	1			1	1	2				1				
13 Germany, East	556	2	2%				1	1	1	1	1						1		
14 Switzerland	426	1	1%				1		1	1									
15 UN Special Fund	113	1	1%	1%				1				1		1					
16 United Nations	233	1	1%			1						1		1		1	2	1	
17 UNICEF (Children)	122	1	1%	1%	1					1				1					
18 Philippines	236	1	1%																
19 Norway	461	1	1%			1				1									
20 Netherlands	548	1	1%			1				1					1				
21 Israel	232	1	1%				1					1					1		
22 Germany, West	890	1	1%					1											
23 Denmark	380	1	1%			1				1					1				
24 Czechoslovakia	393	1	1%				1			1					1			1	
25 Ceylon (Sri Lanka)	123	1	1%	1%						1					1				
26 Belgium	499	1	1%		1				1										
27 Accept UN Charter	68	1	1%	1%	1									1					
28																			
29																			
30																			
31 All Others (0)																			
GROUPS																			
32 African Group	968																		
33 Arab Group	937																		
34 Asian Group	1937	11	11%	1%	3	4	3	1	5	4	2				2		1	1	
35 Commonwealth	1641	8	8%		3	1	3	1	1	1	6				1	1	1		
36 Communist Group	3310	32	31%	1%	1	9	12	10	10	8	10				1			1	
37 Latin America	1674											4							1
38 Western Europe	5906	8	8%	1%	1	3	3	1	2	6	1	1			6		2		
39 Intl Organs	1399	15	15%	1%	1	8	4	2	1	7		7		4	3	4	4	1	1
TOTALS																			
40 All Data	13748	102	100%		15	32	38	17	21	28	22	26	5	10	14	7	10	5	4
41 UNTS Only		70																		
COMPARISONS																			
42 Party Total					15%	31%	37%	17%	21%	27%	22%	25%	5%	14%	20%	10%	14%	7%	6%
43 Group Total					16%	23%	31%	30%	21%	23%	20%	30%	7%	10%	15%	8%	8%	6%	16%
44 World Total					18%	23%	29%	29%	22%	25%	25%	20%	7%	8%	12%	6%	7%	12%	100%

78 • Table 30

TREATY PROFILE OF BURUNDI

Partners (1)	Partner's World Total (2)	Dyads Absolutes (3)	Ratios Self (4)	Ratios Other (5)	Time 1946-1950 (6)	Time 1951-1955 (7)	Time 1956-1960 (8)	Time 1961-1965 (9)	Admin & Dipl (10)	Social Coop (11)	Econ Coop (12)	Aid (13)	Milit (14)	UN (15)	Spec Ag's (16)	Intl Court (17)	Arbitration (18)	Other (19)	Self-Registered (20)
TOP THIRTY																			
1 USSR (Soviet Union)	1356	2	17%					2	2										
2 WHO (World Health)	187	2	17%	1%				2	1								2		
3 Germany, West	890	2	17%					2				1		1	1		1		
4 UN Special Fund	113	1	8%	1%				1				2				1			
5 United Nations	233	1	8%					1	1			1		1			2		
6 UNICEF (Children)	122	1	8%	1%				1	1										
7 France	1033	1	8%					1		1									
8 China People's Rep	766	1	8%					1			1								
9 Accept UN Charter	68	1	8%	1%				1	1					1					
10																			
11-29																			
30																			
31 All Others (0)																			
GROUPS																			
32 African Group	968																		
33 Arab Group	937																		
34 Asian Group	1937																		
35 Commonwealth	1641																		
36 Communist Group	3310	3	25%					3	2		1								
37 Latin America	1674																		
38 Western Europe	5906	3	25%					3	2	1		2							
39 Intl Organs	1399	5	42%					5				3		2	1	1	5	*	
TOTALS																			
40 All Data	4768	12	100%					12	5	1	1	5		3	1	1	5		
41 UNTS Only		6																		
COMPARISONS																			
42 Party Total					1%	5%	18%	100%	42%	8%	8%	42%	4%	50%	17%	17%	83%	4%	1%
43 Group Total					1%	23%	18%	75%	22%	21%	18%	35%	4%	19%	13%	10%	15%	4%	1%
44 World Total					18%	23%	29%	29%	22%	25%	25%	20%	7%	8%	12%	6%	7%	12%	100%

Table 31 • 79

TREATY PROFILE OF CAMBODIA

Partners (1)	Partner's World Total (2)	Dyads Absolutes (3)	Ratios Self (4)	Ratios Other (5)	Time 1946-1950 (6)	Time 1951-1955 (7)	Time 1956-1960 (8)	Time 1961-1965 (9)	Admin & Dipl (10)	Social Coop (11)	Econ Coop (12)	Aid (13)	Milit (14)	UN (15)	Spec Ag's (16)	Intl Court (17)	Arbitration (18)	Other (19)	Self-Registered (20)
TOP THIRTY																			
1 China People's Rep	766	10	18%	1%			5	5	2	4	3	1							
2 USSR (Soviet Union)	1356	9	16%	1%		3	8	1	1	1	2	5							
3 USA (United States)	2599	5	9%			3	2		1	1		1							
4 France	1033	5	9%	3%	1	2	2	2	3	1		1	2						
5 Thailand	132	4	7%	1%			4		3	1									
6 Germany, East	556	4	7%	1%			3	1	3	1	2								
7 Japan	443	3	5%	2%		1	2		1		2	1							
8 Vietnam, South	106	2	4%	1%		2	1		1	1	1								
9 WHO (World Health)	187	2	4%	2%		1	1					2				1			
10 United Nations	233	2	4%	1%			2					2		1					
11 UNICEF (Children)	122	2	4%	2%			2					2							
12 Czechoslovakia	393	2	4%	3%		1	1		1	1				1					
13 ICJ Option Clause	62	2	4%	1%			1	1	2							2			
14 UN Special Fund	113	1	2%				1					1		1	1	1			
15 Poland	493	1	2%				1											1	
16 Accept UN Charter	68	1	2%	1%		1			1					1					
17																			
...																			
31 All Others (0)																			
GROUPS																			
32 African Group	968																		
33 Arab Group	937																		
34 Asian Group	1937	6	11%			2	4		3	2	1			3					
35 Commonwealth	1641																		
36 Communist Group	3310	26	47%	1%			19	7	4	7	7	8							
37 Latin America	1674																		
38 Western Europe	5906	5	9%		1	2	2	2	3	1		1		2	1	2	1		
39 Intl Organs	1399	7	13%	1%			5	2		1		7		6	1	4		1	
TOTALS																			
40 All Data	8662	55	100%		1	12	33	9	15	11	10	17	2						
41 UNTS Only		22																		
COMPARISONS																			
42 Party Total					2%	22%	60%	16%	27%	20%	18%	31%	4%	27%	5%	18%	5%	5%	16%
43 Group Total					16%	23%	31%	30%	21%	23%	20%	30%	7%	10%	15%	8%	8%	6%	16%
44 World Total					18%	23%	29%	29%	22%	25%	25%	20%	7%	8%	12%	6%	7%	12%	100%

TREATY PROFILE OF CAMEROON

Table 32

	Partners (1)	Partner's World Total (2)	Dyads Absolutes (3)	Ratios Self (4)	Ratios Other (5)	Time 1946 1950 (6)	Time 1951 1955 (7)	Time 1956 1960 (8)	Time 1961 1965 (9)	Topics Admin & Dipl (10)	Topics Social Coop (11)	Topics Econ Coop (12)	Topics Aid (13)	Topics Milit (14)	Institutions UN (15)	Institutions Spec Ag's (16)	Institutions Intl Court (17)	Institutions Arbitration (18)	Other (19)	Self-Registered (20)
	TOP THIRTY																			
1	France	1033	18	35%	2%			11	7	6	5	5		2		1				
2	Germany, West	890	10	19%	1%			3	7		2	2	3	3						
3	USSR (Soviet Union)	1356	3	6%					3			3								
4	Netherlands	548	3	6%	1%				3				3							
5	Israel	232	3	6%	1%				3		2		1			1	1	1		
6	USA (United States)	2599	2	4%					2			1	2							
7	UK Great Britain	981	2	4%					2		1	1					1		1	
8	Poland	493	2	4%					2		1		1							
9	Switzerland	426	1	2%					1											
10	WHO (World Health)	187	1	2%	1%				1							1				
11	UN Special Fund	113	1	2%	1%				1				1		1			1		
12	United Nations	233	1	2%					1									2		
13	UNICEF (Children)	122	1	2%	1%				1		1	1				1		1		
14	Mali	54	1	2%	2%				1			1								
15	Greece	318	1	2%					1			1								
16	Denmark	380	1	2%					1											
17	Accept UN Charter	68	1	2%	1%			1		1					1					
18																				
19																				
20																				
21																				
22																				
23																				
24																				
25																				
26																				
27																				
28																				
29																				
30																				
31	All Others (0)																			
	GROUPS																			
32	African Group	968	1	2%					1		1					1		1		
33	Arab Group	937																		
34	Asian Group	1937																		
35	Commonwealth	1641	2	4%					2		1	1					1			
36	Communist Group	3310	5	10%					5		1	3	1							
37	Latin America	1674																		
38	Western Europe	5906	34	65%	1%			14	20	6	7	10	6	5	1	1	1	3	1	
39	Intl Organs	1399	4	8%					4				4		1					
	TOTALS																			
40	All Data	10033	52	100%				15	37	7	12	14	14	5	2	3	3	6	1	
41	UNTS Only		31																	
	COMPARISONS																			
42	Party Total					1%	5%	29%	71%	13%	23%	27%	27%	10%	6%	10%	10%	19%	3%	
43	Group Total							18%	75%	22%	21%	18%	35%	4%	19%	13%	10%	15%	4%	1%
44	World Total					18%	23%	29%	29%	22%	25%	25%	20%	7%	8%	12%	6%	7%	12%	100%

Table 33 • 81

TREATY PROFILE OF CANADA

	Partners (1)	Partner's World Total (2)	Dyads Absolutes (3)	Dyads Ratios Self (4)	Dyads Ratios Other (5)	Time 1946 1950 (6)	Time 1951 1955 (7)	Time 1956 1960 (8)	Time 1961 1965 (9)	Topics Admin & Dipl (10)	Topics Social Coop (11)	Topics Econ Coop (12)	Topics Aid (13)	Topics Milit (14)	Institutions UN (15)	Institutions Spec Ag's (16)	Institutions Intl Court (17)	Institutions Arbitration (18)	Institutions Other (19)	Self-Registered (20)
	TOP THIRTY																			
1	USA (United States)	2599	113	36%	4%	30	29	23	31	31	35	15	2	30	1	5	1		25	9
2	France	1033	19	6%	2%	7	4	2	6	1	7	5		6		2		1	1	14
3	UK Great Britain	981	17	5%	2%	6	1	7	3		6	5	1	5		4		2	2	4
4	Netherlands	548	10	3%	2%	7	1	2		1	1	3		5		1			2	7
5	Norway	461	9	3%	2%	4	2	3		2	2	1		5					2	6
6	Japan	443	8	3%	2%		3	2	3	2	1	2	1	1		3				2
7	Italy	755	8	3%	1%	2	3	1	2	3	2	1		1				1		4
8	India	299	8	3%	3%		3	3	2	2	3	2	4			1				8
9	Denmark	380	7	2%	2%	3	1	1	2	1		1		2		2			2	2
10	USSR (Soviet Union)	1356	5	2%	1%	1		3		2	3	2							1	2
11	Switzerland	426	5	2%	4%	1	1	4		2	1	1	1			1		1		3
12	South Africa	120	5	2%	4%		3	2			1	2								1
13	Pakistan	245	5	2%	2%		2	3			1	4	2			2				2
14	Germany, West	890	5	2%	1%		2	3		1	1	1		1		1		1	1	4
15	Finland	245	5	2%	2%	1		3	1	2	1	2								2
16	Belgium	499	5	2%	1%	4	1			1	1			3		1	1			2
17	Turkey	298	4	1%	1%	2	1	1		3		1								4
18	Sweden	483	4	1%	1%	2	1		1	1	1		1			2				2
19	Spain	437	4	1%	1%		2	1		1		2								3
20	Mexico	138	4	1%	3%	1	1		2		3	1				1		1		2
21	Greece	318	4	1%	1%	1		2	1	2		1		1						4
22	Australia	201	4	1%	2%	1		3			1	1	1			2		1		2
23	Venezuela	47	3	1%	6%				1			1								3
24	Portugal	131	3	1%	2%	1	1	1		1	1	2				1				2
25	Ireland	103	3	1%	3%	1	2			1	1									2
26	Taiwan	172	3	1%	2%	3						2								1
27	Ceylon (Sri Lanka)	123	3	1%	2%		2	1				2	1							3
28	Vietnam, South	106	2	1%	2%			1	1	1			2						2	
29	United Nations	233	2	1%	1%			1			1						1			
30	New Zealand	101	2	1%	2%	2					1			1		1	1	1		
31	All Others (30)	4142	31	10%	1%	8	7	6	10	9	6	11	1	4	1	2	2	2		25
	GROUPS																			
32	African Group	968	3	1%		3	1		2			1		2						3
33	Arab Group	937	1				1				1	1								1
34	Asian Group	1937	22	7%	1%	3	7	8	4	5	1	5	11			3		1	5	15
35	Commonwealth	1641	30	10%	2%	10	4	13	3		10	13	2	5		8	1	3	2	8
36	Communist Group	3310	8	3%		2	1	4	1	2	1	5								5
37	Latin America	1674	17	5%	1%	6	2	2	7	1	8	7		1		2		1		13
38	Western Europe	5906	101	33%	2%	37	23	25	16	29	22	23	3	24		13	1	7		67
39	Intl Organs	1399	5	2%		1	1	3		1	2		1	1	1		3	2	7	1
	TOTALS																			
40	All Data	18313	310	100%		90	73	80	67	72	81	72	20	65	2	34	6	15	39	125
41	UNTS Only		291																	
	COMPARISONS																			
42	Party Total					29%	24%	26%	22%	23%	26%	23%	6%	21%	1%	12%	2%	5%	13%	43%
43	Group Total					27%	25%	24%	24%	25%	24%	27%	10%	14%	4%	13%	4%	5%	12%	63%
44	World Total					18%	23%	29%	29%	22%	25%	25%	20%	7%	8%	12%	6%	7%	12%	100%

82 • Table 34

TREATY PROFILE OF CENTRAL AFRI REP

			Dyads			Time				Topics						Institutions			Self-Registered
Partners	Partner's World Total	Absolutes	Ratios Self	Other	1946 1950	1951 1955	1956 1960	1961 1965	Admin & Dipl	Social Coop	Econ Coop	Aid	Milit	UN	Spec Ag's	Intl Court	Arbitration	Other	
(1)	(2)	(3)	(4)	(5)	(6)	(7)	(8)	(9)	(10)	(11)	(12)	(13)	(14)	(15)	(16)	(17)	(18)	(19)	(20)
TOP THIRTY																			
1 France	1033	5	23%				2	3	4		1								
2 Germany, West	890	4	18%					4			2	2							
3 China People's Rep	766	4	18%	1%				4		1	1	2							
4 USA (United States)	2599	2	9%					2	1			1							
5 Israel	232	2	9%	1%			1	2	1										
6 USSR (Soviet Union)	1356	1	5%																
7 WHO (World Health)	187	1	5%	1%				1				1		1	1				
8 UN Special Fund	113	1	5%	1%				1				1		1					
9 UNICEF (Children)	122	1	5%	1%				1	1			1		1					
10 Accept UN Charter	68	1	5%	1%			1												
11																			
31 All Others (0)																			
GROUPS																			
32 African Group	968																		
33 Arab Group	937																		
34 Asian Group	1937																		
35 Commonwealth	1641																		
36 Communist Group	3310	5	23%				1	4	1	1	1	2							
37 Latin America	1674	9	41%				2	7	4										
38 Western Europe	5906	3	14%					3	4		3	2		3	1	1	1		
39 Intl Organs	1399																		
TOTALS																			
40 All Data	7366	22	100%				4	18	7	1	5	9		4	1	1	1		
41 UNTS Only		8																	
COMPARISONS																			
42 Party Total					1%	5%	18%	82%	32%	5%	23%	41%	4%	50%	13%	13%	13%	4%	1%
43 Group Total					1%	5%	18%	75%	22%	21%	18%	35%	4%	19%	13%	10%	15%	4%	1%
44 World Total					18%	23%	29%	29%	22%	25%	25%	20%	7%	8%	12%	6%	7%	12%	100%

Table 35 • 83

TREATY PROFILE OF CERN (NUC RESRCH)

	Partners (1)	Partner's World Total (2)	Dyads Absolutes (3)	Ratios Self (4)	Ratios Other (5)	Time 1946 1950 (6)	Time 1951 1955 (7)	Time 1956 1960 (8)	Time 1961 1965 (9)	Topics Admin & Dipl (10)	Topics Social Coop (11)	Topics Econ Coop (12)	Topics Aid (13)	Topics Milit (14)	Institutions UN (15)	Institutions Spec Ag's (16)	Institutions Intl Court (17)	Institutions Arbi-tration (18)	Institutions Other (19)	Self-Regis-tered (20)
	TOP THIRTY																			
1	France	1033	2	67%			1		2	1			1							
2	Switzerland	426	1	33%						1						1				
3																				
4																				
5																				
6																				
7																				
8																				
9																				
10																				
11																				
12																				
13																				
14																				
15																				
16																				
17																				
18																				
19																				
20																				
21																				
22																				
23																				
24																				
25																				
26																				
27																				
28																				
29																				
30																				
31	All Others (0)																			
	GROUPS																			
32	African Group	968																		
33	Arab Group	937																		
34	Asian Group	1937																		
35	Commonwealth	1641																		
36	Communist Group	3310																		
37	Latin America	1674																		
38	Western Europe	5906	3	100%			1		2	2			1				1			
39	Intl Organs	1399																			
	TOTALS																			
40	All Data	1459	3	100%			1		2	2			1					1		
41	UNTS Only		2	100%																
	COMPARISONS																			
42	Party Total						33%		67%	67%			33%		27%		50%	15%		
43	Group Total					12%	25%	23%	40%	19%	7%	1%	71%	1%	11%	13%	7%	4%	74%
44	World Total					18%	23%	29%	29%	22%	25%	25%	20%	7%	8%	12%	6%	12%	100%

84 • Table 36

TREATY PROFILE OF CEYLON (SRI LANKA)

			Dyads	Ratios		Time				Topics							Institutions			Self-Registered
Partners	Partner's World Total	Absolutes	Self	Other	1946 1950	1951 1955	1956 1960	1961 1965	Admin & Dipl	Social Coop	Econ Coop	Aid	Milit	UN	Spec Ag's	Intl Court	Arbitration	Other	
(1)	(2)	(3)	(4)	(5)	(6)	(7)	(8)	(9)	(10)	(11)	(12)	(13)	(14)	(15)	(16)	(17)	(18)	(19)	(20)
TOP THIRTY																			
1 China People's Rep	766	28	23%	4%		3	12	13	1	2	19	6							2
2 USA (United States)	2599	15	12%	1%	2	4	6	3	2	5		7	1					1	1
3 USSR (Soviet Union)	1356	11	9%	1%			6	5	1	2	5	3						2	1
4 UK Great Britain	981	8	7%	1%	7		1		2	2	2		2						3
5 WHO (World Health)	187	5	4%	3%	1	3	2					3		1	3		1		
6 India	299	5	4%	2%	2	1				2	3				1		1		2
7 Germany, West	890	4	3%			2		2		2	3	1						1	1
8 Sweden	483	3	2%	1%			3		1	1	1	1			1		1		
9 ILO (Labor Org)	59	3	2%	5%		2		1				2		3					
10 IBRD (World Bank)	452	3	2%	1%		1	1	1	1			3			1				
11 Pakistan	245	3	2%	1%	2		1		1	2	1				2				
12 Canada	310	3	2%	1%		2	1					2						2	
13 Yugoslavia	525	2	2%	1%	1	1				1	1				1				1
14 United Arab Rep	232	2	2%	1%		1	1			1	1				1				1
15 United Nations	233	2	2%	1%				1				2		1		1		1	
16 Romania	251	2	2%	1%			2				2								2
17 Norway	461	2	2%			1	1	1		1	1				1		1		1
18 Japan	443	2	2%			1		1		1	1				1				1
19 Italy	755	2	2%				2			1	1							2	
20 Denmark	380	2	2%	1%			1	1		1		1		1	1				2
21 Bulgaria	236	2	2%	1%			2				2							2	
22 Australia	201	2	2%	1%	1	1			1	1					1	1	1		
23 Thailand	132	2	2%	1%	1			1		1					1		1		
24 Spain	437	1	1%			1					1								
25 UN Special Fund	113	1	1%	1%				1				1		1	1	1	1		1
26 UNICEF (Children)	122	1	1%	1%			1							1	1		1		1
27 Netherlands	548	1	1%			1				1					1				
28 Ireland	103	1	1%																
29 Hungary	290	1	1%				1				1							1	
30 Germany, East	556	1	1%					1			1				1				
31 All Others (4)	477	4	3%	1%	2	1		1	2	2				1					
GROUPS																			
32 African Group	968	2	2%		1	1				1	1				1				1
33 Arab Group	937	10	8%	1%	6	2	2			6	4	2			5		4		2
34 Asian Group	1937	13	11%	1%	8	3	2		4	3	2	9			4	1	2	2	3
35 Commonwealth	1641	13	11%	1%		3	23	19	2	4	30		2						8
36 Communist Group	3310	45	37%															6	
37 Latin America	1674																		
38 Western Europe	5906	17	14%			5	7	5		6	9	2			4	1	4	3	4
39 Intl Organs	1399	15	12%	1%	2	7	2	4	2	2		11		6	3	1	2		
TOTALS																			
40 All Data	15122	123	100%		20	28	43	32	12	29	48	31	3	7	17	4	12	12	21
41 UNTS Only		83																	
COMPARISONS																			
42 Party Total					16%	23%	35%	26%	10%	24%	39%	25%	2%	8%	20%	5%	14%	14%	25%
43 Group Total					16%	23%	31%	30%	21%	23%	20%	30%	7%	10%	15%	8%	8%	6%	16%
44 World Total					18%	23%	29%	29%	22%	25%	25%	20%	7%	8%	12%	6%	7%	12%	100%

Table 37 • 85

TREATY PROFILE OF CHAD

Partners (1)	Partner's World Total (2)	Dyads Absolutes (3)	Ratios Self (4)	Ratios Other (5)	Time 1946 1950 (6)	Time 1951 1955 (7)	Time 1956 1960 (8)	Time 1961 1965 (9)	Topics Admin & Dipl (10)	Topics Social Coop (11)	Topics Econ Coop (12)	Topics Aid (13)	Topics Milit (14)	Institutions UN (15)	Institutions Spec Ag's (16)	Institutions Intl Court (17)	Institutions Arbitration (18)	Institutions Other (19)	Self-Registered (20)
TOP THIRTY																			
1 France	1033	13	54%	1%			2	11	4	4	1	2	2						
2 Germany, West	890	3	13%					3			1	2							
3 USA (United States)	2599	1	4%	1%				1			1								
4 WHO (World Health)	187	1	4%	1%				1				1		1					
5 UN Special Fund	113	1	4%	1%				1				1							
6 UNICEF (Children)	122	1	4%					1				1		1					
7 Japan	443	1	4%					1			1								
8 Italy	755	1	4%					1				1							
9 Israel	232	1	4%					1											
10 Accept UN Charter	68	1	4%	1%					1					1		1			
11																			
12																			
13																			
14																			
15																			
16																			
17																			
18																			
19																			
20																			
21																			
22																			
23																			
24																			
25																			
26																			
27																			
28																			
29																			
30																			
31 All Others (0)																			
GROUPS																			
32 African Group	968																		
33 Arab Group	937																		
34 Asian Group	1937																		
35 Commonwealth	1641																		
36 Communist Group	3310																		
37 Latin America	1674																		
38 Western Europe	5906	17	71%				2	15	4	4	2	5	2	2		1			
39 Intl Organs	1399	3	12%					3				3							
TOTALS																			
40 All Data	6442	24	100%				3	21	5	4	4	9	2	4		1			
41 UNTS Only		10																	
COMPARISONS																			
42 Party Total					1%	5%	12%	87%	21%	17%	17%	37%	8%	40%	13%	10%	15%	4%	
43 Group Total					5%	18%	75%	22%	21%	18%	35%	4%	19%	12%	10%	7%	4%	1%	
44 World Total					18%	23%	29%	29%	22%	25%	25%	20%	7%	8%	12%	6%	7%	12%	100%

86 • Table 38

TREATY PROFILE OF CHILE

(1) Partners	(2) Partner's World Total	(3) Abso- lutes	Dyads Ratios		Time					Topics						Institutions				(20) Self- Regis- tered
			(4) Self	(5) Other	(6) 1946 1950	(7) 1951 1955	(8) 1956 1960	(9) 1961 1965	(10) Admin & Dipl	(11) Social Coop	(12) Econ Coop	(13) Aid	(14) Milit	(15) UN	(16) Spec Ag's	(17) Intl Court	(18) Arbi- tration	(19) Other	
TOP THIRTY																			
1 USA (United States)	2599	43	36%	2%	6	18	13	6	4	8	3	21	7	1	2		1	2	
2 IBRD (World Bank)	452	13	11%	3%	2	2	4	5				13							
3 Germany, West	890	10	8%	1%		3	3	4	2	3	5								
4 UK Great Britain	981	8	7%	1%	4	1	1	2	1	1	2	2	2		1				
5 Italy	755	6	5%	1%	2		2	2	1	2	2	1	1						
6 Spain	437	4	3%	1%	1		2	1		3	1								
7 WHO (World Health)	187	4	3%	2%		4				3		1		3	2		1		
8 Netherlands	548	4	3%	1%		1		3	3	1					1				
9 Belgium	499	4	3%	1%	2		1	1	2		2								
10 Norway	461	3	3%	1%		2		1	1	1	1								
11 Switzerland	426	2	2%			1		1	1			1							
12 UNICEF (Children)	122	2	2%	2%	1			1	1	1				1					
13 France	1033	2	2%			1		1		1									
14 Denmark	380	2	2%	1%		2				1			1		1				
15 Argentina	164	2	2%	1%	1		1		1	1					1				
16 Sweden	483	1	1%				1			1									
17 UN Special Fund	113	1	1%	1%		1					1	1		1	1	1			
18 United Nations	233	1	1%					1	1					1					
19 ILO (Labor Org)	59	1	1%	2%				1		1									
20 IDA (Devel Assoc)	82	1	1%					1				1							
21 Mexico	138	1	1%	1%			1												
22 Japan	443	1	1%					1		1	1								
23 Israel	232	1	1%					1		1									
24 Canada	310	1	1%					1											
25 Austria	445	1	1%			1			1										
26																				
27																				
28																				
29																				
30																				
31 All Others (0)																				
GROUPS																				
32 African Group	968																		
33 Arab Group	937																		
34 Asian Group	1937																		
35 Commonwealth	1641	9	8%	1%	4	1	1	3	1	2	2	2	2		1			1	
36 Communist Group	3310																		
37 Latin America	1674	3	3%		1		1	1		2									
38 Western Europe	5906	39	33%	1%	5	12	8	14	10	13	11	3			1		1		
39 Intl Organs	1399	23	19%	2%	3	8	5	7	2	3		18	2	6	3	1			
TOTALS																				
40 All Data	12472	119	100%		19	39	28	33	18	29	17	44	11	7	10	1	2	3	
41 UNTS Only		92																		
COMPARISONS																				
42 Party Total					16%	33%	24%	28%	15%	24%	14%	37%	9%	8%	11%	1%	2%	3%	
43 Group Total					18%	27%	24%	31%	16%	25%	18%	31%	9%	7%	10%	5%	6%	7%	6%
44 World Total					18%	23%	29%	29%	22%	25%	25%	20%	7%	8%	12%	6%	7%	12%	100%

TREATY PROFILE OF CHINA PEOPLE'S REP

	Partners (1)	Partner's World Total (2)	Abso- lutes (3)	Dyads Ratios Self (4)	Dyads Ratios Other (5)	Time 1946 1950 (6)	Time 1951 1955 (7)	Time 1956 1960 (8)	Time 1961 1965 (9)	Topics Admin & Dipl (10)	Topics Social Coop (11)	Topics Econ Coop (12)	Topics Aid (13)	Topics Milit (14)	Institutions UN (15)	Institutions Spec Ag's (16)	Institutions Intl Court (17)	Institutions Arbi- tration (18)	Institutions Other (19)	Self- Regis- tered (20)
	TOP THIRTY																			
1	USSR (Soviet Union)	1356	108	14%	8%	27	35	32	14	29	36	21	18	4	1				2	
2	Germany, East	556	59	8%	11%	1	29	17	12	6	31	22								
3	Vietnam, North	81	38	5%	47%		9	14	15	1	20	13	4							
4	Korea, North	99	36	5%	36%	4	3	16	13	5	21	10								
5	Czechoslovakia	393	36	5%	9%	1	13	11	11	3	16	17								
6	Poland	493	31	4%	6%		14	11	6		19	12								
7	Mongolia	119	28	4%	24%		6	13	9	4	10	12	2							
8	Ceylon (Sri Lanka)	123	28	4%	23%		3	12	13	1	2	19	6						1	
9	Albania	125	28	4%	22%		5	9	14	1	10	12	5							
10	Romania	251	26	3%	10%		8	6	12		12	14								
11	Hungary	290	26	3%	9%		9	8	9	1	11	14								
12	Bulgaria	236	23	3%	10%		9	7	7		9	14								
13	Burma	102	22	3%	22%		8	8	6	7	6	8	1							
14	Yugoslavia	525	21	3%	4%			16	5	3	8	10								
15	United Arab Rep	232	21	3%	9%		2	9	10		5	14	2							
16	Indonesia	126	21	3%	17%		4	3	14	3	4	7	7							
17	Nepal	36	17	2%	47%			9	8	8	3	2	4							
18	Finland	245	16	2%	7%		5	5	6			16								
19	Cuba	111	14	2%	13%			4	10		6	5	3							
20	Japan	443	13	2%	3%		5	1	7	8	1	4								
21	Syria	84	10	1%	12%		2	2	5		4	5	1							
22	Pakistan	245	10	1%	4%		1	3	6	2	2	3	3							
23	Guinea	75	10	1%	13%			3	6	1	6	2	1							
24	Cambodia	55	10	1%	18%			4	5	2	4	3	1							
25	Ghana	81	9	1%	11%			5	5	1	3	2	1							
26	Mali	54	8	1%	15%				9	2	2	1	2	2						
27	Algeria	52	8	1%	15%				8		3	3	1							
28	Yemen	35	7	1%	20%				8		4	1	1							
29	Tanzania	45	7	1%	16%			3	4	2	3	1	1							
30	India	299	7	1%	2%		7				1	2	3							
31	All Others (21)	8324	68	9%	1%		9	24	35	10	11	39	7	1						
	GROUPS																			
32	African Group	968	51	7%	5%		7	4	47	6	19	11	13	2						
33	Arab Group	937	59	8%	6%			20	32	2	17	35	5							
34	Asian Group	1937	122	16%	6%		23	42	57	29	22	48	23	1						
35	Commonwealth	1641	3				2	1				2								
36	Communist Group	3310	439	57%	13%	33	140	144	122	50	195	161	29	4	1				3	
37	Latin America	1674	14	2%	1%			4	10		6	5	3							
38	Western Europe	5906	43	6%	1%		8	21	14	5	3	35								
39	Intl Organs	1399																		
	TOTALS																			
40	All Data	15291	766	100%		33	186	253	294	104	271	311	73	7	1				3	
41	UNTS Only		22																	
	COMPARISONS																			
42	Party Total					4%	24%	33%	38%	14%	35%	41%	10%	1%	5%	4%		3%	14%	
43	Group Total					16%	17%	38%	29%	20%	32%	32%	13%	2%	4%	12%	6%	7%	17%	33%
44	World Total					18%	23%	29%	29%	22%	25%	25%	20%	7%	8%	12%			12%	100%

88 • Table 40

TREATY PROFILE OF COLOMBIA

Partners	Partner's World Total	Dyads Absolutes	Ratios Self	Ratios Other	Time 1946-1950	Time 1951-1955	Time 1956-1960	Time 1961-1965	Topics Admin & Dipl	Topics Social Coop	Topics Econ Coop	Topics Aid	Topics Milit	Institutions UN	Institutions Spec Ag's	Institutions Intl Court	Institutions Arbitration	Institutions Other	Self-Registered
(1)	(2)	(3)	(4)	(5)	(6)	(7)	(8)	(9)	(10)	(11)	(12)	(13)	(14)	(15)	(16)	(17)	(18)	(19)	(20)
TOP THIRTY																			
1 USA (United States)	2599	44	39%	2%	8	13	10	13	2	12	6	17	7	2	2	1	1		
2 IBRD (World Bank)	452	25	22%	6%	3	7	7	8				25			1		1		
3 Germany, West	890	9	8%	1%		1	3	5		1	6	2							
4 Italy	755	4	4%	1%	1	2		1	3		1				1				
5 UK Great Britain	981	3	3%		2				1	1	1				1	1	1		
6 Spain	437	3	3%	1%		3				3									
7 WHO (World Health)	187	3	3%	2%		3				1		2		1				1	
8 United Nations	233	2	2%	1%		1		1	1	1		1				1		1	
9 Netherlands	548	2	2%				1	2											
10 Israel	232	2	2%	1%			1	2	1										
11 France	1033	2	2%				1	1	1			1							
12 Brazil	195	2	2%	1%		1	1	1	1			1						1	
13 Belgium	499	2	2%				1	1	2										
14 Switzerland	426	1	1%										1						
15 Sweden	483	1	1%			1	1				1								
16 UN Special Fund	113	1	1%	1%	1							1		1	1				
17 UNICEF (Children)	122	1	1%	1%			1			1		1		1					
18 IDA (Devel Assoc)	82	1	1%	1%				1							1				
19 Portugal	131	1	1%			1			1										
20 Norway	461	1	1%				1		1										
21 Denmark	380	1	1%			1													
22 Argentina	164	1	1%					1	1		1						1		
31 All Others (0)																			
GROUPS																			
32 African Group	968																		
33 Arab Group	937																		
34 Asian Group	1937																		
35 Commonwealth	1641	3	3%					1	1	1	1				1		1		
36 Communist Group	3310																		
37 Latin America	1674	3	3%				1	2	2			1						1	
38 Western Europe	5906	27	24%			10	6	10	7	5	10	4	1		2		2		
39 Intl Organs	1399	33	29%	2%	4	11	8	10		2		31		3	4	2	1	2	
TOTALS																			
40 All Data	11403	112	100%		15	34	25	38	13	20	17	54	8	5	9	3	5	3	
41 UNTS Only		93																	
COMPARISONS																			
42 Party Total					13%	30%	22%	34%	12%	18%	15%	48%	7%	5%	10%	3%	5%	3%	
43 Group Total					18%	27%	24%	31%	16%	25%	18%	31%	9%	7%	10%	5%	6%	7%	6%
44 World Total					18%	23%	29%	29%	22%	25%	25%	20%	7%	8%	12%	6%	7%	12%	100%

Table 41

TREATY PROFILE OF COMECON (ECON AID)

Partners (1)	Partner's World Total (2)	Dyads Absolutes (3)	Ratios Self (4)	Ratios Other (5)	Time 1946-1950 (6)	Time 1951-1955 (7)	Time 1956-1960 (8)	Time 1961-1965 (9)	Admin & Dipl (10)	Social Coop (11)	Econ Coop (12)	Aid (13)	Milit (14)	UN (15)	Spec Ag's (16)	Intl Court (17)	Arbitration (18)	Other (19)	Self-Registered (20)
TOP THIRTY																			
1 USSR (Soviet Union)	1356	1	20%					1	1										1
2 Poland	493	1	20%					1	1										1
3 Hungary	290	1	20%					1	1										1
4 Czechoslovakia	393	1	20%					1	1										1
5 Bulgaria	236	1	20%					1	1										1
6																			
7																			
8																			
9																			
10																			
11																			
12																			
13																			
14																			
15																			
16																			
17																			
18																			
19																			
20																			
21																			
22																			
23																			
24																			
25																			
26																			
27																			
28																			
29																			
30																			
31 All Others (0)																			
GROUPS																			
32 African Group	968																		
33 Arab Group	937																		
34 Asian Group	1937																		
35 Commonwealth	1641																		
36 Communist Group	3310	5	100%					5	5										5
37 Latin America	1674																		
38 Western Europe	5906																		
39 Intl Organs	1399																		
TOTALS																			
40 All Data		5	100%					5	5										5
41 UNTS Only	2768	5																	
COMPARISONS																			
42 Party Total								100%	100%										100%
43 Group Total					12%	25%	23%	40%	19%	7%	1%	71%	1%	27%	11%	13%	15%	4%	74%
44 World Total					18%	23%	29%	29%	22%	25%	25%	20%	7%	8%	12%	6%	7%	12%	100%

90 • Table 42

TREATY PROFILE OF CONGO (BRAZZAVILLE)

			Dyads			Time				Topics					Institutions				
		Partner's World Total	Absolutes	Ratios Self	Other	1946 1950	1951 1955	1956 1960	1961 1965	Admin & Dipl	Social Coop	Econ Coop	Aid	Milit	UN	Spec Ag's	Intl Court	Arbitration	Other	Self-Registered
	Partners (1)	(2)	(3)	(4)	(5)	(6)	(7)	(8)	(9)	(10)	(11)	(12)	(13)	(14)	(15)	(16)	(17)	(18)	(19)	(20)
	TOP THIRTY																			
1	China People's Rep	766	7	27%	1%				7	1	3	1	2							
2	Germany, West	890	5	19%	1%				5	1	1	2	2							
3	France	1033	5	19%				2	3	2	1	1		1						
4	USA (United States)	2599	2	8%				2	2	1		1						1			
5	Switzerland	426	1	4%	1%				1											
6	WHO (World Health)	187	1	4%				1					1		1					
7	UN Special Fund	113	1	4%	1%				1				1		1					
8	UNICEF (Children)	122	1	4%					1				1			1				
9	IBRD (World Bank)	452	1	4%	1%			1					1							
10	Germany, East	556	1	4%					1											
11	Accept UN Charter	68	1	4%	1%			1		1					1		1			
31	All Others (0)																			
	GROUPS																			
32	African Group	968																		
33	Arab Group	937																		
34	Asian Group	1937																		
35	Commonwealth	1641																		
36	Communist Group	3310	8	31%					8	1	3	1	3							
37	Latin America	1674																		
38	Western Europe	5906	11	42%				2	9	2	2	4	2	1			1			
39	Intl Organs	1399	4	15%				2	2				4		3	1	1			
	TOTALS																			
40	All Data	7212	26	100%				5	21	5	5	6	9	1	4	1	2			
41	UNTS Only		7																	
	COMPARISONS																			
42	Party Total					1%	5%	19%	81%	19%	19%	23%	35%	4%	57%	14%	29%	15%	4%	1%
43	Group Total					1%	5%	18%	75%	22%	21%	18%	35%	4%	19%	13%	10%	7%	4%	1%
44	World Total					18%	23%	29%	29%	22%	25%	25%	20%	7%	8%	12%	6%	7%	12%	100%

TREATY PROFILE OF CONGO (ZAIRE)

Table 43 • 91

	Partners (1)	Partner's World Total (2)	Dyads Absolutes (3)	Dyads Ratios Self (4)	Dyads Ratios Other (5)	Time 1946-1950 (6)	Time 1951-1955 (7)	Time 1956-1960 (8)	Time 1961-1965 (9)	Topics Admin & Dipl (10)	Topics Social Coop (11)	Topics Econ Coop (12)	Topics Aid (13)	Topics Milit (14)	Institutions UN (15)	Institutions Spec Ag's (16)	Institutions Intl Court (17)	Institutions Arbitration (18)	Institutions Other (19)	Self-Registered (20)
	TOP THIRTY																			
1	USA (United States)	2599	8	28%	2%				8			1	6	1	2				2	
2	United Nations	233	4	14%				1	3	1			2	1		1	1			
3	USSR (Soviet Union)	1356	3	10%	1%			2	1	2		1				1			1	
4	Belgium	499	3	10%				1	2			3				1	2			
5	Germany, West	890	2	7%					2		2		2							
6	France	1033	2	7%					2											
7	UK Great Britain	981	1	3%					1			1	1							
8	Switzerland	426	1	3%				1												
9	UN Special Fund	113	1	3%	1%				1				1		1	1	1			
10	IAEA (Atom Energy)	44	1	3%	2%				1		1							1		
11	Italy	755	1	3%					1	1										
12	Israel	232	1	3%					1	1										
13	Accept UN Charter	68	1	3%	1%				1						1					
31	All Others (0)																			
	GROUPS																			
32	African Group	968																		
33	Arab Group	937																		
34	Asian Group	1937																		
35	Commonwealth	1641	1	3%				2	1	2		1								
36	Communist Group	3310	3	10%				2	1											
37	Latin America	1674																		
38	Western Europe	5906	9	31%				2	7		3	4	2			1	2		1	
39	Intl Organs	1399	6	21%				1	5	1			4	1	1	2	2	1	2	
	TOTALS																			
40	All Data	9229	29	100%				5	24	5	3	6	13	2	4	3	4	1	3	
41	UNTS Only		21																	
	COMPARISONS																			
42	Party Total					1%	5%	17%	83%	17%	10%	21%	45%	7%	19%	14%	19%	5%	14%	
43	Group Total							18%	75%	22%	21%	18%	35%	4%	19%	13%	10%	15%	4%	1%
44	World Total					18%	23%	29%	29%	22%	25%	25%	20%	7%	8%	12%	6%	7%	12%	100%

92 • Table 44

TREATY PROFILE OF COSTA RICA

Partners (1)	Partner's World Total (2)	Dyads Abso-lutes (3)	Ratios Self (4)	Ratios Other (5)	Time 1946-1950 (6)	Time 1951-1955 (7)	Time 1956-1960 (8)	Time 1961-1965 (9)	Topics Admin & Dipl (10)	Topics Social Coop (11)	Topics Econ Coop (12)	Topics Aid (13)	Topics Milit (14)	Institutions UN (15)	Institutions Spec Ag's (16)	Institutions Intl Court (17)	Institutions Arbi-tration (18)	Institutions Other (19)	Self-Regis-tered (20)
TOP THIRTY																			
1 USA (United States)	2599	18	35%	1%	5	7	2	4	3	5	2	6	2		1			2	2
2 IBRD (World Bank)	452	7	14%	2%			3	4				7			1				
3 WHO (World Health)	187	3	6%	2%		3				3				1			1	2	2
4 Norway	461	3	6%	1%		1	2	1	2		1								
5 France	1033	3	6%			2		1	1	1	1								
6 Spain	437	3	4%			1		2	2	1		1							
7 Israel	232	2	4%	1%				1	1			1							
8 UN Special Fund	113	1	2%	1%		1						1				1			
9 United Nations	233	1	2%		1									1					
10 UNICEF (Children)	122	1	2%	1%								1							
11 IDA (Devel Assoc)	82	1	2%	1%	1						1				1				
12 Mexico	138	1	2%			1					1								
13 Italy	755	1	2%			1													
14 Guatemala	50	1	2%	2%				1			1						1	1	
15 Germany, West	890	1	2%								1	1							
16 Denmark	380	1	2%				1			1									
17 Taiwan	172	1	2%	1%			1												
18 Canada	310	1	2%					1		1									
19 Brazil	195	1	2%	1%				1		1						1	1	1	
20 Argentina	164	1	2%	1%				1											
31 All Others (0)																			
GROUPS																			
32 African Group	968																		
33 Arab Group	937																		
34 Asian Group	1937	1	2%				1			1									
35 Commonwealth	1641	1	2%		1														
36 Communist Group	3310																		
37 Latin America	1674	4	8%		1	1		2		2	2								
38 Western Europe	5906	11	22%			5	3	3	5	1	4	1						1	
39 Intl Organs	1399	14	27%	1%	1	4	3	6		3		11		2	2	1	1	2	
TOTALS																			
40 All Data	9005	51	100%		8	17	9	17	9	13	9	18	2	2	3	1	2	5	
41 UNTS Only		40																		
COMPARISONS																			
42 Party Total					16%	33%	18%	33%	18%	25%	18%	35%	4%	5%	8%	3%	5%	13%	
43 Group Total					18%	27%	24%	31%	16%	25%	18%	31%	9%	7%	10%	5%	6%	7%	6%
44 World Total					18%	23%	29%	29%	22%	25%	25%	20%	7%	8%	12%	6%	7%	12%	100%

Table 45 • 93

TREATY PROFILE OF COUNCIL OF EUROPE

Partners (1)	Partner's World Total (2)	Dyads Absolutes (3)	Ratios Self (4)	Ratios Other (5)	Time 1946-1950 (6)	Time 1951-1955 (7)	Time 1956-1960 (8)	Time 1961-1965 (9)	Admin & Dipl (10)	Social Coop (11)	Econ Coop (12)	Aid (13)	Milit (14)	UN (15)	Spec Ag's (16)	Intl Court (17)	Arbitration (18)	Other (19)	Self-Registered (20)
TOP THIRTY																			
1 ILO (Labor Org)	59	2	50%	3%	1	1			2					1					
2 France	1033	2	50%				1		1	1									1
3																			
4																			
5																			
6																			
7																			
8																			
9																			
10																			
11																			
12																			
13																			
14																			
15																			
16																			
17																			
18																			
19																			
20																			
21																			
22																			
23																			
24																			
25																			
26																			
27																			
28																			
29																			
30																			
31 All Others (0)																			
GROUPS																			
32 African Group	968																		
33 Arab Group	937																		
34 Asian Group	1937																		
35 Commonwealth	1641																		
36 Communist Group	3310																		
37 Latin America	1674																		
38 Western Europe	5906	2	50%		1	1	1		1	1									1
39 Intl Organs	1399	2	50%				1		2					1					
TOTALS																			
40 All Data	1092	4	100%		1	1	2		3	1				1					1
41 UNTS Only		3																	
COMPARISONS																			
42 Party Total					25%	25%	50%		75%	25%		71%	1%	33%	11%	13%	15%	4%	33%
43 Group Total					12%	25%	23%	40%	19%	7%	1%		1%	27%	11%	13%	15%	4%	74%
44 World Total					18%	23%	29%	29%	22%	25%	25%	20%	7%	8%	12%	6%	7%	12%	100%

TREATY PROFILE OF CUBA

	Partners	Partner's World Total	Abso- lutes	Dyads Ratios Self	Dyads Ratios Other	Time 1946 1950	Time 1951 1955	Time 1956 1960	Time 1961 1965	Topics Admin & Dipl	Topics Social Coop	Topics Econ Coop	Topics Aid	Topics Milit	Institutions UN	Institutions Spec Ag's	Institutions Intl Court	Institutions Arbi- tration	Institutions Other	Self- Regis- tered
	(1)	(2)	(3)	(4)	(5)	(6)	(7)	(8)	(9)	(10)	(11)	(12)	(13)	(14)	(15)	(16)	(17)	(18)	(19)	(20)
	TOP THIRTY																			
1	USSR (Soviet Union)	1356	25	23%	2%			11	14	3	6	8	8						1	
2	USA (United States)	2599	19	17%	1%	4	10	4	1	4	4	1	2	8	2	2		1	1	
3	China People's Rep	766	14	13%	2%			4	10		6	5	3							1
4	Germany, East	556	12	11%	2%			2	10	1	5	2	2							
5	UK Great Britain	981	5	5%	1%	2	3	1		2	1	2	4			1				
6	Spain	437	5	5%	1%		4	1			1	4								
7	Czechoslovakia	393	5	5%	1%		3	2	3		4	1							1	3
8	Germany, West	890	4	4%				1		1	1	3								
9	Poland	493	3	3%	1%	2		1	2	1	2		1							
10	Italy	755	3	3%					1	1			1	1						2
11	Korea, North	99	2	2%	2%			2		1	1									
12	Bulgaria	236	2	2%	1%				2	1	1									
13	Switzerland	426	1	1%			1		1			1					1			
14	UN Special Fund	113	1	1%	1%			1					1		1					
15	UNICEF (Children)	122	1	1%	1%								1		1					
16	ILO (Labor Org)	59	1	1%	2%		1				1									
17	Romania	251	1	1%				1			1									
18	Portugal	131	1	1%	1%		1													
19	Philippines	236	1	1%			1			1										
20	Norway	461	1	1%						1										
21	Japan	443	1	1%				1				1				2				1
22	France	1033	1	1%			1					1								
23	Belgium	499	1	1%								1								
24	Albania	125	1	1%	1%				1					1						1
25																				
26																				
27																				
28																				
29																				
30																				
31	All Others (0)																			
	GROUPS																			
32	African Group	968																		
33	Arab Group	937																		
34	Asian Group	1937	1	1%			1			1										
35	Commonwealth	1641	5	5%		2	3			2	1					1				
36	Communist Group	3310	65	59%	2%			23	42	6	26	17	16						2	7
37	Latin America	1674										2								
38	Western Europe	5906	17	15%		2	12	2	1	3	3	9	1	1		1	1			
39	Intl Organs	1399	3	3%			1	1	1				3		2			1		
40	TOTALS All Data	13460	111	100%		8	27	31	45	16	34	30	22	9	4	6	1	1	3	8
41	UNTS Only		49																	
	COMPARISONS																			
42	Party Total					7%	24%	28%	41%	14%	31%	27%	20%	8%	8%	12%	2%	2%	6%	16%
43	Group Total					18%	27%	24%	31%	16%	25%	18%	31%	9%	7%	10%	5%	6%	7%	6%
44	World Total					18%	23%	29%	29%	22%	25%	25%	20%	7%	8%	12%	6%	7%	12%	100%

TREATY PROFILE OF CYPRUS

Table 47 • 95

Part-ners (1)	Part-ner's World Total (2)	Abso-lutes (3)	Dyads Ratios Self (4)	Other (5)	Time 1946-1950 (6)	1951-1955 (7)	1956-1960 (8)	1961-1965 (9)	Topics Admin & Dipl (10)	Social Coop (11)	Econ Coop (12)	Aid (13)	Milit (14)	Institutions UN (15)	Spec Ag's (16)	Intl Court (17)	Arbi-tration (18)	Other (19)	Self-Regis-tered (20)
TOP THIRTY																			
1 UK Great Britain	981	11	22%	1%			10	1	7		3	1			1			1	
2 USA (United States)	2599	10	20%				1	9	1	2	2	5						1	
3 USSR (Soviet Union)	1356	6	12%				2	4	2	1	3								
4 United Nations	233	3	6%	1%				3	2						1	1	3		
5 Norway	461	3	6%	1%		1		2		1	1	1			1		1		
6 Germany, West	890	3	6%					3	2	1	2								
7 Greece	318	2	4%	1%				2	1	1	1					1	1		
8 Syria	84	1	2%	1%				1											
9 UN Special Fund	113	1	2%	1%				1				1							
10 UNICEF (Children)	122	1	2%	1%				1				1		1					
11 IBRD (World Bank)	452	1	2%					1											
12 Israel	232	1	2%					1	1										
13 Hungary	290	1	2%					1		1					1				
14 Germany, East	556	1	2%					1			1				1		1		
15 Denmark	380	1	2%					1		1									
16 Bulgaria	236	1	2%					1		1					1				
17 Belgium	499	1	2%					1							1				
18 Accept UN Charter	68	1	2%	1%				1	1					1					
19																			
20																			
21																			
22																			
23																			
24																			
25																			
26																			
27																			
28																			
29																			
30																			
31 All Others (0)																			
GROUPS																			
32 African Group	968																		
33 Arab Group	937	1	2%					1											
34 Asian Group	1937																		
35 Commonwealth	1641	11	22%	1%			10	1	7		3				1				
36 Communist Group	3310	9	18%				2	7	2	3	4	1			1			1	
37 Latin America	1674																		
38 Western Europe	5906	10	20%			1		9	1	4	4	1			4	2	3		
39 Intl Organs	1399	6	12%					6	2			4		1			3		
TOTALS																			
40 All Data	9870	49	100%			1	13	35	15	10	13	11		2	7	2	6	2	
41 UNTS Only		40																	
COMPARISONS																			
42 Party Total					22%	2%	27%	71%	31%	20%	27%	22%	8%	5%	18%	5%	15%	5%	
43 Group Total					18%	25%	27%	26%	24%	26%	32%	10%		4%	14%	6%	8%	17%	32%
44 World Total					18%	23%	29%	29%	22%	25%	25%	20%	7%	8%	12%	6%	7%	12%	100%

96 • Table 48

TREATY PROFILE OF CZECHOSLOVAKIA

			Dyads			Time				Topics						Institutions			
Partners	Partner's World Total	Absolutes	Ratios Self	Other	1946 1950	1951 1955	1956 1960	1961 1965	Admin & Dipl	Social Coop	Econ Coop	Aid	Milit	UN	Spec Ag's	Intl Court	Arbitration	Other	Self-Registered
(1)	(2)	(3)	(4)	(5)	(6)	(7)	(8)	(9)	(10)	(11)	(12)	(13)	(14)	(15)	(16)	(17)	(18)	(19)	(20)
TOP THIRTY																			
1 Germany, East	556	56	14%	10%	10	17	23	6	13	24	18	1						2	11
2 USSR (Soviet Union)	1356	48	12%	4%	14	4	23	7	9	13	16	10						1	4
3 Poland	493	46	12%	9%	14	6	17	9	15	21	7		3	1	2			6	7
4 China People's Rep	766	36	9%	5%	1	13	11	11	3	16	7			1			2		1
5 Yugoslavia	525	25	6%	5%	12		7	6	6	9	17		1					8	9
6 Hungary	290	18	5%	6%	2	2	8	6	6	6	9							2	13
7 Sweden	483	15	4%	3%	12	2		1	10	2	2				1				
8 France	1033	11	3%	1%	6		3	5	1	3	12	1	2						1
9 Austria	445	11	3%	2%	2	1	3	6	2	6	4						2	2	6
10 Romania	251	9	2%	4%	2	1	5	1	3	5	3							2	4
11 Bulgaria	236	9	2%	4%	2		4	2	3	5	1							1	8
12 UK Great Britain	981	8	2%	1%	7	1	1		4	2					2		1	2	1
13 Italy	755	7	2%	1%	2		2	3	2		3	1							1
14 Denmark	380	7	2%	2%	3	3		1		1	6				1			2	
15 Belgium	499	7	2%	1%	4	1	2		2	2	3							1	
16 USA (United States)	2599	6	2%	2%	5			1	1	2	1		3		2				
17 Greece	318	6	2%	2%	4	2				2	5							3	
18 United Arab Rep	232	5	1%	2%			4	1		3	1	1	2		2		1	1	4
19 Switzerland	426	5	1%	1%	2	1	2		2	2	3		1		1		2		1
20 Netherlands	548	5	1%	1%	4			1	1	1	4				1				
21 Cuba	111	5	1%	5%			2	3		4	1								
22 Norway	461	3	1%	1%	1			2			3							1	1
23 Mongolia	119	3	1%	3%		1	1	1	2	3		1		1			1	1	3
24 Ghana	81	3	1%	4%			2	1		2	3								2
25 Ethiopia	98	3	1%	3%			3		1	2	4								3
26 Somalia	37	2	1%	5%				2		1	3								2
27 New Zealand	101	2	1%	2%	2														
28 Japan	443	2	1%	1%			2		1	2	2			1	1				1
29 India	299	2	1%	1%			2			2	1				1				1
30 Guinea	75	2	1%	3%			1	1		2					1			1	
31 All Others (22)	2705	26	7%	1%	6	1	8	11	6	18	1	1		1	7		4		10
GROUPS																			
32 African Group	968	12	3%	1%			6	6	1	9		2			3		2	2	8
33 Arab Group	937	11	3%	1%			6	5		9	1	1			3		2	1	6
34 Asian Group	1937	8	2%				5	3	2	6					2			1	5
35 Commonwealth	1641	12	3%	1%	10	1	1		2	3	6		3		3		1	2	1
36 Communist Group	3310	229	58%	7%	45	44	95	45	62	92	61	11	3	1	2		2	14	55
37 Latin America	1674	5	1%				2	3		4	1							1	1
38 Western Europe	5906	80	20%	1%	43	10	9	18	8	20	47	2	3		8		6	1	9
39 Intl Organs	1399	3	1%		2			1	1	1		1		1				9	
TOTALS																			
40 All Data	17702	393	100%		117	55	133	88	82	155	127	17	12	4	24		13	35	95
41 UNTS Only		222																	
COMPARISONS																			
42 Party Total					30%	14%	34%	22%	21%	39%	32%	4%	3%	2%	11%		6%	16%	43%
43 Group Total					16%	17%	38%	29%	20%	32%	32%	13%	2%	4%	4%		3%	17%	33%
44 World Total					18%	23%	29%	29%	22%	25%	25%	20%	7%	8%	12%	6%	7%	12%	100%

TREATY PROFILE OF DAHOMEY

Table 49

Partners (1)	Partner's World Total (2)	Dyads Absolutes (3)	Dyads Ratios Self (4)	Dyads Ratios Other (5)	Time 1946-1950 (6)	Time 1951-1955 (7)	Time 1956-1960 (8)	Time 1961-1965 (9)	Admin & Dipl (10)	Social Coop (11)	Econ Coop (12)	Aid (13)	Milit (14)	UN (15)	Spec Ag's (16)	Intl Court (17)	Arbitration (18)	Other (19)	Self-Registered (20)
TOP THIRTY																			
1 France	1033	6	24%	1%			1	5	2	1	3								
2 USA (United States)	2599	4	16%					4	2	1	1	2	1	1					
3 Germany, West	890	4	16%					4	1	1	2	1							
4 USSR (Soviet Union)	1356	3	12%					3	1	1	1							1	
5 Israel	232	2	8%	1%				2	1			1							
6 WHO (World Health)	187	1	4%	1%			1					1		1					
7 UN Special Fund	113	1	4%	1%				1	1			1		1					
8 UNICEF (Children)	122	1	4%	1%				1	1						1	1			
9 Poland	493	1	4%					1											
10 Italy	755	1	4%					1		1									
11 Accept UN Charter	68	1	4%	1%			1		1					1					
12																			
31 All Others (0)																			
GROUPS																			
32 African Group	968																		
33 Arab Group	937																		
34 Asian Group	1937																		
35 Commonwealth	1641																		
36 Communist Group	3310	4	16%					4	1		1							1	
37 Latin America	1674																		
38 Western Europe	5906	11	44%				1	10	2	2	5	2							
39 Intl Organs	1399	3	12%				1	2	1	2		2		2	1	1	1		
TOTALS																			
40 All Data	7848	25	100%				3	22	6	4	7	7	1	4	1	1	1	1	
41 UNTS Only		12																	
COMPARISONS																			
42 Party Total					1%	5%	12%	88%	24%	16%	28%	28%	4%	33%	8%	8%	8%	8%	1%
43 Group Total					18%	23%	18%	75%	22%	21%	18%	35%	4%	19%	13%	10%	15%	4%	1%
44 World Total					18%	23%	29%	29%	22%	25%	25%	20%	7%	8%	12%	6%	7%	12%	100%

TREATY PROFILE OF DENMARK

Partners (1)	Partner's World Total (2)	Dyads Absolutes (3)	Ratios Self (4)	Ratios Other (5)	Time 1946-1950 (6)	Time 1951-1955 (7)	Time 1956-1960 (8)	Time 1961-1965 (9)	Admin & Dipl (10)	Social Coop (11)	Econ Coop (12)	Aid (13)	Milit (14)	UN (15)	Spec Ag's (16)	Intl Court (17)	Arbitration (18)	Other (19)	Self-Registered (20)
TOP THIRTY																			
1 USA (United States)	2599	33	9%	1%	9	14	7	3	3	9	7	3	11	1	6	2		8	8
2 UK Great Britain	981	28	7%	3%	11	4	8	5	6	6	9	1	6		4		1	7	6
3 Sweden	483	23	6%	5%	11	9	3		1	5	17							2	5
4 Germany, West	890	22	6%	2%	1	4	9	8	10	6	4		2		2	1	1	2	15
5 Norway	461	18	5%	4%	7	2	5	4	4	4	10							4	12
6 USSR (Soviet Union)	1356	16	4%	1%	5	3	6	2	5	4	7								4
7 Italy	755	11	3%	1%	3	4	3	1	1	1	8		1					11	7
8 Switzerland	426	10	3%	2%	3	3	3	1		4	6				1			1	7
9 Finland	245	10	3%	4%	4	3	1	2	2	2	6			1	1		1	2	5
10 Austria	445	10	3%	2%	4	2	1	3	3	2	5				1	2	1	4	7
11 Poland	493	9	2%	2%	4	3	1	1		2	7							3	7
12 Greece	318	9	2%	3%	3	3	1	2		1	8			1	1			2	2
13 Netherlands	548	8	2%	1%	2	1	4	1	2	1	6		1		1		1	4	2
14 Japan	443	8	2%	2%		5	3			2	3		2						1
15 France	1033	8	2%	1%	3	1	1	2	4	1	4				1		1	1	5
16 Belgium	499	8	2%	2%	5	2	1	1		2	3				1			2	4
17 Spain	437	7	2%	2%	4	2		2		1	6				1		2	4	5
18 Portugal	131	7	2%	5%	4		2				6				2				6
19 India	299	7	2%	2%	1	1	1	5		1	1	4	1		1		1		7
20 Czechoslovakia	393	7	2%	2%	3	3		1		1	6				2			2	6
21 Canada	310	7	2%	2%	3		1	2	1	3	1		2				1	1	4
22 WHO (World Health)	187	6	2%	3%		5	1		1	5				3					
23 Pakistan	245	6	2%	2%	1	1	2	2	1	2	1	1			2	1	2		3
24 China People's Rep	766	6	2%	1%			4	2	2		6								2
25 Israel	232	5	1%	2%		5			1		3								4
26 Argentina	164	5	1%	3%	3		1	1		1	4		1		1				4
27 Yugoslavia	525	4	1%	1%	1	1	1	1	2	1	1				1			1	3
28 Turkey	298	4	1%	1%	3		1			1	2	1			1				2
29 South Africa	120	4	1%	3%	2	1	1			2	2				2				1
30 Ireland	103	4	1%	4%	2	1	1		1		2						1		2
31 All Others (43)	4976	70	18%	1%	17	15	19	19	9	26	26	7	2	4	18	5	13	2	46
GROUPS																			
32 African Group	968	7	2%	1%	1	3	3		1	1	4	1		2	7	1	3		7
33 Arab Group	937	10	3%	1%	1	3	3	3		8	1		1	1	9	2	6	1	8
34 Asian Group	1937	25	7%	1%	4	4	6	11	4	9	5	6			8		2	1	14
35 Commonwealth	1641	43	11%	3%	19	7	10	7	9	11	14	1	8		8			8	12
36 Communist Group	3310	45	12%	1%	15	10	14	6	5	10	30			1	1			6	26
37 Latin America	1674	20	5%	1%	5	6	7	2		4	13		2	1	4	2	2		17
38 Western Europe	5906	167	44%	3%	60	38	38	31	28	37	95	1	6	2	13	2	8	39	92
39 Intl Organs	1399	11	3%	1%	2	5	3	1	1	6		3	1	3		2	2	1	
TOTALS																			
40 All Data	21161	380	100%		117	98	93	72	58	98	177	17	30	10	50	12	24	64	192
41 UNTS Only		330																	
COMPARISONS																			
42 Party Total					31%	26%	24%	19%	15%	26%	47%	4%	8%	3%	15%	4%	7%	19%	58%
43 Group Total					22%	25%	27%	26%	24%	26%	32%	10%	8%	4%	14%	6%	8%	17%	32%
44 World Total					18%	23%	29%	29%	22%	25%	25%	20%	7%	8%	12%	6%	7%	12%	100%

TREATY PROFILE OF DOMINICAN REPUBLIC

Table 51

	Partners (1)	Partner's World Total (2)	Dyads Absolutes (3)	Ratios Self (4)	Ratios Other (5)	Time 1946 1950 (6)	Time 1951 1955 (7)	Time 1956 1960 (8)	Time 1961 1965 (9)	Topics Admin & Dipl (10)	Topics Social Coop (11)	Topics Econ Coop (12)	Topics Aid (13)	Topics Milit (14)	Institutions UN (15)	Institutions Spec Ag's (16)	Institutions Intl Court (17)	Institutions Arbitration (18)	Institutions Other (19)	Self-Registered (20)
	TOP THIRTY																			
1	USA (United States)	2599	27	55%	1%	4	8	4	11	2	8	2	9	6	1	1	1	1	2	1
2	Spain	437	4	8%	1%		3	1		1	2	1								
3	UK Great Britain	981	2	4%			1	1		1				1						
4	WHO (World Health)	187	2	4%	1%		2		1		2				2	1		1		
5	United Nations	233	2	4%	1%		1			1			1					2		
6	Norway	461	2	4%		1		2		2										
7	Italy	755	2	4%			1		1	1		1		1						
8	Turkey	298	1	2%			1													
9	UN Special Fund	113	1	2%	1%				1				1		1	1	1	1		
10	UNICEF (Children)	122	1	2%	1%		1				1				1					
11	ILO (Labor Org)	59	1	2%	2%		1						1		1					
12	Philippines	236	1	2%				1		1										
13	Japan	443	1	2%					1	1										
14	Israel	232	1	2%				1					1							
15	Germany, West	890	1	2%					1	1										
31	All Others (0)																			
	GROUPS																			
32	African Group	968																		
33	Arab Group	937																		
34	Asian Group	1937	1	2%			1			1										
35	Commonwealth	1641	2	4%			1	1		1										
36	Communist Group	3310												1						
37	Latin America	1674																		
38	Western Europe	5906	10	20%		1	5	4		5	2	2		1						
39	Intl Organs	1399	7	14%	1%		5		2	1	3		3		5	1	1	4		
40	TOTALS All Data	8046	49	100%		5	20	10	14	11	13	4	13	8	6	2	2	5	2	1
41	UNTS Only		39																		
	COMPARISONS																			
42	Party Total					10%	41%	20%	29%	22%	27%	8%	27%	16%	15%	5%	5%	13%	5%	3%
43	Group Total					18%	27%	24%	31%	16%	25%	18%	31%	9%	7%	10%	5%	6%	7%	6%
44	World Total					18%	23%	29%	29%	22%	25%	25%	20%	7%	8%	12%	6%	7%	12%	100%

TREATY PROFILE OF EAST AFRI SERVICE

Table 52

	Partners (1)	Partner's World Total (2)	Dyads Absolutes (3)	Dyads Ratios Self (4)	Dyads Ratios Other (5)	Time 1946-1950 (6)	Time 1951-1955 (7)	Time 1956-1960 (8)	Time 1961-1965 (9)	Topics Admin & Dipl (10)	Topics Social Coop (11)	Topics Econ Coop (12)	Topics Aid (13)	Topics Milit (14)	Institutions UN (15)	Institutions Spec Ag's (16)	Institutions Intl Court (17)	Institutions Arbitration (18)	Institutions Other (19)	Self-Registered (20)
	TOP THIRTY																			
1	United Nations	233	1	50%					1		1									
2	IBRD (World Bank)	452	1	50%					1				1							
3																				
4																				
5																				
6																				
7																				
8																				
9																				
10																				
11																				
12																				
13																				
14																				
15																				
16																				
17																				
18																				
19																				
20																				
21																				
22																				
23																				
24																				
25																				
26																				
27																				
28																				
29																				
30																				
31	All Others (0)																			
	GROUPS																			
32	African Group	968																		
33	Arab Group	937																		
34	Asian Group	1937																		
35	Commonwealth	1641																		
36	Communist Group	3310																		
37	Latin America	1674																		
38	Western Europe	5906																		
39	Intl Organs	1399	2	100%					2		1		1							
	TOTALS																			
40	All Data	685	2	100%					2		1		1							
41	UNTS Only																			
	COMPARISONS																			
42	Party Total					12%	25%	23%	100%	19%	50%	1%	50%	1%	27%	11%	13%	15%	4%	74%
43	Group Total					18%	23%	29%	40%	22%	7%	25%	71%	7%	8%	12%	6%	7%	12%	100%
44	World Total							29%	29%		25%		20%								

TREATY PROFILE OF ECSC (COAL/STEEL)

Table 53 • 101

Partners (1)	Partner's World Total (2)	Dyads Abso-lutes (3)	Dyads Ratios Self (4)	Dyads Ratios Other (5)	Time 1946 1950 (6)	Time 1951 1955 (7)	Time 1956 1960 (8)	Time 1961 1965 (9)	Topics Admin & Dipl (10)	Topics Social Coop (11)	Topics Econ Coop (12)	Topics Aid (13)	Topics Milit (14)	Institutions UN (15)	Institutions Spec Ag's (16)	Institutions Intl Court (17)	Institutions Arbi-tration (18)	Institutions Other (19)	Self-Regis-tered (20)
TOP THIRTY																			
1 USA (United States)	2599	1	33%			1													
2 ILO (Labor Org)	59	1	33%			1						1			1				
3 Austria	445	1	33%	2%			1		1	1									
4																			
5																			
6																			
7																			
8																			
9																			
10																			
11																			
12																			
13																			
14																			
15																			
16																			
17																			
18																			
19																			
20																			
21																			
22																			
23																			
24																			
25																			
26																			
27																			
28																			
29																			
30																			
31 All Others (0)																			
GROUPS																			
32 African Group	968																		
33 Arab Group	937																		
34 Asian Group	1937																		
35 Commonwealth	1641																		
36 Communist Group	3310																		
37 Latin America	1674																		
38 Western Europe	5906	1	33%				1		1	1									
39 Intl Organs	1399	1	33%			1													
TOTALS																			
40 All Data	3103	3	100%			2	1		1	1		1			1				
41 UNTS Only		2					1					1				1			
COMPARISONS																			
42 Party Total					12%	67%	33%	40%	33%	33%	33%	33%	1%	27%	50%	13%	15%	4%	74%
43 Group Total					12%	25%	23%	29%	19%	7%	1%	71%	7%	8%	11%	6%	7%	12%	100%
44 World Total					18%	23%	29%	29%	22%	25%	25%	20%	7%	8%	12%	6%	7%	12%	

102 • Table 54

TREATY PROFILE OF ECUADOR

Part-ners (1)	Partner's World Total (2)	Dyads Absolutes (3)	Dyads Ratios Self (4)	Dyads Ratios Other (5)	Time 1946-1950 (6)	Time 1951-1955 (7)	Time 1956-1960 (8)	Time 1961-1965 (9)	Topics Admin & Dipl (10)	Topics Social Coop (11)	Topics Econ Coop (12)	Topics Aid (13)	Topics Milit (14)	Institutions UN (15)	Institutions Spec Ag's (16)	Institutions Intl Court (17)	Institutions Arbitration (18)	Institutions Other (19)	Self-Registered (20)
TOP THIRTY																			
1 USA (United States)	2599	40	41%	2%	10	10	11	9	3	10	1	17	9	1	1	1		3	
2 Germany, West	890	9	9%	1%		4	1	4	2	1	5	1			1	1	1		
3 Spain	437	7	7%	2%		5		1	1	3	3				1			2	1
4 IBRD (World Bank)	452	6	6%	1%			4	1				6							
5 France	1033	5	5%		1		2	2	1	1	2	1							
6 Taiwan	172	4	5%	2%	1	1	1	2		1	2								
7 Brazil	195	4	4%	2%	1	1		2	2	1	2							2	
8 Netherlands	548	3	4%	1%	1	1	1		2	2				1	1	1			1
9 Italy	755	3	3%			1		2	2	1									1
10 United Nations	233	2	2%	1%		1		1	1		1	2					2		
11 Norway	461	2	2%				1	1	1										
12 Belgium	499	2	2%						2										
13 UK Great Britain	981	1	1%					1			1								
14 Switzerland	426	1	1%			1	1										1		
15 WHO (World Health)	187	1	1%	1%	1							1		1	1				
16 UN Special Fund	113	1	1%	1%			1					1		1					
17 UNICEF (Children)	122	1	1%	1%		1						1		1					
18 ILO (Labor Org)	59	1	1%	2%											1				
19 IDA (Devel Assoc)	82	1	1%	1%				1											
20 Philippines	236	1	1%		1														
21 Mexico	138	1	1%	1%	1					1									
22 Canada	310	1	1%		1														
23																			
24																			
25																			
26																			
27																			
28																			
29																			
30																			
31 All Others (0)																			
GROUPS																			
32 African Group	968																		
33 Arab Group	937																		
34 Asian Group	1937	5	5%		2		1	2	2	1	2								
35 Commonwealth	1641	2	2%		1			1	1		1								
36 Communist Group	3310																		
37 Latin America	1674	5	5%		2	1	1	1	2	1	2			1	2	1	1	2	1
38 Western Europe	5906	32	33%	1%	2	12	6	12	10	8	12	2		4	3	1	3	2	1
39 Intl Organs	1399	13	13%	1%	1	4	5	3				13							
TOTALS																			
40 All Data	10928	97	100%		18	27	24	28	18	20	18	32	9	6	6	3	4	7	2
41 UNTS Only		70																		
COMPARISONS																			
42 Party Total					19%	28%	25%	29%	19%	21%	19%	33%	9%	9%	9%	4%	6%	10%	3%
43 Group Total					18%	27%	24%	31%	16%	25%	18%	31%	9%	7%	10%	5%	6%	7%	6%
44 World Total					18%	23%	29%	29%	22%	25%	25%	20%	7%	8%	12%	6%	7%	12%	100%

Table 55 • 103

TREATY PROFILE OF EEC (ECON COMMNTY)

Partners (1)	Partner's World Total (2)	Dyads Absolutes (3)	Ratios Self (4)	Ratios Other (5)	Time 1946-1950 (6)	Time 1951-1955 (7)	Time 1956-1960 (8)	Time 1961-1965 (9)	Topics Admin & Dipl (10)	Topics Social Coop (11)	Topics Econ Coop (12)	Topics Aid (13)	Topics Milit (14)	Institutions UN (15)	Institutions Spec Ag's (16)	Institutions Intl Court (17)	Institutions Arbitration (18)	Institutions Other (19)	Self-Registered (20)
TOP THIRTY																			
1 USA (United States)	2599	3	50%					3			3				3			1	
2 Turkey	298	1	17%					1			1								
3 ILO (Labor Org)	59	1	17%	2%			1		1					1					
4 Iran	170	1	17%	1%				1			1								
5																			
6																			
7																			
8																			
9																			
10																			
11																			
12																			
13																			
14																			
15																			
16																			
17																			
18																			
19																			
20																			
21																			
22																			
23																			
24																			
25																			
26																			
27																			
28																			
29																			
30																			
31 All Others (0)																			
GROUPS																			
32 African Group	968																		
33 Arab Group	937																		
34 Asian Group	1937	1	17%					1											
35 Commonwealth	1641										1								
36 Communist Group	3310																		
37 Latin America	1674																		
38 Western Europe	5906	1	17%				1												
39 Intl Organs	1399	1	17%					1	1		1			1					
TOTALS																			
40 All Data		6	100%				1	5	1		5			1	3			1	
41 UNTS Only	3126	4																	
COMPARISONS																			
42 Party Total					12%	25%	17%	83%	17%	7%	83%	71%	1%	25%	75%	13%	15%	25%	25%
43 Group Total					18%	23%	23%	40%	19%	7%	1%	20%	7%	27%	11%	6%	7%	4%	74%
44 World Total					18%	23%	29%	29%	22%	25%	25%			8%	12%			12%	100%

104 • Table 56

TREATY PROFILE OF EFTA (FREE TRADE)

Part-ners	Part-ner's World Total	Dyads Abso-lutes	Ratios Self	Ratios Other	Time 1946-1950	Time 1951-1955	Time 1956-1960	Time 1961-1965	Topics Admin & Dipl	Topics Social Coop	Topics Econ Coop	Topics Aid	Topics Milit	Institutions UN	Institutions Spec Ag's	Institutions Intl Court	Institutions Arbi-tration	Institutions Other	Self-Regis-tered
(1)	(2)	(3)	(4)	(5)	(6)	(7)	(8)	(9)	(10)	(11)	(12)	(13)	(14)	(15)	(16)	(17)	(18)	(19)	(20)
TOP THIRTY																			
1 Switzerland	426	1	100%					1	1										
2																			
3																			
4																			
5																			
6																			
7																			
8																			
9																			
10																			
11																			
12																			
13																			
14																			
15																			
16																			
17																			
18																			
19																			
20																			
21																			
22																			
23																			
24																			
25																			
26																			
27																			
28																			
29																			
30																			
31 All Others (0)																			
GROUPS																			
32 African Group	968																		
33 Arab Group	937																		
34 Asian Group	1937																		
35 Commonwealth	1641																		
36 Communist Group	3310																		
37 Latin America	1674																		
38 Western Europe	5906	1	100%					1											
39 Intl Organs	1399																		
TOTALS																			
40 All Data	426	1	100%					1	1										
41 UNTS Only		0																		
COMPARISONS																			
42 Party Total								100%	100%			1%	71%	1%	27%	11%	13%	15%	4%	74%
43 Group Total					12%	25%	23%	40%	19%	7%	25%	20%	7%	8%	12%	6%	7%	4%	74%
44 World Total					18%	23%	29%	29%	22%	25%	25%	20%	7%	8%	12%	6%	7%	12%	100%

Table 57 • 105

TREATY PROFILE OF EL SALVADOR

Partners (1)	Partner's World Total (2)	Dyads Abso-lutes (3)	Dyads Ratios Self (4)	Dyads Ratios Other (5)	Time 1946-1950 (6)	Time 1951-1955 (7)	Time 1956-1960 (8)	Time 1961-1965 (9)	Topics Admin & Dipl (10)	Topics Social Coop (11)	Topics Econ Coop (12)	Topics Aid (13)	Topics Milit (14)	Institutions UN (15)	Institutions Spec Ag's (16)	Institutions Intl Court (17)	Institutions Arbi-tration (18)	Institutions Other (19)	Self-Registered (20)
TOP THIRTY																			
1 USA (United States)	2599	31	44%	1%	4	17	3	7	2	6	2	16	5			1		3	
2 IBRD (World Bank)	452	7	10%	2%	1	1	3	2			2	7					1		
3 Spain	437	4	6%	1%		4			2		2								
4 Israel	232	3	4%	1%			2	1	2	1	1								
5 Austria	445	3	4%	1%			2	1	2										
6 UK Great Britain	981	2	3%		1			1	1										
7 WHO (World Health)	187	2	3%	1%		1		1		2					1			1	
8 Germany, West	890	2	3%			1		1			1	1							
9 France	1033	2	3%			1		1	1	1	1								
10 Taiwan	172	2	3%	1%		1		1			1								
11 Switzerland	426	1	1%				1												
12 UN Special Fund	113	1	1%	1%	1							1		1	1	1		1	
13 UNICEF (Children)	122	1	1%	1%			1					1		1	1				
14 IDA (Devel Assoc)	82	1	1%	1%								1							
15 Norway	461	1	1%				1		1										
16 Mexico	138	1	1%	1%	1						1								
17 Japan	443	1	1%					1			1				1				
18 Italy	755	1	1%			1					1								
19 Guatemala	50	1	1%	2%		1					1								
20 Denmark	380	1	1%				1												
21 Canada	310	1	1%					1		1									
22 Brazil	195	1	1%	1%				1		1									
23																			
24																			
25																			
26																			
27																			
28																			
29																			
30																			
31 All Others (0)																			
GROUPS																			
32 African Group	968																		
33 Arab Group	937																		
34 Asian Group	1937	2	3%			1		1	1	1									
35 Commonwealth	1641	3	4%					2	1	1	1								
36 Communist Group	3310																		
37 Latin America	1674	3	4%		1	1		1		1	2							1	
38 Western Europe	5906	15	21%			8	4	3	5	1	8	1			2	1	1	1	
39 Intl Organs	1399	12	17%	1%	3	2	4	3		2	1	10		2	2	1	2	1	
TOTALS																			
40 All Data	10903	70	100%		9	29	13	19	11	13	14	27	5	2	3	2	3	5	
41 UNTS Only		56																		
COMPARISONS																			
42 Party Total					13%	41%	19%	27%	16%	19%	20%	39%	7%	4%	5%	4%	5%	9%	
43 Group Total					18%	27%	24%	31%	16%	25%	18%	31%	9%	7%	10%	5%	6%	7%	6%
44 World Total					18%	23%	29%	29%	22%	25%	25%	20%	7%	8%	12%	6%	7%	12%	100%

TREATY PROFILE OF ETHIOPIA

	Partners (1)	Partner's World Total (2)	Dyads Absolutes (3)	Ratios Self (4)	Ratios Other (5)	Time 1946 1950 (6)	Time 1951 1955 (7)	Time 1956 1960 (8)	Time 1961 1965 (9)	Topics Admin & Dipl (10)	Topics Social Coop (11)	Topics Econ Coop (12)	Topics Aid (13)	Topics Milit (14)	Institutions UN (15)	Institutions Spec Ag's (16)	Institutions Intl Court (17)	Institutions Arbitration (18)	Other (19)	Self-Registered (20)
	TOP THIRTY																			
1	USA (United States)	2599	31	32%	1%	2	17	2	10	1	6	2	16	6	2	3			3	
2	USSR (Soviet Union)	1356	10	10%	1%			8	2	2	2	2	4							
3	IBRD (World Bank)	452	8	8%	2%	2	1	1	4				8							
4	UK Great Britain	981	7	7%	1%	1	5	1		3	1	1		2	1	1				
5	Greece	318	5	5%	2%		2	1	2			3								
6	Germany, West	890	5	5%	1%			1	4		2	2						1		
7	WHO (World Health)	187	4	4%	2%		1	1	2	1	3		3		1	1		1		
8	United Nations	233	4	4%	2%		1	2	1	1	3		3		1	1		1		
9	Czechoslovakia	393	3	3%	1%			3		1	2									
10	Yugoslavia	525	2	2%			1	1				1	1							
11	Sweden	483	2	2%			1	1					2							
12	UNICEF (Children)	122	2	2%	2%			1	1				1							
13	Pakistan	245	2	2%	1%		1		1	1	2				1	2		1		
14	France	1033	2	2%		1		2		1	1				1	1		1		
15	UN Special Fund	113	1	1%	1%			1					1		1					
16	ILO (Labor Org)	59	1	1%	2%				1											
17	IDA (Devel Assoc)	82	1	1%	1%				1				1			1				
18	ICAO (Civil Aviat)	23	1	1%	4%		1						1							
19	Poland	493	1	1%					1				1							
20	Netherlands	548	1	1%					1				1							
21	Japan	443	1	1%				1		1										
22	Italy	755	1	1%							1			1						
23	India	299	1	1%					1		1									
24	Hungary	290	1	1%			1					1								
25	Canada	310	1	1%					1											
26																				
27																				
28																				
29																				
30																				
31	All Others (0)																			
	GROUPS																			
32	African Group	968	3	3%		2	1			3	3	2				3	1	1		
33	Arab Group	937																		
34	Asian Group	1937	8	8%		1	6	1		3	1	2		2	1	1				
35	Commonwealth	1641																		
36	Communist Group	3310	15	15%				11	4	3	5	2	5							
37	Latin America	1674																		
38	Western Europe	5906	16	16%			3	6	7	1	6	5	3	1		2	1	2	1	
39	Intl Organs	1399	22	22%	2%	2	5	5	10	4			18		5	2	2	3		
	TOTALS																			
40	All Data	13232	98	100%		7	33	27	31	13	21	12	43	9	8	11	3	6	4	
41	UNTS Only		83																	
	COMPARISONS																			
42	Party Total					7%	34%	28%	32%	13%	21%	12%	44%	9%	10%	13%	4%	7%	5%	
43	Group Total					1%	5%	18%	75%	22%	21%	18%	35%	4%	19%	13%	10%	15%	4%	1%
44	World Total					18%	23%	29%	29%	22%	25%	25%	20%	7%	8%	12%	6%	7%	12%	100%

TREATY PROFILE OF EUR PLANT PROTECT

Table 59 • 107

	Partners (1)	Partner's World Total (2)	Abso-lutes (3)	Dyads Ratios Self (4)	Dyads Ratios Other (5)	Time 1946-1950 (6)	Time 1951-1955 (7)	Time 1956-1960 (8)	Time 1961-1965 (9)	Topics Admin & Dipl (10)	Topics Social Coop (11)	Topics Econ Coop (12)	Topics Aid (13)	Topics Milit (14)	Institutions UN (15)	Institutions Spec Ag's (16)	Institutions Intl Court (17)	Institutions Arbi-tration (18)	Institutions Other (19)	Self-Regis-tered (20)
	TOP THIRTY																			
1	France	1033	1	100%					1	1										
2																				
3																				
4																				
5																				
6																				
7																				
8																				
9																				
10																				
11																				
12																				
13																				
14																				
15																				
16																				
17																				
18																				
19																				
20																				
21																				
22																				
23																				
24																				
25																				
26																				
27																				
28																				
29																				
30																				
31	All Others (0)																			
	GROUPS																			
32	African Group	968																		
33	Arab Group	937																		
34	Asian Group	1937																		
35	Commonwealth	1641																		
36	Communist Group	3310																		
37	Latin America	1674																		
38	Western Europe	5906	1	100%					1											
39	Intl Organs	1399																			
	TOTALS																			
40	All Data	1033	1	100%					1	1										
41	UNTS Only		0																		
	COMPARISONS																			
42	Party Total					12%	25%	23%	100%	100%	7%	1%	71%	1%	27%	11%	13%	15%	4%	74%
43	Group Total					18%	23%	29%	40%	19%	25%	25%	20%	7%	8%	12%	6%	7%	12%	100%
44	World Total							29%	29%	22%										

108 • Table 60

TREATY PROFILE OF EUR SPACE RESEARCH

			Dyads			Time				Topics						Institutions			
Partners	Partner's World Total	Abso- lutes	Ratios Self	Other	1946 1950	1951 1955	1956 1960	1961 1965	Admin & Dipl	Social Coop	Econ Coop	Aid	Milit	UN	Spec Ag's	Intl Court	Arbi- tration	Other	Self- Regis- tered
(1)	(2)	(3)	(4)	(5)	(6)	(7)	(8)	(9)	(10)	(11)	(12)	(13)	(14)	(15)	(16)	(17)	(18)	(19)	(20)
TOP THIRTY																			
1 France	1033	2	40%					2	1							1	1		1
2 Sweden	483	1	20%					1	1	1						1	1	1	1
3 Norway	461	1	20%					1	1										1
4 Italy	755	1	20%					1	1										1
5																			
6																			
7																			
8																			
9																			
10																			
11																			
12																			
13																			
14																			
15																			
16																			
17																			
18																			
19																			
20																			
21																			
22																			
23																			
24																			
25																			
26																			
27																			
28																			
29																			
30																			
31 All Others (0)																			
GROUPS																			
32 African Group	968																		
33 Arab Group	937																		
34 Asian Group	1937																		
35 Commonwealth	1641																		
36 Communist Group	3310																		
37 Latin America	1674																		
38 Western Europe	5906	5	100%					5	4	1						2	2	1	4
39 Intl Organs	1399																			
TOTALS																			
40 All Data	2732	5	100%					5	4	1						2	2	1	4
41 UNTS Only		4																		
COMPARISONS																			
42 Party Total					12%	25%	23%	100%	80%	20%	1%	71%	1%	27%	11%	50%	50%	25%	100%
43 Group Total					18%	23%	29%	40%	19%	7%	25%	20%	7%	8%	12%	13%	15%	4%	74%
44 World Total					18%	23%	29%	29%	22%	25%	25%	20%	7%	8%	12%	6%	7%	12%	100%

TREATY PROFILE OF EUR SPACE VEHICLE

Table 61 • 109

	Partners (1)	Partner's World Total (2)	Dyads Abso-lutes (3)	Ratios Self (4)	Ratios Other (5)	Time 1946 1950 (6)	Time 1951 1955 (7)	Time 1956 1960 (8)	Time 1961 1965 (9)	Topics Admin & Dipl (10)	Topics Social Coop (11)	Topics Econ Coop (12)	Topics Aid (13)	Topics Milit (14)	Institutions UN (15)	Institutions Spec Ag's (16)	Institutions Intl Court (17)	Institutions Arbi-tration (18)	Institutions Other (19)	Self-Regis-tered (20)
	TOP THIRTY																			
1	France	1033	1	50%					1		1									
2	Australia	201	1	50%					1								1			1
3																				
4																				
5																				
6																				
7																				
8																				
9																				
10																				
11																				
12																				
13																				
14																				
15																				
16																				
17																				
18																				
19																				
20																				
21																				
22																				
23																				
24																				
25																				
26																				
27																				
28																				
29																				
30																				
31	All Others (0)																			
	GROUPS																			
32	African Group	968																		
33	Arab Group	937																		
34	Asian Group	1937																		
35	Commonwealth	1641	1	50%					1	1									1	1
36	Communist Group	3310																		
37	Latin America	1674																		
38	Western Europe	5906	1	50%					1	1	1									
39	Intl Organs	1399																		
	TOTALS																			
40	All Data	1234	2	100%					2	1	1						1			1
41	UNTS Only		1																	
	COMPARISONS																			
42	Party Total					12%	25%	23%	100%	50%	50%	1%	71%	1%	27%	11%	100%	15%	4%	100%
43	Group Total					18%	23%	29%	40%	19%	7%	25%	20%	7%	8%	12%	13%	7%	12%	74%
44	World Total							29%	29%	22%	25%						6%			100%

110 • Table 62

TREATY PROFILE OF EURATOM

Partners	Partner's World Total	Dyads Absolutes	Ratios Self	Ratios Other	Time 1946-1950	Time 1951-1955	Time 1956-1960	Time 1961-1965	Admin & Dipl	Social Coop	Econ Coop	Aid	Milit	UN	Spec Ag's	Intl Court	Arbitration	Other	Self-Registered
(1)	(2)	(3)	(4)	(5)	(6)	(7)	(8)	(9)	(10)	(11)	(12)	(13)	(14)	(15)	(16)	(17)	(18)	(19)	(20)
TOP THIRTY																			
1 USA (United States)	2599	2	29%				2					2			1	1			
2 Netherlands	548	2	29%				1	2	1	1					1			4	
3 UK Great Britain	981	1	14%					1	1			1						1	
4 ILO (Labor Org)	59	1	14%	2%			1			1									
5 Canada	310	1	14%				1												
6																			
7																			
8																			
9																			
10																			
11																			
12																			
13																			
14																			
15																			
16																			
17																			
18																			
19																			
20																			
21																			
22																			
23																			
24																			
25																			
26																			
27																			
28																			
29																			
30																			
31 All Others (0)																			
GROUPS																			
32 African Group	968																		
33 Arab Group	937																		
34 Asian Group	1937																		
35 Commonwealth	1641	2	29%				2											1	
36 Communist Group	3310																		
37 Latin America	1674																		
38 Western Europe	5906	2	29%					2	1	1								4	
39 Intl Organs	1399	1	14%					1	1			1							
TOTALS																			
40 All Data	4497	7	100%				4	3	2	2		3			2			5	
41 UNTS Only		7																	
COMPARISONS																			
42 Party Total					12%	25%	57%	43%	29%	29%	1%	43%	1%	27%	29%	13%	15%	71%	74%
43 Group Total					18%	23%	23%	40%	19%	7%	1%	71%	7%	8%	11%	6%	7%	4%	74%
44 World Total					18%	23%	29%	29%	22%	25%	25%	20%	7%	8%	12%	6%	7%	12%	100%

TREATY PROFILE OF FAO (FOOD AGRI)

Table 63 • 111

			Dyads			Time				Topics					Institutions				
Partners (1)	Partner's World Total (2)	Absolutes (3)	Ratios Self (4)	Other (5)	1946 1950 (6)	1951 1955 (7)	1956 1960 (8)	1961 1965 (9)	Admin & Dipl (10)	Social Coop (11)	Econ Coop (12)	Aid (13)	Milit (14)	UN (15)	Spec Ag's (16)	Intl Court (17)	Arbitration (18)	Other (19)	Self-Registered (20)
TOP THIRTY																			
1 Philippines	236	4	21%	2%		4						4							
2 UK Great Britain	981	2	11%		2		1		2					1					
3 United Nations	233	2	11%	1%	2				2					2		1			
4 UNESCO (Educ/Cult)	19	2	11%	11%	2	1	1		2					1				1	
5 Australia	201	2	11%	1%		1	1					2						1	
6 Vietnam, South	106	1	5%	1%		1						1							
7 USA (United States)	2599	1	5%					1	1					1					
8 Turkey	298	1	5%			1						1							
9 WHO (World Health)	187	1	5%	1%	1				1					1					
10 UN Special Fund	113	1	5%	1%			1		1					1					
11 ILO (Labor Org)	59	1	5%	2%	1				1					1					
12 IAEA (Atom Energy)	44	1	5%	2%			1		1					1	1				
13																			
14–30																			
31 All Others (0)																			
GROUPS																			
32 African Group	968																		
33 Arab Group	937																		
34 Asian Group	1937	5	26%			5						5							
35 Commonwealth	1641	4	21%			1	2	1	2			2		1				1	
36 Communist Group	3310																		
37 Latin America	1674																		
38 Western Europe	5906	1	5%			1						1							
39 Intl Organs	1399	8	42%	1%	6		2		8					7	1	1		1	
TOTALS																			
40 All Data	5076	19	100%		6	7	4	2	11			8		9	1	1		2	
41 UNTS Only		13																		
COMPARISONS																			
42 Party Total					32%	37%	21%	11%	58%	7%	1%	42%	1%	69%	8%	8%	15%	15%	
43 Group Total					12%	25%	23%	40%	19%	25%	25%	71%	7%	27%	11%	13%	15%	4%	74%
44 World Total					18%	23%	29%	29%	22%	25%	25%	20%		8%	12%	6%	7%	12%	100%

TREATY PROFILE OF FED OF MALAYA

Table 64

	Partners (1)	Partner's World Total (2)	Dyads Absolutes (3)	Ratios Self (4)	Ratios Other (5)	Time 1946-1950 (6)	Time 1951-1955 (7)	Time 1956-1960 (8)	Time 1961-1965 (9)	Admin & Dipl (10)	Social Coop (11)	Econ Coop (12)	Aid (13)	Milit (14)	UN (15)	Spec Ag's (16)	Intl Court (17)	Arbitration (18)	Other (19)	Self-Registered (20)
	TOP THIRTY																			
1	UK Great Britain	981	9	39%	1%			8	1	4	3		1	1		1	1	1		1
2	USA (United States)	2599	4	17%				3	1	1			2	1		1				1
3	Australia	201	3	13%	1%			2	1	1	1	1								
4	WHO (World Health)	187	1	4%	1%				1				1		1		1	1		
5	UN Special Fund	113	1	4%	1%			1					1							
6	United Nations	233	1	4%				1					1							
7	IBRD (World Bank)	452	1	4%				1				1				2				
8	Japan	443	1	4%				1		1										
9	Belgium	499	1	4%				1		1										
10	Accept UN Charter	68	1	4%	1%			1							1					
11																				
12																				
13																				
14																				
15																				
16																				
17																				
18																				
19																				
20																				
21																				
22																				
23																				
24																				
25																				
26																				
27																				
28																				
29																				
30																				
31	All Others (0)																			
	GROUPS																			
32	African Group	968																		
33	Arab Group	937																		
34	Asian Group	1937																		
35	Commonwealth	1641	12	52%	1%			10	2	5	4	1	1	1		2				2
36	Communist Group	3310																		
37	Latin America	1674																		
38	Western Europe	5906	1	4%				1												
39	Intl Organs	1399	4	17%				3	1	1		1	1		1		1	1		
40	TOTALS All Data	5776	23	100%				19	4	8	4	2	7	2	2	4	2	2	2	2
41	UNTS Only		23	100%																
	COMPARISONS																			
42	Party Total					16%	23%	83%	17%	35%	17%	9%	30%	9%	9%	17%	9%	9%	9%	9%
43	Group Total					18%	23%	31%	30%	21%	23%	20%	30%	7%	10%	15%	8%	8%	6%	16%
44	World Total					18%	23%	29%	29%	22%	25%	25%	20%	7%	8%	12%	6%	7%	12%	100%

Table 65

TREATY PROFILE OF FED RHOD/NYASALAND

Partners	Partner's World Total	Dyads Absolutes	Dyads Ratios Self	Dyads Ratios Other	Time 1946-1950	Time 1951-1955	Time 1956-1960	Time 1961-1965	Admin & Dipl	Social Coop	Econ Coop	Aid	Milit	UN	Spec Ag's	Intl Court	Arbitration	Other	Self-Registered
(1)	(2)	(3)	(4)	(5)	(6)	(7)	(8)	(9)	(10)	(11)	(12)	(13)	(14)	(15)	(16)	(17)	(18)	(19)	(20)
TOP THIRTY																			
1 South Africa	120	6	55%	5%		1	4	1	1	2	3								
2 IBRD (World Bank)	452	1	9%	1%			1		1			1							
3 Portugal	131	1	9%				1				1								
4 Netherlands	548	1	9%			1				1									
5 Canada	310	1	9%				1				1								
6 Australia	201	1	9%			1					1								
7																			
...																			
31 All Others (0)																			
GROUPS																			
32 African Group	968																		
33 Arab Group	937																		
34 Asian Group	1937																		
35 Commonwealth	1641	8	73%			2	5	1	1	2	5								
36 Communist Group	3310																		
37 Latin America	1674																		
38 Western Europe	5906	2	18%			1	1		1	1	1								
39 Intl Organs	1399	1	9%				1				1	1							
TOTALS																			
40 All Data	1762	11	100%			3	7	1	1	3	6	1							
41 UNTS Only		11	100%			3	7	1	1	3	6	1							
COMPARISONS																			
42 Party Total					27%	27%	64%	9%	9%	27%	55%	9%	14%	4%	13%	4%	5%	12%	63%
43 Group Total					25%	25%	24%	24%	25%	24%	27%	10%	7%	8%	12%	6%	7%	12%	
44 World Total					18%	23%	29%	29%	22%	25%	25%	20%							100%

TREATY PROFILE OF FINLAND

Table 66

	Partners (1)	Partner's World Total (2)	Dyads Absolutes (3)	Dyads Ratios Self (4)	Dyads Ratios Other (5)	Time 1946-1950 (6)	Time 1951-1955 (7)	Time 1956-1960 (8)	Time 1961-1965 (9)	Topics Admin & Dipl (10)	Topics Social Coop (11)	Topics Econ Coop (12)	Topics Aid (13)	Topics Milit (14)	Institutions UN (15)	Institutions Spec Ag's (16)	Institutions Intl Court (17)	Institutions Arbitration (18)	Institutions Other (19)	Self-Registered (20)
	TOP THIRTY																			
1	USSR (Soviet Union)	1356	43	18%	3%	20	6	10	7	19	7	10	4	3	1	1		1	4	8
2	USA (United States)	2599	21	9%	1%	4	7	6	4	4	3	8	6			6	1	1	2	1
3	Sweden	483	21	9%	4%	8	4	6	3	6	6	9				1	2		3	5
4	Norway	461	19	8%	4%	5	8	4	2	10	2	5	1	1		1		3	1	3
5	China People's Rep	766	16	7%	2%	3	5	5	6		2	16								
6	UK Great Britain	981	11	4%	1%	3	2	1	5	5	2	3		1	1	2		1		2
7	IBRD (World Bank)	452	11	4%	2%	2	2	2	5				11			1	2	2		
8	Denmark	380	10	4%	3%	4	3	1	2	2	2	6			1	1	2	1	1	4
9	Turkey	298	7	3%	2%	3	2	2		1		6								
10	Netherlands	548	7	3%	1%	1	6			1	1	4				1		1		2
11	Switzerland	426	6	2%	2%		2	4			1	5								3
12	Austria	445	6	2%	1%		1		5	2	2	2								
13	Germany, East	556	5	2%	1%	1		4				5								3
14	Canada	310	5	2%	2%	1	1	3	1	2			3		1					
15	Spain	437	4	2%	1%			4				4								
16	South Africa	120	4	2%	3%	1	1	1	1	3	1				1		1			1
17	IAEA (Atom Energy)	44	4	2%	9%			1	3		1	2	3					1		
18	Ireland	103	4	2%	4%		2		2	1	2	1			1					
19	France	1033	4	2%		1		2	1			1				1				
20	Australia	201	4	2%	2%	1	1	1	2	3	1	1								
21	Italy	755	3	1%		1	1	1		1	1						1	1		1
22	Belgium	499	3	1%	1%	1	2			1	1									
23	United Nations	233	2	1%	1%			1	1	1				1	1					2
24	Poland	493	2	1%					2		2									
25	Israel	232	2	1%	1%		1	1				1	1							
26	India	299	2	1%	1%			1	1	1		1								
27	Hungary	290	2	1%	1%				2		2								1	2
28	Greece	318	2	1%	1%	2					1	2							1	
29	Germany, West	890	2	1%			1	1		2					1		2			1
30	ICJ Option Clause	62	2	1%	3%		1	1												
31	All Others (11)	2015	11	4%	1%	2	1	2	6	3	5	1	1	1	2	3	2	2		4
	GROUPS																			
32	African Group	968							1		1	1		1	3	2		1	1	1
33	Arab Group	937	1	1%				1	2											
34	Asian Group	1937	3					5	10	13	5	6		1	1	1		2		3
35	Commonwealth	1641	25	10%	2%	6	4	5	10	13	5	6		1	1	1		2		3
36	Communist Group	3310	69	28%	2%	22	11	20	16	19	12	31	4	3					5	6
37	Latin America	1674	1						1					1						10
38	Western Europe	5906	101	41%	2%	25	32	25	19	26	23	50	1	1	1	8	4	7	6	19
39	Intl Organs	1399	19	8%	1%	4	3	4	8	1	2		15	1	2		2	4		
	TOTALS																			
40	All Data	18085	245	100%		61	59	63	62	67	46	98	27	7	8	17	9	15	13	42
41	UNTS Only		162																	
	COMPARISONS																			
42	Party Total					25%	24%	26%	25%	27%	19%	40%	11%	3%	5%	10%	6%	9%	8%	26%
43	Group Total					22%	25%	27%	26%	24%	26%	32%	10%	8%	4%	14%	6%	8%	17%	32%
44	World Total					18%	23%	29%	29%	22%	25%	25%	20%	7%	8%	12%	6%	7%	12%	100%

Table 67

TREATY PROFILE OF FRANCE

Partners	Partner's World Total	Dyads Absolutes	Dyads Ratios Self	Dyads Ratios Other	Time 1946-1950	Time 1951-1955	Time 1956-1960	Time 1961-1965	Admin & Dipl	Social Coop	Econ Coop	Aid	Milit	UN	Spec Ag's	Intl Court	Arbitration	Other	Self-Registered
(1)	(2)	(3)	(4)	(5)	(6)	(7)	(8)	(9)	(10)	(11)	(12)	(13)	(14)	(15)	(16)	(17)	(18)	(19)	(20)
TOP THIRTY																			
1 USA (United States)	2599	79	8%	3%	40	14	19	6	8	12	17	14	28	5	9	2	1	6	
2 Spain	437	69	7%	16%	2	10	24	33	12	39	17	1					1		4
3 Italy	755	62	6%	8%	13	19	20	10	13	28	15		6		1	2		5	2
4 Germany, West	890	56	5%	6%	5	11	19	21	30	16	6		4			1	1		2
5 Switzerland	426	50	5%	12%	10	8	16	16	24	14	10	1	1						1
6 UK Great Britain	981	49	5%	5%	21	11	5	12	15	17	12		5	1	5	4	1	9	
7 Belgium	499	42	4%	8%	15	11	10	6	16	13	7	1	5			2	1	5	1
8 Vietnam, South	106	38	4%	36%	4	19	9	6	11	14	6	2	5		1				1
9 Algeria	52	25	2%	48%				25	6	8	1	10			1				7
10 Sweden	483	24	2%	5%	12	8	3	1	4	4	16				1	2			
11 Netherlands	548	22	2%	4%	12	7	3		4	5	10		3		1		1	8	
12 Canada	310	19	2%	6%	7	4	2	6	1	7	5		6		2			1	
13 Greece	318	18	2%	6%	4	9	3	2		4	10	2	2		1			14	
14 Cameroon	52	18	2%	35%			11	7	6	5	5		2		1				11
15 USSR (Soviet Union)	1356	16	2%	1%	1	3	9	3	3	5	11		1					4	
16 Norway	461	16	1%	3%	7	5	2	2	3	3	9		1		1				
17 Luxembourg	136	15	1%	11%	3	2	3	7	4	8	2		1		1		1		2
18 Israel	232	15	1%	6%		5	6	4	5	4	5					1		2	
19 Tunisia	97	14	1%	14%		2	3	9	4	8	2								1
20 Poland	493	14	1%	3%	6	1	3	4	1	7	4	1	1						2
21 Morocco	94	14	1%	15%			8	6	5	8	1	1			1				6
22 Senegal	40	13	1%	33%			2	11	6	4	3				1		1		1
23 Chad	24	13	1%	54%		4	1	11	4	4	1	2	2						4
24 Taiwan	172	12	1%	7%	7	4	2		2	5	4	1	1		3	1	1	1	
25 Japan	443	11	1%	2%				5	4	2	4	1							1
26 Czechoslovakia	393	11	1%	3%	6		1	5	1	3	4	1	2		1				2
27 Turkey	298	10	1%	3%	4	3		2		4	6								
28 Togo	28	10	1%	36%				10	4	4	2	2	1						8
29 Monaco	36	10	1%	28%	4	1		5	3	1	5								2
30 Mauritania	18	10	1%	56%			1	9	5	4		1	1						1
31 All Others (84)	9177	258	25%	3%	42	37	56	123	76	89	66	19	8	7	15	8	10	4	17
GROUPS																			
32 African Group	968	129	12%	13%	3	3	30	99	54	36	27	6	6		4		3	1	28
33 Arab Group	937	63	6%	7%	3	28	13	44	18	26	8	11		1	4	1	1	1	17
34 Asian Group	1937	80	8%	4%	17	20	18	17	27	27	15	4	7		2	1	1	1	3
35 Commonwealth	1641	82	8%	5%	34	7	7	21	18	30	19		15		9	4	2	10	
36 Communist Group	3310	60	6%	2%	15	6	16	23	4	24	27	2	3			1			6
37 Latin America	1674	44	4%	3%	6	11	9	18	6	17	16	5			2	1	2		3
38 Western Europe	5906	430	42%	7%	102	98	114	116	118	157	124	5	26		9	7	10	37	17
39 Intl Organs	1399	29	3%	2%	5	8	7	9	13	6		10		6	1	3	1		1
TOTALS																			
40 All Data	21954	1033	100%		225	198	243	367	277	346	266	58	86	13	44	23	22	59	77
41 UNTS Only		409																	
COMPARISONS																			
42 Party Total					22%	19%	24%	36%	27%	33%	26%	6%	8%	3%	11%	6%	5%	14%	19%
43 Group Total					22%	25%	27%	26%	24%	26%	32%	10%	8%	4%	14%	6%	8%	17%	32%
44 World Total					18%	23%	29%	29%	22%	25%	25%	20%	7%	8%	12%	6%	7%	12%	100%

116 • Table 68

TREATY PROFILE OF GABON

Partners (1)	Partner's World Total (2)	Dyads Absolutes (3)	Ratios Self (4)	Ratios Other (5)	Time 1946-1950 (6)	Time 1951-1955 (7)	Time 1956-1960 (8)	Time 1961-1965 (9)	Topics Admin & Dipl (10)	Topics Social Coop (11)	Topics Econ Coop (12)	Topics Aid (13)	Topics Milit (14)	Institutions UN (15)	Institutions Spec Ag's (16)	Institutions Intl Court (17)	Institutions Arbitration (18)	Institutions Other (19)	Self-Registered (20)
TOP THIRTY																			
1 France	1033	6	27%	1%			2	4	4	1	1								
2 Germany, West	890	4	18%					4		1	1	2							
3 Israel	232	3	14%	1%				3	2		1	1							
4 USA (United States)	2599	2	9%				1	1				2							
5 IBRD (World Bank)	452	2	9%					1				2							
6 WHO (World Health)	187	1	5%	1%				1				1		1	1				
7 UN Special Fund	113	1	5%	1%				1	1					1	1	1		1	
8 United Nations	233	1	5%					1						1					
9 UNICEF (Children)	122	1	5%	1%			1		1			1		1					
10 Accept UN Charter	68	1	5%	1%				1											
11																			
12																			
13																			
14																			
15																			
16																			
17																			
18																			
19																			
20																			
21																			
22																			
23																			
24																			
25																			
26																			
27																			
28																			
29																			
30																			
31 All Others (0)																			
GROUPS																			
32 African Group	968																		
33 Arab Group	937																		
34 Asian Group	1937																		
35 Commonwealth	1641																		
36 Communist Group	3310																		
37 Latin America	1674																		
38 Western Europe	5906	10	45%				2	8	4	2	2	2							
39 Intl Organs	1399	6	27%				1	5	1			5		3	1	1		1	
TOTALS																			
40 All Data		22	100%				4	18	8	2	3	9		4	1	1		1	
41 UNTS Only		12																		
COMPARISONS																			
42 Party Total					1%	5%	18%	82%	36%	9%	14%	41%		33%	8%	8%	15%	8%	1%
43 Group Total					1%	5%	18%	75%	22%	21%	18%	35%	4%	19%	13%	10%		4%	1%
44 World Total					18%	23%	29%	29%	22%	25%	25%	20%	7%	8%	12%	6%	7%	12%	100%

Table 69 • 117

TREATY PROFILE OF GAMBIA

Partners (1)	Partner's World Total (2)	Dyads Absolutes (3)	Ratios Self (4)	Ratios Other (5)	Time 1946-1950 (6)	Time 1951-1955 (7)	Time 1956-1960 (8)	Time 1961-1965 (9)	Admin & Dipl (10)	Social Coop (11)	Econ Coop (12)	Aid (13)	Milit (14)	UN (15)	Spec Ag's (16)	Intl Court (17)	Arbitration (18)	Other (19)	Self-Registered (20)
TOP THIRTY																			
1 Norway	461	2	29%			1		1	1										
2 UK Great Britain	981	1	14%	1%				1	1		1								
3 UN Special Fund	113	1	14%	1%				1	1										
4 UNICEF (Children)	122	1	14%					1	1										
5 Italy	755	1	14%					1	1										
6 Accept UN Charter	68	1	14%	1%				1	1					1					
7																			
8																			
9																			
10																			
11																			
12																			
13																			
14																			
15																			
16																			
17																			
18																			
19																			
20																			
21																			
22																			
23																			
24																			
25																			
26																			
27																			
28																			
29																			
30																			
31 All Others (0)																			
GROUPS																			
32 African Group	968																		
33 Arab Group	937																		
34 Asian Group	1937																		
35 Commonwealth	1641	1	14%					1	1										
36 Communist Group	3310																		
37 Latin America	1674																		
38 Western Europe	5906	3	43%			1		2	2		1								
39 Intl Organs	1399	2	29%					2	2		1			1					
TOTALS																			
40 All Data	2500	7	100%			1		6	6		1			1					
41 UNTS Only		4																		
COMPARISONS																			
42 Party Total					1%	14%	18%	86%	86%	21%	14%	35%	4%	25%	13%	10%	15%	4%	1%
43 Group Total					18%	5%	18%	75%	22%	25%	18%	35%	4%	19%	13%	10%	15%	4%	1%
44 World Total					18%	23%	29%	29%	22%	25%	25%	20%	7%	8%	12%	6%	7%	12%	100%

TREATY PROFILE OF GERMANY, EAST

Table 70

	Partners (1)	Partner's World Total (2)	Absolutes (3)	Dyads Ratios Self (4)	Dyads Ratios Other (5)	Time 1946 1950 (6)	Time 1951 1955 (7)	Time 1956 1960 (8)	Time 1961 1965 (9)	Admin & Dipl (10)	Social Coop (11)	Econ Coop (12)	Aid (13)	Milit (14)	UN (15)	Spec Ag's (16)	Intl Court (17)	Arbi- tration (18)	Other (19)	Self- Regis- tered (20)
	TOP THIRTY																			
1	USSR (Soviet Union)	1356	75	13%	6%	7	23	32	13	19	22	15	12	7	1				3	
2	Poland	493	71	13%	14%	7	24	28	12	20	35	14	2						3	
3	China People's Rep	766	59	11%	8%	1	29	17	12	6	31	22		1						
4	Czechoslovakia	393	56	10%	14%	10	17	23	6	13	24	18	1						2	
5	Hungary	290	42	8%	14%	5	13	18	6	5	19	17	1							
6	Bulgaria	236	39	7%	17%	3	16	13	7	4	17	17	1							
7	Romania	251	30	5%	12%	3	10	9	7	5	17	7	1							
8	Albania	125	19	3%	15%	4	6	10	3	4	7	7	4							
9	Yugoslavia	525	16	3%	3%			5	11	4	6	6								
10	United Arab Rep	232	15	3%	6%		2	9	4	3	4	5	3							
11	Mongolia	119	15	3%	13%		3	8	4	4	7	3	2							
12	Korea, North	99	13	2%	13%		4	7	2	1	7	3	2							
13	Cuba	111	12	2%	11%			2	10	1	5	2	4							
14	Syria	84	11	2%	13%		2	3	6	1	4	5	1							
15	Vietnam, North	81	10	2%	12%			8	2	1	4	3	1							
16	Guinea	75	10	2%	13%			5	5	1	3	6								
17	Ghana	81	9	2%	11%			1	8	1	3	3	2							
18	Mali	54	8	1%	15%				8	1	3	1	3							
19	India	299	7	1%	2%		2	2	3	1	2	4	1							
20	Indonesia	126	5	1%	4%			1	4		2	3								
21	Finland	245	5	1%	2%	1		4				5								
22	Tunisia	97	4	1%	4%				4		1	3								
23	Iraq	96	4	1%	4%			3	1	2	1	1								
24	Cambodia	55	4	1%	7%			3	1		1	2	1							
25	Tanzania	45	3	1%	7%				3				2							
26	Morocco	94	3	1%	3%			1	2	1		3								
27	Sweden	483	2		5%	2						2								
28	Sudan	37	2		5%		1	1		1	1	1								
29	Burma	102	2		2%			1	1	1	1									
30	Yemen	35	1		3%				1			1								
31	All Others (4)	273	4	1%	1%				4		1	3	1							
	GROUPS																			
32	African Group	368	31	6%	3%		5	6	25	4	9	10	8							
33	Arab Group	937	41	7%	4%		5	17	19	7	11	19	4							
34	Asian Group	937	19	3%	1%		2	7	10	1	6	10	2							
35	Commonwealth	1641																		
36	Communist Group	3310	429	77%	13%	37	145	173	74	82	190	123	26	8	1				8	
37	Latin America	1674	12	2%	1%			2	10	1	5	2	4							
38	Western Europe	5906	8	1%		3		4	1			8								
39	Intl Organs	1399													1					
40	**TOTALS** All Data	7358	556	100%		40	152	214	150	99	227	178	44	8	1				8	
41	UNTS Only		46																	
	COMPARISONS																			
42	Party Total					7%	27%	38%	27%	18%	41%	32%	8%	1%	2%				17%	
43	Group Total					16%	17%	38%	29%	20%	32%	32%	13%	2%	4%	4%	6%	3%	17%	33%
44	World Total					18%	23%	29%	29%	22%	25%	25%	20%	7%	8%	12%	6%	7%	12%	100%

TREATY PROFILE OF GERMANY, WEST

Table 71

Partners (1)	Partner's World Total (2)	Dyads Absolutes (3)	Ratios Self (4)	Ratios Other (5)	Time 1946-1950 (6)	Time 1951-1955 (7)	Time 1956-1960 (8)	Time 1961-1965 (9)	Topics Admin & Dipl (10)	Topics Social Coop (11)	Topics Econ Coop (12)	Topics Aid (13)	Topics Milit (14)	Institutions UN (15)	Institutions Spec Ag's (16)	Institutions Intl Court (17)	Institutions Arbitration (18)	Institutions Other (19)	Self-Registered (20)
TOP THIRTY																			
1 USA (United States)	2599	67	8%	3%	1	34	24	8	11	13	11	8	24	3	6	2	2	16	
2 France	1033	56	6%	5%	5	11	19	21	30	16	6		4		1	1	1		
3 Netherlands	548	43	5%	8%	1	12	17	13	20	13	3		7		2	1	1	8	
4 Belgium	499	43	5%	9%		20	14	9	24	11	4		4		1	1	2	4	
5 Austria	445	41	5%	9%		23	10	8	25	11	5								
6 UK Great Britain	981	33	4%	3%	1	7	16	9	9	5	7	1	11	1	5	3	3	17	
7 Switzerland	426	33	4%	8%	2	17	8	6	9	11	13				1		1		
8 Spain	437	30	3%	7%		4	22	4	1	14	15								
9 Italy	755	25	3%	3%		10	6	9	5	10	7	1	2					6	
10 Turkey	298	24	3%	8%	4	7	7	6	4	6	10	4							
11 Denmark	380	22	2%	6%	1	4	9	8	10	6	4		2		2	1	1	2	
12 Sweden	483	20	2%	4%	5	5	9	1	5	3	10		2		1				
13 Greece	318	20	2%	6%	2	4	6	8	3	7	9		1		1			2	
14 Norway	461	19	2%	4%	3	6	6	4	4	3	6	1	5		1			1	
15 Luxembourg	136	18	2%	13%		2	7	9	8	9	1								
16 Yugoslavia	525	16	2%	3%		5	9	2	4	3	8	1			1			1	
17 Portugal	131	12	1%	9%	1	1	5	5	2	4	6				1		1		
18 Japan	443	12	1%	3%		4	5	3	5	3	4				1		1	1	
19 Brazil	195	12	1%	6%	1	3	2	6	3	2	5	2							
20 Thailand	132	10	1%	8%			1	9		3	1	6						1	
21 Philippines	236	10	1%	4%		1	9		4	1	3	2			2		1		
22 Chile	119	10	1%	8%		3	3	4	2	3	5								
23 Cameroon	52	10	1%	19%			3	7	4	2	2	3	3		1				
24 Australia	201	10	1%	5%		2	4	4	2	5	2		1		1	1	1		
25 Ecuador	97	9	1%	9%		4	1	4	2	1	5	1							
26 Colombia	112	9	1%	8%		1	3	5		1	6	2							
27 Ireland	103	8	1%	8%	1	3	2	2	5	2	5		1		1		1		
28 Iran	170	8	1%	5%		1	4	3	1	2	3	4							
29 Guinea	75	8	1%	11%			1	7		2	2	3							
30 USSR (Soviet Union)	1356	7	1%	1%		1	6		3	2	2								
31 All Others (74)	7345	245	28%	3%	4	34	57	150	27	48	95	68	7	1	7	2	7	4	
GROUPS																			
32 African Group	968	110	12%	11%		6	11	99	1	24	34	48	3		2	2	2		
33 Arab Group	937	33	4%	4%			10	17	4	6	14	8	1		5		3		
34 Asian Group	1937	67	8%	3%	1	8	19	39	6	15	22	22	2		7	4	5	1	
35 Commonwealth	1641	56	6%	3%	1	14	27	14	15	12	13	1	15	1				19	
36 Communist Group	3310	19	2%	1%	1	1	12	5	5	3	11								
37 Latin America	1674	73	8%	4%	1	23	18	31	12	15	34	12			1		1		
38 Western Europe	5906	431	48%	4%	27	132	151	121	157	128	111	7	28		14	4	12	23	
39 Intl Organs	1399	2		7%				2	1		1								
TOTALS																			
40 All Data	21091	890	100%		32	229	286	343	223	222	264	107	74	5	37	14	28	61	
41 UNTS Only		286																	
COMPARISONS																			
42 Party Total					4%	26%	32%	39%	25%	25%	30%	12%	8%	2%	13%	5%	10%	21%	
43 Group Total					22%	25%	27%	26%	24%	26%	32%	10%	8%	4%	14%	6%	8%	17%	32%
44 World Total					18%	23%	29%	29%	22%	25%	25%	20%	7%	8%	12%	6%	7%	12%	100%

120 • Table 72

TREATY PROFILE OF GHANA

Partners (1)	Partner's World Total (2)	Dyads Absolutes (3)	Ratios Self (4)	Ratios Other (5)	Time 1946 1950 (6)	Time 1951 1955 (7)	Time 1956 1960 (8)	Time 1961 1965 (9)	Topics Admin & Dipl (10)	Topics Social Coop (11)	Topics Econ Coop (12)	Topics Aid (13)	Topics Milit (14)	Institutions UN (15)	Institutions Spec Ag's (16)	Institutions Intl Court (17)	Institutions Arbitration (18)	Institutions Other (19)	Self-Registered (20)
TOP THIRTY																			
1 USSR (Soviet Union)	1356	17	21%	1%			5	12	3	2	9	3							
2 Germany, East	556	9	11%	2%			1	8	1	3	3	2							
3 China People's Rep	766	9	11%	1%				9	1	3	2	1	2						
4 USA (United States)	2599	7	9%				4	3	2	2	1	2	1	1					2
5 UK Great Britain	981	5	6%	1%			5		3	1					1	1	1		
6 Germany, West	890	5	6%	1%			2	3		2	1	2							
7 Poland	493	3	4%	1%				3		2		1							
8 Czechoslovakia	393	3	4%	1%			2	1		1	1	1				1		1	
9 Switzerland	426	2	2%					2								1		2	
10 United Nations	233	2	2%	1%			1	1				2		1					
11 Romania	251	2	2%	1%				2		2		1							
12 Japan	443	2	2%					2		1		2							
13 Israel	232	2	2%	1%				2											
14 United Arab Rep	232	1	1%	1%			1			1					1	1		1	
15 Tunisia	97	1	1%	1%				1		1					1			1	
16 WHO (World Health)	187	1	1%	1%			1					1		1					
17 UN Special Fund	113	1	1%	1%			1					1		1					
18 UNICEF (Children)	122	1	1%	1%			1					1			1			1	
19 IBRD (World Bank)	452	1	1%					1							1	1			
20 Netherlands	548	1	1%				1			1									
21 Mali	54	1	1%	2%				1		1									
22 Malawi	11	1	1%	9%				1		1									
23 Italy	755	1	1%					1		1									
24 Hungary	290	1	1%					1	1										
25 Canada	310	1	1%				1						1						
26 Accept UN Charter	68	1	1%	1%			1							1					
27																			
28																			
29																			
30																			
31 All Others (0)																			
GROUPS																			
32 African Group	968	2	2%					2		2					2		1		
33 Arab Group	937	2	2%				1	1		2					2		2		
34 Asian Group	1937																		
35 Commonwealth	1641	6	7%				5	1	3	1			2		1		1		2
36 Communist Group	3310	44	54%	1%			8	36	5	15	14	8	2		1				
37 Latin America	1674																		
38 Western Europe	5906	9	11%				3	6		5	2	2			2	1	1		
39 Intl Organs	1399	6	7%				4	2				6		3	1		3	1	
TOTALS																			
40 All Data	12858	81	100%				26	55	11	28	17	21	4	5	9	2	9	1	2
41 UNTS Only		41																	
COMPARISONS																			
42 Party Total					1%	5%	32%	68%	14%	35%	21%	26%	5%	12%	22%	5%	22%	2%	5%
43 Group Total					1%	5%	18%	75%	22%	21%	18%	35%	4%	19%	13%	10%	15%	4%	1%
44 World Total					18%	23%	29%	29%	22%	25%	25%	20%	7%	8%	12%	6%	7%	12%	100%

TREATY PROFILE OF GREECE

Table 73

Partners (1)	Partner's World Total (2)	Dyads Absolutes (3)	Ratios Self (4)	Ratios Other (5)	Time 1946-1950 (6)	Time 1951-1955 (7)	Time 1956-1960 (8)	Time 1961-1965 (9)	Admin & Dipl (10)	Social Coop (11)	Econ Coop (12)	Aid (13)	Milit (14)	UN (15)	Spec Ag's (16)	Intl Court (17)	Arbitration (18)	Other (19)	Self-Registered (20)
TOP THIRTY																			
1 USA (United States)	2599	52	16%	2%	18	15	11	8	3	6	10	18	15	2	6	2		6	9
2 UK (Great Britain)	981	22	7%	2%	9	8	2	3	8	3	7		4		1	2	2	6	3
3 Germany, West	890	20	6%	2%	2	4	6	8	3	7	9		1		1			5	8
4 Yugoslavia	525	18	6%	3%		3	13	2	8	7	3				1	1	2	8	6
5 France	1033	18	6%	2%	4	9	3	2		4	10	2	2		1	1		14	14
6 Italy	755	14	4%	2%	4	6	1	2	3	4	6		1		3		1	11	7
7 Sweden	483	13	4%	3%	4	7	1	1		2	11				1		1	3	7
8 Netherlands	548	10	3%	2%	1	8	1		2	2	6				1	1		8	4
9 Denmark	380	9	3%	2%	3	3	1	2		1	8				1			2	6
10 Belgium	499	9	3%	2%	3	5	1		1	3	5				1		1	4	4
11 Turkey	298	8	3%	3%	3	4			2	2	4				1		1	5	6
12 Norway	461	7	2%	2%		2	1	1	1	1	2	1			1		1	1	2
13 Bulgaria	236	7	2%	3%		2	1	4	1	4	4							1	2
14 USSR (Soviet Union)	1356	6	2%	1%	3	3	1	2	1	2	2								3
15 Spain	437	6	2%	1%		4	2			1	6							1	3
16 Czechoslovakia	393	6	2%	2%	4	2				1	5		1					3	6
17 Austria	445	6	2%	1%	1	3	1	2	2		3							3	3
18 Australia	201	6	2%	3%	2	3	1		3	1	1	1			1			4	1
19 United Arab Rep	232	5	2%	2%	2	2		1		2	2		1		1		1	2	4
20 Romania	251	5	2%	2%			2	3		1	3							2	5
21 Poland	493	5	2%	1%		2	2	1		1	4							2	5
22 Ethiopia	98	5	2%	5%		2	1	2		2	3								3
23 Switzerland	426	4	1%	1%	2	1		1	1	1	3				1		1		
24 United Nations	233	4	1%	2%		1	1	2	2	2		2				1	2	2	4
25 Lebanon	75	4	1%	5%	4				1		3								
26 Japan	443	4	1%	1%		1	1	2	2	1	1			1	1			2	2
27 Hungary	290	4	1%	1%		2		2	1		3		1					1	2
28 Canada	310	4	1%	1%	1		2	1	2		1		1						4
29 South Africa	120	3	1%	3%	1	1		1			2							1	2
30 Portugal	131	3	1%	2%	2	1					3							1	
31 All Others (22)	3121	31	10%	1%	7	6	9	9	5	6	16	3	1	3	6	2	2	5	16
TOTALS																			
40 All Data	18743	318	100%		82	110	65	61	49	66	147	27	29	7	32	9	17	94	
41 UNTS Only		277																	147
GROUPS																			
32 African Group	968	6	2%	1%	7	2	1	3	2	2	4	1			1		1	6	6
33 Arab Group	937	14	4%	1%	2	3	2	2	2	5	5		1		3	1	1	5	12
34 Asian Group	1937	9	3%		2	1	4	2	2	2	4		1		2	1		8	5
35 Commonwealth	1641	36	11%	2%	13	12	5	6		4	11	1	6	1	2	2	2	5	6
36 Communist Group	3310	33	10%	1%	4	11	6	12	14	9	21		2		1			9	25
37 Latin America	1674	3	1%		1		2		1		3								2
38 Western Europe	5906	134	42%	2%	35	58	19	22	17	29	81	3	4	1	15	1	8	57	74
39 Intl Organs	1399	7	2%	1%	2	2	1	2	1	2	3	4		3	1	1	3		
COMPARISONS																			
42 Party Total					26%	35%	20%	19%	15%	21%	46%	8%	9%	3%	12%	3%	6%	34%	53%
43 Group Total					22%	25%	27%	26%	24%	26%	32%	10%	8%	4%	14%	6%	8%	17%	32%
44 World Total					18%	23%	29%	29%	22%	25%	25%	20%	7%	8%	12%	6%	7%	12%	100%

122 • Table 74

TREATY PROFILE OF GUATEMALA

			Dyads	Ratios		Time				Topics						Institutions				Self-Registered
Partners	Partner's World Total	Absolutes	Self	Other	1946 1950	1951 1955	1956 1960	1961 1965	Admin & Dipl	Social Coop	Econ Coop	Aid	Milit	UN	Spec Ag's	Intl Court	Arbi- tration	Other	
(1)	(2)	(3)	(4)	(5)	(6)	(7)	(8)	(9)	(10)	(11)	(12)	(13)	(14)	(15)	(16)	(17)	(18)	(19)	(20)
TOP THIRTY																			
1 USA (United States)	2599	23	46%	1%	6	8	4	5	2	2	4	7	8	2		1	1		1
2 Spain	437	3	6%	1%		1		2	1	1	1							1	
3 WHO (World Health)	187	3	6%	2%	1	2				3		2		2	1				
4 UNICEF (Children)	122	2	4%	2%	1	1								2					
5 Norway	461	2	4%				1	2	2		1								
6 Switzerland	426	1	2%				1												
7 UN Special Fund	113	1	2%	1%		1						1		1	1	1			
8 United Nations	233	1	2%			1						1		1					
9 ILO (Labor Org)	59	1	2%	2%															
10 IBRD (World Bank)	452	1	2%									1							
11 Mexico	138	1	2%	1%	1			1		1									1
12 Italy	755	1	2%					1	1	1						1			
13 Israel	232	1	2%	2%			1				1							1	
14 Honduras	43	1	2%		1	1				1	1						1		1
15 France	1033	1	2%	1%				1			1								
16 El Salvador	70	1	2%		1	1			1		1							1	
17 Denmark	380	1	2%	2%			1												
18 Costa Rica	51	1	2%	1%				1											
19 Taiwan	172	1	2%													1			1
20 Austria	445	1	2%																
21 Argentina	164	1	2%	1%															
22 ICJ Option Clause	62	1	2%	2%	1														
31 All Others (0)																			
GROUPS																			
32 African Group	968																		
33 Arab Group	937																		
34 Asian Group	1937	1	2%					1			1								
35 Commonwealth	1641																		
36 Communist Group	3310																		
37 Latin America	1674	5	10%		3	2	1	2		2	3					1	2	3	3
38 Western Europe	5906	10	20%		2	2	1	4	4	2	4				2	1	1	1	2
39 Intl Organs	1399	9	18%	1%		6	1			3		6		6	2				
TOTALS																			
40 All Data	8634	50	100%		12	18	7	13	7	10	12	13	8	8	2	4	4	4	6
41 UNTS Only		42																		
COMPARISONS																			
42 Party Total					24%	36%	14%	26%	14%	20%	24%	26%	16%	19%	5%	10%	10%	10%	14%
43 Group Total					18%	27%	24%	31%	16%	25%	18%	31%	9%	7%	10%	5%	6%	7%	6%
44 World Total					18%	23%	29%	29%	22%	25%	25%	20%	7%	8%	12%	6%	7%	12%	100%

TREATY PROFILE OF GUINEA

Table 75 • 123

			Dyads			Time				Topics							Institutions			Self-Registered
Partners	Partner's World Total	Absolutes	Ratios Self	Other	1946 1950	1951 1955	1956 1960	1961 1965	Admin & Dipl	Social Coop	Econ Coop	Aid	Milit	UN	Spec Ag's	Intl Court	Arbitration	Other	
(1)	(2)	(3)	(4)	(5)	(6)	(7)	(8)	(9)	(10)	(11)	(12)	(13)	(14)	(15)	(16)	(17)	(18)	(19)	(20)
TOP THIRTY																			
1 USSR (Soviet Union)	1356	14	19%	1%			10	4	2	2	2	8							
2 Germany, East	556	10	13%	2%			5	5	1	3	6								
3 China People's Rep	766	10	13%	1%			4	6	1	6	2	1							
4 USA (United States)	2599	9	12%				2	7		2	1	5		1					
5 Germany, West	890	8	11%	1%			1	7		2	3	3	1						
6 Italy	755	4	5%	1%				4		2	1	1							
7 France	1033	4	5%					4		2	1	1							
8 Switzerland	426	2	3%					2		1	1				1		1		
9 Czechoslovakia	393	2	3%	1%			1	1		2					1				
10 UK Great Britain	981	1	1%				1				1							2	
11 Sweden	483	1	1%				1			1					1	1	1		
12 WHO (World Health)	187	1	1%	1%			1					1		1	1				
13 UN Special Fund	113	1	1%	1%			1					1		1		1	1		
14 United Nations	233	1	1%				1					1		1	1		2		
15 UNICEF (Children)	122	1	1%	1%			1					1							
16 Poland	493	1	1%					1		1					1	1	1		
17 Norway	461	1	1%					1		1						1			
18 Netherlands	548	1	1%				1			1							2		
19 Ivory Coast	32	1	1%	3%					1								1		
20 Hungary	290	1	1%				1												
21 Accept UN Charter	68	1	1%	1%										1					
22																				
23																				
24																				
25																				
26																				
27																				
28																				
29																				
30																				
31 All Others (0)																				
GROUPS																			
32 African Group	968	1	1%					1		1						1			
33 Arab Group	937																		
34 Asian Group	1937																		
35 Commonwealth	1641	1	1%				1				1								
36 Communist Group	3310	38	51%	1%			21	17	4	14	10	10			1		1	2	
37 Latin America	1674																			
38 Western Europe	5906	21	28%				2	19		10	6	5			4	3	3		
39 Intl Organs	1399	4	5%				3	1				4		3	1	1	3		
TOTALS																				
40 All Data	12785	75	100%				30	45	5	27	18	24	1	5	7	4	7	2	
41 UNTS Only		23																		
COMPARISONS																				
42 Party Total					1%	5%	40%	60%	7%	36%	24%	32%	1%	22%	30%	17%	30%	9%	
43 Group Total					18%	23%	18%	75%	22%	21%	18%	35%	4%	19%	13%	10%	15%	4%	1%
44 World Total					18%		29%	29%	22%	25%	25%	20%	7%	8%	12%	6%	7%	12%	100%

TREATY PROFILE OF HAGUE PRIVATE IL

	Partners (1)	Partner's World Total (2)	Dyads Absolutes (3)	Ratios Self (4)	Ratios Other (5)	Time 1946-1950 (6)	Time 1951-1955 (7)	Time 1956-1960 (8)	Time 1961-1965 (9)	Topics Admin & Dipl (10)	Topics Social Coop (11)	Topics Econ Coop (12)	Topics Aid (13)	Topics Milit (14)	Institutions UN (15)	Institutions Spec Ag's (16)	Institutions Intl Court (17)	Institutions Arbitration (18)	Institutions Other (19)	Self-Registered (20)
	TOP THIRTY																			
1	Netherlands	548	1	100%				1		1										
2																				
3																				
4																				
5																				
6																				
7																				
8																				
9																				
10																				
11																				
12																				
13																				
14																				
15																				
16																				
17																				
18																				
19																				
20																				
21																				
22																				
23																				
24																				
25																				
26																				
27																				
28																				
29																				
30																				
31	All Others (0)																			
	GROUPS																			
32	African Group	968																		
33	Arab Group	937																		
34	Asian Group	1937																		
35	Commonwealth	1641																		
36	Communist Group	3310																		
37	Latin America	1674																		
38	Western Europe	5906	1	100%				1												
39	Intl Organs	1399																		
	TOTALS																			
40	All Data	548	1	100%				1		1										
41	UNTS Only		1																		
	COMPARISONS																			
42	Party Total									100%										
43	Group Total					12%	25%	23%	40%	19%	7%	1%	71%	1%	27%	11%	13%	15%	4%	74%
44	World Total					18%	23%	29%	29%	22%	25%	25%	20%	7%	8%	12%	6%	7%	12%	100%

TREATY PROFILE OF HAITI

Table 77 • 125

	Partners (1)	Partner's World Total (2)	Dyads Absolutes (3)	Ratios Self (4)	Ratios Other (5)	Time 1946 1950 (6)	1951 1955 (7)	1956 1960 (8)	1961 1965 (9)	Topics Admin & Dipl (10)	Social Coop (11)	Econ Coop (12)	Aid (13)	Milit (14)	Institutions UN (15)	Spec Ag's (16)	Intl Court (17)	Arbitration (18)	Other (19)	Self-Registered (20)
	TOP THIRTY																			
1	USA (United States)	2599	29	71%	1%	11	10	7	1	5	3	3	10	8	1	1			1	
2	WHO (World Health)	187	2	5%	1%	2					1		1		1	1	1		1	
3	France	1033	2	5%			1		1		2									
4	UN Special Fund	113	1	2%	1%				1				1		1	1				
5	United Nations	233	1	2%		1			1				1		1		1	2		
6	UNICEF (Children)	122	1	2%	1%				1				1							
7	IDA (Devel Assoc)	82	1	2%	1%			1					1							
8	IBRD (World Bank)	452	1	2%				1		1										
9	Norway	461	1	2%			1													
10	Japan	443	1	2%								1								
11	Italy	755	1	2%								1								
12-30																				
31	All Others (0)																			
	GROUPS																			
32	African Group	968																		
33	Arab Group	937																		
34	Asian Group	1937																		
35	Commonwealth	1641																		
36	Communist Group	3310																		
37	Latin America	1674																		
38	Western Europe	5906	4	10%		3	2	1		1	2	1								
39	Intl Organs	1399	7	17%	1%				2 3		1		6		2	2	2	3	1	
	TOTALS																			
40	All Data	6480	41	100%		14	12	9	6	6	6	5	16	8	3	3	2	3	2	
41	UNTS Only		38																	
	COMPARISONS																			
42	Party Total					34%	29%	22%	15%	15%	15%	12%	39%	20%	8%	8%	5%	8%	5%	6%
43	Group Total					18%	27%	24%	31%	16%	25%	18%	31%	9%	7%	10%	5%	6%	7%	6%
44	World Total					18%	23%	29%	29%	22%	25%	25%	20%	7%	8%	12%	6%	7%	12%	100%

TREATY PROFILE OF HONDURAS

Partners (1)	Partner's World Total (2)	Dyads Absolutes (3)	Ratios Self (4)	Ratios Other (5)	Time 1946-1950 (6)	Time 1951-1955 (7)	Time 1956-1960 (8)	Time 1961-1965 (9)	Admin & Dipl (10)	Social Coop (11)	Econ Coop (12)	Aid (13)	Milit (14)	UN (15)	Spec Ag's (16)	Intl Court (17)	Arbitration (18)	Other (19)	Self-Registered (20)
TOP THIRTY																			
1 USA (United States)	2599	21	49%	1%	4	10	3	4	1	3	3	7	7	1	1	1			
2 IBRD (World Bank)	452	5	12%	1%		1	3	1				5			1		1	1	
3 IDA (Devel Assoc)	82	2	5%	2%				2				2			2				
4 UK Great Britain	981	1	2%					1	1										
5 Spain	437	1	2%				1			1									
6 WHO (World Health)	187	1	2%	1%		1						1		1		1			
7 UN Special Fund	113	1	2%	1%				1				1		1					
8 UNICEF (Children)	122	1	2%	1%	1				1										
9 Norway	461	1	2%					1	1										
10 Nicaragua	50	1	2%	2%	1				1					1					1
11 Italy	755	1	2%				1		1										
12 Israel	232	1	2%					1					1						
13 Guatemala	50	1	2%	2%			1				1							1	
14 Germany, West	890	1	2%			1			1										
15 France	1033	1	2%				1			1	1								
16 Canada	310	1	2%																
17 Argentina	164	1	2%	1%															
18 ICJ Option Clause	62	1	2%	2%	1				1							1			
19																			
20-30																			
31 All Others (0)																			
GROUPS																			
32 African Group	968																		
33 Arab Group	937																		
34 Asian Group	1937																		
35 Commonwealth	1641	2	5%				1	1	1										
36 Communist Group	3310																		
37 Latin America	1674	3	7%		1	1	2	1	1	1	1			1		1		2	1
38 Western Europe	5906	5	12%			2	1	2	1	1		1			2	3	1	1	
39 Intl Organs	1399	10	23%	1%	1		4	3				10	1	3	3	3			1
TOTALS																			
40 All Data	8980	43	100%		7	13	11	12	7	5	5	18	8	5	3	6	1	3	1
41 UNTS Only		38																		
COMPARISONS																			
42 Party Total					16%	30%	26%	28%	16%	12%	12%	42%	19%	13%	8%	16%	3%	8%	3%
43 Group Total					18%	27%	24%	31%	16%	25%	18%	31%	9%	7%	10%	5%	6%	7%	6%
44 World Total					18%	23%	29%	29%	22%	25%	25%	20%	7%	8%	12%	6%	7%	12%	100%

Table 79 • 127

TREATY PROFILE OF HUNGARY

Partners (1)	Partner's World Total (2)	Dyads Absolutes (3)	Ratios Self (4)	Ratios Other (5)	Time 1946-1950 (6)	Time 1951-1955 (7)	Time 1956-1960 (8)	Time 1961-1965 (9)	Topics Admin & Dipl (10)	Topics Social Coop (11)	Topics Econ Coop (12)	Topics Aid (13)	Topics Milit (14)	Institutions UN (15)	Institutions Spec Ag's (16)	Institutions Intl Court (17)	Institutions Arbitration (18)	Institutions Other (19)	Self-Registered (20)
TOP THIRTY																			
1 USSR (Soviet Union)	1356	60	21%	4%	21	7	24	8	15	16	14	9	6				1		6
2 Germany, East	556	42	14%	8%	5	13	18	6	5	19	17		1					3	9
3 China People's Rep	766	26	9%	3%		9	8	9	1	11	14			1					
4 Yugoslavia	525	24	8%	5%	13		5	6	4	7	7		5					7	10
5 Poland	493	18	6%	4%	6	2	9	6	4	12	2			1			4	3	2
6 Czechoslovakia	393	18	6%	5%	2	1	8	3	10	6	2			1				2	5
7 Austria	445	16	6%	4%		2	3	12	7	5	4				1		1	1	6
8 Sweden	483	8	3%	2%	5	1	1			1	7								
9 Romania	251	8	3%	3%	1	1	4	2	4	4									4
10 Bulgaria	236	7	2%	3%	1		4	2	2	5									7
11 UK Great Britain	981	5	2%	1%	2	1	2		1	1	3								
12 Netherlands	548	5	1%	1%	2	1	1	2		1	4								
13 Norway	461	4	1%	1%	1		2	1		1									
14 Greece	318	4	1%	1%	3	2		2		1	3			1				1	
15 Switzerland	426	3	1%	1%	1		1	1			3								
16 Italy	755	3	1%		1	1	1			1	2								
17 France	1033	3	1%		1	1	1				3								
18 Denmark	380	3	1%	1%	1		1	1		1	2								
19 Australia	201	3	1%	1%	2				1		2								
20 USA (United States)	2599	2	1%	2%	2				1			1	1	1	1			1	2
21 Mongolia	119	2	1%	2%			1	1	2					1				1	2
22 Iraq	96	2	1%				1	1		2	2								
23 Germany, West	890	2	1%	1%			1	1		2								1	2
24 Finland	245	2	1%			1		1		2									
25 Belgium	499	2	1%	3%			1	1											1
26 Yemen	35	1						1											
27 Turkey	298	1		1%	1				1										
28 Syria	84	1						1		1	1								
29 COMECON (Econ Aid)	5	1		20%					1										
30 South Africa	120	1			1				1										
31 All Others (13)	1745	13	4%	1%	2		4	7	4	6	3			2	1			1	7
GROUPS																			
32 African Group	968	3	1%				1	2	1	3	2							1	3
33 Arab Group	937	4	1%				1	3	1	3									3
34 Asian Group	1937	4	1%				1	3		1	4	1						1	3
35 Commonwealth	1641	10	3%	1%	5	2	3		3	2	2			3	1		1	2
36 Communist Group	3310	183	63%	6%	36	32	76	39	44	74	49	1	7	1			1	8	37
37 Latin America	1674																		
38 Western Europe	5906	57	20%	1%	14	7	13	23	7	16	34			1	2		1	3	8
39 Intl Organs	1399	2	1%		1			1	2					1					
TOTALS																			
40 All Data	17342	290	100%		72	41	100	77	64	106	96	11	13	9	3		6	21	63
41 UNTS Only		150																	
COMPARISONS																			
42 Party Total					25%	14%	34%	27%	22%	37%	33%	4%	4%	6%	2%		4%	14%	42%
43 Group Total					16%	17%	38%	29%	20%	32%	32%	13%	2%	4%	4%		3%	17%	33%
44 World Total					18%	23%	29%	29%	22%	25%	25%	20%	7%	8%	12%	6%	7%	12%	100%

128 • Table 80

TREATY PROFILE OF IAEA (ATOM ENERGY)

Partners	Partner's World Total	Abso-lutes	Dyads Ratios Self	Dyads Ratios Other	Time 1946-1950	Time 1951-1955	Time 1956-1960	Time 1961-1965	Topics Admin & Dipl	Topics Social Coop	Topics Econ Coop	Topics Aid	Topics Milit	Institutions UN	Institutions Spec Ag's	Institutions Intl Court	Institutions Arbi-tration	Institutions Other	Self-Regis-tered
(1)	(2)	(3)	(4)	(5)	(6)	(7)	(8)	(9)	(10)	(11)	(12)	(13)	(14)	(15)	(16)	(17)	(18)	(19)	(20)
TOP THIRTY																			
1 USA (United States)	2599	5	11%				2	3	1		1	3		2		1	2		4
2 Yugoslavia	525	4	9%	1%				4		2		2				2	1		4
3 Finland	245	4	9%	2%			1	3	1	1		3				1	1		4
4 United Arab Rep	232	2	5%	1%			2	2				2				2			2
5 United Nations	233	2	5%	1%			2		2					1		1			
6 Austria	445	2	5%				1	1				2							2
7 USSR (Soviet Union)	1356	1	2%				1		1			1		1			1		1
8 Uruguay	63	1	2%	2%				1				1							1
9 UK Great Britain	981	1	2%									1							1
10 Thailand	132	1	2%	1%			1		1					1					1
11 WMO (Meteorology)	6	1	2%	17%			1		1					1					
12 WHO (World Health)	187	1	2%	1%			1		1					1					1
13 UN Special Fund	113	1	2%	1%			1		1					1					
14 UNESCO (Educ/Cult)	19	1	2%	5%				1	1					1					1
15 OECD (Econ Coop)	3	1	2%	33%				1	1		1				1				1
16 IMCO (Maritime Org)	5	1	2%	20%				1	1					1					1
17 ILO (Labor Org)	59	1	2%	2%			1		1	1					1				1
18 ICAO (Civil Aviat)	23	1	2%	4%			1		1					1					1
19 FAO (Food Agri)	19	1	2%	5%			1		1					1					1
20 Pakistan	245	1	2%					1								1	1		1
21 Norway	461	1	2%					1				1				1			1
22 Morocco	94	1	2%	1%				1				1							1
23 Mexico	138	1	2%	1%				1								1	1		1
24 Japan	443	1	2%				1		1										1
25 Italy	755	1	2%				1		1										1
26 Inter-Am Nuc Energ	1	1	2%	100%				1		1						1			1
27 Congo (Zaire)	29	1	2%	3%			1					1							1
28 Canada	310	1	2%					1	1			1		1					1
29 Argentina	164	1	2%	1%				1											1
30 Subsahara Tech Com	2	1	2%	50%				1											1
31 All Others (1)	83	1	2%	1%				1											1
GROUPS																			
32 African Group	968	1	2%					1				3		1		3			1
33 Arab Group	937	3	7%				1	3		1		2				2	1		3
34 Asian Group	1937	3	7%				2	2				1				1	1		3
35 Commonwealth	1641	2	5%				1					2		1					2
36 Communist Group	3310	1	2%									1							
37 Latin America	1674	3	7%					3				3				1			3
38 Western Europe	5906	8	18%				2	6	1	2		5		1		4	2		8
39 Intl Organs	1399	13	30%	1%			10	3	13					10	2	1			8
TOTALS																			
40 All Data	9970	44	100%				19	25	15	5	1	23		14	2	16	8		38
41 UNTS Only		44																	
COMPARISONS																			
42 Party Total					12%	25%	43%	57%	34%	11%	2%	52%	1%	32%	5%	36%	18%	2%	86%
43 Group Total					18%	23%	23%	40%	19%	7%	1%	71%		27%	11%	13%	15%	4%	74%
44 World Total					18%	23%	29%	29%	22%	25%	25%	20%	7%	8%	12%	6%	7%	12%	100%

TREATY PROFILE OF IBRD (WORLD BANK)

Table 81

	Partners	Partner's World Total	Dyads Absolutes	Dyads Ratios Self	Dyads Ratios Other	Time 1946-1950	Time 1951-1955	Time 1956-1960	Time 1961-1965	Topics Admin & Dipl	Topics Social Coop	Topics Econ Coop	Topics Aid	Topics Milit	Institutions UN	Institutions Spec Ag's	Institutions Intl Court	Institutions Arbitration	Institutions Other	Self-Registered
(1)		(2)	(3)	(4)	(5)	(6)	(7)	(8)	(9)	(10)	(11)	(12)	(13)	(14)	(15)	(16)	(17)	(18)	(19)	(20)
	TOP THIRTY																			
1	India	299	31	7%	10%	3	4	15	9				31					3		31
2	Japan	443	30	7%	7%		5	16	9			1	29							30
3	Colombia	112	25	6%	22%	3	7	7	8				25			1		1		25
4	Pakistan	245	21	5%	9%		6	7	8				21		1	1	1			21
5	Peru	109	20	4%	18%		7	5	8				20							20
6	Mexico	138	17	4%	12%	4	2	3	8				17					3		17
7	UK Great Britain	981	16	4%	2%		3	5	8				16							16
8	Thailand	132	14	3%	11%	3	1	2	8				14							14
9	Brazil	195	14	3%	7%	2	1	3	8				14					1		14
10	Chile	119	13	3%	11%	2	2	4	5				13							13
11	Nicaragua	50	11	2%	22%		8	2	1				11							11
12	Finland	245	11	2%	4%	2	2	2	5				11					2		11
13	South Africa	120	10	2%	8%		5	3	2				10							10
14	Netherlands	548	10	2%	2%	8	1	1					10					2		10
15	Belgium	499	10	2%	2%	1	3	6					10					1		10
16	Austria	445	9	2%	2%		2	6	1				9							9
17	Yugoslavia	525	8	2%	2%	1	2		5				8					1		8
18	Philippines	236	8	2%	3%			1	7				8							8
19	Italy	755	8	2%	1%		3	4	1				8							8
20	Iran	170	8	2%	5%			4	4				8		1					8
21	Ethiopia	98	8	2%	8%	2	1	1	4				8							8
22	El Salvador	70	7	2%	10%	1	1	3	2				7							7
23	Costa Rica	51	7	2%	14%			3	4				7					1		7
24	Australia	201	7	2%	3%	1	3	3					7			1				7
25	Uruguay	63	6	1%	10%	1	1	2	2				6			2		1		6
26	Turkey	298	6	1%	2%	3	2		1				6					2		6
27	Norway	461	6	1%	1%		2	3	1			1	6							6
28	Iceland	99	6	1%	6%		5		1				6							6
29	France	1033	6	1%	1%	1	2	3					6							6
30	Ecuador	97	6	1%	6%		1	4	1				6						2	6
31	All Others (41)	4104	93	21%	2%	4	9	20	60	4		2	87		2	5	2	6	1	90
	GROUPS																			
32	African Group	968	23	5%	2%	2	1	4	16				23			1		2		23
33	Arab Group	937	13	3%	1%	1	1	3	8			1	12			2	1	3	1	13
34	Asian Group	1937	96	21%	5%	6	12	33	45				96		2					96
35	Commonwealth	1641	38	8%	2%	1	11	11	15				38							38
36	Communist Group	3310																		
37	Latin America	1674	149	33%	9%	13	42	41	53	1			149			3		7	3	149
38	Western Europe	5906	86	19%	1%	17	23	27	19				85			1	2	11		86
39	Intl Organs	1399	4	1%		1		1	2	3			1			2				1
	TOTALS																			
40	All Data	12941	452	100%		42	97	137	176	4		3	445		2	9	3	24	4	449
41	UNTS Only		452																	
	COMPARISONS																			
42	Party Total					9%	21%	30%	39%	1%		1%	98%	1%		2%	1%	5%	1%	99%
43	Group Total					12%	25%	23%	40%	19%	7%	1%	71%	7%	27%	11%	13%	15%	4%	74%
44	World Total					18%	23%	29%	29%	22%	25%	25%	20%	8%	8%	12%	6%	7%	12%	100%

130 • Table 82

TREATY PROFILE OF ICAO (CIVIL AVIAT)

Partners (1)	Partner's World Total (2)	Dyads Absolutes (3)	Ratios Self (4)	Ratios Other (5)	Time 1946 1950 (6)	Time 1951 1955 (7)	Time 1956 1960 (8)	Time 1961 1965 (9)	Topics Admin & Dipl (10)	Topics Social Coop (11)	Topics Econ Coop (12)	Topics Aid (13)	Topics Milit (14)	Institutions UN (15)	Institutions Spec Ag's (16)	Institutions Intl Court (17)	Institutions Arbitration (18)	Institutions Other (19)	Self-Registered (20)
TOP THIRTY																			
1 United Arab Rep	232	2	9%	1%		2			1			1		2		1	1		2
2 Thailand	132	2	9%	2%		1		1	1	1		1		1					2
3 United Nations	233	2	9%	1%	1	1			2					2		1			
4 Mexico	138	2	9%	1%		1	1		1			1		1					2
5 Iceland	99	2	9%	2%	1	1				1		1		1					2
6 Yugoslavia	525	1	4%			1						1		1					1
7 Syria	84	1	4%	1%		1								1					
8 UN Special Fund	113	1	4%	2%			1		1					1	1				1
9 IAEA (Atom Energy)	44	1	4%	2%			1		1					1					
10 Peru	109	1	4%	1%	1									1		1			1
11 Lebanon	75	1	4%	1%		1						1		1					1
12 Israel	232	1	4%																
13 Iraq	96	1	4%	1%		1						1		1					1
14 India	299	1	4%																
15 France	1033	1	4%		1				1										1
16 Ethiopia	98	1	4%	1%		1													1
17 Denmark	380	1	4%		1					1						1			1
18 Canada	310	1	4%						1					1					1
19																			
20																			
21																			
22																			
23																			
24																			
25																			
26																			
27																			
28																			
29																			
30																			
31 All Others (0)																			
GROUPS																			
32 African Group	968	1	4%			1						1							1
33 Arab Group	937	5	22%	1%		5			1			4		5		1	1		5
34 Asian Group	1937	3	13%			2		1		1		2		1		1			3
35 Commonwealth	1641	1	4%			1			1					1					1
36 Communist Group	3310																		
37 Latin America	1674	3	13%		1	1	1		2			1		2		2			3
38 Western Europe	5906	4	17%		3	1			1	2				1					4
39 Intl Organs	1399	4	17%		1	1	2		4					3	1				
TOTALS																			
40 All Data	4232	23	100%		5	14	3	1	9	3		11		14	1	4	1		19
41 UNTS Only		23																		
COMPARISONS																			
42 Party Total					22%	61%	13%	4%	39%	13%		48%		61%	4%	17%	4%	4%	83%
43 Group Total					12%	25%	23%	40%	19%	7%	1%	71%	1%	27%	11%	13%	15%		74%
44 World Total					18%	23%	29%	29%	22%	25%	25%	20%	7%	8%	12%	6%	7%	12%	100%

TREATY PROFILE OF ICELAND

Table 83 • 131

	Partners (1)	Partner's World Total (2)	Dyads Absolutes (3)	Ratios Self (4)	Ratios Other (5)	Time 1946-1950 (6)	Time 1951-1955 (7)	Time 1956-1960 (8)	Time 1961-1965 (9)	Admin & Dipl (10)	Social Coop (11)	Econ Coop (12)	Aid (13)	Milit (14)	UN (15)	Spec Ag's (16)	Intl Court (17)	Arbitration (18)	Other (19)	Self-Registered (20)
	TOP THIRTY																			
1	USA (United States)	2599	32	32%	1%	4	6	11	11	3	2	5	15	7	2	3	2		6	
2	USSR (Soviet Union)	1356	11	11%	1%		4	5	2	4	1	5	1			1				
3	Sweden	483	10	10%	2%	4	6	1		1	1	8								
4	UK Great Britain	981	6	6%	1%	3		1	2	4		1			1	1		1		1
5	IBRD (World Bank)	452	6	6%	1%		5	2	1				6			2				
6	Germany, West	890	6	6%	1%	2	1	2	1	3	1	2				1		1		
7	Denmark	380	4	4%	1%	2	1		1	1	2	1				1				1
8	Spain	437	3	3%	1%		2	1				3								
9	Netherlands	548	3	3%	1%	1	1	1			1	2							4	
10	ICAO (Civil Aviat)	23	2	2%	9%	1	1								1	1		1		
11	Norway	461	2	2%	1%		2	1		1	1	1								
12	Israel	232	2	2%	1%		1		1	1		1								
13	Ireland	103	2	2%	2%	2		1		1										
14	Thailand	132	1	1%	1%			1			1								1	
15	WHO (World Health)	187	1	1%	1%	1			1				1			1		1		
16	UN Special Fund	113	1	1%	1%				1	1					1					
17	United Nations	233	1	1%		1		1		1							1			
18	Luxembourg	136	1	1%	1%		1				1							1		
19	Finland	245	1	1%				1			1									
20	Canada	310	1	1%					1	1										
21	Belgium	499	1	1%			1					1								
22	Australia	201	1	1%			1			1										
23	Accept UN Charter	68	1	1%	1%	1									1					
24–30																				
31	All Others (0)																			
	GROUPS																			
32	African Group	968																		
33	Arab Group	937																		
34	Asian Group	1937	1	1%			1	1	3	5	1	2			1	1		1	2	1
35	Commonwealth	1641	8	8%		3	1	1	2	4	1	5	1			3				
36	Communist Group	3310	11	11%			4	5												
37	Latin America	1674																		
38	Western Europe	5906	33	33%	1%	11	15	5	2	6	8	19				7	1	6	5	1
39	Intl Organs	1399	11	11%	1%	3	6		2	1	2		8		2	1	1	1		
	TOTALS																			
40	All Data	11069	99	100%		22	33	24	20	21	15	32	24	7	6	15	3	8	13	2
41	UNTS Only		73																	
	COMPARISONS																			
42	Party Total					22%	33%	24%	20%	21%	15%	32%	24%	7%	8%	21%	4%	11%	18%	3%
43	Group Total					22%	25%	27%	26%	24%	26%	32%	10%	8%	4%	14%	6%	8%	17%	32%
44	World Total					18%	23%	29%	29%	22%	25%	25%	20%	7%	8%	12%	6%	7%	12%	100%

TREATY PROFILE OF ICJ (INT COURT)

Table 84

	Partners (1)	Partner's World Total (2)	Dyads Absolutes (3)	Dyads Ratios Self (4)	Dyads Ratios Other (5)	Time 1946-1950 (6)	Time 1951-1955 (7)	Time 1956-1960 (8)	Time 1961-1965 (9)	Topics Admin & Dipl (10)	Topics Social Coop (11)	Topics Econ Coop (12)	Topics Aid (13)	Topics Milit (14)	Institutions UN (15)	Institutions Spec Ag's (16)	Institutions Intl Court (17)	Institutions Arbitration (18)	Institutions Other (19)	Self-Registered (20)
	TOP THIRTY																			
1	Netherlands	548	1	100%		1				1					1					
2																				
3																				
4																				
5																				
6																				
7																				
8																				
9																				
10																				
11																				
12																				
13																				
14																				
15																				
16																				
17																				
18																				
19																				
20																				
21																				
22																				
23																				
24																				
25																				
26																				
27																				
28																				
29																				
30																				
31	All Others (0)																			
	GROUPS																			
32	African Group	968																		
33	Arab Group	937																		
34	Asian Group	1937																		
35	Commonwealth	1641																		
36	Communist Group	3310																		
37	Latin America	1674																		
38	Western Europe	5906	1	100%		1														
39	Intl Organs	1399								1					1					
	TOTALS																			
40	All Data	548	1	100%		1														
41	UNTS Only		1																	
	COMPARISONS																			
42	Party Total					100%				100%					100%					
43	Group Total					12%	25%	23%	40%	19%	7%	1%	71%	1%	27%	11%	13%	15%	4%	74%
44	World Total					18%	23%	29%	29%	22%	25%	25%	20%	7%	8%	12%	6%	7%	12%	100%

TREATY PROFILE OF IDA (DEVEL ASSOC)

Table 85

	Partners (1)	Partner's World Total (2)	Absolutes (3)	Dyads Ratios Self (4)	Dyads Ratios Other (5)	Time 1946-1950 (6)	Time 1951-1955 (7)	Time 1956-1960 (8)	Time 1961-1965 (9)	Topics Admin & Dipl (10)	Topics Social Coop (11)	Topics Econ Coop (12)	Topics Aid (13)	Topics Milit (14)	Institutions UN (15)	Institutions Spec Ag's (16)	Institutions Intl Court (17)	Institutions Arbitration (18)	Institutions Other (19)	Self-Registered (20)
	TOP THIRTY																			
1	Pakistan	245	18	22%	7%				18				18			1				18
2	India	299	17	21%	6%				17				17			2			1	16
3	Turkey	298	6	7%	2%				6				6							6
4	Taiwan	172	4	5%	2%				4				4							4
5	Kenya	26	3	4%	12%				3				3							3
6	Jordan	65	3	4%	5%				3				3							3
7	UK Great Britain	981	2	2%					2				2							2
8	Tanzania	45	2	2%	4%				2				2							2
9	Paraguay	75	2	2%	3%				2				2							2
10	Nigeria	27	2	2%	7%				2				2							2
11	Honduras	43	2	2%	5%				2				2							2
12	Bolivia	58	2	2%	3%				2				2							2
13	Tunisia	97	1	1%	1%				1				1							1
14	Syria	84	1	1%	1%				1				1							1
15	Sudan	37	1	1%	3%				1				1				1				1
16	Somalia	37	1	1%	3%				1				1							1
17	United Nations	233	1	1%					1	1						2	1	1		
18	Niger	25	1	1%	4%				1				1							1
19	Nicaragua	50	1	1%	2%				1				1							1
20	Morocco	94	1	1%	1%				1				1							1
21	Mauritania	18	1	1%	6%				1				1							1
22	Mali	54	1	1%	2%				1				1							1
23	Korea, South	80	1	1%	1%				1				1							1
24	Haiti	41	1	1%	2%				1				1				1				1
25	Ethiopia	98	1	1%	1%				1				1							1
26	El Salvador	70	1	1%	1%				1				1							1
27	Ecuador	97	1	1%	1%				1				1				1				1
28	Costa Rica	51	1	1%	2%				1				1				1				1
29	Colombia	112	1	1%	1%				1				1							1
30	Chile	119	1	1%	1%				1				1							1
31	All Others (1)	83	1	1%	1%				1				1			2				1
	GROUPS																			
32	African Group	968	12	15%	1%				12				12			1			1	12
33	Arab Group	937	7	9%	1%				7				7			1				7
34	Asian Group	1937	41	50%	2%				41				41			5			1	40
35	Commonwealth	1641	2	2%					2				2							2
36	Communist Group	3310																		
37	Latin America	1674	13	16%	1%				13				13			5	1	1	1	13
38	Western Europe	5906	6	7%					6				6							6
39	Intl Organs	1399	1	1%					1	1					1	2				
	TOTALS																			
40	All Data	3814	82	100%					82	1			81		1	14	1	1	4	80
41	UNTS Only		82																	
	COMPARISONS																			
42	Party Total					12%	25%	23%	100%	1%	7%	1%	99%	1%	1%	17%	1%	1%	5%	98%
43	Group Total					18%	23%	29%	40%	19%	25%	25%	71%	7%	27%	11%	13%	15%	4%	74%
44	World Total					18%	23%	29%	29%	22%	25%	25%	20%	7%	8%	12%	6%	7%	12%	100%

TREATY PROFILE OF ILO (LABOR ORG)

			Dyads			Time				Topics						Institutions			Self-Registered
				Ratios															
Partners	Partner's World Total	Absolutes	Self	Other	1946 1950	1951 1955	1956 1960	1961 1965	Admin & Dipl	Social Coop	Econ Coop	Aid	Milit	UN	Spec Ag's	Intl Court	Arbitration	Other	
(1)	(2)	(3)	(4)	(5)	(6)	(7)	(8)	(9)	(10)	(11)	(12)	(13)	(14)	(15)	(16)	(17)	(18)	(19)	(20)
TOP THIRTY																			
1 United Nations	233	4	7%	2%	4				4					3	1				3
2 Ceylon (Sri Lanka)	123	3	5%	2%		2		1	1			2		2					1
3 Thailand	132	2	3%	2%		1	1		1			1		1					2
4 Peru	109	2	3%	2%		1		1	1			1		1					2
5 Mexico	138	2	3%	1%		2			1			1		1					2
6 Italy	755	2	3%			1	1		2					1		1			2
7 Council of Europe	4	2	3%	50%		1	1					1		1					1
8 Vietnam, South	106	1	2%	1%		1			1					1					1
9 Venezuela	47	1	2%	2%		1			1										1
10 Uruguay	63	1	2%	2%		1													
11 USA (United States)	2599	1	2%					1	1										1
12 UK Great Britain	981	1	2%				1												
13 Turkey	298	1	2%					1	1			1		1	1				1
14 Tanzania	45	1	2%	2%		1													
15 Syria	84	1	2%	1%		1													
16 Switzerland	426	1	2%		1				1					1	1			1	1
17 WHO (World Health)	187	1	2%	1%	1														1
18 UN Special Fund	113	1	2%	1%			1					1		1					1
19 UN Relief Palestin	9	1	2%	11%				1	1					1					
20 Org Ctrl Am States	1	1	2%	100%		1													
21 OAU (Afri Unity)	2	1	2%	50%			1												1
22 OAS (Am States)	5	1	2%	20%	1														1
23 LAFTA (Free Trade)	1	1	2%	100%				1											1
24 IMCO (Maritime Org)	5	1	2%	20%			1												1
25 IAEA (Atom Energy)	44	1	2%	2%		1			1					1					1
26 FAO (Food Agri)	19	1	2%	5%	1														1
27 Euratom	7	1	2%	14%				1	1										1
28 EEC (Econ Commnty)	6	1	2%	17%		1			1										1
29 ECSC (Coal/Steel)	3	1	2%	33%		1			1										1
30 Paraguay	75	1	2%	1%				1				1		1					1
31 All Others (19)	1972	19	32%	1%	1	13	2	3	6			13		17		1	3		19
TOTALS																			
40 All Data	8592	59	100%		9	29	9	12	33			26		37	3	2	3	1	51
41 UNTS Only		58																		
GROUPS																			
32 African Group	968	3	5%			1		2	2			1		3	1	1	1		3
33 Arab Group	937	2	3%			2						2		2					2
34 Asian Group	1937	9	15%			7	1	2	2			7		9	1				8
35 Commonwealth	1641	1	2%				1		1					1					1
36 Communist Group	3310																		
37 Latin America	1674	13	22%	1%	1	12	1		2			11		10		1	2		13
38 Western Europe	5906	5	8%			3		1	2			3		2	1			1	4
39 Intl Organs	1399	24	41%	2%	8	3	7	6	23			1		9					19
COMPARISONS																			
42 Party Total					15%	49%	15%	20%	56%	7%	1%	44%	1%	64%	5%	3%	5%	2%	88%
43 Group Total					12%	25%	23%	40%	19%	25%	25%	71%	7%	27%	11%	13%	15%	4%	74%
44 World Total					18%	23%	29%	29%	22%			20%		8%	12%	6%	7%	12%	100%

Table 87 • 135

TREATY PROFILE OF IMCO (MARITIME ORG)

Partners (1)	Partner's World Total (2)	Dyads Absolutes (3)	Ratios Self (4)	Ratios Other (5)	Time 1946-1950 (6)	Time 1951-1955 (7)	Time 1956-1960 (8)	Time 1961-1965 (9)	Topics Admin & Dipl (10)	Topics Social Coop (11)	Topics Econ Coop (12)	Topics Aid (13)	Topics Milit (14)	Institutions UN (15)	Institutions Spec Ag's (16)	Institutions Intl Court (17)	Institutions Arbitration (18)	Other (19)	Self Registered (20)
TOP THIRTY																			
1 United Nations	233	3	60%	1%			2	1	3					1		1		1	
2 ILO (Labor Org)	59	1	20%	2%			1		1					1					
3 IAEA (Atom Energy)	44	1	20%	2%				1	1					1					
4																			
5																			
6																			
7																			
8																			
9																			
10																			
11																			
12																			
13																			
14																			
15																			
16																			
17																			
18																			
19																			
20																			
21																			
22																			
23																			
24																			
25																			
26																			
27																			
28																			
29																			
30																			
31 All Others (0)																			
GROUPS																			
32 African Group	968																		
33 Arab Group	937																		
34 Asian Group	1937																		
35 Commonwealth	1641																		
36 Communist Group	3310																		
37 Latin America	1674																		
38 Western Europe	5906																		
39 Intl Organs	1399	5	100%				3	2	5					3		1		1	
TOTALS																			
40 All Data	336	5	100%				3	2	5					3		1		1	
41 UNTS Only		5																	
COMPARISONS																			
42 Party Total					12%	25%	60%	40%	100%	7%	1%	71%	1%	60%	11%	20%	15%	20%	
43 Group Total					18%	23%	23%	40%	19%	25%	25%	20%	7%	27%	12%	13%	7%	4%	74%
44 World Total					18%	23%	29%	29%	22%	25%	25%	20%	7%	8%	12%	6%	7%	12%	100%

136 • Table 88

TREATY PROFILE OF IMF (FUND)

Partners (1)	Partner's World Total (2)	Dyads Absolutes (3)	Ratios Self (4)	Ratios Other (5)	Time 1946-1950 (6)	Time 1951-1955 (7)	Time 1956-1960 (8)	Time 1961-1965 (9)	Topics Admin & Dipl (10)	Topics Social Coop (11)	Topics Econ Coop (12)	Topics Aid (13)	Topics Milit (14)	Institutions UN (15)	Institutions Spec Ag's (16)	Institutions Intl Court (17)	Institutions Arbitration (18)	Institutions Other (19)	Self-Registered (20)
TOP THIRTY																			
1 United Nations	233	2	100%	1%	1		1		2							1			
2																			
3																			
4																			
5																			
6																			
7																			
8																			
9																			
10																			
11																			
12																			
13																			
14																			
15																			
16																			
17																			
18																			
19																			
20																			
21																			
22																			
23																			
24																			
25																			
26																			
27																			
28																			
29																			
30																			
31 All Others (0)																			
GROUPS																			
32 African Group	968																		
33 Arab Group	937																		
34 Asian Group	1937																		
35 Commonwealth	1641																		
36 Communist Group	3310																		
37 Latin America	1674																		
38 Western Europe	5906			100%															
39 Intl Organs	1399	2			1		1		2							1			
TOTALS																			
40 All Data		2	100%		1		1		2							1			
41 UNTS Only	233	2																	
COMPARISONS																			
42 Party Total					50%	50%	50%	40%	100%	7%	1%	71%	1%	27%	11%	50%	15%	4%	
43 Group Total					12%	25%	23%	29%	19%	25%	25%	20%	7%	8%	12%	13%	7%	12%	74%
44 World Total					18%	23%	29%	29%	22%							6%			100%

TREATY PROFILE OF INDIA

Table 89 • 137

Partners (1)	Partner's World Total (2)	Dyads Absolutes (3)	Ratios Self (4)	Ratios Other (5)	Time 1946-1950 (6)	Time 1951-1955 (7)	Time 1956-1960 (8)	Time 1961-1965 (9)	Admin & Dipl (10)	Social Coop (11)	Econ Coop (12)	Aid (13)	Milit (14)	UN (15)	Spec Ag's (16)	Intl Court (17)	Arbitration (18)	Other (19)	Self-Registered (20)
TOP THIRTY																			
1 USA (United States)	2599	40	13%	2%	7	7	11	15	2	9	5	18	6	2	5	1	1	2	
2 IBRD (World Bank)	452	31	10%	7%	3	4	15	9				31					3		
3 USSR (Soviet Union)	1356	29	10%	2%	1	5	17	6	5	5	7	12						1	
4 IDA (Devel Assoc)	82	17	6%	21%				17				17							
5 Pakistan	245	17	6%	7%	8	5	3	1	8	3	5		1	2	2		1	3	5
6 WHO (World Health)	187	15	5%	8%	1	14			1	6		8		7	3	5	4	1	
7 Japan	443	12	4%	3%		2	4	6		7	3	1	1		1	1		1	
8 UK Great Britain	981	10	3%	1%	3	3		4		3	5		1		4				1
9 Canada	310	8	3%	3%		3	3	2	2		2	4	2		1			2	
10 United Nations	233	7	2%	3%		3	1	3		2		4	1			1	1	2	
11 Netherlands	548	7	2%	1%	1	2	2	2		3		3	1		3	1	1		
12 Germany, West	890	7	2%	1%		2	3	2		2	4		1						
13 Germany, East	556	7	2%	1%		2	2	3		2	4	1			1				
14 Denmark	380	7	2%	2%	1		1	5		1	1	4	1		2			1	
15 China People's Rep	766	7	2%	1%		7			3		4								1
16 Sweden	483	6	2%	1%	3	2	1			1	5				1	1	1		
17 Iran	170	5	2%	3%	1		1	1	1	2	2				1		1		1
18 Ceylon (Sri Lanka)	123	5	2%	4%	2	1	2			1	3		1		1		1		2
19 Switzerland	426	4	1%	1%	2		2		1	2	1								1
20 Italy	755	4	1%	1%		1	2	1	1	1			1		1		1	1	
21 France	1033	4	1%	1%	1	1	1	1	3							1			1
22 Turkey	298	3	1%	1%		2	1		1	1	1								1
23 Poland	493	3	1%	1%		3				3									1
24 Norway	461	3	1%	1%	1		3			1	2							1	
25 Greece	318	3	1%	1%		1	1	1			2								
26 Burma	102	3	1%	3%		2	1		1		2		1						3
27 Australia	201	3	1%	1%	1			2		1	1	1	1		1	1	1	1	
28 Afghanistan	83	3	1%	4%	3				1	1									
29 Philippines	236	2	1%	1%	1	1			1	1						1	1		
30 Nepal	36	2	1%	6%	2				1		1								2
31 All Others (21)	4137	25	8%	1%	3	8	8	6	8	8	3	5	1	5	5	4	2	1	4
GROUPS																			
32 African Group	968	1																	
33 Arab Group	937	3	1%							1					1				2
34 Asian Group	1937	40	13%	2%	17	13	8	2	2	10	14		1	2	7	2	5	3	16
35 Commonwealth	1641	22	7%	1%	4	6	3	9	15	4	8	5	3		6	1	1	2	1
36 Communist Group	3310	51	17%	2%	1	14	25	11	2	15	15	13			1			3	2
37 Latin America	1674																		
38 Western Europe	5906	53	18%	1%	10	13	15	15	7	12	20	8	6		9	3	4	2	5
39 Intl Organs	1399	74	25%	5%	5	23	17	29	2	8		63	1	11	3	7	8	3	
TOTALS																			
40 All Data	19383	299	100%		45	82	85	87	40	67	66	108	18	16	34	17	20	16	26
41 UNTS Only		236																	
COMPARISONS																			
42 Party Total					15%	27%	28%	29%	13%	22%	22%	36%	6%	7%	14%	7%	8%	7%	11%
43 Group Total					16%	23%	31%	30%	21%	23%	20%	30%	7%	10%	15%	8%	8%	6%	16%
44 World Total					18%	23%	29%	29%	22%	25%	25%	20%	7%	8%	12%	6%	7%	12%	100%

TREATY PROFILE OF INDONESIA

	Partners (1)	Partner's World Total (2)	Dyads Absolutes (3)	Ratios Self (4)	Ratios Other (5)	Time 1946-1950 (6)	Time 1951-1955 (7)	Time 1956-1960 (8)	Time 1961-1965 (9)	Admin & Dipl (10)	Social Coop (11)	Econ Coop (12)	Aid (13)	Milit (14)	UN (15)	Spec Ag's (16)	Intl Court (17)	Arbitration (18)	Other (19)	Self-Registered (20)
	TOP THIRTY																			
1	USSR (Soviet Union)	1356	25	20%	2%	2	1	14	8	4	5	4	11	1						
2	China People's Rep	766	21	17%	3%		4	3	14	3	4	7	7							
3	USA (United States)	2599	16	13%	1%	4	2	6	4	2	2		10	2	2	1			1	
4	Philippines	236	11	9%	5%		1	2	8	5	1	2	1	2						
5	Japan	443	8	6%	2%		1	5	2			2	2	3		1	2	1	1	
6	Netherlands	548	7	6%	1%	2	3		2	3		2	1	1	2	3	1		1	
7	Germany, East	556	5	4%				1	4		2	3								
8	UK Great Britain	981	4	3%	1%			3	1		1	3				1		1	1	
9	Sweden	483	2	2%			2					2								
10	WHO (World Health)	187	2	2%	1%		1	1					2		1		1			
11	United Nations	233	2	2%	1%		1		1				2		1		2	2		
12	UNICEF (Children)	122	2	2%	2%	1	1			2										
13	Poland	493	2	2%			1		1			1	1							
14	Norway	461	2	2%			2					2								
15	Germany, West	890	2	2%			1	1				1	1							
16	Yugoslavia	525	1	1%				1				1								
17	Turkey	298	1	1%	1%			1										1	1	
18	Thailand	132	1	1%					1	1										
19	Switzerland	426	1	1%	1%		1					1					1	1		
20	UN Special Fund	113	1	1%				1					1		1					
21	Pakistan	245	1	1%					1	1					1					
22	Mexico	138	1	1%	1%			1		1										
23	Malaysia	26	1	1%	4%			1		1										
24	Italy	755	1	1%					1	1										
25	Iran	170	1	1%	1%		1			1										
26	India	299	1	1%				1		1										
27	Hungary	290	1	1%					1	1										
28	Czechoslovakia	393	1	1%				1				1								
29	Australia	201	1	1%					1			1			1	1			1	
30	Accept UN Charter																			
31	All Others (0)	68	1	1%	1%	1				1										
	GROUPS																			
32	African Group	968																		
33	Arab Group	937																		
34	Asian Group	1937	16	13%	1%		4	4	8	10	1	2	1	2	1		1			
35	Commonwealth	1641	5	4%				4	1		1	4				2		1	2	
36	Communist Group	3310	55	44%	2%	2	6	18	29	9	11	15	19	1						
37	Latin America	1674	1	1%					1			1								
38	Western Europe	5906	16	13%		2	9	2	3	4		2	2		2		1		1	
39	Intl Organs	1399	7	6%	1%	1	3	3		2		9	5		3		3	3		
	TOTALS																			
40	All Data	14433	126	100%		10	25	43	48	29	16	33	39	9	9	6	7	5	6	
41	UNTS Only		49																	
	COMPARISONS																			
42	Party Total					8%	20%	34%	38%	23%	13%	26%	31%	7%	18%	12%	14%	10%	12%	16%
43	Group Total					16%	23%	31%	30%	21%	23%	20%	30%	7%	10%	15%	8%	8%	6%	16%
44	World Total					18%	23%	29%	29%	22%	25%	25%	20%	7%	8%	12%	6%	7%	12%	100%

TREATY PROFILE OF INT BUREAU EDUC

Table 91 • 139

Partners (1)	Partner's World Total (2)	Dyads Abso-lutes (3)	Ratios Self (4)	Ratios Other (5)	Time 1946-1950 (6)	Time 1951-1955 (7)	Time 1956-1960 (8)	Time 1961-1965 (9)	Topics Admin & Dipl (10)	Topics Social Coop (11)	Topics Econ Coop (12)	Topics Aid (13)	Topics Milit (14)	Institutions UN (15)	Institutions Spec Ag's (16)	Institutions Intl Court (17)	Institutions Arbi-tration (18)	Institutions Other (19)	Self-Registered (20)
TOP THIRTY																			
1 Switzerland	426	1	100%		1				1										
2–30																				
31 All Others (0)																				
GROUPS																				
32 African Group	968																		
33 Arab Group	937																		
34 Asian Group	1937																		
35 Commonwealth	1641																		
36 Communist Group	3310																		
37 Latin America	1674																		
38 Western Europe	5906	1	100%		1														
39 Intl Organs	1399	1	100%		1				1										
TOTALS																				
40 All Data	426	1																		
41 UNTS Only		0																		
COMPARISONS																				
42 Party Total					100%				100%											
43 Group Total					12%	25%	23%	40%	19%	7%	1%	71%	1%	27%	11%	13%	15%	4%	74%
44 World Total					18%	23%	29%	29%	22%	25%	25%	20%	7%	8%	12%	6%	7%	12%	100%

140 • Table 92

TREATY PROFILE OF INT EXHIBIT BUREAU

Partners (1)	Partner's World Total (2)	Dyads Absolutes (3)	Ratios Self (4)	Other (5)	Time 1946 1950 (6)	1951 1955 (7)	1956 1960 (8)	1961 1965 (9)	Topics Admin & Dipl (10)	Social Coop (11)	Econ Coop (12)	Aid (13)	Milit (14)	Institutions UN (15)	Spec Ag's (16)	Intl Court (17)	Arbi- tration (18)	Other (19)	Self- Regis- tered (20)
TOP THIRTY																			
1 France	1033	1	100%					1	1										
2																			
3																			
4																			
5																			
6																			
7																			
8																			
9																			
10																			
11																			
12																			
13																			
14																			
15																			
16																			
17																			
18																			
19																			
20																			
21																			
22																			
23																			
24																			
25																			
26																			
27																			
28																			
29																			
30																			
31 All Others (0)																			
GROUPS																			
32 African Group	968																		
33 Arab Group	937																		
34 Asian Group	1937																		
35 Commonwealth	1641																		
36 Communist Group	3310																		
37 Latin America	1674																		
38 Western Europe	5906	1	100%					1	1										
39 Intl Organs	1399																			
TOTALS																			
40 All Data	1033	1	100%					1	1										
41 UNTS Only		0																		
COMPARISONS																			
42 Party Total					12%	25%	23%	100%	100%	7%	1%	71%	1%	27%	11%	13%	15%	4%	74%
43 Group Total					18%	23%	29%	40%	19%	25%	25%	20%	7%	8%	12%	6%	7%	12%	100%
44 World Total							29%	29%	22%										

TREATY PROFILE OF INT ORG METROLOGY

Table 93

Partners (1)	Partner's World Total (2)	Dyads Absolutes (3)	Ratios Self (4)	Ratios Other (5)	Time 1946-1950 (6)	Time 1951-1955 (7)	Time 1956-1960 (8)	Time 1961-1965 (9)	Topics Admin & Dipl (10)	Topics Social Coop (11)	Topics Econ Coop (12)	Topics Aid (13)	Topics Milit (14)	Institutions UN (15)	Institutions Spec Ag's (16)	Institutions Intl Court (17)	Institutions Arbitration (18)	Institutions Other (19)	Self-Registered (20)
TOP THIRTY																			
1 France	1033	1	100%					1	1										
2																			
3																			
4																			
5																			
6																			
7																			
8																			
9																			
10																			
11																			
12																			
13																			
14																			
15																			
16																			
17																			
18																			
19																			
20																			
21																			
22																			
23																			
24																			
25																			
26																			
27																			
28																			
29																			
30																			
31 All Others (0)																			
GROUPS																			
32 African Group	968																		
33 Arab Group	937																		
34 Asian Group	1937																		
35 Commonwealth	1641																		
36 Communist Group	3310																		
37 Latin America	1674																		
38 Western Europe	5906	1	100%					1											
39 Intl Organs	1399								1										
TOTALS																			
40 All Data	1033	1	100%					1	1										
41 UNTS Only		0																		
COMPARISONS																			
42 Party Total					12%	25%	23%	100%	100%	7%	1%	71%	1%	27%	11%	13%	15%	4%	74%
43 Group Total					18%	23%	29%	40%	19%	25%	25%	20%	7%	8%	12%	6%	7%	12%	100%
44 World Total								29%	22%	25%									

142 • Table 94

TREATY PROFILE OF INT RAIL TRANSPORT

	Partners (1)	Partner's World Total (2)	Dyads Absolutes (3)	Ratios Self (4)	Ratios Other (5)	Time 1946-1950 (6)	Time 1951-1955 (7)	Time 1956-1960 (8)	Time 1961-1965 (9)	Admin & Dipl (10)	Social Coop (11)	Econ Coop (12)	Aid (13)	Milit (14)	UN (15)	Spec Ag's (16)	Intl Court (17)	Arbitration (18)	Other (19)	Self-Registered (20)
	TOP THIRTY																			
1	Switzerland	426	1	100%				1		1										
2–30																				
31	All Others (0)																			
	GROUPS																			
32	African Group	968																		
33	Arab Group	937																		
34	Asian Group	1937																		
35	Commonwealth	1641																		
36	Communist Group	3310																		
37	Latin America	1674																		
38	Western Europe	5906	1	100%				1		1										
39	Intl Organs	1399																		
	TOTALS																			
40	All Data	426	1	100%				1		1										
41	UNTS Only		0																	
	COMPARISONS																			
42	Party Total									100%										
43	Group Total					12%	25%	23%	40%	19%	7%	1%	71%	1%	27%	11%	13%	15%	4%	74%
44	World Total					18%	23%	29%	29%	22%	25%	25%	20%	7%	8%	12%	6%	7%	12%	100%

Table 95 • 143

TREATY PROFILE OF INT WINE OFFICE

	Partner's World Total	Dyads Ratios			Time					Topics						Institutions				Self-Registered
Partners		Absolutes	Self	Other	1946 1950	1951 1955	1956 1960	1961 1965	Admin & Dipl	Social Coop	Econ Coop	Aid	Milit	UN	Spec Ag's	Intl Court	Arbitration	Other	
(1)	(2)	(3)	(4)	(5)	(6)	(7)	(8)	(9)	(10)	(11)	(12)	(13)	(14)	(15)	(16)	(17)	(18)	(19)	(20)
TOP THIRTY																			
1 France	1033	1	100%					1	1										
2																				
...																				
31 All Others (0)																				
GROUPS																				
32 African Group	968																			
33 Arab Group	937																			
34 Asian Group	1937																			
35 Commonwealth	1641																			
36 Communist Group	3310																			
37 Latin America	1674																			
38 Western Europe	5906	1	100%					1	1										
39 Intl Organs	1399																			
TOTALS																				
40 All Data	1033	1	100%					1	1										
41 UNTS Only		0																		
COMPARISONS																				
42 Party Total					12%	25%	23%	100%	100%	7%	1%	71%	1%	27%	11%	13%	15%	4%	74%
43 Group Total					18%	23%	29%	40%	19%	25%	25%	20%	7%	8%	12%	6%	7%	12%	100%
44 World Total								29%	22%											

TREATY PROFILE OF INTER-AM DEVEL BNK

Table 96

Partners (1)	Partner's World Total (2)	Dyads Absolutes (3)	Ratios Self (4)	Ratios Other (5)	Time 1946 1950 (6)	Time 1951 1955 (7)	Time 1956 1960 (8)	Time 1961 1965 (9)	Topics Admin & Dipl (10)	Topics Social Coop (11)	Topics Econ Coop (12)	Topics Aid (13)	Topics Milit (14)	Institutions UN (15)	Institutions Spec Ag's (16)	Institutions Intl Court (17)	Institutions Arbi-tration (18)	Institutions Other (19)	Self-Regis-tered (20)
TOP THIRTY																			
1 USA (United States)	2599	1	100%					1				1						1	
2																			
3																			
4																			
5																			
6																			
7																			
8																			
9																			
10																			
11																			
12																			
13																			
14																			
15																			
16																			
17																			
18																			
19																			
20																			
21																			
22																			
23																			
24																			
25																			
26																			
27																			
28																			
29																			
30																			
31 All Others (0)																			
GROUPS																			
32 African Group	968																		
33 Arab Group	937																		
34 Asian Group	1937																		
35 Commonwealth	1641																		
36 Communist Group	3310																		
37 Latin America	1674																		
38 Western Europe	5906																		
39 Intl Organs	1399																		
TOTALS																			
40 All Data	2599	1	100%					1				1						1	
41 UNTS Only		1																	
COMPARISONS																			
42 Party Total					12%	25%	23%	40%	19%	7%	1%	71%	1%	27%	11%	13%	15%	4%	74%
43 Group Total					100%			100%				100%						100%	100%
44 World Total					18%	23%	29%	29%	22%	25%	25%	20%	7%	8%	12%	6%	7%	12%	100%

TREATY PROFILE OF INTER-AM NUC ENERG

Table 97 • 145

	Part-ners (1)	Partner's World Total (2)	Dyads Abso-lutes (3)	Dyads Ratios Self (4)	Dyads Ratios Other (5)	Time 1946-1950 (6)	Time 1951-1955 (7)	Time 1956-1960 (8)	Time 1961-1965 (9)	Topics Admin & Dipl (10)	Topics Social Coop (11)	Topics Econ Coop (12)	Topics Aid (13)	Topics Milit (14)	Institutions UN (15)	Institutions Spec Ag's (16)	Institutions Intl Court (17)	Institutions Arbi-tration (18)	Institutions Other (19)	Self-Regis-tered (20)
	TOP THIRTY																			
1	IAEA (Atom Energy)	44	1	100%	2%			1		1					1					
2–30																				
31	All Others (0)																			
	GROUPS																			
32	African Group	968																		
33	Arab Group	937																		
34	Asian Group	1937																		
35	Commonwealth	1641																		
36	Communist Group	3310																		
37	Latin America	1674																		
38	Western Europe	5906																		
39	Intl Organs	1399	1	100%				1		1					1					
	TOTALS																			
40	All Data	44	1	100%				1		1					1					
41	UNTS Only		1																	
	COMPARISONS																			
42	Party Total					12%	25%	100% 23%	100% 40%	100% 19%	7%	1%	71%	1%	100% 27%	11%	13%	15%	4%	74%
43	Group Total					18%	23%	29%	29%	22%	25%	25%	20%	7%	8%	12%	6%	7%	12%	100%
44	World Total																			

146 • Table 98

TREATY PROFILE OF INTGOV EUR MIGRAT

Partners (1)	Partner's World Total (2)	Dyads Absolutes (3)	Ratios Self (4)	Ratios Other (5)	Time 1946-1950 (6)	Time 1951-1955 (7)	Time 1956-1960 (8)	Time 1961-1965 (9)	Admin & Dipl (10)	Social Coop (11)	Econ Coop (12)	Aid (13)	Milit (14)	UN (15)	Spec Ag's (16)	Intl Court (17)	Arbitration (18)	Other (19)	Self-Registered (20)
TOP THIRTY																			
1 Switzerland	426	1	100%			1			1										
2–30																				
31 All Others (0)																				
GROUPS																				
32 African Group	968																			
33 Arab Group	937																			
34 Asian Group	1937																			
35 Commonwealth	1641																			
36 Communist Group	3310																			
37 Latin America	1674																			
38 Western Europe	5906	1	100%						1										
39 Intl Organs	1399						1			1										
TOTALS																				
40 All Data	426	1	100%																	
41 UNTS Only		0																		
COMPARISONS																				
42 Party Total					12%	100%	23%	40%	100%	7%	1%	71%	1%	27%	11%	13%	15%	4%	74%
43 Group Total					18%	25%	29%	29%	19%	25%	25%	20%	7%	8%	12%	6%	7%	12%	100%
44 World Total						23%			22%											

TREATY PROFILE OF IRAN

Partners (1)	Partner's World Total (2)	Dyads Absolutes (3)	Ratios Self (4)	Ratios Other (5)	Time 1946-1950 (6)	Time 1951-1955 (7)	Time 1956-1960 (8)	Time 1961-1965 (9)	Admin & Dipl (10)	Social Coop (11)	Econ Coop (12)	Aid (13)	Milit (14)	UN (15)	Spec Ag's (16)	Intl Court (17)	Arbitration (18)	Other (19)	Self-Registered (20)
TOP THIRTY																			
1 USA (United States)	2599	26	15%	1%	5	5	8	8	1	2	3	14	6		1			1	
2 USSR (Soviet Union)	1356	25	15%	2%	3	6	12	4	13	3	8	1						2	1
3 Pakistan	245	10	6%	4%	1		7	2	5	4	1							1	1
4 Turkey	298	8	5%	3%	3	2	2	1	1	4	3								
5 IBRD (World Bank)	452	8	5%	2%			4	4				8		1					
6 Germany, West	890	8	5%	1%		1	4	3	1	2	1	4				1			
7 Netherlands	548	7	4%	1%	2		4	1	2	4	4								
8 Italy	755	7	4%	1%	1	1	5		2	1	3				1				
9 Afghanistan	83	7	4%	8%	1		1	5	2	2	3								
10 France	1033	6	4%	1%			3	3	2	2	2					1	1	1	
11 Japan	443	5	3%	1%		1	4		1	2	2	1							
12 India	299	5	3%	2%	1	2	1	1	1	2	2								
13 UK Great Britain	981	4	2%			1	3			2	1				1	1	1	1	
14 Belgium	499	4	2%	1%			2	2	1	2	1				1				
15 Switzerland	426	3	2%	1%		1	1	1		1	2				1				
16 UNICEF (Children)	122	3	2%	2%		1	1	2	1			2		2					
17 Jordan	65	3	2%	5%	1		1	1	1	1	1								
18 Sweden	483	2	1%		1		1			1	1								
19 Spain	437	2	1%				2		1	1									
20 WHO (World Health)	187	2	1%	1%		2						2		1	1				
21 UN Special Fund	113	2	1%	2%			2					2		1					
22 United Nations	233	2	1%	1%			2	2	2							1	1	1	
23 Norway	461	2	1%		1		1			1	1								
24 Lebanon	75	2	1%	3%		1	1		1	1					1				
25 Denmark	380	2	1%	1%		1	1			1	1								
26 Yugoslavia	525	1	1%					1		1									
27 United Arab Rep	232	1	1%				1												
28 EEC (Econ Commnty)	6	1	1%	17%				1	1		1								
29 Romania	251	1	1%					1			1								
30 Poland	493	1	1%					1			1								
31 All Others (10)	2252	10	6%				5	5	5	4	1								
GROUPS																			
32 African Group	968	7	4%	1%	1	1	3	2	3	3	1							1	
33 Arab Group	937	24	14%	1%	3	2	11	8	9	9	6							1	2
34 Asian Group	1937	5	3%			1	3	1	1	2	2							1	
35 Commonwealth	1641	28	16%	1%	3	6	12	7	13	3	11	1			1	1	1	2	1
36 Communist Group	3310	2	1%				1	1		3									
37 Latin America	1674	54	32%	1%	8	6	28	12	12	2	17	4		4	5	3	2		
38 Western Europe	5906	18	11%	1%		3	6	9	3	21	1	14		4	1	1	1	1	
39 Intl Organs	1399																		
TOTALS																			
40 All Data	17222	170	100%		20	24	76	50	43	45	42	34	6	4	7	5	4	6	3
41 UNTS Only		62																		
COMPARISONS																			
42 Party Total					12%	14%	45%	29%	25%	26%	25%	20%	4%	6%	11%	8%	6%	10%	5%
43 Group Total					16%	23%	31%	30%	21%	23%	20%	30%	7%	10%	15%	8%	8%	6%	16%
44 World Total					18%	23%	29%	29%	22%	25%	25%	20%	7%	8%	12%	6%	7%	12%	100%

148 • Table 100

TREATY PROFILE OF IRAQ

Partners (1)	Partner's World Total (2)	Dyads Absolutes (3)	Dyads Ratios Self (4)	Dyads Ratios Other (5)	Time 1946-1950 (6)	Time 1951-1955 (7)	Time 1956-1960 (8)	Time 1961-1965 (9)	Topics Admin & Dipl (10)	Topics Social Coop (11)	Topics Econ Coop (12)	Topics Aid (13)	Topics Milit (14)	Institutions UN (15)	Institutions Spec Ag's (16)	Institutions Intl Court (17)	Institutions Arbitration (18)	Institutions Other (19)	Self-Registered (20)
TOP THIRTY																			
1 USA (United States)	2599	21	22%	1%		15	4	2	2	2		14	3	3				1	
2 USSR (Soviet Union)	1356	12	13%	1%			11	1	2	1	2	7			1			2	2
3 UK Great Britain	981	10	10%	1%	2	6	1	1	2	2	5		1	1	1		1	2	4
4 Turkey	298	5	5%	2%	4	1			3	1							1	1	
5 China People's Rep	766	5	5%	1%			3	2		1	4								
6 Germany, East	556	4	4%	1%			3	1	2	2	1								
7 Poland	493	3	3%	1%			2	1		2								1	
8 Pakistan	245	3	3%		3				2	1									
9 Spain	437	2	2%			2			1						1				
10 WHO (World Health)	187	2	2%	1%		1		1	1			2		1		1			
11 UNICEF (Children)	122	2	2%	2%		1						1		2					
12 Romania	251	2	2%	1%			2			1	1							1	
13 Italy	755	2	2%				1	2			1	1						1	
14 Hungary	290	2	2%	1%			1	1	1	2	1								
15 Germany, West	890	2	2%			1	1		1						1				
16 United Arab Rep	232	1	1%					1		1	1				1				
17 Syria	84	1	1%				1				1								
18 Switzerland	426	1	1%			1				1									
19 Sweden	483	1	1%			1				1									
20 UN Special Fund	113	1	1%	1%			1					1		1			1		
21 United Nations	233	1	1%					1	1			1		1			1		
22 ICAO (Civil Aviat)	23	1	1%	4%											1				
23 IBRD (World Bank)	452	1	1%		1							1							
24 Norway	461	1	1%		1				1										
25 Netherlands	548	1	1%					1	1										
26 Kuwait	10	1	1%	10%				1	1										1
27 Jordan	65	1	1%	2%	1								1						
28 Japan	443	1	1%					1											
29 Iran	170	1	1%	1%		1		1	1										
30 India	299	1	1%			1			1										
31 All Others (4)	1444	4	4%		1	1	2			3	1				1				
GROUPS																			
32 African Group	968	4	4%		1	1		2	2	1	1				1				
33 Arab Group	937	6	6%		3	1	1	1	4	2					1				1
34 Asian Group	1937	10	10%	1%	2	6	1	1	2	2	5		1		1		1	2	2
35 Commonwealth	1641	10	10%	1%			2	6	4	9	9	7						3	
36 Communist Group	3310	29	30%				23	6					1						
37 Latin America	1674																		
38 Western Europe	5906	17	18%	1%	6	8	1	2	5	7	3	1	1	1	4	1	2	1	4
39 Intl Organs	1399	8	8%		1	3	1	3	1			7		5			3		
TOTALS																			
40 All Data	15712	96	100%		13	34	31	18	20	23	19	29	5	9	7	1	6	7	7
41 UNTS Only		67																		
COMPARISONS																			
42 Party Total					14%	35%	32%	19%	21%	24%	20%	30%	5%	13%	10%	1%	9%	10%	10%
43 Group Total					9%	24%	31%	36%	18%	27%	22%	29%	4%	15%	20%	8%	15%	9%	5%
44 World Total					18%	23%	29%	29%	22%	25%	25%	20%	7%	8%	12%	6%	7%	12%	100%

Table 101 • 149

TREATY PROFILE OF IRELAND

	Partners (1)	Partner's World Total (2)	Dyads Absolutes (3)	Ratios Self (4)	Ratios Other (5)	Time 1946 1950 (6)	Time 1951 1955 (7)	Time 1956 1960 (8)	Time 1961 1965 (9)	Admin & Dipl (10)	Social Coop (11)	Econ Coop (12)	Aid (13)	Milit (14)	UN (15)	Spec Ag's (16)	Intl Court (17)	Arbitration (18)	Other (19)	Self-Registered (20)
	TOP THIRTY																			
1	USA (United States)	2599	14	14%	1%	8	1	2	3	3	2	5	4		1	3	2			
2	UK Great Britain	981	8	8%	1%	3	1	1	3		3	5				2		1		4
3	Germany, West	890	8	8%	1%	1	3	2	2		2	5		1		1		1		7
4	Netherlands	548	7	7%	1%	5		2		1	2	4				1		1	2	2
5	Sweden	483	6	6%	1%	3	1	2		1	2	3				1		1	1	2
6	Switzerland	426	5	5%	1%	3	1	1		1	2	2				1		1	1	4
7	Norway	461	5	5%	1%	2	2		1	1	2	2				1		1	1	2
8	Italy	755	5	5%	1%	2	1	2		2	2	2				1		1	1	2
9	France	1033	5	5%	1%	4	1			1	2	2				1		1	1	4
10	Belgium	499	5	5%	1%	2	2	1		2	2	1				2		1	1	1
11	Portugal	131	4	4%	3%		2	2		1	1	2				1		1		3
12	Finland	245	4	4%	2%		2		2	1	1	1							1	1
13	Denmark	380	4	4%	1%	2		1	1	1	1	2						1		4
14	Spain	437	3	3%	1%	1	1	1		1	1	1								1
15	Canada	310	3	3%	1%	1	2				1	2								3
16	South Africa	120	2	2%	2%			2			1	1								
17	Luxembourg	136	2	2%	1%	1	1			1	1					1				1
18	Iceland	99	2	2%	2%	2				1	1	1							1	2
19	Vietnam, South	106	1	1%	1%				1	1										1
20	Turkey	298	1	1%	1%		1			1										1
21	UN Special Fund	113	1	1%	1%				1				1		1		1			
22	Monaco	36	1	1%	3%		1											1		
23	Greece	318	1	1%				1			1					1				
24	Czechoslovakia	393	1	1%	1%	1				1		1								
25	Ceylon (Sri Lanka)	123	1	1%					1			1								
26	Austria	445	1	1%		1						1								
27	Australia	201	1	1%	1%			1			1					1		1		1
28	Argentina	164	1	1%	1%				1	1				1						
29	Accept UN Charter	68	1	1%	1%			1		1					1					
30																				
31	All Others (0)																			
	GROUPS																			
32	African Group	968																		
33	Arab Group	937																		
34	Asian Group	1937	2	2%								2								1
35	Commonwealth	1641	14	14%	1%	4	1	4	1		6	8				4		3		4
36	Communist Group	3310	1	1%		1	3		3		1					1		1		
37	Latin America	1674	1	1%					1	1										
38	Western Europe	5906	69	67%	1%	29	21	13	6	18	21	29		1	1	12	1	9	9	42
39	Intl Organs	1399	1	1%					1				1			1				
	TOTALS																			
40	All Data	12798	103	100%		42	26	20	15	23	30	44	5	1	3	21	3	13	9	47
41	UNTS Only		99																	
	COMPARISONS																			
42	Party Total					41%	25%	19%	15%	22%	29%	43%	5%	1%	3%	21%	3%	13%	9%	47%
43	Group Total					22%	25%	27%	26%	24%	26%	32%	10%	8%	4%	14%	6%	8%	17%	32%
44	World Total					18%	23%	29%	29%	22%	25%	25%	20%	7%	8%	12%	6%	7%	12%	100%

TREATY PROFILE OF IRO (REFUGEE ORG)

Partners (1)	Partner's World Total (2)	Dyads Absolutes (3)	Ratios Self (4)	Ratios Other (5)	Time 1946-1950 (6)	Time 1951-1955 (7)	Time 1956-1960 (8)	Time 1961-1965 (9)	Admin & Dipl (10)	Social Coop (11)	Econ Coop (12)	Aid (13)	Milit (14)	UN (15)	Spec Ag's (16)	Intl Court (17)	Arbitration (18)	Other (19)	Self-Registered (20)
TOP THIRTY																			
1 Netherlands	548	2	67%		1	1			2					2					
2 United Nations	233	1	33%		1				1					1		1			
3																			
4																			
5																			
6																			
7																			
8																			
9																			
10																			
11																			
12																			
13																			
14																			
15																			
16																			
17																			
18																			
19																			
20																			
21																			
22																			
23																			
24																			
25																			
26																			
27																			
28																			
29																			
30																			
31 All Others (0)																			
GROUPS																			
32 African Group	968																		
33 Arab Group	937																		
34 Asian Group	1937																		
35 Commonwealth	1641																		
36 Communist Group	3310																		
37 Latin America	1674																		
38 Western Europe	5906	2	67%		1	1			2					2					
39 Intl Organs	1399	1	33%		1				1					1		1			
TOTALS																			
40 All Data	781	3	100%		2	1			3					3		1			
41 UNTS Only		3																	
COMPARISONS																			
42 Party Total					67%	33%			100%					100%		33%			
43 Group Total					12%	25%	23%	40%	19%	7%	1%	71%	1%	27%	11%	13%	15%	4%	74%
44 World Total					18%	23%	29%	29%	22%	25%	25%	20%	7%	8%	12%	6%	7%	12%	100%

TREATY PROFILE OF ISRAEL

Table 103

Partners (1)	Partner's World Total (2)	Dyads Absolutes (3)	Ratios Self (4)	Ratios Other (5)	Time 1946-1950 (6)	Time 1951-1955 (7)	Time 1956-1960 (8)	Time 1961-1965 (9)	Topics Admin & Dipl (10)	Topics Social Coop (11)	Topics Econ Coop (12)	Topics Aid (13)	Topics Milit (14)	Institutions UN (15)	Institutions Spec Ag's (16)	Institutions Intl Court (17)	Institutions Arbitration (18)	Institutions Other (19)	Self-Registered (20)
TOP THIRTY																			
1 USA (United States)	2599	40	17%	2%	3	17	6	14	5	7	4	21	3		7	1	1	1	8
2 France	1033	15	6%	1%		5	6	4	5	4	5		1		1	1		2	14
3 UK Great Britain	981	11	5%	1%	4	1	3	3	1	3	7				1	1	1		2
4 Netherlands	548	7	3%	1%	1	3	1	2	5	1					2				5
5 Italy	755	7	3%	1%		5	1	1	3	2	4								5
6 Belgium	499	7	3%	1%		6	1		6	1					1				5
7 USSR (Soviet Union)	1356	6	3%		2	3		1	5		1								2
8 Sweden	483	6	3%	1%		1	3	2	3	2	3				1	1			6
9 Switzerland	426	5	2%	1%		2	2	1	2	2	1				1		1		3
10 South Africa	120	5	2%	4%		3	1		2		1								1
11 IBRD (World Bank)	452	5	2%	1%			1	4				4							
12 Philippines	236	5	2%	2%		1	2	2	2	1	1	2			1				1
13 Liberia	46	5	2%	11%			1	4	2	2						1			5
14 Denmark	380	5	2%	1%		5			1		4								1
15 Austria	445	5	2%	1%			2	2	2	3					1				2
16 Yugoslavia	525	4	2%	1%		1	2	1	1		3	1							2
17 Norway	461	4	2%	1%		2	1	1	1	1	2								3
18 Germany, West	890	4	2%		1	2		2	2		1	1	1	1		1	1	1	4
19 Turkey	298	3	1%	1%		1		2		1					1				2
20 Sierra Leone	27	3	1%	11%				3	1			1							3
21 Malagasy	27	3	1%	11%				3	2			1							3
22 Luxembourg	136	3	1%	2%		2	1		3										3
23 Gabon	22	3	1%	14%				3	2			1							3
24 El Salvador	70	3	1%	4%			2	1	2						1		1		2
25 Cameroon	52	3	1%	6%				3		2		1			1				3
26 Australia	201	3	1%	1%		2		1	1	1	1								1
27 Tanzania	45	2	1%	4%				2	1			1					1		2
28 WHO (World Health)	187	2	1%	1%		1	1					2		2					
29 United Nations	233	2	1%	1%		1		1											
30 Peru	109	2	1%	2%				2				1					2		
31 All Others (44)	3808	54	23%	1%	7	8	12	27	19	8	5	18	4	10	1	3	1	4	46
GROUPS																			
32 African Group	968	35	15%	4%	4	1	3	32	14	6		15	4	1	2		1		34
33 Arab Group	937	4	2%											4				4	
34 Asian Group	1937	8	3%			1	4	3	3	1	1				1	1			4
35 Commonwealth	1641	21	9%	1%	4	7	6	4	6	6	9	3		4	3				4
36 Communist Group	3310	6	3%		2	3		1	5		1								6
37 Latin America	1674	18	8%	1%		1	5	12	6	9		3							2
38 Western Europe	5906	78	34%	1%	2	39	19	18	36	14	25	1	2	1	7	4	4	3	18
39 Intl Organs	1399	15	6%	1%	1	4	4	6			1	14		5	1	1	3		56
TOTALS																			2
40 All Data	17450	232	100%		18	73	50	91	79	43	44	57	9	13	21	9	10	9	136
41 UNTS Only		221																	
COMPARISONS																			
42 Party Total					8%	31%	22%	39%	34%	19%	19%	25%	4%	6%	10%	4%	5%	4%	62%
43 Group Total					18%	23%	29%	29%	22%	25%	25%	20%	7%	8%	12%	6%	7%	12%	100%
44 World Total																			

152 • Table 104

TREATY PROFILE OF ITALY

			Dyads			Time				Topics						Institutions				Self-Registered
Partners	Partner's World Total	Absolutes		Ratios		1946 1950	1951 1955	1956 1960	1961 1965	Admin & Dipl	Social Coop	Econ Coop	Aid	Milit	UN	Spec Ag's	Intl Court	Arbitration	Other	
			Self	Other																
(1)	(2)	(3)	(4)	(5)	(6)	(7)	(8)	(9)	(10)	(11)	(12)	(13)	(14)	(15)	(16)	(17)	(18)	(19)	(20)
TOP THIRTY																				
1 USA (United States)	2599	63	8%	2%	17	22	14	10	9	7	7	21	19	4	5	3	1	8	3
2 France	1033	62	8%	6%	13	19	20	10	13	28	15		6			2		5	13
3 Switzerland	426	41	5%	10%	5	11	15	10	12	16	12	1			1	1	2	7	9
4 UK Great Britain	981	40	5%	4%	14	13	8	5	12	10	12	1	5	5	2	1	1	6	1
5 Yugoslavia	525	38	5%	7%	11	6	13	8	16	8	9		5		1		1	6	4
6 Austria	445	28	4%	6%	7	13	5	3	10	10	7		1		2			3	6
7 Germany, West	890	25	3%	3%		10	6	9	5	10	7	1	2					6	4
8 Belgium	499	24	3%	5%	8	9	3	4	6	15	5		4					4	4
9 Netherlands	548	23	3%	4%	3	10	8	2	4	10	5		4	1	1			8	1
10 USSR (Soviet Union)	1356	19	3%	1%	6		9	4	6	2	10		1					1	
11 Spain	437	19	3%	4%	2	3	13	1		10	9							1	
12 Turkey	298	18	2%	6%	4	5	3	6	2	2	10	4	1		1	1		1	4
13 Argentina	164	17	2%	10%	4	2	7	4	1	9	5	2						1	2
14 Brazil	195	16	2%	8%	4	2	8	2	4	4	4	1	3				1	1	2
15 Sweden	483	15	2%	3%	7	4	3	1	1	3	11								1
16 Poland	493	14	2%	3%	1		5	8	3	4	8	1							
17 Greece	318	14	2%	4%	4	6	2	2	1	4	6		1		3	1		11	1
18 United Arab Rep	232	12	2%	5%	1	1	6	4	2	2	6	1						2	2
19 Norway	461	11	1%	2%	5	3	2	1	1	2	8						1	3	2
20 Denmark	380	11	1%	3%	3	4	3	1	1	1	8		1					11	3
21 Australia	201	11	1%	5%	3	5	3		2	4	1	1	3	3	1				
22 IBRD (World Bank)	452	8	1%	2%	2	3	3					8					2		
23 Canada	310	8	1%	3%		3	4	1	3	3	1		1					5	2
24 Tunisia	97	7	1%	7%		1	1	2	3	3	2	2	1			1		1	3
25 Monaco	36	7	1%	19%		1	4	2	2	4									
26 Mexico	138	7	1%	5%	1			6	2	1	2	2							
27 Israel	232	7	1%	3%		5	1	1	3		4						1		
28 Iran	170	7	1%	4%	1	1	5		2	1	4			1	1	2		2	2
29 Czechoslovakia	393	7	1%	2%	2		2	3	1		4	1		4		4	3		
30 Albania	125	7	1%	6%			5	2	1	2	2		2						1
31 All Others (67)	6627	169	22%	3%	34	30	47	58	51	41	45	19	13	7	9	7	3	8	18
GROUPS																				
32 African Group	968	21	3%	2%	4	7	6	15	4	6	3	7	8		1	1		9	1
33 Arab Group	937	43	6%	5%	4	7	14	18	8	11	15	8	1		3	2		9	9
34 Asian Group	1937	29	4%	1%	6	4	14	5	9	5	12	1	2		3	1	1	3	4
35 Commonwealth	1641	67	9%	4%	21	25	12	9	19	19	16	2	11	10	3		3	6	1
36 Communist Group	3310	61	8%	2%	12	12	25	24	10	11	34	3	3					2	4
37 Latin America	1674	77	10%	5%	22	12	23	20	22	20	20	6	8	1	10	2	1	3	8
38 Western Europe	5906	325	43%	6%	68	105	96	56	68	126	106	7	19	4	3	4	6	62	50
39 Intl Organs	1399	18	2%	1%	1	4	6	7	6	1		11				3			
TOTALS																				
40 All Data	21544	755	100%		162	192	226	175	177	216	226	66	70	20	27	16	14	99	85
41 UNTS Only		322																		
COMPARISONS																				
42 Party Total					21%	25%	30%	23%	23%	29%	30%	9%	9%	6%	8%	5%	4%	31%	26%
43 Group Total					22%	25%	27%	26%	24%	26%	32%	10%	8%	4%	14%	6%	8%	17%	32%
44 World Total					18%	23%	29%	29%	22%	25%	25%	20%	7%	8%	12%	6%	7%	12%	100%

TREATY PROFILE OF ITU (TELECOMMUN)

Partners (1)	Partner's World Total (2)	Dyads Absolutes (3)	Ratios Self (4)	Ratios Other (5)	Time 1946-1950 (6)	Time 1951-1955 (7)	Time 1956-1960 (8)	Time 1961-1965 (9)	Admin & Dipl (10)	Social Coop (11)	Econ Coop (12)	Aid (13)	Milit (14)	UN (15)	Spec Ag's (16)	Intl Court (17)	Arbitration (18)	Other (19)	Self-Registered (20)
TOP THIRTY																			
1 United Nations	233	2	50%	1%	1		1		2					1					
2 Switzerland	426	1	25%		1				1						1				
3 UN Special Fund	113	1	25%	1%			1		1										
4																			
5																			
6																			
7																			
8																			
9																			
10																			
11																			
12																			
13																			
14																			
15																			
16																			
17																			
18																			
19																			
20																			
21																			
22																			
23																			
24																			
25																			
26																			
27																			
28																			
29																			
30																			
31 All Others (0)																			
GROUPS																			
32 African Group	968																		
33 Arab Group	937																		
34 Asian Group	1937																		
35 Commonwealth	1641																		
36 Communist Group	3310																		
37 Latin America	1674																		
38 Western Europe	5906	1	25%		1				1										
39 Intl Organs	1399	3	75%		1		2		3					1	1				
TOTALS																			
40 All Data		4	100%		2		2		4					1	1				
41 UNTS Only	772	3																	
COMPARISONS																			
42 Party Total					50%	25%	50%	40%	100%	7%	1%	71%	1%	33%	33%	13%	15%	4%	74%
43 Group Total					12%	25%	23%	29%	19%	25%	25%	20%	7%	27%	11%	6%	7%	12%	100%
44 World Total					18%	23%	29%	29%	22%	25%	25%	20%	7%	8%	12%				

154 • Table 106

TREATY PROFILE OF IVORY COAST

Partners (1)	Partner's World Total (2)	Dyads Absolutes (3)	Dyads Ratios Self (4)	Dyads Ratios Other (5)	Time 1946 1950 (6)	Time 1951 1955 (7)	Time 1956 1960 (8)	Time 1961 1965 (9)	Topics Admin & Dipl (10)	Topics Social Coop (11)	Topics Econ Coop (12)	Topics Aid (13)	Topics Milit (14)	Institutions UN (15)	Institutions Spec Ag's (16)	Institutions Intl Court (17)	Institutions Arbitration (18)	Institutions Other (19)	Self-Registered (20)
TOP THIRTY																			
1 France	1033	6	19%	1%			1	5	3	2	1				1		1		
2 USA (United States)	2599	5	16%					5			1	4			1	1	1		
3 Netherlands	548	4	13%	1%				4	1	2	1				1	1	1		
4 Germany, West	890	4	13%					4	1	1	1	2			1				
5 Switzerland	426	2	6%					2		1	1				1	1	1		
6 UK Great Britain	981	1	3%					1	1						1				
7 Sweden	483	1	3%					1		1									
8 WHO (World Health)	187	1	3%	1%				1				1		1					
9 UN Special Fund	113	1	3%	1%				1				1				1			
10 United Nations	233	1	3%					1									2		
11 UNICEF (Children)	122	1	3%					1				1		1					
12 Mali	54	1	3%	2%				1	1	1					1		1		
13 Israel	232	1	3%					1											
14 Guinea	75	1	3%	1%				1	1	1					1				
15 Belgium	499	1	3%					1	1										
16 Accept UN Charter	68	1	3%	1%			1							1					
17																			
18																			
19																			
20																			
21																			
22																			
23																			
24																			
25																			
26																			
27																			
28																			
29																			
30																			
31 All Others (0)																			
GROUPS																			
32 African Group	968	2	6%					2		2					2		2		
33 Arab Group	937																		
34 Asian Group	1937																		
35 Commonwealth	1641	1	3%					1	1										
36 Communist Group	3310																		
37 Latin America	1674																		
38 Western Europe	5906	18	56%				1	17	5	7	4	2			4	2	3		
39 Intl Organs	1399	4	13%					4				4		2		1	2		
TOTALS																			
40 All Data	8543	32	100%				2	30	8	9	5	10		3	6	4	7		
41 UNTS Only	24																			
COMPARISONS																			
42 Party Total					1%	5%	6%	94%	25%	28%	16%	31%	4%	12%	25%	17%	29%	4%	1%
43 Group Total					18%	23%	18%	75%	22%	21%	18%	35%	7%	19%	13%	10%	15%	12%	1%
44 World Total					18%	29%	29%	29%	22%	25%	25%	20%		8%	12%	6%	7%	12%	100%

TREATY PROFILE OF JAMAICA

Table 107 • 155

Partners (1)	Partner's World Total (2)	Dyads Absolutes (3)	Ratios Self (4)	Ratios Other (5)	Time 1946 1950 (6)	Time 1951 1955 (7)	Time 1956 1960 (8)	Time 1961 1965 (9)	Admin & Dipl (10)	Social Coop (11)	Econ Coop (12)	Aid (13)	Milit (14)	UN (15)	Spec Ag's (16)	Intl Court (17)	Arbi- tration (18)	Other (19)	Self- Regis- tered (20)
TOP THIRTY																			
1 USA (United States)	2599	5	24%					5		1	2	1	1						1
2 UK Great Britain	981	4	19%					4	1	1	1		2						2
3 Germany, West	890	3	14%					3		2		1							3
4 USSR (Soviet Union)	1356	1	5%					1	1										
5 WHO (World Health)	187	1	5%	1%				1				1			1				
6 UN Special Fund	113	1	5%	1%				1	1			1			1				
7 United Nations	233	1	5%					1						1		1	1		
8 UNICEF (Children)	122	1	5%	1%				1							1		2		
9 IBRD (World Bank)	452	1	5%					1				1							
10 Japan	443	1	5%					1	1										
11 Canada	310	1	5%					1											
12 Accept UN Charter	68	1	5%	1%				1	1				1	1					1
13																			
14																			
15																			
16																			
17																			
18																			
19																			
20																			
21																			
22																			
23																			
24																			
25																			
26																			
27																			
28																			
29																			
30																			
31 All Others (0)																			
GROUPS																			
32 African Group	968																		
33 Arab Group	937																		
34 Asian Group	1937																		
35 Commonwealth	1641	5	24%					5	1		1		3						3
36 Communist Group	3310	1	5%					1	1										
37 Latin America	1674																		
38 Western Europe	5906	3	14%					3		2		1							
39 Intl Organs	1399	5	24%					5	2			3		1	2	1	3		3
TOTALS																			
40 All Data	7754	21	100%					21	6	3	3	5	4	2	2	1	3		7
41 UNITS Only		19																		
COMPARISONS																			
42 Party Total					18%	27%	24%	100%	29%	14%	14%	24%	19%	11%	11%	5%	16%	7%	37%
43 Group Total					18%	23%	29%	31%	16%	25%	18%	31%	9%	7%	10%	5%	6%	7%	6%
44 World Total					18%	23%	29%	29%	22%	25%	25%	20%	7%	8%	12%	6%	7%	12%	100%

TREATY PROFILE OF JAPAN

Table 108

Part-ners (1)	Partner's World Total (2)	Abso-lutes (3)	Dyads Ratios Self (4)	Dyads Ratios Other (5)	Time 1946-1950 (6)	Time 1951-1955 (7)	Time 1956-1960 (8)	Time 1961-1965 (9)	Admin & Dipl (10)	Social Coop (11)	Econ Coop (12)	Aid (13)	Milit (14)	UN (15)	Spec Ag's (16)	Intl Court (17)	Arbi-tration (18)	Other (19)	Self-Regis-tered (20)
TOP THIRTY																			
1 USA (United States)	2599	84	19%	3%	1	36	23	24	16	9	14	25	20	4	8	1	1	7	8
2 IBRD (World Bank)	452	30	7%	7%		5	16	9			1	29							
3 UK Great Britain	981	21	5%	2%		9	4	8	8	2	7	1	3		4		1	1	2
4 USSR (Soviet Union)	1356	18	4%	1%	1		15	2	8	3	7			1			1		1
5 Philippines	236	18	4%	8%	1	7	8	2	3	3	6	2	4				1	1	3
6 China People's Rep	766	13	3%	2%		5	1	7	8	1	4				1				
7 Sweden	483	12	3%	2%	2	7	3		2	7	7		1		1		1		2
8 India	299	12	3%	4%		2	4	6	5	3	3	1	1		1	1		1	7
9 Germany, West	890	12	3%	1%		4	5	3	5	3	4				1	1	1		2
10 Pakistan	245	11	2%	4%		1	6	4	4	5	2				3				5
11 France	1033	11	2%	1%		4	2	5	4	2	4				2	1	1		3
12 Argentina	164	10	2%	6%				10	3	4	3			1	2		1		4
13 Thailand	132	9	2%	7%		4	2	3	5	6	3	1			1			1	2
14 United Nations	233	9	2%	4%		5	1	3		1			2			1		1	
15 Morocco	94	8	2%	9%			5	8	1	1	1	2	1		3	2	1		5
16 Indonesia	126	8	2%	6%		1	5	2	2	1	3	2	3		1				2
17 Denmark	380	8	2%	2%		5	3		2	2	3	1	1		3		1		4
18 Canada	310	8	2%	3%		3	2	3	5	2	2				3	1	3		6
19 Korea, South	80	7	2%	9%			1	6	2	3	1				3		1	1	6
20 Australia	201	7	2%	3%		2	2	3	5	1	3	1			1	2			3
21 Netherlands	548	6	1%	1%		3	3		2	2	1					1			
22 Taiwan	172	6	1%	3%		5	1		2	1	3		1						
23 Brazil	195	6	1%	3%	2		2	4	1	1	3				2			1	3
24 Belgium	499	6	1%	1%			4		2	1	3		1		2	1	1	1	
25 Vietnam, South	106	5	1%	5%		1	3	1	2			2							3
26 New Zealand	101	5	1%	5%	1		1	4	2	1	4		1		2				3
27 Italy	755	5	1%	1%		2	1	2	2	2	1		1		1		1		
28 Iran	170	5	1%	3%	1		4		2		1	1		3					3
29 Burma	102	5	1%	5%		3	2		2		3	1	2			2		1	1
30 Switzerland	426	4	1%	1%	4	2	2	1	1	1	2			2	1		1		23
31 All Others (44)	6388	74	17%	1%		16	31	27	24	14	28	7	1	8	13	10	5	4	
GROUPS																			
32 African Group	968	6	1%	1%		2	1	5	1	2	2	1	1		2	2	2		1
33 Arab Group	937	16	4%	2%		2	2	12	2	7	4	2							1
34 Asian Group	1937	98	22%	5%	1	26	39	32	19	32	25	10	12	2	10	8	8	8	41
35 Commonwealth	1641	43	10%	3%		15	9	19	13	9	14	3	4		13	3	2	1	12
36 Communist Group	3310	35	8%	1%	1	5	20	9	18	4	13			3	1				
37 Latin America	1674	27	6%	2%		1	8	18	7	9	10	1			7	5	4	2	12
38 Western Europe	5906	85	19%	1%	4	32	34	15	29	15	36	1	4	2	12	3	2	3	12
39 Intl Organs	1399	43	10%	3%		12	18	13	5	1	1	34	2		2			1	17
TOTALS																			
40 All Data	20522	443	100%		7	132	156	148	115	88	120	77	43	15	55	26	20	22	96
41 UNTS Only		283																	
COMPARISONS																			
42 Party Total					2%	30%	35%	33%	26%	20%	27%	17%	10%	5%	19%	9%	7%	8%	34%
43 Group Total					18%	23%	29%	29%	22%	25%	25%	20%	7%	8%	12%	6%	7%	12%	100%
44 World Total																			

TREATY PROFILE OF JORDAN

Table 109

Partners (1)	Partner's World Total (2)	Dyads Absolutes (3)	Ratios Self (4)	Ratios Other (5)	Time 1946-1950 (6)	Time 1951-1955 (7)	Time 1956-1960 (8)	Time 1961-1965 (9)	Topics Admin & Dipl (10)	Topics Social Coop (11)	Topics Econ Coop (12)	Topics Aid (13)	Topics Milit (14)	Institutions UN (15)	Institutions Spec Ag's (16)	Institutions Intl Court (17)	Institutions Arbitration (18)	Institutions Other (19)	Self-Registered (20)
TOP THIRTY																			
1 UK Great Britain	981	13	20%	1%	2	1	4	6	1			9	1	2	1	2			
2 USA (United States)	2599	12	18%			7	4	1		1	1	11	1		1	1		1	
3 WHO (World Health)	187	4	6%	2%		3	1					4			2				
4 United Nations	233	3	5%	1%		1	1	1	1			2			2	1			
5 IDA (Devel Assoc)	82	3	5%	4%				3				3			4		1		
6 Italy	755	3	5%			1		2	1	2									
7 Iran	170	3	5%	2%	1			1	1	1									1
8 United Arab Rep	232	2	3%	1%	1	1			1	1	1								
9 Turkey	298	2	3%	1%	2					1	1								
10 Syria	84	2	3%	2%		2			1								1		
11 UN Relief Palestin	9	2	3%	22%		2	1		2			1		1				1	
12 UNICEF (Children)	122	2	3%	2%		1		1	1			2		1	1				
13 Taiwan	172	2	3%	1%			1	1											
14 Sweden	483	1	2%		1					1									
15 Spain	437	1	2%					1	1							1			
16 UN Special Fund	113	1	2%	1%			1				1	1		1	1				
17 ILO (Labor Org)	59	1	2%	2%				1		1						1			
18 Norway	461	1	2%					1											
19 Netherlands	548	1	2%		1					1							1		
20 Israel	232	1	2%	1%	1								1					1	
21 Iraq	96	1	2%		1				1										
22 France	1033	1	2%					1											
23 Denmark	380	1	2%				1												
24 Belgium	499	1	2%	1%				1	1								1	1	
25 Accept UN Charter	68	1	2%			1								1					1
31 All Others (0)																			
GROUPS																			
32 African Group	968	5	8%	1%	2	3			3	1	1				1				
33 Arab Group	937	5	8%	1%	1		2	2	2	2	1				1		1	1	
34 Asian Group	1937																		
35 Commonwealth	1641	13	20%	1%	2	1	4	6	1	1	1	9	1	2	1	2	1		
36 Communist Group	3310																		
37 Latin America	1674																		
38 Western Europe	5906	12	18%		3	1	1	7	3						6	2	4		
39 Intl Organs	1399	16	25%	1%		8	4	4	2	9		14		4	7	2	2		1
TOTALS																			
40 All Data	10333	65	100%		9	21	15	20	12	13	3	34	3	8	16	7	7	3	1
41 UNTS Only		58																		
COMPARISONS																			
42 Party Total					14%	32%	23%	31%	18%	20%	5%	52%	5%	14%	28%	12%	12%	5%	2%
43 Group Total					9%	24%	31%	36%	18%	27%	22%	29%	4%	15%	20%	8%	15%	9%	5%
44 World Total					18%	23%	29%	29%	22%	25%	25%	20%	7%	8%	12%	6%	7%	12%	100%

TREATY PROFILE OF KENYA

Table 110

	Partners	Partner's World Total	Dyads Abso-lutes	Ratios Self	Ratios Other	Time 1946-1950	Time 1951-1955	Time 1956-1960	Time 1961-1965	Topics Admin & Dipl	Topics Social Coop	Topics Econ Coop	Topics Aid	Topics Milit	Institutions UN	Institutions Spec Ag's	Institutions Intl Court	Institutions Arbi-tration	Institutions Other	Self-Regis-tered
	(1)	(2)	(3)	(4)	(5)	(6)	(7)	(8)	(9)	(10)	(11)	(12)	(13)	(14)	(15)	(16)	(17)	(18)	(19)	(20)
	TOP THIRTY																			
1	USA (United States)	2599	4	15%					4	1		1	2		1					1
2	Germany, West	890	4	15%					4			2	2							
3	UK Great Britain	981	3	12%					3	1		1		1		1				
4	IDA (Devel Assoc)	82	3	12%	4%				3				3							
5	Norway	461	2	8%					2			1	1							
6	UN Special Fund	113	1	4%	1%				1	1					1					
7	United Nations	233	1	4%					1	1							1	1		
8	IBRD (World Bank)	452	1	4%					1				1					2		
9	Poland	493	1	4%					1		1									
10	Japan	443	1	4%					1		1									
11	France	1033	1	4%					1											
12	Denmark	380	1	4%					1				1							
13	China People's Rep	766	1	4%	2%				1	1					1		1			
14	ICJ Option Clause	62	1	4%	2%				1	1					1					
15	Accept UN Charter	68	1	4%	1%				1											
16																				
...																				
31	All Others (0)																			
	GROUPS																			
32	African Group	968																		
33	Arab Group	937																		
34	Asian Group	1937																		
35	Commonwealth	1641	3	12%					3	1		1		1		1				
36	Communist Group	3310	2	8%					2		2		2							
37	Latin America	1674																		
38	Western Europe	5906	8	31%					8		2	3	3							
39	Intl Organs	1399	6	23%					6	2			4		1		1	3		
	TOTALS																			
40	All Data	9056	26	100%					26	6	3	5	11	1	4	1	2	3	1	
41	UNTS Only		16																	
	COMPARISONS																			
42	Party Total					1%	5%	18%	100%	23%	12%	19%	42%	4%	25%	6%	13%	19%	6%	
43	Group Total					18%	23%	18%	75%	22%	21%	18%	35%	4%	19%	13%	10%	15%	4%	1%
44	World Total					18%	23%	29%	29%	22%	25%	25%	20%	7%	8%	12%	6%	7%	12%	100%

TREATY PROFILE OF KOREA, NORTH

Table 111 • 159

Partners (1)	Partner's World Total (2)	Dyads Absolutes (3)	Ratios Self (4)	Other (5)	Time 1946-1950 (6)	1951-1955 (7)	1956-1960 (8)	1961-1965 (9)	Topics Admin & Dipl (10)	Social Coop (11)	Econ Coop (12)	Aid (13)	Milit (14)	Institutions UN (15)	Spec Ag's (16)	Intl Court (17)	Arbitration (18)	Other (19)	Self-Registered (20)
TOP THIRTY																			
1 USSR (Soviet Union)	1356	38	38%	3%	4	8	22	4	7	9	8	13	1				1	1	
2 China People's Rep	766	36	36%	5%	4	3	16	13	5	21	10								
3 Germany, East	556	13	13%	2%		4	7	2	1	7	3	2							
4 Poland	493	5	5%	1%		3	2			4		1							
5 Romania	251	3	3%	1%		2	1			3									
6 Cuba	111	2	2%	2%			2		1	1									
7 Hungary	290	1	1%					1		1									
8 Czechoslovakia	393	1	1%				1			1									
9																			
10-30																			
31 All Others (0)																			
GROUPS																			
32 African Group	968																		
33 Arab Group	937																		
34 Asian Group	1937																		
35 Commonwealth	1641																		
36 Communist Group	3310	97	98%	3%	8	20	49	20	13	46	21	16	1				1	1	
37 Latin America	1674	2	2%				2		1	1									
38 Western Europe	5906																		
39 Intl Organs	1399																		
TOTALS																			
40 All Data	4216	99	100%		8	20	51	20	14	47	21	16	1				1	1	
41 UNTS Only		15																	
COMPARISONS																			
42 Party Total					8%	20%	52%	20%	14%	47%	21%	16%	1%	4%	4%		7%	7%	
43 Group Total					16%	17%	38%	29%	20%	32%	32%	13%	2%	8%	12%	6%	3%	17%	33%
44 World Total					18%	23%	29%	29%	22%	25%	25%	20%	7%				7%	12%	100%

160 • Table 112

TREATY PROFILE OF KOREA, SOUTH

Partners	Partner's World Total	Dyads Absolutes	Ratios Self	Ratios Other	Time 1946-1950	Time 1951-1955	Time 1956-1960	Time 1961-1965	Admin & Dipl	Social Coop	Econ Coop	Aid	Milit	UN	Spec Ag's	Intl Court	Arbitration	Other	Self-Registered
(1)	(2)	(3)	(4)	(5)	(6)	(7)	(8)	(9)	(10)	(11)	(12)	(13)	(14)	(15)	(16)	(17)	(18)	(19)	(20)
TOP THIRTY																			
1 USA (United States)	2599	43	54%	2%	10	8	15	10	3	7	4	17	12	9	2		1	2	2
2 Japan	443	7	9%	2%				6	5	1	1	1				5	3		
3 Germany, West	890	6	8%	1%				6	1	2	2								
4 France	1033	3	4%					3		1	2								
5 Taiwan	172	3	4%	2%		1		2	1	1	1				1				
6 Vietnam, South	106	2	3%	2%				2					1						
7 WHO (World Health)	187	2	3%	1%		1	1			1		1		1					
8 United Nations	233	2	3%			1		1	1				1	1		1			
9 Philippines	236	2	3%	1%			1	1	1		1								
10 Netherlands	548	2	3%					2			2								
11 Italy	755	2	3%					1						1					
12 Thailand	132	1	1%	1%				1						1	1		1		
13 UN Special Fund	113	1	1%	1%	1							1							
14 UNICEF (Children)	122	1	1%	1%				1				1							
15 IDA (Devel Assoc)	82	1	1%					1											
16 Norway	461	1	1%					1			1								
17 Australia	201	1	1%					1						1					
18																			
19																			
20																			
21																			
22																			
23																			
24																			
25																			
26																			
27																			
28																			
29																			
30																			
31 All Others (0)																			
GROUPS																			
32 African Group	968																		
33 Arab Group	937																		
34 Asian Group	1937	8	10%			1	1	6	2	1	4		1	2	1				
35 Commonwealth	1641	1	1%					1			1			1	1				
36 Communist Group	3310																		
37 Latin America	1674																		
38 Western Europe	5906	14	18%			1	1	13	1	4	8	1				1			
39 Intl Organs	1399	7	9%	1%	1	2	1	3	2	1		3	1	2	1	1	2		
TOTALS																			
40 All Data	8313	80	100%		11	12	18	39	13	14	18	21	14	14	5	6	6	2	
41 UNTS Only		64																	
COMPARISONS																			
42 Party Total					14%	15%	23%	49%	16%	18%	23%	26%	18%	22%	8%	9%	9%	3%	16%
43 Group Total					16%	23%	31%	30%	21%	23%	20%	30%	7%	10%	15%	8%	8%	6%	16%
44 World Total					18%	23%	29%	29%	22%	25%	25%	20%	7%	8%	12%	6%	7%	12%	100%

Table 113 • 161

TREATY PROFILE OF KUWAIT

	Partners (1)	Partner's World Total (2)	Dyads Absolutes (3)	Ratios Self (4)	Ratios Other (5)	Time 1946-1950 (6)	Time 1951-1955 (7)	Time 1956-1960 (8)	Time 1961-1965 (9)	Topics Admin & Dipl (10)	Topics Social Coop (11)	Topics Econ Coop (12)	Topics Aid (13)	Topics Milit (14)	Institutions UN (15)	Institutions Spec Ag's (16)	Institutions Intl Court (17)	Institutions Arbitration (18)	Institutions Other (19)	Self-Registered (20)
	TOP THIRTY																			
1	USA (United States)	2599	2	20%				1								1				
2	UK Great Britain	981	2	20%				1	1	1	1					1		1		
3	WHO (World Health)	187	1	10%	1%				1						1					
4	UN Special Fund	113	1	10%	1%			1		1			1		1	1				
5	United Nations	233	1	10%				1					1				1	1		
6	Japan	443	1	10%					1		1					1	1	1		
7	Iraq	96	1	10%	1%				1	1										1
8	Accept UN Charter	68	1	10%	1%					1					1					
9																				
10																				
11																				
12																				
13																				
14																				
15																				
16																				
17																				
18																				
19																				
20																				
21																				
22																				
23																				
24																				
25																				
26																				
27																				
28																				
29																				
30																				
31	All Others (0)																			
	GROUPS																			
32	African Group	968																		
33	Arab Group	937	1	10%					1	1										1
34	Asian Group	1937																		
35	Commonwealth	1641	2	20%				1	1	1						1		1		
36	Communist Group	3310																		
37	Latin America	1674																		
38	Western Europe	5906																		
39	Intl Organs	1399	3	30%				2	1	1	1				2	1	1	1		1
40	TOTALS All Data	4720	10	100%				4	6	4	3		3		3	4	2	3		
41	UNTS Only		10	100%																
	COMPARISONS																			
42	Party Total					9%	24%	40%	60%	40%	30%		30%	4%	30%	40%	20%	30%	9%	10%
43	Group Total					18%	23%	31%	36%	18%	27%	22%	29%	4%	15%	20%	8%	15%	9%	5%
44	World Total					18%	23%	29%	29%	22%	25%	25%	20%	7%	8%	12%	6%	7%	12%	100%

162 • Table 114

TREATY PROFILE OF LAFTA (FREE TRADE)

Partners (1)	Partner's World Total (2)	Dyads Abso- lutes (3)	Ratios Self (4)	Ratios Other (5)	Time 1946 1950 (6)	Time 1951 1955 (7)	Time 1956 1960 (8)	Time 1961 1965 (9)	Topics Admin & Dipl (10)	Topics Social Coop (11)	Topics Econ Coop (12)	Topics Aid (13)	Topics Milit (14)	Institutions UN (15)	Institutions Spec Ag's (16)	Institutions Intl Court (17)	Institutions Arbi- tration (18)	Institutions Other (19)	Self- Regis- tered (20)
TOP THIRTY																			
1 ILO (Labor Org)	59	1	100%	2%				1	1										
2																			
3																			
4																			
5																			
6																			
7																			
8																			
9																			
10																			
11																			
12																			
13																			
14																			
15																			
16																			
17																			
18																			
19																			
20																			
21																			
22																			
23																			
24																			
25																			
26																			
27																			
28																			
29																			
30																			
31 All Others (0)																			
GROUPS																			
32 African Group	968																		
33 Arab Group	937																		
34 Asian Group	1937																		
35 Commonwealth	1641																		
36 Communist Group	3310																		
37 Latin America	1674																		
38 Western Europe	5906																		
39 Intl Organs	1399	1	100%					1	1										
TOTALS																			
40 All Data	59	1	100%																
41 UNTS Only		1																		
COMPARISONS																			
42 Party Total					12%	25%	23%	100% 40%	100% 19%	7%	1%	71%	1%	27%	11%	13%	15%	4%	74%
43 Group Total					18%	23%	29%	29%	22%	25%	25%	20%	7%	8%	12%	6%	7%	12%	100%
44 World Total																				

Table 115 • 163

TREATY PROFILE OF LAOS

Partners (1)	Partner's World Total (2)	Dyads Absolutes (3)	Dyads Ratios Self (4)	Dyads Ratios Other (5)	Time 1946-1950 (6)	Time 1951-1955 (7)	Time 1956-1960 (8)	Time 1961-1965 (9)	Topics Admin & Dipl (10)	Topics Social Coop (11)	Topics Econ Coop (12)	Topics Aid (13)	Topics Milit (14)	Institutions UN (15)	Institutions Spec Ag's (16)	Institutions Intl Court (17)	Institutions Arbitration (18)	Institutions Other (19)	Self-Registered (20)
TOP THIRTY																			
1 USSR (Soviet Union)	1356	5	18%			3	1	4	1		2	2							
2 USA (United States)	2599	4	14%	3%			1	1	1		1	3			1	1		1	
3 Vietnam, South	106	3	11%			1	2		2	1	1	1							
4 UK Great Britain	981	2	7%	2%		1		2	1									1	
5 Thailand	132	2	7%	2%		1	1	1	1	1	1	1							1
6 UNICEF (Children)	122	2	7%				1							1					
7 Japan	443	2	7%				1	1				1							
8 France	1033	2	7%			1	1		2									1	
9 WHO (World Health)	187	1	4%	1%			1							1	1				
10 UN Special Fund	113	1	4%				1					1							
11 United Nations	233	1	4%				1				1	1				1			
12 Australia	201	1	4%					1									1		
13 ICJ Option Clause	62	1	4%	2%		1			1					1				1	
14 Accept UN Charter	68	1	4%	1%		1			1										
15–30																			
31 All Others (0)																			
GROUPS																			
32 African Group	968																		
33 Arab Group	937																		
34 Asian Group	1937	5	18%			2	2	1	3	2	2	1						1	1
35 Commonwealth	1641	3	11%				1	3	1		2	2							
36 Communist Group	3310	5	18%			2		4	1									2	
37 Latin America	1674																		
38 Western Europe	5906	2	7%			1	1												
39 Intl Organs	1399	5	18%			1	4		2		1	4		2	1	1	1		
TOTALS																			
40 All Data	7636	28	100%			9	9	10	8	3	6	11		3	2	3	1	3	1
41 UNTS Only		20																	
COMPARISONS																			
42 Party Total					16%	32%	32%	36%	29%	11%	21%	39%		15%	10%	15%	5%	15%	5%
43 Group Total					18%	23%	31%	30%	21%	23%	20%	30%	7%	10%	15%	8%	8%	6%	16%
44 World Total					18%	23%	29%	29%	22%	25%	25%	20%	7%	8%	12%	6%	7%	12%	100%

164 • Table 116

TREATY PROFILE OF LEAGUE OF NATIONS

Partners (1)	Partner's World Total (2)	Absolutes (3)	Dyads Ratios Self (4)	Other (5)	Time 1946-1950 (6)	1951-1955 (7)	1956-1960 (8)	1961-1965 (9)	Topics Admin & Dipl (10)	Social Coop (11)	Econ Coop (12)	Aid (13)	Milit (14)	UN (15)	Institutions Spec Ag's (16)	Intl Court (17)	Arbitration (18)	Other (19)	Self-Registered (20)
TOP THIRTY																			
1 United Nations	233	8	89%	3%	8				8						3			1	
2 ILO (Labor Org)	59	1	11%	2%	1				1										
3																			
4																			
5																			
6																			
7																			
8																			
9																			
10																			
11																			
12																			
13																			
14																			
15																			
16																			
17																			
18																			
19																			
20																			
21																			
22																			
23																			
24																			
25																			
26																			
27																			
28																			
29																			
30																			
31 All Others (0)																			
GROUPS																			
32 African Group	968																		
33 Arab Group	937																		
34 Asian Group	1937																		
35 Commonwealth	1641																		
36 Communist Group	3310																		
37 Latin America	1674																		
38 Western Europe	5906																		
39 Intl Organs	1399	9	100%	1%	9				9						3		1		
TOTALS																			
40 All Data	292	9	100%		9				9						3		1		
41 UNTS Only		9			9														
COMPARISONS																			
42 Party Total					100%	25%	23%	40%	100%	7%	1%	71%	1%	27%	33%	11%	11%		74%
43 Group Total					12%	25%	29%	29%	19%	25%	25%	20%	7%	8%	11%	13%	15%	4%	
44 World Total					18%	23%	29%		22%						12%	6%	7%	12%	100%

TREATY PROFILE OF LEBANON

Table 117

Partners (1)	Partner's World Total (2)	Dyads Absolutes (3)	Ratios Self (4)	Ratios Other (5)	Time 1946-1950 (6)	Time 1951-1955 (7)	Time 1956-1960 (8)	Time 1961-1965 (9)	Admin & Dipl (10)	Social Coop (11)	Econ Coop (12)	Aid (13)	Milit (14)	UN (15)	Spec Ag's (16)	Intl Court (17)	Arbitration (18)	Other (19)	Self-Registered (20)
TOP THIRTY																			
1 USA (United States)	2599	13	17%	1%	2	7	4			3		8	2	3	1				
2 Italy	755	6	8%	1%	3	2	1		2	2	1	1			1			1	
3 United Nations	233	5	7%	2%			4	1	2	1		1	1		1	1	1		
4 Germany, West	890	5	7%	1%	1	2	1	2	1	1	3				1				
5 UK Great Britain	981	4	5%		1	1	1	1		2	1				1				
6 Turkey	298	4	5%	1%	3		1		3	1									
7 Greece	318	4	5%	1%	4				2	2									1
8 WHO (World Health)	187	3	4%	2%		2	1			1		2		2		1		2	
9 Pakistan	245	3	4%		1	1		1	2										
10 China People's Rep	766	3	4%	1%		3					3								
11 Switzerland	426	2	3%			1	1		1	1	1				1				
12 Spain	437	2	3%		2				1	1									
13 Iran	170	2	3%	1%		1	1		1	1								1	
14 France	1033	2	3%		1			1			2			1	1	1	1		
15 Belgium	499	2	3%			2			1	1									
16 Yugoslavia	525	1	1%			1					1								
17 USSR (Soviet Union)	1356	1	1%			1													
18 Sweden	483	1	1%			1				1									
19 UN Special Fund	113	1	1%				1					1		1	1				
20 UN Relief Palestin	9	1	1%	11%								1		1					
21 UNICEF (Children)	122	1	1%			1						1		1					
22 ICAO (Civil Aviat)	23	1	1%	4%		1									1				
23 IBRD (World Bank)	452	1	1%				1								1				
24 Norway	461	1	1%		1					1									
25 Netherlands	548	1	1%		1					1									
26 Mexico	138	1	1%		1														
27 Israel	232	1	1%					1			1		1					1	
28 Germany, East	556	1	1%					1			1								
29 Denmark	380	1	1%				1			1									
30 Taiwan	172	1	1%	1%								1	1						
31 All Others (0)																			
GROUPS																			
32 African Group	968	6	8%		1	2	2	1		2	1				1				
33 Arab Group	937	4	5%		1	1	1	1	3	2	1								
34 Asian Group	1937	5	7%			4		1			5								
35 Commonwealth	1641																		
36 Communist Group	3310	5	7%			4	1				5		1						
37 Latin America	1674	1	1%		1					1									
38 Western Europe	5906	31	41%	1%	14	9	5	3	10	13	7	1		1	9	5	5	4	1
39 Intl Organs	1399	13	17%	1%		5	7	1	2	2		8	1	5	2	1	2		
TOTALS																			
40 All Data	15407	75	100%		20	29	19	7	15	24	14	17	5	10	14	6	8	5	1
41 UNTS Only		52																		
COMPARISONS																			
42 Party Total					27%	39%	25%	9%	20%	32%	19%	23%	7%	19%	27%	12%	15%	10%	2%
43 Group Total					9%	24%	31%	36%	18%	27%	22%	29%	4%	15%	20%	8%	15%	9%	5%
44 World Total					18%	23%	29%	29%	22%	25%	25%	20%	7%	8%	12%	6%	7%	12%	100%

166 • Table 118

TREATY PROFILE OF LIBERIA

Partners (1)	Partner's World Total (2)	Dyads Absolutes (3)	Ratios Self (4)	Ratios Other (5)	Time 1946-1950 (6)	Time 1951-1955 (7)	Time 1956-1960 (8)	Time 1961-1965 (9)	Topics Admin & Dipl (10)	Topics Social Coop (11)	Topics Econ Coop (12)	Topics Aid (13)	Topics Milit (14)	Institutions UN (15)	Institutions Spec Ag's (16)	Institutions Intl Court (17)	Institutions Arbitration (18)	Other (19)	Self-Registered (20)
TOP THIRTY																			
1 USA (United States)	2599	23	50%	1%	5	8	5	5	5	5	1	8	4	3	1			6	
2 Israel	232	5	11%	2%			1	4	2	2		1			1				
3 Germany, West	890	4	9%				1	3		1	1	2							
4 Spain	437	2	4%			2													
5 Switzerland	426	1	2%				1		1	1					1	1	1		
6 Sweden	483	1	2%				1			1					1	1	1		
7 WHO (World Health)	187	1	2%	1%		1						1		1	1				
8 UN Special Fund	113	1	2%	1%		1						1		1					
9 United Nations	233	1	2%			1						1		1					
10 UNICEF (Children)	122	1	2%			1						1			1				
11 ILO (Labor Org)	59	1	2%			1									1				
12 IBRD (World Bank)	452	1	2%	2%				1							1				
13 Norway	461	1	2%				1			1									
14 Netherlands	548	1	2%	1%			1			1						1	1		
15 Taiwan	172	1	2%	2%		1		1	1								1		
16 ICJ Option Clause	62	1	2%																
17																			
18																			
19																			
20																			
21																			
22																			
23																			
24																			
25																			
26																			
27																			
28																			
29																			
30																			
31 All Others (0)																			
GROUPS																			
32 African Group	968																		
33 Arab Group	937																		
34 Asian Group	1937	1	2%					1											
35 Commonwealth	1641																		
36 Communist Group	3310																		
37 Latin America	1674																		
38 Western Europe	5906	10	22%			2	3	5	1	5	2	2			2	4	4		
39 Intl Organs	1399	6	13%			4	1	1				6		3	1	1			
TOTALS																			
40 All Data	7476	46	100%		5	15	10	16	9	13	3	17	4	6	5	6	4	6	
41 UNTS Only		40																		
COMPARISONS																			
42 Party Total					11%	33%	22%	35%	20%	28%	7%	37%	9%	15%	13%	15%	10%	15%	
43 Group Total					1%	5%	18%	75%	22%	21%	18%	35%	4%	19%	13%	10%	15%	4%	1%
44 World Total					18%	23%	29%	29%	22%	25%	25%	20%	7%	8%	12%	6%	7%	12%	100%

Table 119 • 167

TREATY PROFILE OF LIBYA

Partners (1)	Partner's World Total (2)	Dyads Absolutes (3)	Ratios Self (4)	Ratios Other (5)	Time 1946-1950 (6)	Time 1951-1955 (7)	Time 1956-1960 (8)	Time 1961-1965 (9)	Topics Admin & Dipl (10)	Topics Social Coop (11)	Topics Econ Coop (12)	Topics Aid (13)	Topics Milit (14)	Institutions UN (15)	Institutions Spec Ag's (16)	Institutions Intl Court (17)	Institutions Arbitration (18)	Institutions Other (19)	Self-Registered (20)
TOP THIRTY																			
1 USA (United States)	2599	21	47%	1%		16	5					18	2	2				3	
2 UK Great Britain	981	9	20%	1%		9				1		1	2	2	1	2	2		
3 WHO (World Health)	187	2	4%	1%		1	1	1	2	2	2	2		1					
4 Italy	755	2	4%				1				1								
5 France	1033	2	4%			1	1		2			1							
6 USSR (Soviet Union)	1356	1	2%			1	1		1	1									
7 Turkey	298	1	2%				1			1									
8 Spain	437	1	2%				1												
9 UN Special Fund	113	1	2%	1%			1					1		1	1	1	1		
10 United Nations	233	1	2%			1						1		1					
11 UNICEF (Children)	122	1	2%			1				1		1							
12 Netherlands	548	1	2%																
13 Germany, West	890	1	2%				1					1							
14 Accept UN Charter	68	1	2%	1%		1			1					1					
15																			
31 All Others (0)																			
GROUPS																			
32 African Group	968																		
33 Arab Group	937																		
34 Asian Group	1937																		
35 Commonwealth	1641	9	20%	1%		9			2	2	2	1	2	2	1	2	2		
36 Communist Group	3310	1	2%			1			1										
37 Latin America	1674							1											
38 Western Europe	5906	8	18%			2	5	1	2	3	1	2			1	1	1		
39 Intl Organs	1399	5	11%			2	2	1				5		3	1				
TOTALS																			
40 All Data	9620	45	100%			31	12	2	6	6	3	26	4	8	2	3	3	3	
41 UNTS Only		37																		
COMPARISONS																			
42 Party Total					9%	69%	27%	4%	13%	13%	7%	58%	9%	22%	5%	8%	8%	8%	5%
43 Group Total					18%	24%	31%	36%	18%	27%	22%	29%	4%	15%	20%	8%	15%	9%	9%
44 World Total					18%	23%	29%	29%	22%	25%	25%	20%	7%	8%	12%	6%	7%	12%	5%
																			100%

168 • Table 120

TREATY PROFILE OF LIECHTENSTEIN

			Dyads			Time				Topics					Institutions				
Partners	Partner's World Total	Abso-lutes	Ratios Self	Other	1946 1950	1951 1955	1956 1960	1961 1965	Admin & Dipl	Social Coop	Econ Coop	Aid	Milit	UN	Spec Ag's	Intl Court	Arbi-tration	Other	Self-Regis-tered
(1)	(2)	(3)	(4)	(5)	(6)	(7)	(8)	(9)	(10)	(11)	(12)	(13)	(14)	(15)	(16)	(17)	(18)	(19)	(20)
TOP THIRTY																			
1 Switzerland	426	6	38%	1%		2		4	3	1	2								
2 Austria	445	5	31%	1%		3	1	1	4		1								
3 Germany, West	890	2	13%			1	1		1										
4 ICJ Option Clause	62	2	13%	3%	2				2					1		2			
5 Norway	461	1	6%					1	1										
6																			
7																			
8																			
9																			
10																			
11																			
12																			
13																			
14																			
15																			
16																			
17																			
18																			
19																			
20																			
21																			
22																			
23																			
24																			
25																			
26																			
27																			
28																			
29																			
30																			
31 All Others (0)																			
GROUPS																			
32 African Group	968																		
33 Arab Group	937																		
34 Asian Group	1937																		
35 Commonwealth	1641																		
36 Communist Group	3310																		
37 Latin America	1674																		
38 Western Europe	5906	14	88%			6	6	6	9	1	4								
39 Intl Organs	1399						2												
TOTALS																			
40 All Data	2284	16	100%		2	6	2	6	11	1	4			1		2			
41 UNTS Only		2																		
COMPARISONS																			
42 Party Total					13%	38%	13%	38%	69%	6%	25%	10%	8%	50%	14%	100%	8%	17%	32%
43 Group Total					22%	25%	27%	26%	24%	26%	32%	20%	7%	4%	12%	6%	7%	12%	
44 World Total					18%	23%	29%	29%	22%	25%	25%			8%	12%	6%			100%

TREATY PROFILE OF LUXEMBOURG

Table 121 • 169

Partners (1)	Partner's World Total (2)	Dyads Absolutes (3)	Ratios Self (4)	Ratios Other (5)	Time 1946-1950 (6)	Time 1951-1955 (7)	Time 1956-1960 (8)	Time 1961-1965 (9)	Topics Admin & Dipl (10)	Topics Social Coop (11)	Topics Econ Coop (12)	Topics Aid (13)	Topics Milit (14)	Institutions UN (15)	Institutions Spec Ag's (16)	Institutions Intl Court (17)	Institutions Arbitration (18)	Other (19)	Self-Registered (20)
TOP THIRTY																			
1 Belgium	499	22	16%	4%	11	3	1	7	8	3	8	2	1					4	
2 Germany, West	890	18	13%	2%		2	7	9	8	9	1		1						
3 USA (United States)	2599	16	12%	1%	5	7	1	3	1	2	3	1	9	2	2	2		5	
4 France	1033	15	11%	1%	3	2	3	7	4	8	2		1		1			1	
5 Netherlands	548	9	7%	2%	4	2	2	1	4	4			1						
6 UK Great Britain	981	8	6%	1%	4	2	1	1	4	3	1		1				1	1	1
7 Italy	755	5	4%	1%	1	2	2		3										
8 Norway	461	4	3%	1%	1	2	1		1	1	2				1				
9 Austria	445	4	3%	1%	1	1	1	2	1	2	2				1				
10 Sweden	483	3	2%	1%		1	2		2	1					1				
11 Spain	437	3	2%	1%				3	3	3									
12 Israel	232	3	2%	1%			1		1						1		1		
13 Switzerland	426	2	1%	2%		2		2	1	2									1
14 South Africa	120	2	1%	2%	1	2		1	1	1					1				
15 Portugal	131	2	1%	2%			2		2	2	1				1		1		
16 Japan	443	2	1%	1%					2	1									
17 Ireland	103	2	1%	2%	1	1			1	1					1				
18 Denmark	380	2	1%	1%			1		1	1									
19 Yugoslavia	525	1	1%				1				1								
20 USSR (Soviet Union)	1356	1	1%				1		1	1									
21 Tunisia	97	1	1%	1%				1	1	1					1				
22 Thailand	132	1	1%	1%		1			1	1					1				
23 IBRD (World Bank)	452	1	1%		1							1					1		
24 Philippines	236	1	1%				1												
25 New Zealand	101	1	1%	2%					1										
26 Iran	170	1	1%	1%					1								1		
27 Iceland	99	1	1%	1%		1				1									
28 Greece	318	1	1%			1			1						1				
29 Finland	245	1	1%					1	1										
30 Taiwan	172	1	1%	1%				1	1										
31 All Others (2)	511	2	1%		1	1			2										
GROUPS																			
32 African Group	968	1	1%							1									
33 Arab Group	937	4	3%				1	2	2	2					1				
34 Asian Group	1937	13	10%	1%	5	4	2	3	7	4					1		1	1	
35 Commonwealth	1641	1	1%				1		1		1		1						
36 Communist Group	3310																		
37 Latin America	1674																		
38 Western Europe	5906	94	69%	2%	23	20	20	31	28	44	16	2	4		12	2	4	5	1
39 Intl Organs	1399	1	1%		1							1					1		1
TOTALS																			
40 All Data	15380	136	100%		34	33	30	39	44	54	20	4	14	2	17	2	7	11	2
41 UNTS Only		92																		
COMPARISONS																			
42 Party Total					25%	24%	22%	29%	32%	40%	15%	3%	10%	2%	18%	2%	8%	12%	2%
43 Group Total					22%	25%	27%	26%	24%	26%	32%	10%	8%	4%	14%	6%	8%	17%	32%
44 World Total			100%		18%	23%	29%	29%	22%	25%	25%	20%	7%	8%	12%	6%	7%	12%	100%

TREATY PROFILE OF MALAGASY

Table 122

Partners (1)	Partner's World Total (2)	Dyads Absolutes (3)	Ratios Self (4)	Ratios Other (5)	Time 1946-1950 (6)	Time 1951-1955 (7)	Time 1956-1960 (8)	Time 1961-1965 (9)	Topics Admin & Dipl (10)	Topics Social Coop (11)	Topics Econ Coop (12)	Topics Aid (13)	Topics Milit (14)	Institutions UN (15)	Institutions Spec Ag's (16)	Institutions Intl Court (17)	Institutions Arbitration (18)	Other (19)	Self-Registered (20)
TOP THIRTY																			
1 France	1033	8	30%	1%			2	6	5		3								
2 Germany, West	890	4	15%					4		1	2	1							
3 USA (United States)	2599	3	11%	1%				3		1	1	1							
4 Israel	232	3	11%					3	2			1							
5 Italy	755	2	7%					2			1	1							
6 USSR (Soviet Union)	1356	1	4%	1%				1											
7 WHO (World Health)	187	1	4%	1%				1				1		1	1				
8 UN Special Fund	113	1	4%	1%				1				1		1					
9 UNICEF (Children)	122	1	4%					1											
10 Denmark	380	1	4%	1%				1	1		1					1			
11 Taiwan	172	1	4%				1		1										
12 Accept UN Charter	68	1	4%	1%			1							1		1			
13																			
14																			
15																			
16																			
17																			
18																			
19																			
20																			
21																			
22																			
23																			
24																			
25																			
26																			
27																			
28																			
29																			
30																			
31 All Others (0)																			
GROUPS																			
32 African Group	968																		
33 Arab Group	937																		
34 Asian Group	1937	1	4%					1	1							1			
35 Commonwealth	1641																		
36 Communist Group	3310	1	4%					1			1								
37 Latin America	1674																		
38 Western Europe	5906	15	56%				2	13	5	1	7	2		2	1	1			
39 Intl Organs	1399	3	11%					3				3		2					
TOTALS																			
40 All Data	7907	27	100%				3	24	9	2	9	7		3	1	2			
41 UNTS Only		13																	
COMPARISONS																			
42 Party Total					1%	5%	11%	89%	33%	7%	33%	26%	4%	23%	8%	15%	15%	4%	1%
43 Group Total					1%	5%	18%	75%	22%	21%	18%	35%	7%	19%	13%	10%	7%	12%	100%
44 World Total					18%	23%	29%	29%	22%	25%	25%	20%		8%	12%	6%			

TREATY PROFILE OF MALAWI

Table 123

	Partners (1)	Partner's World Total (2)	Dyads Absolutes (3)	Ratios Self (4)	Ratios Other (5)	Time 1946-1950 (6)	Time 1951-1955 (7)	Time 1956-1960 (8)	Time 1961-1965 (9)	Topics Admin & Dipl (10)	Topics Social Coop (11)	Topics Econ Coop (12)	Topics Aid (13)	Topics Milit (14)	Institutions UN (15)	Institutions Spec Ag's (16)	Institutions Intl Court (17)	Institutions Arbitration (18)	Institutions Other (19)	Self-Registered (20)
	TOP THIRTY																			
1	UK Great Britain	981	2	18%					2	1		1				1				
2	WHO (World Health)	187	2	18%	1%				2	1			2							
3	Germany, West	890	2	18%				1	1	1			1					1		
4	USA (United States)	2599	1	9%					1				1							
5	UN Special Fund	113	1	9%	1%				1				1		1	1	1			
6	Norway	461	1	9%					1			1			1	1				
7	Ghana	81	1	9%	1%				1		1									
8	Accept UN Charter	68	1	9%	1%				1	1										1
9-30																				
31	All Others (0)																			
	GROUPS																			
32	African Group	968	1	9%					1											1
33	Arab Group	937																		
34	Asian Group	1937																		
35	Commonwealth	1641	2	18%					2	1		1				1				
36	Communist Group	3310																		
37	Latin America	1674																		
38	Western Europe	5906	3	27%				1	2	1		1	1			1	1	1		
39	Intl Organs	1399	3	27%					3		1		3		1	1		1		1
	TOTALS																			
40	All Data	5380	11	100%				1	10	3	1	2	5		2	3	1	1		
41	UNTS Only		8																	
	COMPARISONS																			
42	Party Total					1%	5%	9%	91%	27%	9%	18%	45%		25%	38%	13%	13%	13%	13%
43	Group Total					5%	18%	75%	22%	21%	18%	35%	4%	19%	13%	10%	15%	4%	1%	
44	World Total					18%	23%	29%	29%	22%	25%	25%	20%	7%	8%	12%	6%	7%	12%	100%

172 • Table 124

TREATY PROFILE OF MALAYSIA

Partners (1)	Partner's World Total (2)	Dyads Absolutes (3)	Ratios Self (4)	Ratios Other (5)	Time 1946-1950 (6)	Time 1951-1955 (7)	Time 1956-1960 (8)	Time 1961-1965 (9)	Topics Admin & Dipl (10)	Topics Social Coop (11)	Topics Econ Coop (12)	Topics Aid (13)	Topics Milit (14)	Institutions UN (15)	Institutions Spec Ag's (16)	Institutions Intl Court (17)	Institutions Arbitration (18)	Other (19)	Self-Registered (20)
TOP THIRTY																			
1 UK Great Britain	981	4	15%	1%				4	4										
2 IBRD (World Bank)	452	4	15%	1%				4				4							
3 Japan	443	3	12%					3		2	1				1				
4 Germany, West	890	3	12%				1	2			1	2			1				
5 Norway	461	2	8%				1	1	1	1					1				
6 Netherlands	548	2	8%				1	1	1	1					1		1		
7 USA (United States)	2599	1	4%					1	1	1								1	
8 Singapore	3	1	4%	33%				1	1					1					
9 UNICEF (Children)	122	1	4%	1%				1	1										
10 Philippines	236	1	4%					1	1										
11 New Zealand	101	1	4%					1		1	1								
12 Indonesia	126	1	4%	1%			1	1		1					1				1
13 Denmark	380	1	4%																
14 Australia	201	1	4%																
31 All Others (0)																			
GROUPS																			
32 African Group	968																		
33 Arab Group	937																		
34 Asian Group	1937	3	12%				1	2	3										
35 Commonwealth	1641	6	23%					6	4	1	1								
36 Communist Group	3310																		
37 Latin America	1674																		
38 Western Europe	5906	8	31%				3	5	2	3	1	2			3		1		1
39 Intl Organs	1399	5	19%					5	1			4		1					
TOTALS																			
40 All Data	7543	26	100%		4		4	22	10	7	3	6		1	3		1	1	1
41 UNTS Only		21																		
COMPARISONS																			
42 Party Total					16%	23%	15%	85%	38%	27%	12%	23%	7%	5%	14%	5%	5%	5%	5%
43 Group Total					18%	23%	31%	30%	21%	23%	20%	30%	7%	10%	15%	8%	8%	6%	16%
44 World Total					18%	23%	29%	29%	22%	25%	25%	20%		8%	12%	6%	7%	12%	100%

Table 125 • 173

TREATY PROFILE OF MALDIVE ISLANDS

			Dyads			Time				Topics						Institutions			Self-Registered
Partners	Partner's World Total	Absolutes	Ratios Self	Other	1946 1950	1951 1955	1956 1960	1961 1965	Admin & Dipl	Social Coop	Econ Coop	Aid	Milit	UN	Spec Ag's	Intl Court	Arbitration	Other	
(1)	(2)	(3)	(4)	(5)	(6)	(7)	(8)	(9)	(10)	(11)	(12)	(13)	(14)	(15)	(16)	(17)	(18)	(19)	(20)
TOP THIRTY																			
1 UK Great Britain	981	1	50%					1	1										
2 Accept UN Charter	68	1	50%	1%				1	1					1					
3																			
4																			
5																			
6																			
7																			
8																			
9																			
10																			
11																			
12																			
13																			
14																			
15																			
16																			
17																			
18																			
19																			
20																			
21																			
22																			
23																			
24																			
25																			
26																			
27																			
28																			
29																			
30																			
31 All Others (0)																			
GROUPS																			
32 African Group	968																		
33 Arab Group	937																		
34 Asian Group	1937																		
35 Commonwealth	1641	1	50%					1	1										
36 Communist Group	3310																		
37 Latin America	1674																		
38 Western Europe	5906																		
39 Intl Organs	1399																		
TOTALS																			
40 All Data		2	100%					2	2					1					
41 UNTS Only	1049	2																		
COMPARISONS																			
42 Party Total								100%	100%					50%					
43 Group Total					16%	23%	31%	30%	21%	23%	20%	30%	7%	10%	15%	8%	8%	6%	16%
44 World Total					18%	23%	29%	29%	22%	25%	25%	20%	7%	8%	12%	6%	7%	12%	100%

174 • Table 126

TREATY PROFILE OF MALI

Part-ners (1)	Partner's World Total (2)	Dyads Abso-lutes (3)	Ratios Self (4)	Ratios Other (5)	Time 1946-1950 (6)	1951-1955 (7)	1956-1960 (8)	1961-1965 (9)	Topics Admin & Dipl (10)	Social Coop (11)	Econ Coop (12)	Aid (13)	Milit (14)	Institutions UN (15)	Spec Ag's (16)	Intl Court (17)	Arbi-tration (18)	Other (19)	Self-Regis-tered (20)
TOP THIRTY																			
1 USSR (Soviet Union)	1356	8	15%	1%			1	7	2	2	2	2							
2 Germany, East	556	8	15%	1%				8	1	3	1	3							
3 China People's Rep	766	8	15%	1%				8	2	3	1	2							
4 USA (United States)	2599	4	7%					4			1	2	1			1	1		
5 France	1033	4	7%	1%				4	2	1	1								
6 Poland	493	3	6%	1%				3		2		1							
7 Israel	232	2	4%	1%			2			1									
8 Tunisia	97	1	2%	1%				1		1					1		1		
9 Senegal	40	1	2%	3%				1		1					1				
10 WHO (World Health)	187	1	2%	1%				1						1					
11 UN Special Fund	113	1	2%	1%				1									1		
12 United Nations	233	1	2%				1									1			
13 UNICEF (Children)	122	1	2%	1%				1							1				
14 IDA (Devel Assoc)	82	1	2%	1%				1							1				
15 Romania	251	1	2%					1		1							1		
16 Niger	25	1	2%	4%				1		1							1		
17 Ivory Coast	32	1	2%	3%				1									1		
18 Italy	755	1	2%					1				1							
19 Ghana	81	1	2%	1%				1		1					1				
20 Germany, West	890	1	2%					1				1							
21 Czechoslovakia	393	1	2%					1		1					1		1		
22 Cameroon	52	1	2%	2%				1		1					1		1		
23 Algeria	52	1	2%	2%				1		1									
24 Accept UN Charter	68	1	2%	1%			1		1					1			1		
25																			
26																			
27																			
28																			
29																			
30																			
31 All Others (0)																			
GROUPS																			
32 African Group	968	5	9%	1%				5		5					5		5		
33 Arab Group	937	2	4%					2		2					2		1		
34 Asian Group	1937																		
35 Commonwealth	1641																		
36 Communist Group	3310	29	54%	1%			1	28	5	12	4	8							
37 Latin America	1674																		
38 Western Europe	5906	6	11%					6	2	1	1	2							
39 Intl Organs	1399	5	9%				1	4				5		1		1	1		
TOTALS																			
40 All Data	10508	54	100%				5	49	8	21	6	18	1	2	7	2	8		
41 UNTS Only		24																	
COMPARISONS																			
42 Party Total					1%	5%	9%	91%	15%	39%	1%	33%	2%	8%	29%	8%	33%	4%	1%
43 Group Total					18%	23%	18%	75%	22%	21%	18%	35%	4%	19%	13%	10%	15%	4%	1%
44 World Total					29%	29%	29%	29%	22%	25%	25%	20%	7%	8%	12%	6%	7%	12%	100%

Table 127 • 175

TREATY PROFILE OF MALTA

Partners (1)	Partner's World Total (2)	Dyads Absolutes (3)	Ratios Self (4)	Ratios Other (5)	Time 1946 1950 (6)	Time 1951 1955 (7)	Time 1956 1960 (8)	Time 1961 1965 (9)	Topics Admin & Dipl (10)	Topics Social Coop (11)	Topics Econ Coop (12)	Topics Aid (13)	Topics Milit (14)	Institutions UN (15)	Institutions Spec Ag's (16)	Institutions Intl Court (17)	Institutions Arbitration (18)	Institutions Other (19)	Self-Registered (20)
TOP THIRTY																			
1 UK Great Britain	981	3	20%					3	1				1						1
2 Yugoslavia	525	1	7%					1			1								1
3 Switzerland	426	1	7%					1			1								1
4 Sweden	483	1	7%					1	1										1
5 UNICEF (Children)	122	1	7%	1%				1				1		1					
6 Norway	461	1	7%					1	1										1
7 Italy	755	1	7%					1	1										1
8 Greece	318	1	7%					1	1							1			1
9 Germany, West	890	1	7%					1			1								1
10 Finland	245	1	7%					1	1										1
11 Denmark	380	1	7%					1	1										1
12 Australia	201	1	7%					1		1									
13 Accept UN Charter	68	1	7%	1%				1	1					1					
14																			
15																			
16																			
17																			
18																			
19																			
20																			
21																			
22																			
23																			
24																			
25																			
26																			
27																			
28																			
29																			
30																			
31 All Others (0)																			
GROUPS																			
32 African Group	968																		
33 Arab Group	937																		
34 Asian Group	1937																		
35 Commonwealth	1641	4	27%					4	1	1		1	1						2
36 Communist Group	3310																		
37 Latin America	1674																		
38 Western Europe	5906	8	53%					8	6		2					1			7
39 Intl Organs	1399	1	7%					1	1					1					
TOTALS																			
40 All Data	5855	15	100%					15	9	1	3	1	1	2		1			10
41 UNTS Only	14																			
COMPARISONS																			
42 Party Total					22%	25%	27%	100%	60%	7%	20%	7%	7%	14%	14%	7%	8%	17%	71%
43 Group Total					18%	23%	29%	26%	24%	26%	32%	10%	8%	4%	12%	6%	7%	12%	32%
44 World Total							29%	29%	22%	25%	25%	20%	7%	8%	12%	6%			100%

176 • Table 128

TREATY PROFILE OF MAURITANIA

		Partner's World Total	Dyads Abso- lutes	Dyads Ratios Self	Dyads Ratios Other	Time 1946 1950	Time 1951 1955	Time 1956 1960	Time 1961 1965	Topics Admin & Dipl	Topics Social Coop	Topics Econ Coop	Topics Aid	Topics Milit	Institutions UN	Institutions Spec Ag's	Institutions Intl Court	Institutions Arbi- tration	Institutions Other	Self- Regis- tered
	Partners (1)	(2)	(3)	(4)	(5)	(6)	(7)	(8)	(9)	(10)	(11)	(12)	(13)	(14)	(15)	(16)	(17)	(18)	(19)	(20)
	TOP THIRTY																			
1	France	1033	10	56%	1%			1	9	5	4		1							
2	USA (United States)	2599	1	6%					1			1					1	1		
3	Spain	437	1	6%	1%				1		1					1				
4	WHO (World Health)	187	1	6%	1%				1				1		1	1	1			
5	UN Special Fund	113	1	6%	1%				1				1		1					
6	UNICEF (Children)	122	1	6%	1%				1				1							
7	IDA (Devel Assoc)	82	1	6%				1												
8	IBRD (World Bank)	452	1	6%	1%				1										1	
9	Accept UN Charter	68	1	6%					1	1					1					
10																				
11																				
12																				
13																				
14																				
15																				
16																				
17																				
18																				
19																				
20																				
21																				
22																				
23																				
24																				
25																				
26																				
27																				
28																				
29																				
30																				
31	All Others (0)																			
	GROUPS																			
32	African Group	968																		
33	Arab Group	937																		
34	Asian Group	1937																		
35	Commonwealth	1641																		
36	Communist Group	3310																		
37	Latin America	1674																		
38	Western Europe	5906	11	61%				1	10	5	5		1			1	1			
39	Intl Organs	1399	5	28%				1	4				5		3	1			1	
	TOTALS																			
40	All Data	5093	18	100%				2	16	6	5	1	6		4	2	2	1	1	
41	UNTS Only		9																	
	COMPARISONS																			
42	Party Total					1%	5%	11%	89%	33%	28%	6%	33%	4%	44%	22%	22%	11%	11%	
43	Group Total					1%	23%	18%	75%	22%	21%	18%	35%	7%	19%	13%	10%	15%	4%	1%
44	World Total					18%	23%	29%	29%	22%	25%	25%	20%		8%	12%	6%	7%	12%	100%

TREATY PROFILE OF MEXICO

Table 129

	Partners (1)	Partner's World Total (2)	Dyads Absolutes (3)	Ratios Self (4)	Ratios Other (5)	Time 1946 1950 (6)	Time 1951 1955 (7)	Time 1956 1960 (8)	Time 1961 1965 (9)	Topics Admin & Dipl (10)	Topics Social Coop (11)	Topics Econ Coop (12)	Topics Aid (13)	Topics Milit (14)	Institutions UN (15)	Institutions Spec Ag's (16)	Institutions Intl Court (17)	Institutions Arbitration (18)	Institutions Other (19)	Self-Registered (20)
	TOP THIRTY																			
1	USA (United States)	2599	47	34%	2%	13	13	10	11	7		4	10	1		5	1	1	7	
2	IBRD (World Bank)	452	17	12%	4%	4	2	3	8				17					3	7	
3	Italy	755	7	5%	1%	1			6	2	1	2	2							
4	UK Great Britain	981	5	4%	1%	2	2	1		3	1	1					1			
5	Netherlands	548	5	4%	1%	2	1	1	2	1	3					2	1	2		
6	United Nations	233	4	3%	2%		1		2	3									1	
7	France	1033	4	3%		1	2		1		1	2	1			1				
8	Canada	310	4	3%	1%	1	1	1	2		3	1				1				
9	Yugoslavia	525	3	2%	1%	1		1	1		1	2								
10	WHO (World Health)	187	3	2%	2%		3				1		2		3					
11	Germany, West	890	3	2%			1	2		2		1								
12	Belgium	499	3	2%	1%	1		1	1	1	1	1								
13	United Arab Rep	232	2	1%	1%				1		1	1				1	1	1		
14	ILO (Labor Org)	59	2	1%	3%		2			1	1		1		1					
15	ICAO (Civil Aviat)	23	2	1%	9%		1	1		1			1		2					
16	Venezuela	47	1	1%	2%	1														
17	Switzerland	426	1	1%		1						1								
18	UN Special Fund	113	1	1%	1%				1				1		1					
19	UNICEF (Children)	122	1	1%	1%		1				1		1							
20	IAEA (Atom Energy)	44	1	1%	2%				1							1		1		
21	Portugal	131	1	1%	1%				1		1									
22	Peru	109	1	1%	1%	1		1			1									
23	Paraguay	75	1	1%		1														
24	Norway	461	1	1%				1		1										
25	Nicaragua	50	1	1%	2%	1					1									
26	Lebanon	75	1	1%	1%	1					1									
27	Japan	443	1	1%			1				1									
28	Israel	232	1	1%				1			1									
29	Indonesia	126	1	1%	1%				1		1									
30	Guatemala	50	1	1%	2%				1			1								
31	All Others (12)	2131	12	9%	1%	4	1	5	2	2	5	5								
	GROUPS																			
32	African Group	968	3	2%		1			1			1								
33	Arab Group	937	2	1%					2		2	2								
34	Asian Group	1937	9	7%	1%	3	3	1	2	3	4	2				1	1			
35	Commonwealth	1641																		
36	Communist Group	3310																		
37	Latin America	1674	12	9%	1%	5		5	2		10	2								
38	Western Europe	5906	28	20%		7	5	6	10	8	7	10	3			4	2	3		
39	Intl Organs	1399	31	22%	2%	4	10	5	12	5	2		24		7		2	3	1	
	TOTALS																			
40	All Data	13961	138	100%		35	32	30	41	24	53	23	37	1	7	10	7	7	8	
41	UNTS Only		100																	
	COMPARISONS																			
42	Party Total					25%	23%	22%	30%	17%	38%	17%	27%	1%	7%	10%	7%	7%	8%	
43	Group Total					18%	27%	24%	31%	16%	25%	18%	31%	9%	7%	10%	5%	6%	7%	6%
44	World Total					18%	23%	29%	29%	22%	25%	25%	20%	7%	8%	12%	6%	7%	12%	100%

TREATY PROFILE OF MONACO

	Partners (1)	Partner's World Total (2)	Dyads Absolutes (3)	Ratios Self (4)	Ratios Other (5)	Time 1946-1950 (6)	Time 1951-1955 (7)	Time 1956-1960 (8)	Time 1961-1965 (9)	Admin & Dipl (10)	Social Coop (11)	Econ Coop (12)	Aid (13)	Milit (14)	UN (15)	Spec Ag's (16)	Intl Court (17)	Arbitration (18)	Other (19)	Self-Registered (20)
	TOP THIRTY																			
1	France	1033	10	28%	1%	4	1		5	3	1	5		1						
2	Italy	755	7	19%	1%		1	4	2	2	4			1					1	
3	Netherlands	548	3	8%	1%	1	1	1		3										
4	Germany, West	890	3	8%				1	2	3										
5	USA (United States)	2599	2	6%			2			1		1								
6	UK Great Britain	981	2	6%		1			1	2										
7	Belgium	499	2	6%		2				2										
8	United Nations	233	1	3%		1				1										
9	Norway	461	1	3%			1		1	1										
10	New Zealand	101	1	3%	1%		1			1										
11	Ireland	103	1	3%	1%		1			1										
12	Canada	310	1	3%				1		1										
13	Austria	445	1	3%						1										
14	Australia	201	1	3%						1										
15																				
31	All Others (0)																			
	GROUPS																			
32	African Group	968																		
33	Arab Group	937																		
34	Asian Group	1937																		
35	Commonwealth	1641	5	14%		1	2	1	1	5										
36	Communist Group	3310																		
37	Latin America	1674																		
38	Western Europe	5906	28	78%		8	5	6	9	16	5	5		2					1	
39	Intl Organs	1399	1	3%					1	1										
40	TOTALS All Data	9159	36	100%		9	9	7	11	23	5	6		2					1	
41	UNTS Only		20																	
	COMPARISONS																			
42	Party Total					25%	25%	19%	31%	64%	14%	17%	10%	6%	4%	14%	6%	8%	5%	32%
43	Group Total					22%	25%	27%	26%	24%	26%	32%	20%	8%	8%	12%	6%	7%	17%	100%
44	World Total					18%	23%	29%	29%	22%	25%	25%		7%	8%	12%	6%	7%	12%	

TREATY PROFILE OF MONGOLIA

Table 131

Partners (1)	Partner's World Total (2)	Dyads Absolutes (3)	Ratios Self (4)	Ratios Other (5)	Time 1946-1950 (6)	Time 1951-1955 (7)	Time 1956-1960 (8)	Time 1961-1965 (9)	Admin & Dipl (10)	Social Coop (11)	Econ Coop (12)	Aid (13)	Milit (14)	UN (15)	Spec Ag's (16)	Intl Court (17)	Arbitration (18)	Other (19)	Self-Registered (20)
TOP THIRTY																			
1 USSR (Soviet Union)	1356	61	51%	4%	9	15	32	5	14	16	7	23	1					1	
2 China People's Rep	766	28	24%	4%		6	13	9	4	10	12	2							
3 Germany, East	556	15	13%	3%		3	8	4	4	7	2	2							1
4 Poland	493	4	3%	1%		1	1	2	1	2		1							
5 Czechoslovakia	393	3	3%	1%			1	2	2	1									
6 Hungary	290	2	2%	1%				2	2										
7 WHO (World Health)	187	1	1%	1%				1	1			1							
8 United Nations	233	1	1%					1	1										
9 UNICEF (Children)	122	1	1%	1%				1											
10 Romania	251	1	1%				1			1									
11 Austria	445	1	1%					1			1								
12 Accept UN Charter	68	1	1%	1%				1	1					1				1	1
13–30																			
31 All Others (0)																			
GROUPS																			
32 African Group	968																		
33 Arab Group	937																		
34 Asian Group	1937																		
35 Commonwealth	1641																		
36 Communist Group	3310	114	96%	3%	9	25	56	24	27	37	21	28	1					2	1
37 Latin America	1674																		
38 Western Europe	5906	1	1%					1	2		1								1
39 Intl Organs	1399	3	3%					3				1							
TOTALS																			
40 All Data	5160	119	100%		9	25	56	29	30	37	22	29	1	1				2	2
41 UNTS Only		20																	
COMPARISONS																			
42 Party Total					8%	21%	47%	24%	25%	31%	18%	24%	1%	5%	4%		3%	10%	10%
43 Group Total					16%	17%	38%	29%	20%	32%	32%	13%	2%	4%	12%	6%	7%	17%	33%
44 World Total					18%	23%	29%	29%	22%	25%	25%	20%	7%	8%				12%	100%

180 • Table 132

TREATY PROFILE OF MOROCCO

Partners (1)	Partner's World Total (2)	Dyads Absolutes (3)	Ratios Self (4)	Ratios Other (5)	Time 1946-1950 (6)	Time 1951-1955 (7)	Time 1956-1960 (8)	Time 1961-1965 (9)	Admin & Dipl (10)	Social Coop (11)	Econ Coop (12)	Aid (13)	Milit (14)	UN (15)	Spec Ag's (16)	Intl Court (17)	Arbitration (18)	Other (19)	Self-Registered (20)
TOP THIRTY																			
1 Spain	437	14	15%	3%			14		6	1	6	1							
2 France	1033	14	15%	1%			8	6	5	7	1	1			1				
3 Japan	443	8	9%	2%				8		4	1	2	1						
4 USSR (Soviet Union)	1356	7	7%	1%			6	1	1	1	4		1						
5 USA (United States)	2599	7	7%				1	6	1	1	2	4			1				
6 Germany, West	890	5	5%	1%			1	4	1	2	2	1					1		
7 Italy	755	4	4%	1%			2	2	1		2	1							
8 Switzerland	426	3	3%	1%			1	2		2	1				2		2		
9 IBRD (World Bank)	452	3	3%	1%				3				2							
10 Germany, East	556	3	3%	1%				2			3								
11 Belgium	499	3	3%	1%			3		2	1	1				1				
12 UK Great Britain	981	2	2%				2		1		2						1		
13 China People's Rep	766	2	2%					2											
14 United Arab Rep	232	1	1%				1				1								
15 Sweden	483	1	1%					1							1				
16 WHO (World Health)	187	1	1%	1%				1				1		1	1				
17 UN Special Fund	113	1	1%	1%			1							1					
18 United Nations	233	1	1%					1	1					1			2		
19 UNICEF (Children)	122	1	1%	1%			1					1		1					
20 UNESCO (Educ/Cult)	19	1	5%	5%				1							1				
21 IDA (Devel Assoc)	82	1	1%	1%				1				1							
22 IAEA (Atom Energy)	44	1	2%	2%				1		1		1				1			
23 Portugal	131	1	1%	1%				1							1				
24 Poland	493	1	1%				1					1							
25 Norway	461	1	1%				1		1										
26 Greece	318	1	1%					1			1							2	
27 Czechoslovakia	393	1	1%	1%			1				1				1				
28 Taiwan	172	1	1%	1%				1		1									
29 Bel-Lux Econ Union	1	1	1%	100%				1	1	1									
30 Argentina	164	1	1%	1%				1		1									
31 All Others (2)	120	2	2%	2%			1	1	1				1	1	1				
GROUPS																			
32 African Group	968	2	2%				1	1		2						2		2	
33 Arab Group	937	1	1%								1								
34 Asian Group	1937	2	2%				2				1								
35 Commonwealth	1641	2	2%				2		1	2	1				1		1		
36 Communist Group	3310	14	15%				7	7	1		9	1	1						
37 Latin America	1674	1	1%					1		1									
38 Western Europe	5906	47	50%	1%			31	16	16	14	14	3			6	2	4		
39 Intl Organs	1399	11	12%	1%			2	9	1	1	2	8		3	1		2		
TOTALS																			
40 All Data	14961	94	100%				46	48	21	24	29	18	2	4	10	2	9	2	
41 UNTS Only		42	100%																
COMPARISONS																			
42 Party Total					9%	24%	49%	51%	22%	26%	31%	19%	2%	10%	24%	5%	21%	5%	5%
43 Group Total					18%	23%	31%	36%	18%	27%	22%	29%	4%	15%	20%	8%	15%	9%	5%
44 World Total					18%	23%	29%	29%	22%	25%	25%	20%	7%	8%	12%	6%	7%	12%	100%

Table 133 • 181

TREATY PROFILE OF MUSCAT AND OMAN

	Partners (1)	Partner's World Total (2)	Absolutes (3)	Dyads Ratios Self (4)	Other (5)	Time 1946-1950 (6)	1951-1955 (7)	1956-1960 (8)	1961-1965 (9)	Topics Admin & Dipl (10)	Social Coop (11)	Econ Coop (12)	Aid (13)	Milit (14)	Institutions UN (15)	Spec Ag's (16)	Intl Court (17)	Arbi-tration (18)	Other (19)	Self-Registered (20)
	TOP THIRTY																			
1	UK Great Britain	981	3	60%		1	1			1	1			1						
2	USA (United States)	2599	1	20%				1		1						1				
3	India	299	1	20%			1			1										
4																				
5																				
6																				
7																				
8																				
9																				
10																				
11																				
12																				
13																				
14																				
15																				
16																				
17																				
18																				
19																				
20																				
21																				
22																				
23																				
24																				
25																				
26																				
27																				
28																				
29																				
30																				
31	All Others (0)																			
	GROUPS																			
32	African Group	968																		
33	Arab Group	937																		
34	Asian Group	1937	1	20%			1			1										
35	Commonwealth	1641	3	60%		1	1	1		1	1									
36	Communist Group	3310												1						
37	Latin America	1674																		
38	Western Europe	5906																		
39	Intl Organs	1399												1		1				
	TOTALS																			
40	All Data	3879	5	100%		1	2	2		3	1									
41	UNTS Only		5																	
	COMPARISONS																			
42	Party Total					20%	40%	40%		60%	20%	20%	20%	20%	10%	20%	8%	8%	6%	16%
43	Group Total					16%	23%	31%	30%	21%	23%	20%	30%	7%	8%	15%	6%	7%	6%	100%
44	World Total					18%	23%	29%	29%	22%	25%	25%	20%	7%		12%			12%	

182 • Table 134

TREATY PROFILE OF NATO (NORTH ATLAN)

Partners	Partner's World Total	Dyads Absolutes	Ratios Self	Ratios Other	1946 1950	1951 1955	Time 1956 1960	1961 1965	Admin & Dipl	Social Coop	Topics Econ Coop	Aid	Milit	UN	Spec Ag's	Institutions Intl Court	Arbitration	Other	Self-Registered
(1)	(2)	(3)	(4)	(5)	(6)	(7)	(8)	(9)	(10)	(11)	(12)	(13)	(14)	(15)	(16)	(17)	(18)	(19)	(20)
TOP THIRTY																			
1 USA (United States)	2599	1	50%			1			1				1						
2 Netherlands	548	1	50%					1											
3																			
4																			
5																			
6																			
7																			
8																			
9																			
10																			
11																			
12																			
13																			
14																			
15																			
16																			
17																			
18																			
19																			
20																			
21																			
22																			
23																			
24																			
25																			
26																			
27																			
28																			
29																			
30																			
31 All Others (0)																			
GROUPS																			
32 African Group	968																		
33 Arab Group	937																		
34 Asian Group	1937																		
35 Commonwealth	1641																		
36 Communist Group	3310																		
37 Latin America	1674																		
38 Western Europe	5906	1	50%					1											
39 Intl Organs	1399																		
TOTALS																			
40 All Data	3147	2	100%			1		1	1				1						
41 UNTS Only		2																		
COMPARISONS																			
42 Party Total					12%	50%		50%	50%				50%						
43 Group Total					12%	25%	23%	40%	19%	7%	1%	71%	1%	27%	11%	13%	15%	4%	74%
44 World Total					18%	23%	29%	29%	22%	25%	25%	20%	7%	8%	12%	6%	7%	12%	100%

Table 135 • 183

TREATY PROFILE OF NEPAL

Partners (1)	Partner's World Total (2)	Dyads Absolutes (3)	Ratios Self (4)	Ratios Other (5)	Time 1946 1950 (6)	Time 1951 1955 (7)	Time 1956 1960 (8)	Time 1961 1965 (9)	Admin & Dipl (10)	Social Coop (11)	Econ Coop (12)	Aid (13)	Milit (14)	UN (15)	Spec Ag's (16)	Intl Court (17)	Arbitration (18)	Other (19)	Self-Registered (20)
TOP THIRTY																			
1 China People's Rep	766	17	47%	2%			9	8	8	3	2	4							
2 USSR (Soviet Union)	1356	5	14%		1	1	4	1	1			4							
3 USA (United States)	2599	5	14%	1%	1	1	1	2	1	1	1	2		1			2		
4 United Nations	233	2	6%	1%			1		1			1		1		1			
5 India	299	2	6%		2				1										
6 UK Great Britain	981	1	3%		1				1										
7 WHO (World Health)	187	1	3%	1%		1						1		1					
8 UN Special Fund	113	1	3%	1%			1					1		1					
9 UNICEF (Children)	122	1	3%	1%			1							1					
10 Accept UN Charter	68	1	3%	1%		1			1										
11																			
12–30																			
31 All Others (0)																			
GROUPS																			
32 African Group	968																		
33 Arab Group	937																		
34 Asian Group	1937	2	6%		2														
35 Commonwealth	1641	1	3%		1				1		1								
36 Communist Group	3310	22	61%	1%			13	9	9	3	2	8							
37 Latin America	1674																		
38 Western Europe	5906																		
39 Intl Organs	1399	5	14%			2	3		1			4		2		1	2		
TOTALS																			
40 All Data	6724	36	100%		4	4	17	11	14	4	4	14		4	4	2	2		
41 UNTS Only		14																	
COMPARISONS																			
42 Party Total					11%	11%	47%	31%	39%	11%	11%	39%	7%	29%	15%	14%	14%	6%	16%
43 Group Total					16%	23%	31%	30%	21%	23%	20%	30%		10%	12%	8%	8%		
44 World Total					18%	23%	29%	29%	22%	25%	25%	20%	7%	8%		6%	7%	12%	100%

TREATY PROFILE OF NETHERLANDS

Partners (1)	Partner's World Total (2)	Dyads Absolutes (3)	Ratios Self (4)	Ratios Other (5)	Time 1946-1950 (6)	Time 1951-1955 (7)	Time 1956-1960 (8)	Time 1961-1965 (9)	Admin & Dipl (10)	Social Coop (11)	Econ Coop (12)	Aid (13)	Milit (14)	UN (15)	Spec Ag's (16)	Intl Court (17)	Arbitration (18)	Other (19)	Self-Registered (20)
TOP THIRTY																			
1 USA (United States)	2599	47	9%	2%	17	18	8	4	7	3	11	9	17	6	6	3		10	20
2 Belgium	499	44	8%	9%	16	13	10	5	18	12	9	1	4			1		8	13
3 Germany, West	890	43	8%	5%	1	12	17	13	20	13	3		7		2	1		8	35
4 UK Great Britain	981	31	6%	3%	15	6	5	5	7	7	9		8		1	1	1	5	14
5 Italy	755	23	4%	3%	3	10	8	2	4	7	5		4	1	1			8	16
6 France	1033	22	4%	2%	12	7	3		4	10	10		3	1	1		1	8	17
7 Sweden	483	19	3%	4%	9	6	3	1	2	4	13					1		2	6
8 Austria	445	17	3%	4%	1	6	8	2	9	5	3				1			2	11
9 Switzerland	426	15	3%	4%	2	8	5		3	5	7				2		2	2	9
10 Norway	461	15	3%	3%	4	5	4	2	1	5	7		2		1		1	7	5
11 Spain	437	14	3%	3%	6	3	1	4	2	7	5				2		2		5
12 Australia	201	12	2%	6%	3	4	4	1	3	6	2		1					1	4
13 IBRD (World Bank)	452	10	2%	2%	8	1	1		2			10						8	5
14 Greece	318	10	2%	3%	1	8	2		2	2	6		5		1		2	2	3
15 Canada	310	10	2%	3%	7	1	2		4	1	3		1					1	9
16 Luxembourg	136	9	2%	7%	4	2	3		4	4		1			1		1		5
17 Turkey	298	8	1%	3%	2	2	3	1	2	3	2		1				1	3	5
18 Denmark	380	8	1%	2%	2	2	4		2	1	6							4	6
19 Portugal	131	7	1%	5%	1	3	2	1	3	2	2				2			3	2
20 Israel	232	7	1%	3%		3	1	2	5	2	4				1				1
21 Ireland	103	7	1%	7%	5	1			1	2	1				1		1	2	2
22 Iran	170	7	1%	4%	2		4	1	2	2	2				1	1			1
23 Indonesia	126	7	1%	6%	2	3		2	3			3	1	2	3	1	1	1	3
24 India	299	7	1%	2%	1	2	2	2		3	1				1	1	1		6
25 Finland	245	7	1%	3%		6			1	2	4						1		2
26 Yugoslavia	525	6	1%	1%	1		3	2		2	3				1				3
27 United Arab Rep	232	6	1%	3%	1	2	2	1		3	3				1	1	1		2
28 Japan	443	6	1%	1%		3	3		2	1	3							3	3
29 Poland	493	5	1%	1%	1	2		1	1	3	1								1
30 Mexico	138	5	1%	4%	2	1	1	1	2	1	4				2	1	2		3
31 All Others (55)	6702	114	21%	2%	25	28	24	37	28	45	27	12	2	7	24	14	17	10	61
GROUPS																			
32 African Group	968	16	3%	2%	3	4	3	13	1	8	2	5			4	4	3		12
33 Arab Group	937	16	3%	2%	3	4	4	5		11	4	1			5	3	4		5
34 Asian Group	1937	39	7%	2%	8	14	9	8	10	15	6	5	3	3	10	5	7	2	19
35 Commonwealth	1641	61	11%	4%	29	15	11	6	13	18	16		14		4	1	1	8	26
36 Communist Group	3310	23	4%	1%	7	3	8	5		6	17				2				7
37 Latin America	1674	29	5%	2%	7	8	4	10	10	13	5	1		1	7	2	5	1	18
38 Western Europe	5906	274	50%	5%	72	95	74	33	79	83	88	2	22	2	14	3	11	70	156
39 Intl Organs	1399	22	4%	2%	10	4	3	5	6	1	1	14	1	5	2	2	3	4	6
TOTALS																			
40 All Data	20943	548	100%		156	167	132	93	136	163	155	37	57	17	58	27	35	95	277
41 UNTS Only		448																	
COMPARISONS																			
42 Party Total					28%	30%	24%	17%	25%	30%	28%	7%	10%	4%	13%	6%	8%	21%	62%
43 Group Total					22%	25%	27%	26%	24%	26%	32%	10%	8%	4%	14%	6%	8%	17%	32%
44 World Total					18%	23%	29%	29%	22%	25%	25%	20%	7%	8%	12%	6%	7%	12%	100%

Table 137

TREATY PROFILE OF NEW ZEALAND

	Partners (1)	Partner's World Total (2)	Dyads Absolutes (3)	Ratios Self (4)	Ratios Other (5)	Time 1946-1950 (6)	Time 1951-1955 (7)	Time 1956-1960 (8)	Time 1961-1965 (9)	Admin & Dipl (10)	Social Coop (11)	Econ Coop (12)	Aid (13)	Milit (14)	UN (15)	Spec Ag's (16)	Intl Court (17)	Arbitration (18)	Other (19)	Self-Registered (20)
	TOP THIRTY																			
1	USA (United States)	2599	17	17%	1%	6	1	5	5	2	3	4	4	4	2	4	1			3
2	UK Great Britain	981	10	10%	1%	2	2	4	2	2	3	4		4		3	1	1	1	7
3	Australia	201	7	7%	3%	2		2	3	2	2	3		3		1		1	1	2
4	Western Samoa	10	5	5%	50%				5	2	2									2
5	Japan	443	5	5%	1%			1	4	2	1	4	1			2				4
6	France	1033	5	5%					1	1	2	1				1				2
7	IBRD (World Bank)	452	4	4%	1%	4							4							3
8	Germany, West	890	4	4%			2	2		2		1		1					1	4
9	Switzerland	426	3	3%	1%	1	1	1		1		2								3
10	Netherlands	548	3	3%	1%	3				1		1								1
11	Italy	755	3	3%		1	1	1		1	1	1								3
12	Yugoslavia	525	2	2%			1	1				1		1						2
13	USSR (Soviet Union)	1356	2	2%					2	1		1			1					1
14	Sweden	483	2	2%		1		1		1		1								2
15	Pakistan	245	2	2%	1%	2					2									
16	Norway	461	2	2%		2				1		1				1				2
17	Denmark	380	2	2%	1%	2				1		1								1
18	Czechoslovakia	393	2	2%	1%	2						2								2
19	Canada	310	2	2%	1%	2						1				1	1			
20	Belgium	499	2	2%			2			1	1									1
21	Austria	445	2	2%			1	1		2										2
22	Turkey	298	1	1%				1		1										1
23	Thailand	132	1	1%	1%			1												
24	Spain	437	1	1%					1			1								
25	UN Special Fund	113	1	1%	1%		1				1		1		1	1		1		1
26	United Nations	233	1	1%					1				1		1					
27	UNICEF (Children)	122	1	1%																
28	Poland	493	1	1%				1												
29	Philippines	236	1	1%															1	1
30	Monaco	36	1	1%	3%		1			1										
31	All Others (6)	1256	6	6%			1	1	4	3	1	1	1							5
	GROUPS																			
32	African Group	968																		
33	Arab Group	937																		
34	Asian Group	1937	11	11%	1%	2		2	7	2	5	2	2			1				6
35	Commonwealth	1641	19	19%	1%	6	2	6	5	2	6	8		3		5		2	2	9
36	Communist Group	3310	5	5%		2			3	1		4					1	2	1	4
37	Latin America	1674																		
38	Western Europe	5906	34	34%	1%	14	9	6	5	17	5	9			1	1	1	1	1	28
39	Intl Organs	1399	7	7%	1%		1		6		1		6	3	2	1				
	TOTALS																			
40	All Data	16791	101	100%		30	14	22	35	25	21	32	12	11	5	14	3	4	4	54
41	UNTS Only		100	100%																
	COMPARISONS																			
42	Party Total					30%	14%	22%	35%	25%	21%	32%	12%	11%	5%	14%	3%	4%	4%	54%
43	Group Total					27%	25%	24%	24%	25%	24%	27%	10%	14%	4%	13%	4%	5%	12%	63%
44	World Total					18%	23%	29%	29%	22%	25%	25%	20%	7%	8%	12%	6%	7%	12%	100%

186 • Table 138

TREATY PROFILE OF NEWFOUNDLAND

Partners (1)	Partner's World Total (2)	Dyads Abso- lutes (3)	Ratios Self (4)	Other (5)	Time 1946 1950 (6)	1951 1955 (7)	1956 1960 (8)	1961 1965 (9)	Topics Admin & Dipl (10)	Social Coop (11)	Econ Coop (12)	Aid (13)	Milit (14)	Institutions UN (15)	Spec Ag's (16)	Intl Court (17)	Arbi- tration (18)	Other (19)	Self- Regis- tered (20)
TOP THIRTY																			
1 Canada	310	1	100%		1					1					1				
2																			
3																			
4																			
5																			
6																			
7																			
8																			
9																			
10																			
11																			
12																			
13																			
14																			
15																			
16																			
17																			
18																			
19																			
20																			
21																			
22																			
23																			
24																			
25																			
26																			
27																			
28																			
29																			
30																			
31 All Others (0)																			
GROUPS																			
32 African Group	968																		
33 Arab Group	937																		
34 Asian Group	1937																		
35 Commonwealth	1641	1	100%		1										1				
36 Communist Group	3310																		
37 Latin America	1674																		
38 Western Europe	5906																		
39 Intl Organs	1399																		
TOTALS																			
40 All Data	310	1	100%		1					1								1	
41 UNTS Only		1																	
COMPARISONS					100%					100%	100%				100%				
42 Party Total					27%	25%	24%	24%	25%	24%	27%	10%	14%	4%	13%	4%	5%	12%	63%
43 Group Total					18%	23%	29%	29%	22%	25%	25%	20%	7%	8%	12%	6%	7%	12%	100%
44 World Total																			

TREATY PROFILE OF NICARAGUA

Table 139

	Partners (1)	Partner's World Total (2)	Dyads Absolutes (3)	Ratios Self (4)	Ratios Other (5)	Time 1946 1950 (6)	Time 1951 1955 (7)	Time 1956 1960 (8)	Time 1961 1965 (9)	Admin & Dipl (10)	Social Coop (11)	Econ Coop (12)	Aid (13)	Milit (14)	UN (15)	Spec Ag's (16)	Intl Court (17)	Arbi- tration (18)	Other (19)	Self- Regis- tered (20)
	TOP THIRTY																			
1	USA (United States)	2599	23	46%	1%	3	11	8	1	4	7	1	5	6	1	1	2	1	1	
2	IBRD (World Bank)	452	11	22%	2%		8	2	1				11			1	1		1	
3	WHO (World Health)	187	2	4%	1%	1	1				1		1						1	
4	UK Great Britain	981	1	2%			1				1									1
5	Spain	437	1	2%					1	1										
6	UN Special Fund	113	1	2%	1%				1	1					1		1			
7	United Nations	233	1	2%					1	1									1	
8	UNICEF (Children)	122	1	2%	1%						1				1			2		
9	IDA (Devel Assoc)	82	1	2%	1%	1							1							
10	Peru	109	1	2%	1%											1				
11	Norway	461	1	2%				1		1										
12	Mexico	138	1	2%	1%	1					1						1			
13	Honduras	43	1	2%	2%			1		1									1	
14	Germany, West	890	1	2%					1	1			1		1	1				
15	Taiwan	172	1	2%	1%						1									
16	Canada	310	1	2%		1						1								
17	Argentina	164	1	2%	1%						1									
18																				
19																				
20																				
21																				
22																				
23																				
24																				
25																				
26																				
27																				
28																				
29																				
30																				
31	All Others (0)																			
	GROUPS																			
32	African Group	968																		
33	Arab Group	937																		
34	Asian Group	1937	1	2%					1						1	1			1	1
35	Commonwealth	1641	2	4%		1	1				1	1							1	
36	Communist Group	3310																		
37	Latin America	1674	4	8%		1		2	1	1	3				1	1	1		1	
38	Western Europe	5906	3	6%				1	2	2			1						2	
39	Intl Organs	1399	17	34%	1%	2	9	2	4	1	1		15		2	1	2	2	2	1
	TOTALS																			
40	All Data	7493	50	100%		7	21	13	9	8	13	2	21	6	5	4	5	3	5	1
41	UNTS Only		46																	
	COMPARISONS																			
42	Party Total					14%	42%	26%	18%	16%	26%	4%	42%	12%	11%	9%	11%	7%	11%	2%
43	Group Total					18%	27%	24%	31%	16%	25%	18%	31%	9%	7%	10%	5%	6%	7%	6%
44	World Total					18%	23%	29%	29%	22%	25%	25%	20%	7%	8%	12%	6%	7%	12%	100%

TREATY PROFILE OF NIGER

	Partners (1)	Partner's World Total (2)	Absolutes (3)	Dyads Ratios Self (4)	Other (5)	Time 1946-1950 (6)	1951-1955 (7)	1956-1960 (8)	1961-1965 (9)	Admin & Dipl (10)	Social Coop (11)	Topics Econ Coop (12)	Aid (13)	Milit (14)	UN (15)	Spec Ag's (16)	Institutions Intl Court (17)	Arbitration (18)	Other (19)	Self-Registered (20)
	TOP THIRTY																			
1	France	1033	6	24%	1%			1	5	3		2								
2	USA (United States)	2599	4	16%					4	3	1	1	2	1	1					
3	Germany, West	890	4	16%					4			2	2							
4	United Nations	233	2	8%	1%				2	1			1			1		2		
5	Switzerland	426	1	4%					1			1								
6	WHO (World Health)	187	1	4%	1%			1					1		1					
7	UN Special Fund	113	1	4%	1%				1	1					1					
8	UNICEF (Children)	122	1	4%	1%				1		1		1							
9	IDA (Devel Assoc)	82	1	4%	1%				1											
10	Poland	493	1	4%					1		1									
11	Mali	54	1	4%	2%				1	1								1		
12	Israel	232	1	4%					1						1	1				
13	Accept UN Charter	68	1	4%	1%			1												
14–30																				
31	All Others (0)																			
	GROUPS																			
32	African Group	968	1	4%					1											
33	Arab Group	937																		
34	Asian Group	1937																		
35	Commonwealth	1641																		
36	Communist Group	3310	1	4%					1											
37	Latin America	1674																		
38	Western Europe	5906	11	44%				1	10	3	1	5	2			1		1		
39	Intl Organs	1399	6	24%				1	5	2	1		4		2	1		2		
	TOTALS																			
40	All Data		25	100%				3	22	7	3	6	8	1	4	2		3		
41	UNTS Only	6532	13																	
	COMPARISONS																			
42	Party Total					1%	5%	12%	88%	28%	12%	24%	32%	4%	31%	15%		23%		1%
43	Group Total							18%	75%	22%	21%	18%	35%	4%	19%	13%	10%	15%	4%	
44	World Total					18%	23%	29%	29%	22%	25%	25%	20%	7%	8%	12%	6%	7%	12%	100%

TREATY PROFILE OF NIGERIA

Table 141 • 189

Partners (1)	Partner's World Total (2)	Dyads Absolutes (3)	Ratios Self (4)	Ratios Other (5)	Time 1946 1950 (6)	Time 1951 1955 (7)	Time 1956 1960 (8)	Time 1961 1965 (9)	Topics Admin & Dipl (10)	Topics Social Coop (11)	Topics Econ Coop (12)	Topics Aid (13)	Topics Milit (14)	Institutions UN (15)	Institutions Spec Ag's (16)	Institutions Intl Court (17)	Institutions Arbitration (18)	Institutions Other (19)	Self-Registered (20)
TOP THIRTY																			
1 IBRD (World Bank)	452	5	19%	1%				5				5							
2 Germany, West	890	4	15%					4		1	1	2							
3 USSR (Soviet Union)	1356	2	7%					2	2	1	1								
4 USA (United States)	2599	2	7%				1	1									1		1
5 UK Great Britain	981	2	7%				1	1	2	1									
6 IDA (Devel Assoc)	82	2	7%	2%				2				2							
7 Netherlands	548	2	7%					2		2									
8 Switzerland	426	1	4%					1		1	1				1				
9 WHO (World Health)	187	1	4%	1%				1				1							
10 UN Special Fund	113	1	4%	1%				1			1	1							
11 United Nations	233	1	4%					1	1								2		
12 Norway	461	1	4%			1			1										
13 Canada	310	1	4%					1	1		1		1						
14 ICJ Option Clause	62	1	4%	2%				1								1			
15 Accept UN Charter	68	1	4%	1%				1						1					
16																			
17																			
18																			
19																			
20																			
21																			
22																			
23																			
24																			
25																			
26																			
27																			
28																			
29																			
30																			
31 All Others (0)																			
GROUPS																			
32 African Group	968																		
33 Arab Group	937																		
34 Asian Group	1937																		
35 Commonwealth	1641	3	11%				1	2	2				1						1
36 Communist Group	3310	2	7%				1	2	2										
37 Latin America	1674																		
38 Western Europe	5906	8	30%			1		7		4	2	2			1	1	2		
39 Intl Organs	1399	10	37%	1%				10				10		1		1			1
TOTALS																			
40 All Data	8768	27	100%			1	2	24	6	5	3	12	1	1	1	1	3		
41 UNTS Only		20																	
COMPARISONS																			
42 Party Total					1%	4%	7%	89%	22%	19%	11%	44%	4%	5%	5%	5%	15%		5%
43 Group Total					18%	5%	18%	75%	22%	21%	18%	35%	4%	19%	13%	10%	15%	4%	1%
44 World Total					18%	23%	29%	29%	22%	25%	25%	20%	7%	8%	12%	6%	7%	12%	100%

TREATY PROFILE OF NORWAY

	Partners (1)	Partner's World Total (2)	Dyads Absolutes (3)	Ratios Self (4)	Ratios Other (5)	Time 1946 1950 (6)	Time 1951 1955 (7)	Time 1956 1960 (8)	Time 1961 1965 (9)	Topics Admin & Dipl (10)	Topics Social Coop (11)	Topics Econ Coop (12)	Topics Aid (13)	Topics Milit (14)	Institutions UN (15)	Institutions Spec Ag's (16)	Institutions Intl Court (17)	Institutions Arbitration (18)	Institutions Other (19)	Self-Registered (20)
	TOP THIRTY																			
1	Sweden	483	39	8%	8%	18	10	8	3	12	8	19				1	1	1	1	13
2	USA (United States)	2599	31	7%	1%	13	10	6	2	2	6	4	5	14	3	4	1	1	4	1
3	USSR (Soviet Union)	1356	30	7%	2%	9	2	12	7	16	6	7		1	1		2		5	10
4	UK Great Britain	981	20	4%	2%	8	4	6	2	8	4	5	1	2		4	1	3	6	2
5	Germany, West	890	19	4%	2%	3	6	6	4	4	3	6	1	5		1		3	1	6
6	Finland	245	19	4%	8%	5	8	4	2	10	2	5	1	1		1		3	1	9
7	Denmark	380	18	4%	5%	7	2	5	4	4	4	10							4	4
8	France	1033	16	3%	2%	7	5	2	2	3	3	9		1					7	9
9	Netherlands	548	15	3%	3%	4	4	6	1	1	5	7		2		2		1	1	4
10	Switzerland	426	13	3%	3%	3	5	3	2	3	1	8		1		1			1	3
11	Spain	437	13	3%	3%		3	8	2	1	2	10							1	2
12	Austria	445	12	3%	3%	5	2	4	1	3	1	8	3			1		1	2	4
13	Turkey	298	11	2%	4%	3	1	5	2	2	3	4				1		1	1	2
14	Italy	755	11	2%	1%	5	3	2	1	1	1	8							3	8
15	Yugoslavia	525	9	2%	2%	2	2	3	2	1	2	6				1	1		2	3
16	Canada	310	9	2%	3%	4	2	3		2	1	1		5		1		1		1
17	Poland	493	8	2%	2%	4	1	1	2	2	2	6							4	4
18	Belgium	499	8	2%	2%	5	2	1		1	2	5							3	1
19	Greece	318	7	2%	2%	3	2	1	1	1	1	4	1							4
20	IBRD (World Bank)	452	6	1%	1%			3	1				6							
21	China People's Rep	766	6	1%	1%			2	4	2	2	2				1			1	1
22	South Africa	120	5	1%	4%		2	3		2	2	1				2	2			1
23	Pakistan	245	5	1%	2%	2	2	1		2	1	2				1		1	1	1
24	Ireland	103	5	1%	5%	2	2	1		1	2	2				1		1		2
25	Brazil	195	5	1%	3%	1	1	2	1	2	1	2				1				
26	Argentina	164	5	1%	3%	3			2	2		2		1					1	
27	Portugal	131	4	1%	3%	3		1		1	1	2								1
28	Luxembourg	136	4	1%	3%	1	2	1		1	1	2						1		2
29	Japan	443	4	1%	1%		1	3		1	1	2				1	2			2
30	Israel	232	4	1%	2%		2	1	1	1	1	2								
31	All Others (60)	5881	100	22%	2%	12	20	32	36	39	26	31	3	1		15	7	13	2	10
	GROUPS																			
32	African Group	968	12	3%	1%	2	3		9	2	2	6	2			1	2	2		1
33	Arab Group	937	12	3%	1%	2		8	2	2	8	2				5	4	4		
34	Asian Group	1937	23	5%	1%	5	6	6	6	4	9	10				6	2	3	8	5
35	Commonwealth	1641	38	8%	2%	15	9	10	4	14	7	9	1	7	1	6	1	3	8	4
36	Communist Group	3310	54	12%	2%	15	4	19	16	18	13	22		1		1			10	17
37	Latin America	1674	40	9%	2%	4	8	15	13	26	5	8		1		4	2	2	1	2
38	Western Europe	5906	222	48%	4%	75	58	58	31	53	42	111	6	10		14	13	13	31	75
39	Intl Organs	1399	10	2%	1%		3	4	3	1	1		7	1			3	2		
	TOTALS																			
40	All Data	21889	461	100%		132	106	134	89	127	97	182	21	34	4	43	16	30	57	110
41	UNTS Only		270																	
	COMPARISONS																			
42	Party Total					29%	23%	29%	19%	28%	21%	39%	5%	7%	1%	16%	6%	11%	21%	41%
43	Group Total					22%	25%	27%	26%	24%	26%	32%	10%	8%	4%	14%	6%	8%	17%	32%
44	World Total					18%	23%	29%	29%	22%	25%	25%	20%	7%	8%	12%	6%	7%	12%	100%

TREATY PROFILE OF OAS (AM STATES)

Table 143

Partners (1)	Partner's World Total (2)	Dyads Absolutes (3)	Ratios Self (4)	Ratios Other (5)	Time 1946-1950 (6)	Time 1951-1955 (7)	Time 1956-1960 (8)	Time 1961-1965 (9)	Admin & Dipl (10)	Social Coop (11)	Econ Coop (12)	Aid (13)	Milit (14)	UN (15)	Spec Ag's (16)	Intl Court (17)	Arbitration (18)	Other (19)	Self-Registered (20)
TOP THIRTY																			
1 USA (United States)	2599	3	60%		1														
2 ILO (Labor Org)	59	1	20%	2%		2		1	1			2							
3 Israel	232	1	20%					1	1			1							
4																			
5																			
...																			
31 All Others (0)																			
GROUPS																			
32 African Group	968																		
33 Arab Group	937																		
34 Asian Group	1937																		
35 Commonwealth	1641																		
36 Communist Group	3310																		
37 Latin America	1674																		
38 Western Europe	5906																		
39 Intl Organs	1399	1	20%		1				1										
TOTALS																			
40 All Data		5	100%		1	2		2	2										
41 UNTS Only	2890	5			1			2	2			3							
COMPARISONS																			
42 Party Total					20%	40%		40%	40%			60%	1%	27%	11%	13%	15%	4%	
43 Group Total					12%	25%	23%	40%	19%	7%	1%	71%	7%	8%	12%	6%	7%	4%	74%
44 World Total					18%	23%	29%	29%	22%	25%	25%	20%						12%	100%

192 • Table 144

TREATY PROFILE OF OAU (AFRI UNITY)

	Partner's World Total	Dyads				Time				Topics						Institutions			Self-Registered
Partners		Absolutes	Ratios Self	Ratios Other		1946 1950	1951 1955	1956 1960	1961 1965	Admin & Dipl	Social Coop	Econ Coop	Aid	Milit	UN	Spec Ag's	Intl Court	Arbitration	Other	
(1)	(2)	(3)	(4)	(5)	(6)	(7)	(8)	(9)	(10)	(11)	(12)	(13)	(14)	(15)	(16)	(17)	(18)	(19)	(20)
TOP THIRTY																			
1 United Nations	233	1	50%					1	1					1					
2 ILO (Labor Org)	59	1	50%	2%				1	1										
3																			
4																			
5																			
6																			
7																			
8																			
9																			
10																			
11																			
12																			
13																			
14																			
15																			
16																			
17																			
18																			
19																			
20																			
21																			
22																			
23																			
24																			
25																			
26																			
27																			
28																			
29																			
30																			
31 All Others (0)																			
GROUPS																			
32 African Group	968																		
33 Arab Group	937																		
34 Asian Group	1937																		
35 Commonwealth	1641																		
36 Communist Group	3310																		
37 Latin America	1674																		
38 Western Europe	5906																		
39 Intl Organs	1399	2	100%					2	2					1					
TOTALS																			
40 All Data		2	100%					2	2					1					
41 UNTS Only	292	2	100%					2	2										
COMPARISONS																			
42 Party Total					12%	25%	23%	100%	100%	7%	1%	71%	1%	50%	11%	13%	15%	4%	74%
43 Group Total					12%	25%	23%	40%	19%	7%	1%	71%	1%	27%	11%	13%	15%	4%	74%
44 World Total					18%	23%	29%	29%	22%	25%	25%	20%	7%	8%	12%	6%	7%	12%	100%

Table 145

TREATY PROFILE OF OECD (ECON COOP)

Part-ners (1)	Partner's World Total (2)	Dyads Abso-lutes (3)	Ratios Self (4)	Ratios Other (5)	Time 1946-1950 (6)	Time 1951-1955 (7)	Time 1956-1960 (8)	Time 1961-1965 (9)	Admin & Dipl (10)	Social Coop (11)	Econ Coop (12)	Aid (13)	Milit (14)	UN (15)	Spec Ag's (16)	Intl Court (17)	Arbi-tration (18)	Other (19)	Self-Regis-tered (20)
TOP THIRTY																			
1 Spain	437	1	33%				1												
2 IAEA (Atom Energy)	44	1	33%	2%			1		1	1				1	1				
3 France	1033	1	33%				1												
4																			
5																			
6																			
7																			
8																			
9																			
10																			
11																			
12																			
13																			
14																			
15																			
16																			
17																			
18																			
19																			
20																			
21																			
22																			
23																			
24																			
25																			
26																			
27																			
28																			
29																			
30																			
31 All Others (0)																			
GROUPS																			
32 African Group	968																		
33 Arab Group	937																		
34 Asian Group	1937																		
35 Commonwealth	1641																		
36 Communist Group	3310																		
37 Latin America	1674																		
38 Western Europe	5906	2	67%				2		1	1				1	1				
39 Intl Organs	1399	1	33%				1		1										
TOTALS																			
40 All Data		3	100%				3		2	1				1	1				
41 UNTS Only	1514	1	100%																
COMPARISONS																			
42 Party Total							100%		67%	33%				100%	100%				
43 Group Total					12%	25%	23%	40%	19%	7%	1%	71%	1%	27%	11%	13%	15%	4%	74%
44 World Total					18%	23%	29%	29%	22%	25%	25%	20%	7%	8%	12%	6%	7%	12%	100%

194 • Table 146

TREATY PROFILE OF ORG CTRL AM STATES

Partners	Partner's World Total	Dyads Abso-lutes	Ratios Self	Ratios Other	Time 1946 1950	Time 1951 1955	Time 1956 1960	Time 1961 1965	Topics Admin & Dipl	Topics Social Coop	Topics Econ Coop	Topics Aid	Topics Milit	Institutions UN	Institutions Spec Ag's	Institutions Intl Court	Institutions Arbi-tration	Institutions Other	Self-Regis-tered
(1)	(2)	(3)	(4)	(5)	(6)	(7)	(8)	(9)	(10)	(11)	(12)	(13)	(14)	(15)	(16)	(17)	(18)	(19)	(20)
TOP THIRTY																			
1 ILO (Labor Org)	59	1	100%	2%				1	1										
2																			
3																			
4																			
5																			
6																			
7																			
8																			
9																			
10																			
11																			
12																			
13																			
14																			
15																			
16																			
17																			
18																			
19																			
20																			
21																			
22																			
23																			
24																			
25																			
26																			
27																			
28																			
29																			
30																			
31 All Others (0)																			
GROUPS																			
32 African Group	968																		
33 Arab Group	937																		
34 Asian Group	1937																		
35 Commonwealth	1641																		
36 Communist Group	3310																		
37 Latin America	1674																		
38 Western Europe	5906																		
39 Intl Organs	1399	1	100%					1	1										
TOTALS																			
40 All Data	59	1	100%																
41 UNTS Only		1						1	1										
COMPARISONS																			
42 Party Total								100%	100%										
43 Group Total					12%	25%	23%	40%	19%	7%	1%	71%	1%	27%	11%	13%	15%	4%	74%
44 World Total					18%	23%	29%	29%	22%	25%	25%	20%	7%	8%	12%	6%	7%	12%	100%

TREATY PROFILE OF ORG RAIL COLLABOR

Table 147

Partners (1)	Partner's World Total (2)	Dyads Absolutes (3)	Ratios Self (4)	Ratios Other (5)	Time 1946-1950 (6)	Time 1951-1955 (7)	Time 1956-1960 (8)	Time 1961-1965 (9)	Topics Admin & Dipl (10)	Social Coop (11)	Econ Coop (12)	Aid (13)	Milit (14)	Institutions UN (15)	Spec Ag's (16)	Intl Court (17)	Arbi-tration (18)	Other (19)	Self-Registered (20)
TOP THIRTY																			
1 Poland	493	1	100%				1		1										
2																				
3																				
4																				
5																				
6																				
7																				
8																				
9																				
10																				
11																				
12																				
13																				
14																				
15																				
16																				
17																				
18																				
19																				
20																				
21																				
22																				
23																				
24																				
25																				
26																				
27																				
28																				
29																				
30																				
31 All Others (0)																				
GROUPS																				
32 African Group	968																			
33 Arab Group	937																			
34 Asian Group	1641																			
35 Commonwealth	3310																			
36 Communist Group	1674	1	100%				1													
37 Latin America	5906																			
38 Western Europe	1399																			
39 Intl Organs		1	100%					1	1											
TOTALS																				
40 All Data	493	1																		
41 UNTS Only		0																			
COMPARISONS																				
42 Party Total					12%	25%	100%	40%	100%	7%	1%	71%	1%	27%	11%	13%	15%	4%	74%
43 Group Total					18%	23%	23%	29%	19%	25%	25%	20%	7%	8%	12%	6%	7%	12%	100%
44 World Total						23%	29%	29%	22%											

TREATY PROFILE OF PAKISTAN

	Partners (1)	Partner's World Total (2)	Abso-lutes (3)	Dyads Ratios Self (4)	Other (5)	Time 1946-1950 (6)	1951-1955 (7)	1956-1960 (8)	1961-1965 (9)	Topics Admin & Dipl (10)	Social Coop (11)	Econ Coop (12)	Aid (13)	Milit (14)	Institutions UN (15)	Spec Ag's (16)	Intl Court (17)	Arbi-tration (18)	Other (19)	Self-Regis-tered (20)
	TOP THIRTY																			
1	USA (United States)	2599	37	15%	1%	4	14	12	7	4	5	4	16	8	2	5	1	1		6
2	IBRD (World Bank)	452	21	9%	5%		6	7	8				21		1	1	1	1	1	
3	IDA (Devel Assoc)	82	18	7%	22%				18				18			1			3	10
4	India	299	17	7%	6%	8	5	3	1	8	3	5		1	2	3	1	1		2
5	Japan	443	11	4%	2%		1	6	4	4	5	2			1	3		1	1	1
6	Iran	170	10	4%	6%	1		7	2	5	4	1					1		1	
7	China People's Rep	766	10	4%	1%		1	3	6	2	2	3	3			3				
8	UK Great Britain	981	9	4%	1%	2	5		2	5	3	4	2				1	1		1
9	USSR (Soviet Union)	1356	8	3%	1%	1		4	3	1	2	4	1			3				
10	Turkey	298	7	3%	2%	1	6			5	2			1	3		1	1		5
11	Germany, West	890	7	3%	1%	1	1	5	1	2	2	4	1			2	1	1		1
12	Denmark	380	6	2%	2%	1	1	2	2	2	2	1	3			2	1	2		2
13	United Nations	233	5	2%	2%	1	2	1	1	1	1							1		
14	Norway	461	5	2%	1%	2	2	3		1	2	2	2			2	2	1	1	1
15	Canada	310	5	2%	2%		2	2	1	1	1	1			1	1	1	1	1	2
16	Belgium	499	5	2%	1%		4	2		2	1	2				3		2		1
17	United Arab Rep	232	4	2%	2%	1	1		2	1	3	3	1		1	3	1			3
18	Sweden	483	4	2%	1%	1	1	2			2	1				1	2	2		
19	Philippines	236	4	1%	2%		2	1	1	2	2		2		2	2	1	1		
20	WHO (World Health)	187	3	1%	2%		2	1		1	1		1			1				
21	Netherlands	548	3	1%	1%	1	2			2	1					1	1	1		2
22	Lebanon	75	3	1%	4%	3				2	1					1				
23	Iraq	96	3	1%	3%	1		1	1	1						1				2
24	France	1033	3	1%	1%	2	1				2	1				2		1		2
25	Ceylon (Sri Lanka)	123	3	1%	2%	2	1			1	2			1		1				2
26	Burma	102	3	1%	3%	2			1	3	2									
27	ICJ Option Clause	62	3	1%	5%	1		2		1							3			1
28	Syria	84	2	1%	2%		1	1		1	1	1				1				
29	Switzerland	426	2	1%	1%		1		1		1	1								
30	New Zealand	101	2	1%	2%	2					2			1						2
31	All Others (17)	3688	22	9%	1%	4	6	9	3	7	8	4	3		6	9	7	4		9
	GROUPS																			
32	African Group	968	2	1%	1%				1		2	1				2	1	1		9
33	Arab Group	937	13	5%	1%	5	7		1	7	5				1	3		1	1	
34	Asian Group	1937	40	16%	2%	14	9	12	5	17	14	8		1	4	8	3	3	4	17
35	Commonwealth	1641	18	7%	1%	5	8	3	2	1	8	5	4			8	1	3	1	6
36	Communist Group	3310	18	7%	1%	1	1	7	9	3	4	7	4							
37	Latin America	1674																		
38	Western Europe	5906	50	20%	1%	7	15	20	8	15	17	14	3		4	18	10	8	3	14
39	Intl Organs	1399	51	21%	4%	2	11	10	28	2	2		47	1	6	5	3	2	3	
	TOTALS																			
40	All Data	17695	245	100%		41	68	72	64	57	62	42	74	10	19	52	23	19	11	55
41	UNTS Only		206																	
	COMPARISONS																			
42	Party Total					17%	28%	29%	26%	23%	25%	17%	30%	4%	9%	25%	11%	9%	5%	27%
43	Group Total					16%	23%	31%	30%	21%	23%	20%	30%	7%	10%	15%	8%	8%	6%	16%
44	World Total					18%	23%	29%	29%	22%	25%	25%	20%	7%	8%	12%	6%	7%	12%	100%

Table 149 • 197

TREATY PROFILE OF PAN AM HEALTH ORG

Part-ners (1)		Part-ner's World Total (2)	Dyads			Time				Topics					Institutions				Self-Regis-tered (20)
			Abso-lutes (3)	Ratios Self (4)	Other (5)	1946 1950 (6)	1951 1955 (7)	1956 1960 (8)	1961 1965 (9)	Admin & Dipl (10)	Social Coop (11)	Econ Coop (12)	Aid (13)	Milit (14)	UN (15)	Spec Ag's (16)	Intl Court (17)	Arbi-tration (18)	Other (19)	
TOP THIRTY																				
1	WHO (World Health)	187	1	100%	1%	1					1									
2																				
3																				
4																				
5																				
6																				
7																				
8																				
9																				
10																				
11																				
12																				
13																				
14																				
15																				
16																				
17																				
18																				
19																				
20																				
21																				
22																				
23																				
24																				
25																				
26																				
27																				
28																				
29																				
30																				
31	All Others (0)																			
GROUPS																				
32	African Group	968																		
33	Arab Group	937																		
34	Asian Group	1937																		
35	Commonwealth	1641																		
36	Communist Group	3310																		
37	Latin America	1674																		
38	Western Europe	5906																		
39	Intl Organs	1399	1	100%		1														
TOTALS																				
40	All Data	187	1	100%		1					1									
41	UNTS Only		1																		
COMPARISONS																				
42	Party Total					100%					100%									
43	Group Total					12%	25%	23%	40%	19%	7%	1%	71%	1%	27%	11%	13%	15%	4%	74%
44	World Total					18%	23%	29%	29%	22%	25%	25%	20%	7%	8%	12%	6%	7%	12%	100%

TREATY PROFILE OF PANAMA

Table 150

	Partners (1)	Partner's World Total (2)	Dyads Absolutes (3)	Ratios Self (4)	Ratios Other (5)	Time 1946-1950 (6)	Time 1951-1955 (7)	Time 1956-1960 (8)	Time 1961-1965 (9)	Topics Admin & Dipl (10)	Topics Social Coop (11)	Topics Econ Coop (12)	Topics Aid (13)	Topics Milit (14)	Institutions UN (15)	Institutions Spec Ag's (16)	Institutions Intl Court (17)	Institutions Arbitration (18)	Institutions Other (19)	Self-Registered (20)
	TOP THIRTY																			
1	USA (United States)	2599	34	60%	1%	12	11	6	5	10	11	2	9	2		1		1	3	
2	IBRD (World Bank)	452	5	9%	1%		3	1	1				5							
3	Italy	755	3	5%		2			1	2				1						
4	United Nations	233	2	4%	1%		1	1	1	1			1					2		
5	Norway	461	2	4%				1	1	2										
6	Germany, West	890	2	4%				1	1	1			1							
7	UK Great Britain	981	1	2%			1									1				
8	Spain	437	1	2%			1			1										
9	WHO (World Health)	187	1	2%	1%				1		1				1			1		
10	UN Special Fund	113	1	2%	1%		1						1		1					
11	UNICEF (Children)	122	1	2%	1%		1						1		1			1		
12	ILO (Labor Org)	59	1	2%	2%		1			1	1									
13	France	1033	1	2%					1		1									
14	Taiwan	172	1	2%	1%															
15	Argentina	164	1	2%	1%															
31	All Others (0)																			
	GROUPS																			
32	African Group	968																		
33	Arab Group	937	1	2%				1												
34	Asian Group	1937	1	2%			1									1				
35	Commonwealth	1641																		
36	Communist Group	3310																		
37	Latin America	1674	1	2%		1	2	2	1	7	1		1							
38	Western Europe	5906	9	16%		2	7	2	3	2										
39	Intl Organs	1399	11	19%	1%				2		1		8	1	4		1	4		
	TOTALS																			
40	All Data	8658	57	100%		14	21	11	11	19	15	2	18	3	4	2	1	5	3	
41	UNTS Only		48																	
	COMPARISONS																			
42	Party Total					25%	37%	19%	19%	33%	26%	4%	32%	5%	8%	4%	2%	10%	6%	
43	Group Total					18%	27%	24%	31%	16%	25%	18%	31%	9%	7%	10%	5%	6%	7%	6%
44	World Total					18%	23%	29%	29%	22%	25%	25%	20%	7%	8%	12%	6%	7%	12%	100%

Table 151 • 199

TREATY PROFILE OF PARAGUAY

Partners	Partner's World Total	Dyads Absolutes	Dyads Ratios Self	Dyads Ratios Other	Time 1946-1950	Time 1951-1955	Time 1956-1960	Time 1961-1965	Topics Admin & Dipl	Topics Social Coop	Topics Econ Coop	Topics Aid	Topics Milit	Institutions UN	Institutions Spec Ag's	Institutions Intl Court	Institutions Arbitration	Institutions Other	Self-Registered
(1)	(2)	(3)	(4)	(5)	(6)	(7)	(8)	(9)	(10)	(11)	(12)	(13)	(14)	(15)	(16)	(17)	(18)	(19)	(20)
TOP THIRTY																			
1 USA (United States)	2599	27	36%	1%	8	4	5	10	1	8	3	10	5		1		1	3	
2 Spain	437	11	15%	3%	2		7	2	4	3	4				1				
3 Argentina	164	4	5%	2%			1	3	2	2					1				
4 IBRD (World Bank)	452	3	4%	1%		1		2				3							
5 Netherlands	548	3	4%			1	2		1	1	1								
6 Germany, West	890	3	4%	1%		3					3								
7 France	1033	3	4%		1		1	2	1		1								
8 UK Great Britain	981	2	3%		1	1				1	2								
9 United Nations	233	2	3%	1%		1	1					2						2	
10 IDA (Devel Assoc)	82	2	3%	2%				2				2							
11 Japan	443	2	3%						1			1							
12 Italy	755	2	3%				2				2								
13 Taiwan	172	2	3%	1%			2			1	1								
14 WHO (World Health)	187	1	1%	1%		1		1				1		1	1				
15 UN Special Fund	113	1	1%	1%		1						1		1		1	1		
16 UNICEF (Children)	122	1	1%	2%		1			1					1					
17 ILO (Labor Org)	59	1	1%					1	1										
18 Norway	461	1	1%				1		1	1									
19 Mexico	138	1	1%	1%				1	1	1									
20 Israel	232	1	1%																
21 Denmark	380	1	1%				1												
22 Belgium	499	1	1%	1%			1		1										
31 All Others (0)																			
GROUPS																			
32 African Group	968																		
33 Arab Group	937																		
34 Asian Group	1937	2	3%		1			2		1	1								
35 Commonwealth	1641	2	3%		1	1					2								
36 Communist Group	3310																		
37 Latin America	1674	5	7%		2		2	3	2	3									
38 Western Europe	5906	25	33%			4	14	5	8	5	12				1	2			
39 Intl Organs	1399	11	15%	1%		5	1	5	1			10		3	2	2	3		
TOTALS																			
40 All Data	10980	75	100%		11	14	24	26	14	17	18	21	5	3	4	2	4	4	
41 UNTS Only		52																		
COMPARISONS																			
42 Party Total					15%	19%	32%	35%	19%	23%	24%	28%	7%	6%	8%	4%	8%	8%	
43 Group Total					18%	27%	24%	31%	16%	25%	18%	31%	9%	7%	10%	5%	6%	7%	6%
44 World Total					18%	23%	29%	29%	22%	25%	25%	20%	7%	8%	12%	6%	7%	12%	100%

TREATY PROFILE OF PERU

Partners (1)	Partner's World Total (2)	Dyads Absolutes (3)	Ratios Self (4)	Ratios Other (5)	Time 1946 1950 (6)	Time 1951 1955 (7)	Time 1956 1960 (8)	Time 1961 1965 (9)	Topics Admin & Dipl (10)	Topics Social Coop (11)	Topics Econ Coop (12)	Topics Aid (13)	Topics Milit (14)	Institutions UN (15)	Institutions Spec Ag's (16)	Institutions Intl Court (17)	Institutions Arbitration (18)	Institutions Other (19)	Self-Registered (20)
TOP THIRTY																			
1 USA (United States)	2599	47	43%	2%	10	12	15	10	2	11	3	19	12	1	3		1	3	
2 IBRD (World Bank)	452	20	18%	4%		7	5	8				20							
3 Germany, West	890	6	6%	1%	1	1	1	4	1	3	1	1							
4 Italy	755	5	5%	1%			3	1	4	1	1			1	1		1		
5 Spain	437	3	3%	1%		2	1		1	1	1				1		1		
6 Denmark	380	3	3%				2	1		1	1	1		1	1		1		
7 UK Great Britain	981	2	2%	1%	2					1									
8 Switzerland	426	2	2%			1	1			1									
9 WHO (World Health)	187	2	2%	1%	2					1		1			1	1			
10 ILO (Labor Org)	59	2	2%	3%		1		2	1					1				1	
11 Norway	461	2	2%				2			1		1							
12 Israel	232	2	2%	1%			1	1	1	1		1							
13 Belgium	499	2	2%				1	1		1					1	1	1		
14 UN Special Fund	113	1	1%	1%			1					1		1					
15 UNICEF (Children)	122	1	1%	1%	1									1					
16 ICAO (Civil Aviat)	23	1	1%	4%	1				1							1			
17 Nicaragua	50	1	1%	2%				1		1									
18 Netherlands	548	1	1%			1				1					1				
19 Mexico	138	1	1%	1%			1												
20 Japan	443	1	1%					1		1									
21 France	1033	1	1%				1		1		1								
22 Taiwan	172	1	1%	1%				1		1							1		
23 Canada	310	1	1%			1													
24 Austria	445	1	1%				1												
25																			
26																			
27																			
28																			
29																			
30																			
31 All Others (0)																			
GROUPS																			
32 African Group	968																		
33 Arab Group	937																		
34 Asian Group	1937	1	1%			1					1								
35 Commonwealth	1641	3	3%		2			1		2	1				2		2		
36 Communist Group	3310																		
37 Latin America	1674	2	2%		1	5	2	7	9	2		3		1	1		5		
38 Western Europe	5906	26	24%		1	5	13	7	9	10	4			1	5	3	5	1	
39 Intl Organs	1399	27	25%	2%	4	8	7	8	2	1		24		3	2	3	1	1	
TOTALS																			
40 All Data	11755	109	100%		17	26	37	29	13	27	10	47	12	5	15	3	9	4	
41 UNTS Only		92																		
COMPARISONS																			
42 Party Total					16%	24%	34%	27%	12%	25%	9%	43%	11%	5%	16%	3%	10%	4%	4%
43 Group Total					18%	27%	24%	31%	16%	25%	18%	31%	9%	7%	10%	5%	6%	7%	6%
44 World Total					18%	23%	29%	29%	22%	25%	25%	20%	7%	8%	12%	6%	7%	12%	100%

TREATY PROFILE OF PETROL EXPORT ORG

Table 153 • 201

Partners (1)	Partner's World Total (2)	Dyads Absolutes (3)	Dyads Ratios Self (4)	Dyads Ratios Other (5)	Time 1946 1950 (6)	Time 1951 1955 (7)	Time 1956 1960 (8)	Time 1961 1965 (9)	Topics Admin & Dipl (10)	Topics Social Coop (11)	Topics Econ Coop (12)	Topics Aid (13)	Topics Milit (14)	Institutions UN (15)	Institutions Spec Ag's (16)	Institutions Intl Court (17)	Institutions Arbitration (18)	Other (19)	Self-Registered (20)
TOP THIRTY																			
1 Austria	445	1	100%					1	1							1	1		
2																			
3																			
4																			
5																			
6																			
7																			
8																			
9																			
10																			
11																			
12																			
13																			
14																			
15																			
16																			
17																			
18																			
19																			
20																			
21																			
22																			
23																			
24																			
25																			
26																			
27																			
28																			
29																			
30																			
31 All Others (0)																			
GROUPS																			
32 African Group	968																		
33 Arab Group	937																		
34 Asian Group	1937																		
35 Commonwealth	1641																		
36 Communist Group	3310																		
37 Latin America	1674																		
38 Western Europe	5906	1	100%					1	1							1	1		
39 Intl Organs	1399																			
TOTALS																				
40 All Data	445	1	100%					1	1							1	1		
41 UNTS Only		1																		
COMPARISONS																				
42 Party Total					12%	25%	23%	100%	100%	7%	1%	71%	1%	27%	11%	100%	100%	4%	74%
43 Group Total					18%	23%	29%	40%	19%	25%	25%	20%	7%	8%	12%	13%	15%	12%	100%
44 World Total							29%	29%	22%							6%	7%		

202 • Table 154

TREATY PROFILE OF PHILIPPINES

	Partners (1)	Partner's World Total (2)	Dyads Absolutes (3)	Ratios Self (4)	Ratios Other (5)	Time 1946 1950 (6)	Time 1951 1955 (7)	Time 1956 1960 (8)	Time 1961 1965 (9)	Topics Admin & Dipl (10)	Topics Social Coop (11)	Topics Econ Coop (12)	Topics Aid (13)	Topics Milit (14)	Institutions UN (15)	Institutions Spec Ag's (16)	Institutions Intl Court (17)	Institutions Arbitration (18)	Institutions Other (19)	Self-Registered (20)
	TOP THIRTY																			
1	USA (United States)	2599	94	40%	4%	40	11	15	28	21	19	13	17	24	4	3			3	9
2	Japan	443	18	8%	4%	1	7	8	2	3	3	6	2	4			1	1	1	2
3	Indonesia	126	11	5%	9%		1	2	8	5	1	2	1	2						1
4	UNTAB (Tech Assis)	10	10	4%	100%		8	2					10							
5	Germany, West	890	10	4%	1%		1		9	4	1	3	2			1		2		1
6	Spain	437	8	3%	2%	5	2	1		4	4								1	3
7	IBRD (World Bank)	452	8	3%	2%				7				8			2		2		
8	UK Great Britain	981	7	3%	1%	3	3	1		3	4	1	1							2
9	Taiwan	172	6	3%	3%	2		3	1	2	2		2			1	1			3
10	Israel	232	5	2%	2%		1	2	2	1	1	1	3		1		2			
11	WHO (World Health)	187	5	2%	2%	1	3	1					3		1					
12	FAO (Food Agri)	19	4	2%	21%		4						4							
13	Pakistan	245	4	2%	2%	1	1	1	2	1	2	1				1	1	1		2
14	Australia	201	4	2%	2%	2	1	1	1	2	2	1								2
15	Thailand	132	3	1%	2%	1	1		1	2	1						1			1
16	Switzerland	426	3	1%	1%	1	1	1		1	1	1					1			
17	United Arab Rep	232	2	1%	1%		1	1		1	1									1
18	Norway	461	2	1%			1	1		1	1									1
19	Netherlands	548	2	1%			1	1		2	1									2
20	Korea, South	80	2	1%	3%			1	1	2	1	1			1	1	1			2
21	Italy	755	2	1%		1	1			2										
22	India	299	2	1%	1%	1			1	1	1					1				
23	Greece	318	2	1%	1%	2				2								1		
24	France	1033	2	1%		1	1			1		1								1
25	Denmark	380	2	1%	1%			1	1	2										
26	Belgium	499	2	1%				2		1										
27	Vietnam, South	106	1	1%	1%			1		1		1								
28	Vatican/Holy See	16	1		6%															1
29	Turkey	298	1				1			1										
30	Sweden	483	1			1					1									
31	All Others (13)	1374	13	6%	1%	3	3	3	4	9	2		2	1	2	1	2	1	1	6
	GROUPS																			
32	African Group	968																		
33	Arab Group	937	2	1%			1	1		1	1									
34	Asian Group	1937	31	13%	2%	5	5	7	14	14	8	5	2	2	1	3	3	2		9
35	Commonwealth	1641	12	5%	1%	5	3	3	1	4	7	1			1	3		2		3
36	Communist Group	3310																		
37	Latin America	1674	5	2%		1	2	1	1	5										3
38	Western Europe	5906	39	17%	1%	11	9	8	11	20	11	5	2			3	3	2	1	12
39	Intl Organs	1399	29	12%	2%	2	15	3	9	2			27	1	3	1	3	1		
	TOTALS																			
40	All Data	14434	236	100%		66	54	47	69	73	50	30	52	31	9	14	12	8	5	41
41	UNTS Only		144																	
	COMPARISONS																			
42	Party Total					28%	23%	20%	29%	31%	21%	13%	22%	13%	6%	10%	8%	6%	3%	28%
43	Group Total					16%	23%	31%	30%	21%	23%	20%	30%	7%	10%	15%	8%	8%	6%	16%
44	World Total					18%	23%	29%	29%	22%	25%	25%	20%	7%	8%	12%	6%	7%	12%	100%

Table 155 • 203

TREATY PROFILE OF POLAND

Partners (1)	Partner's World Total (2)	Dyads Absolutes (3)	Ratios Self (4)	Ratios Other (5)	Time 1946 1950 (6)	Time 1951 1955 (7)	Time 1956 1960 (8)	Time 1961 1965 (9)	Admin & Dipl (10)	Social Coop (11)	Econ Coop (12)	Aid (13)	Milit (14)	UN (15)	Spec Ag's (16)	Intl Court (17)	Arbi- tration (18)	Other (19)	Self- Regis- tered (20)
TOP THIRTY																			
1 USSR (Soviet Union)	1356	84	17%	6%	21	9	36	18	22	20	14	24	4	1				8	12
2 Germany, East	556	71	14%	13%	7	24	28	12	20	35	14	2						3	8
3 Czechoslovakia	393	46	9%	12%	14	6	17	9	15	21	7		3	1	2		2	6	20
4 China People's Rep	766	31	6%	4%		14	11	6	3	19	12	2	1	1				1	1
5 Yugoslavia	525	28	6%	5%	12	2	12	2	3	12	10	2	1					7	7
6 USA (United States)	2599	19	4%	1%	4		8	7	3	3	3	9		1					
7 Hungary	290	18	4%	6%	6		9	3	4	12	2							3	10
8 Bulgaria	236	15	3%	6%	6	1	2	6	5	6	3		1					3	9
9 Italy	755	14	3%	2%	1		5	8	1	4	8			1					
10 France	1033	14	3%	1%	6	1	3	4	1	8	4	1	1						3
11 Sweden	483	12	2%	2%	8	2	2		1	1	10							1	1
12 UK Great Britain	981	10	2%	1%	6	1	3		2	2	5								
13 Denmark	380	9	2%	2%	4	3	2			2	7							3	1
14 Norway	461	8	2%	2%	4	1	2	1		2	6							4	1
15 Romania	251	7	1%	3%	3		1	3	2	3	1		1					1	5
16 Belgium	499	6	1%	1%	1		1	4		4	1	1		1				1	
17 Switzerland	426	5	1%	1%	2			3		1	4								
18 Netherlands	548	5	1%	1%	1	2	1	1		1	4								
19 Korea, North	99	5	1%	5%	1	3				4		1							
20 Greece	318	5	1%	2%			2	3		1	4				1			2	
21 Vietnam, North	81	4	1%	5%			4			4								1	1
22 Mongolia	119	4	1%	3%		1	1	2	1	2	1	1							2
23 Austria	445	4	1%	1%			1	3	1	3									
24 United Arab Rep	232	3	1%	1%			2	1	2	2			1						
25 Turkey	298	3	1%	1%	2	1					3								1
26 Mali	54	3	1%	6%				3		2		1						1	1
27 Iraq	96	3	1%	3%			2	1		2	1							1	1
28 India	299	3	1%	1%			3			3									1
29 Ghana	81	3	1%	4%				3		2		1							1
30 Cuba	111	3	1%	3%			1	2		2		1							4
31 All Others (32)	4483	48	10%	1%	3	5	9	31	5	15	11	17		4	3	1	1	4	4
GROUPS																			
32 African Group	968	16	3%	2%		1	4	16		8	1	7						1	2
33 Arab Group	937	13	3%	1%			4	9		7	1	5						1	2
34 Asian Group	1937	9	2%				5	3	1	4	2	3							1
35 Commonwealth	1641	15	3%	1%	7	2	3	3	3	3	7	1	1		2			1	
36 Communist Group	3310	288	58%	9%	58	59	112	59	69	129	53	28	9	5	2		2	28	71
37 Latin America	1674	6	1%			2	1	3		3	2	2		1					2
38 Western Europe	5906	89	18%	2%	29	10	18	32	4	29	53	1		2	1	1	1	11	6
39 Intl Organs	1399	8	2%	1%	1		2	5	3		1	4		2				1	
TOTALS																			
40 All Data	19254	493	100%		111	76	167	139	86	198	134	62	13	10	6	1	3	50	92
41 UNTS Only		194																	
COMPARISONS																			
42 Party Total					23%	15%	34%	28%	17%	40%	27%	13%	3%	5%	3%	1%	2%	26%	47%
43 Group Total					16%	17%	38%	29%	20%	32%	32%	13%	2%	4%	4%		3%	17%	33%
44 World Total					18%	23%	29%	29%	22%	25%	25%	20%	7%	8%	12%	6%	7%	12%	100%

204 • Table 156

TREATY PROFILE OF PORTUGAL

Partners (1)	Partner's World Total (2)	Dyads Absolutes (3)	Ratios Self (4)	Ratios Other (5)	Time 1946-1950 (6)	Time 1951-1955 (7)	Time 1956-1960 (8)	Time 1961-1965 (9)	Admin & Dipl (10)	Social Coop (11)	Econ Coop (12)	Aid (13)	Milit (14)	UN (15)	Spec Ag's (16)	Intl Court (17)	Arbitration (18)	Other (19)	Self-Registered (20)
TOP THIRTY																			
1 USA (United States)	2599	24	18%	1%	7	6	6	5	2	4	7	4	7	3	3	1		7	
2 UK Great Britain	981	16	12%	2%	3	9	1	3	5	3	4	2	2		2		1	8	
3 Germany, West	890	12	9%	1%	1	1	5	5	2	4	6				1		1		
4 Spain	437	9	7%	2%	1	1	4	3		4	3								
5 Netherlands	548	7	5%	1%	1	3	2	1	3	6	2				1		1	3	
6 Denmark	380	7	5%	2%	4	2		1		2	6				1		1	4	
7 France	1033	6	5%	1%	1		2	3		5					1		1		
8 Belgium	499	5	4%	1%	3	2			1	2	2				1				
9 Sweden	483	4	3%	1%	3	1				1	3								
10 Norway	461	4	3%	1%	3		1			1	2				1				
11 Ireland	103	4	3%	4%		2	2				1						1		
12 Switzerland	426	3	2%	1%	1			3		2	1				1		1		
13 IBRD (World Bank)	452	3	2%	1%			1	3				3							
14 Greece	318	3	2%	1%	2	1					3								
15 Taiwan	172	3	2%	2%	3					1	2				1		1	1	
16 Canada	310	3	2%	1%	1	1	1		1	1	1								
17 Luxembourg	136	2	2%	1%	1		1			2									
18 Italy	755	2	2%		1		1		1	1					1		1		
19 Venezuela	47	1	1%	2%			1			1					1				
20 Turkey	298	1	1%		1										1				
21 South Africa	120	1	1%	1%				1		1		1			1		1		
22 Pakistan	245	1	1%				1			1					1		1		
23 Morocco	94	1	1%	1%			1			1						1			
24 Mexico	138	1	1%	1%	1														
25 Fed Rhod/Nyasaland	11	1	1%	9%				1									1		
26 Cuba	111	1	1%	1%		1				1					1				
27 Colombia	112	1	1%	1%		1			1						1				
28 Brazil	195	1	1%		1						1								
29 Austria	445	1	1%			1				1									
30 Australia	201	1	1%					1	1										
31 All Others (2)	130	2	2%	2%		1		1	2					2		1			
GROUPS																			
32 African Group	968	1	1%																
33 Arab Group	937	4	3%		3		1		1	1	2				1		1		
34 Asian Group	1937	22	17%	1%	4	10	3	5	7	5	6	2	2		4	1	2	8	
35 Commonwealth	1641																			
36 Communist Group	3310																			
37 Latin America	1674	5	4%		2	2	1					1							
38 Western Europe	5906	70	53%	1%	22	14	19	15	11	5		3			5	1	2	9	
39 Intl Organs	1399	3	2%					3		28	30	3		2	11		7		
TOTALS																			
40 All Data	13130	131	100%		38	33	32	28	23	44	45	10	9	5	25	3	13	24	
41 UNTS Only		94																		
COMPARISONS																			
42 Party Total					29%	25%	24%	21%	18%	34%	34%	8%	7%	5%	27%	3%	14%	26%	32%
43 Group Total					22%	25%	27%	26%	24%	26%	32%	10%	8%	4%	14%	6%	8%	17%	
44 World Total					18%	23%	29%	29%	22%	25%	25%	20%	7%	8%	12%	6%	7%	12%	100%

Table 157 • 205

TREATY PROFILE OF ROMANIA

Partners (1)	Partner's World Total (2)	Dyads Absolutes (3)	Ratios Self (4)	Ratios Other (5)	Time 1946-1950 (6)	Time 1951-1955 (7)	Time 1956-1960 (8)	Time 1961-1965 (9)	Admin & Dipl (10)	Social Coop (11)	Econ Coop (12)	Aid (13)	Milit (14)	UN (15)	Spec Ag's (16)	Intl Court (17)	Arbitration (18)	Other (19)	Self-Registered (20)
TOP THIRTY																			
1 USSR (Soviet Union)	1356	75	30%	6%	26	13	31	5	24	15	18	14	4					2	1
2 Germany, East	556	30	12%	5%	4	10	9	7	5	17	7	1							6
3 China People's Rep	766	26	10%	3%		8	6	12		12	14								1
4 Yugoslavia	525	17	7%	3%	7		6	4	5	9	2						2		9
5 Czechoslovakia	393	9	4%	2%	2	1	5	1	3	5	1							5	5
6 Hungary	290	8	3%	3%	1	1	4	2	4	4								2	4
7 Austria	445	8	3%	2%		1	1	6	4	4	2								3
8 USA (United States)	2599	7	3%		2		2	3	2	3	1		1	1					
9 Poland	493	7	3%	1%	3		1	3	2	3	1		1	1				1	1
10 France	1033	7	3%	1%		1		6		4	2	1							
11 Bulgaria	236	6	2%	3%	1	1	4		4	2								1	6
12 Italy	755	5	2%	1%	1		1	3		2	3								2
13 Greece	318	5	2%	2%		2	2	1		1	3		1					2	
14 Korea, North	99	3	1%	3%		2	1			3									3
15 Belgium	499	3	1%	1%			1	2		3									
16 Vietnam, North	81	2	1%	2%			2			2								2	2
17 UK Great Britain	981	2	1%		1		1				1			1				1	
18 United Arab Rep	232	2	1%	1%					1	2	1								2
19 Norway	461	2	1%					1			1								1
20 Netherlands	548	2	1%				2			1	1								
21 Iraq	96	2	1%	2%			2		1	1	1			1					2
22 Ghana	81	2	1%	2%				2		2				1				1	2
23 Ceylon (Sri Lanka)	123	2	1%	2%			2				2				1	1		1	
24 Albania	125	2	1%	2%				1											2
25 Accept UN Charter	68	2	1%	3%		2			2					2					
26 Turkey	298	1				1					1								
27 Switzerland	426	1				1					1								
28 Sweden	483	1					1			1									
29 South Africa	120	1	1%						1					1				1	1
30 UN Special Fund	113	1	1%					1	1					1	1	1	1	1	
31 All Others (10)	2579	10	4%		2		4	4	3	5	2			2				1	4
GROUPS																			
32 African Group	968	3	1%					3		3	1							1	3
33 Arab Group	937	4	2%				4			3	1								4
34 Asian Group	1937	4	2%				3	1		1	3							1	1
35 Commonwealth	1641	4	2%				1				1								
36 Communist Group	3310	169	67%	5%	37	37	64	31	42	66	41	15	5	3				9	32
37 Latin America	1674	1					1			1				1					1
38 Western Europe	5906	37	15%	1%	1	5	11	20	2	18	15	1	1					4	8
39 Intl Organs	1399	3	1%		1			2	3					2	1	1	1		
TOTALS																			
40 All Data	17178	251	100%		51	44	92	64	59	104	64	17	7	9	1	1	3	20	58
41 UNTS Only		124																	
COMPARISONS																			
42 Party Total					20%	18%	37%	25%	24%	41%	25%	7%	3%	7%	1%	1%	2%	16%	47%
43 Group Total					16%	17%	38%	29%	20%	32%	32%	13%	2%	4%	4%		3%	17%	33%
44 World Total					18%	23%	29%	29%	22%	25%	25%	20%	7%	8%	12%	6%	7%	12%	100%

TREATY PROFILE OF RWANDA

Table 158

Part-ners	Part-ner's World Total	Dyads Abso-lutes	Ratios Self	Ratios Other	Time 1946-1950	Time 1951-1955	Time 1956-1960	Time 1961-1965	Topics Admin & Dipl	Topics Social Coop	Topics Econ Coop	Topics Aid	Topics Milit	Institutions UN	Institutions Spec Ag's	Institutions Intl Court	Institutions Arbi-tration	Other	Self-Regis-tered
(1)	(2)	(3)	(4)	(5)	(6)	(7)	(8)	(9)	(10)	(11)	(12)	(13)	(14)	(15)	(16)	(17)	(18)	(19)	(20)
TOP THIRTY																			
1 WHO (World Health)	187	2	14%	1%				2				2							
2 Germany, West	890	2	14%					2				2							
3 Belgium	499	2	14%					2	1			2						1	
4 USSR (Soviet Union)	1356	1	7%					1											
5 USA (United States)	2599	1	7%					1			1								
6 UN Special Fund	113	1	7%	1%				1				1		1	1	1	1		
7 United Nations	233	1	7%					1	1								2		
8 UNICEF (Children)	122	1	7%	1%				1											
9 Israel	232	1	7%					1	1			1							
10 France	1033	1	7%					1	1										
11 Accept UN Charter	68	1	7%	1%				1						1					
31 All Others (0)																			
GROUPS																			
32 African Group	968																		
33 Arab Group	937																		
34 Asian Group	1937																		
35 Commonwealth	1641																		
36 Communist Group	3310	1	7%					1			1								
37 Latin America	1674																		
38 Western Europe	5906	5	36%					5	1			4							
39 Intl Organs	1399	5	36%					5	1			4		1	1	1	3	1	
TOTALS																			
40 All Data	7332	14	100%					14	4		1	9		2	1	1	3	1	
41 UNTS Only		10																		
COMPARISONS																			
42 Party Total					1%	5%	18%	100%	29%	21%	7%	64%	4%	20%	10%	10%	30%	10%	1%
43 Group Total					18%	23%	29%	75%	22%	25%	18%	35%	7%	19%	13%	10%	15%	4%	1%
44 World Total					18%	23%	29%	29%	22%	25%	25%	20%	7%	8%	12%	6%	7%	12%	100%

Table 159 • 207

TREATY PROFILE OF SAN MARINO

Partners (1)	Partner's World Total (2)	Dyads Absolutes (3)	Ratios Self (4)	Ratios Other (5)	Time 1946-1950 (6)	Time 1951-1955 (7)	Time 1956-1960 (8)	Time 1961-1965 (9)	Topics Admin & Dipl (10)	Topics Social Coop (11)	Topics Econ Coop (12)	Topics Aid (13)	Topics Milit (14)	Institutions UN (15)	Institutions Spec Ag's (16)	Institutions Intl Court (17)	Institutions Arbitration (18)	Other (19)	Self-Registered (20)
TOP THIRTY																			
1 Italy	755	5	29%	1%		1	3			2	2		1						
2 UK Great Britain	981	3	18%		1	1		2	2				1						
3 France	1033	3	18%		1	1		1	1	2									
4 Belgium	499	2	12%		1		1		1	1									
5 USSR (Soviet Union)	1356	1	6%		1				1	1									
6 United Nations	233	1	6%					1	1					1					
7 Canada	310	1	6%			1			1										
8 ICJ Option Clause	62	1	6%	2%												1			
9																			
10–30																			
31 All Others (0)																			
GROUPS																			
32 African Group	968																		
33 Arab Group	937																		
34 Asian Group	1937																		
35 Commonwealth	1641	4	24%		1			3	3				1						
36 Communist Group	3310	1	6%				1		1										
37 Latin America	1674																		
38 Western Europe	5906	10	59%		2	3	3	2	2	5	2		1						
39 Intl Organs	1399	1	6%		1					1									
TOTALS																			
40 All Data	5229	17	100%		4	4	4	5	7	6	2		2	1		1			
41 UNTS Only		8																		
COMPARISONS																			
42 Party Total					24%	24%	24%	29%	41%	35%	12%		12%	13%	14%	13%	8%	17%	
43 Group Total					22%	25%	27%	26%	24%	26%	32%	10%	8%	4%	12%	6%	7%	12%	32%
44 World Total					18%	23%	29%	29%	22%	25%	25%	20%	7%	8%	12%	6%	6%	12%	100%

TREATY PROFILE OF SAUDI ARABIA

Partners (1)	Partner's World Total (2)	Dyads Absolutes (3)	Ratios Self (4)	Ratios Other (5)	Time 1946 1950 (6)	Time 1951 1955 (7)	Time 1956 1960 (8)	Time 1961 1965 (9)	Topics Admin & Dipl (10)	Topics Social Coop (11)	Topics Econ Coop (12)	Topics Aid (13)	Topics Milit (14)	Institutions UN (15)	Institutions Spec Ag's (16)	Institutions Intl Court (17)	Institutions Arbitration (18)	Institutions Other (19)	Self-Registered (20)
TOP THIRTY																			
1 USA (United States)	2599	19	61%	1%		12	2	5	1	4		10	4	1	1				1
2 WHO (World Health)	187	2	6%	1%		1	1		1			2		2				1	
3 United Nations	233	2	6%	1%		1		2	1			1				1	1		
4 UK Great Britain	981	1	3%					1											
5 Syria	84	1	3%	1%				1			1								
6 Spain	437	1	3%					1	1										
7 UN Special Fund	113	1	3%	1%				1				1		1					
8 UNICEF (Children)	122	1	3%	1%				1				1		1					
9 Pakistan	245	1	3%			1				1									
10 France	1033	1	3%		1														
11 Taiwan	172	1	3%	1%				1	1										
12																			
...																			
31 All Others (0)																			
GROUPS																			
32 African Group	968																		
33 Arab Group	937	1	3%			1													
34 Asian Group	1937	2	6%		1	1		1	2										
35 Commonwealth	1641	1	3%						1		1								
36 Communist Group	3310																		
37 Latin America	1674																		
38 Western Europe	5906	2	6%			1	1	2	1	1						1	1		
39 Intl Organs	1399	6	19%				1	4	1	1	1	5		4	1	1	1	1	
TOTALS																			
40 All Data	6206	31	100%		1	15	3	12	6	5	1	15	4	5	1	2	2	2	1
41 UNTS Only		29																		
COMPARISONS																			
42 Party Total				3%	3%	48%	10%	39%	19%	16%	3%	48%	13%	17%	3%	7%	7%	7%	3%
43 Group Total				5%	9%	24%	31%	36%	18%	27%	22%	29%	4%	15%	20%	8%	15%	9%	5%
44 World Total				100%	18%	23%	29%	29%	22%	25%	25%	20%	7%	8%	12%	6%	7%	12%	100%

TREATY PROFILE OF SEATO (SE ASIA)

Table 161

	Partners (1)	Partner's World Total (2)	Dyads Abso-lutes (3)	Ratios Self (4)	Ratios Other (5)	Time 1946 1950 (6)	Time 1951 1955 (7)	Time 1956 1960 (8)	Time 1961 1965 (9)	Topics Admin & Dipl (10)	Topics Social Coop (11)	Topics Econ Coop (12)	Topics Aid (13)	Topics Milit (14)	Institutions UN (15)	Institutions Spec Ag's (16)	Institutions Intl Court (17)	Institutions Arbi-tration (18)	Institutions Other (19)	Self-Regis-tered (20)
	TOP THIRTY																			
1	USA (United States)	2599	1	50%				1												
2	UK Great Britain	981	1	50%					1	1	1									
3																				
4																				
5																				
6																				
7																				
8																				
9																				
10																				
11																				
12																				
13																				
14																				
15																				
16																				
17																				
18																				
19																				
20																				
21																				
22																				
23																				
24																				
25																				
26																				
27																				
28																				
29																				
30																				
31	All Others (0)																			
	GROUPS																			
32	African Group	968																		
33	Arab Group	937																		
34	Asian Group	1937																		
35	Commonwealth	1641	1	50%																
36	Communist Group	3310							1											
37	Latin America	1674																		
38	Western Europe	5906																		
39	Intl Organs	1399						1	1	1										
	TOTALS																			
40	All Data	3580	2	100%																
41	UNTS Only		2																		
	COMPARISONS																			
42	Party Total							50%	50%	50%	50%	50%	1%	71%	1%	27%	11%	13%	15%	4%	74%
43	Group Total					12%	25%	23%	40%	19%	7%	25%	20%	7%	8%	12%	6%	7%	12%	100%
44	World Total					18%	23%	29%	29%	22%	25%	25%								

210 • Table 162

TREATY PROFILE OF SENEGAL

Partners (1)	Partner's World Total (2)	Dyads Absolutes (3)	Ratios Self (4)	Ratios Other (5)	Time 1946-1950 (6)	Time 1951-1955 (7)	Time 1956-1960 (8)	Time 1961-1965 (9)	Admin & Dipl (10)	Social Coop (11)	Econ Coop (12)	Aid (13)	Milit (14)	UN (15)	Spec Ag's (16)	Intl Court (17)	Arbitration (18)	Other (19)	Self-Registered (20)
TOP THIRTY																			
1 France	1033	13	33%				2	11	6	4	3				1		1	1	
2 USA (United States)	2599	5	13%					5			1	3	1	1					
3 Germany, West	890	5	13%	1%				5		3	1	1							
4 USSR (Soviet Union)	1356	4	10%					4	1	1	1	1			1				
5 Switzerland	426	2	5%					2		1	1								
6 Poland	493	2	5%					2		1	1								
7 WHO (World Health)	187	1	3%	1%				1				1							
8 UN Special Fund	113	1	3%	1%				1				1		1					
9 UNICEF (Children)	122	1	3%	1%				1	1										
10 Netherlands	548	1	3%					1			1					1		1	
11 Mali	54	1	2%	2%				1		1									
12 Italy	755	1	3%					1			1				1			1	
13 Denmark	380	1	3%					1											
14 Czechoslovakia	393	1	3%				1												
15 Accept UN Charter	68	1	3%	1%				1	1					1					
31 All Others (0)																			
GROUPS																			
32 African Group	968	1	3%					1		1									
33 Arab Group	937																		
34 Asian Group	1937																		
35 Commonwealth	1641																		
36 Communist Group	3310	7	18%					7	1	3	2	1			1		1	1	
37 Latin America	1674																		
38 Western Europe	5906	23	58%				2	21	6	8	7	2				2	1	2	
39 Intl Organs	1399	3	8%					3	1			2		2				1	
TOTALS																			
40 All Data	9417	40	100%				3	37	9	12	10	8	1	4	4	1	5		
41 UNTS Only		18																	
COMPARISONS																			
42 Party Total					1%	5%	8%	93%	23%	30%	25%	20%	3%	22%	22%	6%	28%	4%	1%
43 Group Total					18%	23%	18%	75%	22%	21%	18%	35%	4%	19%	13%	10%	15%	12%	1%
44 World Total					18%	23%	29%	29%	22%	25%	25%	20%	7%	8%	12%	6%	7%	12%	100%

TREATY PROFILE OF SIERRA LEONE

Table 163

Partners (1)	Partner's World Total (2)	Dyads Absolutes (3)	Ratios Self (4)	Ratios Other (5)	Time 1946-1950 (6)	Time 1951-1955 (7)	Time 1956-1960 (8)	Time 1961-1965 (9)	Topics Admin & Dipl (10)	Topics Social Coop (11)	Topics Econ Coop (12)	Topics Aid (13)	Topics Milit (14)	Institutions UN (15)	Institutions Spec Ag's (16)	Institutions Intl Court (17)	Institutions Arbitration (18)	Institutions Other (19)	Self-Registered (20)
TOP THIRTY																			
1 USA (United States)	2599	5	19%					5	1	1		3							
2 Germany, West	890	5	19%	1%				5	1	1	2	2							
3 UK Great Britain	981	3	11%					3	2	1		1			1	1			1
4 Israel	232	3	11%	1%				3	1										
5 USSR (Soviet Union)	1356	2	7%					2	1		1								
6 WHO (World Health)	187	2	7%	1%				2	1			1							
7 UN Special Fund	113	1	4%	1%				1				1		1	1		2		
8 United Nations	233	1	4%					1						1		1	1	1	
9 UNICEF (Children)	122	1	4%	1%				1		1		1					1		
10 IBRD (World Bank)	452	1	4%					1			1								
11 Norway	461	1	4%					1											
12 France	1033	1	4%			1		1	1										
13 Accept UN Charter	68	1	4%	1%										1					
14																			
...																			
31 All Others (0)																			
GROUPS																			
32 African Group	968																		
33 Arab Group	937																		
34 Asian Group	1937																		
35 Commonwealth	1641	3	11%					3	2	1					1				
36 Communist Group	3310	2	7%					2	1		1								
37 Latin America	1674																		
38 Western Europe	5906	7	26%			1		6		2	3	2							
39 Intl Organs	1399	6	22%					6	2			4		2	1	1	4		1
TOTALS																			
40 All Data	8727	27	100%			1		26	8	5	4	10		3	2	2	4		
41 UNTS Only		19																		
COMPARISONS																			
42 Party Total					1%	4%	18%	96%	30%	19%	15%	37%	4%	16%	11%	11%	21%	5%	
43 Group Total					5%	5%	18%	75%	22%	21%	18%	35%	4%	19%	13%	10%	15%	4%	1%
44 World Total					18%	23%	29%	29%	22%	25%	25%	20%	7%	8%	12%	6%	7%	12%	100%

212 • Table 164

TREATY PROFILE OF SINGAPORE

	Partners (1)	Partner's World Total (2)	Dyads Abso-lutes (3)	Ratios Self (4)	Ratios Other (5)	Time 1946 1950 (6)	Time 1951 1955 (7)	Time 1956 1960 (8)	Time 1961 1965 (9)	Topics Admin & Dipl (10)	Topics Social Coop (11)	Topics Econ Coop (12)	Topics Aid (13)	Topics Milit (14)	Institutions UN (15)	Institutions Spec Ag's (16)	Institutions Intl Court (17)	Institutions Arbi-tration (18)	Institutions Other (19)	Self-Regis-tered (20)
	TOP THIRTY																			
1	UN Special Fund	113	1	33%	1%				1	1										1
2	Malaysia	26	1	33%	4%				1	1										
3	Accept UN Charter	68	1	33%	1%				1	1					1					
4																				
5																				
6																				
7																				
8																				
9																				
10																				
11																				
12																				
13																				
14																				
15																				
16																				
17																				
18																				
19																				
20																				
21																				
22																				
23																				
24																				
25																				
26																				
27																				
28																				
29																				
30																				
31	All Others (0)																			
	GROUPS																			
32	African Group	968																		
33	Arab Group	937																		
34	Asian Group	1937	1	33%					1	1										1
35	Commonwealth	1641																		
36	Communist Group	3310																		
37	Latin America	1674																		
38	Western Europe	5906																		
39	Intl Organs	1399	1	33%					1	1										
40	TOTALS All Data		3	100%					3	3					1					1
41	UNTS Only	207	3																	
	COMPARISONS																			
42	Party Total					16%	23%	31%	30%	100%					33%	15%	8%	8%	6%	33%
43	Group Total					18%	23%	29%	29%	21%	23%	20%	30%	7%	10%	12%	6%	7%	6%	16%
44	World Total								22%	25%	25%	20%	7%	8%					12%	100%

Table 165 • 213

TREATY PROFILE OF SOMALIA

(1) Partners	(2) Partner's World Total	Dyads			Time				Topics						Institutions				(20) Self-Registered
		(3) Absolutes	(4) Ratios Self	(5) Other	(6) 1946 1950	(7) 1951 1955	(8) 1956 1960	(9) 1961 1965	(10) Admin & Dipl	(11) Social Coop	(12) Econ Coop	(13) Aid	(14) Milit	(15) UN	(16) Spec Ag's	(17) Intl Court	(18) Arbitration	(19) Other	
TOP THIRTY																			
1 USSR (Soviet Union)	1356	6	16%				1	5	1	1	1	3						1	
2 Italy	755	6	16%	1%			5	1	3	2	1	1							
3 UK Great Britain	981	5	14%	1%			5		1	2	1	2							
4 Germany, West	890	4	11%					4		1	1	2							
5 USA (United States)	2599	3	8%					3			1	2				1	1		
6 China People's Rep	766	3	8%					3	1	2	1								
7 WHO (World Health)	187	3	5%	1%				2									2		
8 Czechoslovakia	393	2	5%	1%				2	1	1		1							
9 UN Special Fund	113	2	3%	1%				1				1							
10 United Nations	233	1	3%					1											
11 UNICEF (Children)	122	1	3%					1				1		1					
12 IDA (Devel Assoc)	82	1	3%					1	1										
13 ICJ Option Clause	62	1	3%	2%				1	1					1		1			
14 Accept UN Charter	68	1	3%	1%				1						1					
GROUPS																			
32 African Group	968																		
33 Arab Group	937																		
34 Asian Group	1937																		
35 Commonwealth	1641	5	14%				5		1	2	1	1							
36 Communist Group	3310	11	30%				1	10	1	4	2	4						1	
37 Latin America	1674																		
38 Western Europe	5906	10	27%				5	5	3	3	2	2					1		
39 Intl Organs	1399	6	16%					6	1			5		1			1	2	
40 TOTALS All Data	8607	37	100%				11	26	8	9	6	14							
41 UNTS Only		21													3	3	3	3	1	
COMPARISONS																			
42 Party Total					1%	5%	30%	70%	22%	24%	16%	38%	4%	14%		14%	14%	5%	
43 Group Total					18%	23%	18%	75%	22%	21%	18%	35%	7%	19%	13%	10%	15%	4%	1%
44 World Total					18%	29%	29%	29%	22%	25%	25%	20%	7%	8%	12%	6%	7%	12%	100%

TREATY PROFILE OF SOUTH AFRICA

Table 166

	Partners (1)	Partner's World Total (2)	Dyads Absolutes (3)	Dyads Ratios Self (4)	Dyads Ratios Other (5)	Time 1946-1950 (6)	Time 1951-1955 (7)	Time 1956-1960 (8)	Time 1961-1965 (9)	Topics Admin & Dipl (10)	Topics Social Coop (11)	Topics Econ Coop (12)	Topics Aid (13)	Topics Milit (14)	Institutions UN (15)	Institutions Spec Ag's (16)	Institutions Intl Court (17)	Institutions Arbitration (18)	Institutions Other (19)	Self-Registered (20)
	TOP THIRTY																			
1	USA (United States)	2599	13	11%	1%	6	4	3		4	3	2	1	3	1	2			2	2
2	UK Great Britain	981	13	11%	1%	7	1	3	2	1	1	10		1		3			1	4
3	IBRD (World Bank)	452	10	8%	2%		5	3	2				10							
4	Belgium	499	7	6%	1%	1	2	3	1	1	4	2				2				1
5	Sweden	483	6	5%	1%		4	1	1		3	3								3
6	Fed Rhod/Nyasaland	11	6	5%	55%		1	4	1	1	2	3								5
7	Switzerland	426	5	4%	1%		3	2			3	2				1				1
8	Norway	461	5	4%	1%		2	3		2	2	1		1	1	1				4
9	Italy	755	5	4%	1%	1	3	1		1	2	2				1				3
10	Israel	232	5	4%	2%		3	2		2	2	1				1				3
11	France	1033	5	4%		1	3		1		3	1								4
12	Canada	310	5	4%	2%		3	2			1	4								1
13	Netherlands	548	4	3%	1%	1	3			1	2	1								3
14	Germany, West	890	4	3%			1	2	1		1	2		1						1
15	Finland	245	4	3%	2%	1	1	1	1	3	1					2				3
16	Denmark	380	4	3%	1%	2	1	1			2	2								2
17	Greece	318	3	3%	1%		1	2						1						3
18	Austria	445	3	3%	1%			2	1	2	1					1				1
19	Luxembourg	136	2	2%					2	1										2
20	Japan	443	2	2%			1		1	1	1									2
21	Ireland	103	2	2%	2%			2		2	1	1								
22	Australia	201	2	2%	1%		1	1			2				1					1
23	Spain	437	1	1%					1	1		1				1				
24	Romania	251	1	1%			1								1					
25	Portugal	131	1	1%	1%			1		1										1
26	Hungary	290	1	1%		1				1										
27	ICJ Option Clause	62	1	1%	2%		1										1			
28																				
29																				
30																				
31	All Others (0)																			
	GROUPS																			
32	African Group	968																		
33	Arab Group	937																		
34	Asian Group	1937																		
35	Commonwealth	1641	26	22%	2%	7	6	10	3	2	6	17		1	2	3			1	13
36	Communist Group	3310	2	2%		2				2										2
37	Latin America	1674																		
38	Western Europe	5906	61	51%	1%	8	24	18	11	11	27	19		4	2	7				29
39	Intl Organs	1399	10	8%	1%		5	3	2				10				1			
	TOTALS																			
40	All Data	13122	120	100%		23	44	36	17	23	39	39	11	8	5	14	1		3	51
41	UNTS Only		113																	
	COMPARISONS																			
42	Party Total					19%	37%	30%	14%	19%	32%	32%	9%	7%	4%	12%	1%		3%	45%
43	Group Total					27%	25%	24%	24%	25%	24%	27%	10%	14%	4%	13%	4%	5%	12%	63%
44	World Total					18%	23%	29%	29%	22%	25%	25%	20%	7%	8%	12%	6%	7%	12%	100%

TREATY PROFILE OF SOUTH PACIFIC COM

Table 167 • 215

Partners (1)	Partner's World Total (2)	Dyads Absolutes (3)	Ratios Self (4)	Ratios Other (5)	Time 1946-1950 (6)	Time 1951-1955 (7)	Time 1956-1960 (8)	Time 1961-1965 (9)	Admin & Dipl (10)	Social Coop (11)	Econ Coop (12)	Aid (13)	Milit (14)	UN (15)	Spec Ag's (16)	Intl Court (17)	Arbitration (18)	Other (19)	Self-Registered (20)
TOP THIRTY																			
1 United Nations	233	2	100%	1%				2				2							
2																			
3																			
4																			
5																			
6																			
7																			
8																			
9																			
10																			
11																			
12																			
13																			
14																			
15																			
16																			
17																			
18																			
19																			
20																			
21																			
22																			
23																			
24																			
25																			
26																			
27																			
28																			
29																			
30																			
31 All Others (0)																			
GROUPS																			
32 African Group	968																		
33 Arab Group	937																		
34 Asian Group	1937																		
35 Commonwealth	1641																		
36 Communist Group	3310																		
37 Latin America	1674																		
38 Western Europe	5906																		
39 Intl Organs	1399	2	100%					2				2							
TOTALS																			
40 All Data	233	2	100%					2				2							
41 UNTS Only		2																	
COMPARISONS																			
42 Party Total								100%			100%		1%	27%	11%	13%	15%	4%	74%
43 Group Total					12%	25%	23%	40%	19%	7%	1%	71%	7%	8%	12%	6%	7%	12%	100%
44 World Total					18%	23%	29%	29%	22%	25%	25%	20%							

216 • Table 168

TREATY PROFILE OF SPAIN

Partners (1)	Partner's World Total (2)	Dyads Absolutes (3)	Ratios Self (4)	Ratios Other (5)	Time 1946-1950 (6)	Time 1951-1955 (7)	Time 1956-1960 (8)	Time 1961-1965 (9)	Admin & Dipl (10)	Social Coop (11)	Econ Coop (12)	Aid (13)	Milit (14)	UN (15)	Spec Ag's (16)	Intl Court (17)	Arbitration (18)	Other (19)	Self-Registered (20)
TOP THIRTY																			
1 France	1033	69	16%	7%	2	10	24	33	12	39	17	1		1				1	
2 USA (United States)	2599	34	8%	1%	4	9	13	8	3	9	4	11	7		3	1	1	1	
3 Germany, West	890	30	7%	3%		4	22	4	1	14	15				1			1	
4 Italy	755	19	4%	3%	2	3	13	1		10	9							1	
5 Belgium	499	19	4%	4%	1	4	14		4	8	7				1			1	
6 Sweden	483	15	3%	3%	6	4	2	3		3	12								
7 UK Great Britain	981	14	3%	1%	4	3	5	2	3	2	8	1			1		1	2	
8 Netherlands	548	14	3%	3%	6	3	1	4	2	7	5				1		2		
9 Morocco	94	14	3%	15%			14		6	1	6	1							
10 Norway	461	13	3%	3%		2	8	3	1	2	10							1	
11 Brazil	195	12	3%	6%	1	1	8	2	3	7	2						1		
12 Austria	445	12	3%	3%		2	7	5	2	6	4						1	2	
13 Switzerland	426	11	3%	3%	2	1	4	4		6	5						1	1	
14 Paraguay	75	11	3%	15%	2		7	2	4	3	4								
15 Portugal	131	9	2%	7%	1	1	4	3		6	3								
16 Argentina	164	9	2%	5%	5		2	2	1	7			1						
17 Philippines	236	8	2%	3%	5	2		1	4	4					1		2	1	
18 Uruguay	63	7	2%	11%		5	2		1	3	7								
19 Ecuador	97	7	2%	7%		5	2			3	3								
20 Denmark	380	7	2%	2%	2	2	2	1		1	6				1			2	
21 Greece	318	6	1%	2%		4	2				6							1	
22 Vatican/Holy See	16	5	1%	31%	2	1	1	1	3	2									
23 Turkey	298	5	1%	2%	1	2	1	1	1	1	3								
24 Cuba	111	5	1%	5%		4	1			1	4								
25 Japan	443	4	1%	1%			2	1	1		2		1						
26 Finland	245	4	1%	2%		1	4		1		4								
27 El Salvador	70	4	1%	6%		4			2	2									
28 Dominican Republic	49	4	1%	8%		3	1		1	2	1								
29 Taiwan	172	4	1%	2%		1	3		1	2	1								
30 Chile	119	4	1%	3%	1		2	1		3	1								
31 All Others (35)	3893	58	13%	1%	4	25	11	18	23	17	11	7		3	5	1	3		
GROUPS																			
32 African Group	968	3	1%		3	2		1	1	1	1	1							
33 Arab Group	937	25	6%	3%	5	6	15	1	12	6	6	1			1		4	1	
34 Asian Group	1937	17	4%	1%	4	4	7	1	8	7	2						1	2	
35 Commonwealth	1641	21	5%	1%	4	5	6	6	6	2	11	2			1				
36 Communist Group	3310																		
37 Latin America	1674	78	18%	5%	9	30	26	13	19	32	26		1		2		3		
38 Western Europe	5906	247	57%	4%	26	44	112	65	27	109	110	1			5		7	9	
39 Intl Organs	1399	7	2%	1%		2	1	4	1			6		2	1	1			
TOTALS																			
40 All Data	16289	437	100%		51	104	182	100	79	166	162	21	9	4	14	2	15	13	
41 UNTS Only		121																		
COMPARISONS																			
42 Party Total					12%	24%	42%	23%	18%	38%	37%	5%	2%	3%	12%	2%	12%	11%	32%
43 Group Total					22%	25%	27%	26%	24%	26%	32%	10%	8%	4%	14%	6%	8%	17%	
44 World Total					18%	23%	29%	29%	22%	25%	25%	20%	7%	8%	12%	6%	7%	12%	100%

TREATY PROFILE OF SUBSAHARA TECH COM

Table 169 • 217

		Partner's World Total		Dyads	Ratios		Time				Topics						Institutions			Self-Registered
	Partners		Absolutes	Self	Other	1946 1950	1951 1955	1956 1960	1961 1965	Admin & Dipl	Social Coop	Econ Coop	Aid	Milit	UN	Spec Ag's	Intl Court	Arbitration	Other	
	(1)	(2)	(3)	(4)	(5)	(6)	(7)	(8)	(9)	(10)	(11)	(12)	(13)	(14)	(15)	(16)	(17)	(18)	(19)	(20)
	TOP THIRTY																			
1	ILO (Labor Org)	59	1	50%	2%			1		1					1					
2	IAEA (Atom Energy)	44	1	50%	2%				1	1					1					
3																				
4																				
5																				
6																				
7																				
8																				
9																				
10																				
11																				
12																				
13																				
14																				
15																				
16																				
17																				
18																				
19																				
20																				
21																				
22																				
23																				
24																				
25																				
26																				
27																				
28																				
29																				
30																				
31	All Others (0)																			
	GROUPS																			
32	African Group	968																		
33	Arab Group	937																		
34	Asian Group	1937																		
35	Commonwealth	1641																		
36	Communist Group	3310																		
37	Latin America	1674																		
38	Western Europe	5906																		
39	Intl Organs	1399	2	100%				1	1	2					2					
	TOTALS																			
40	All Data		2	100%				1	1	2					2					
41	UNTS Only	103	2																	
	COMPARISONS																			
42	Party Total							50%	50%	100%					100%					
43	Group Total					12%	25%	23%	40%	19%	7%	1%	71%	1%	27%	11%	13%	15%	4%	74%
44	World Total					18%	23%	29%	29%	22%	25%	25%	20%	7%	8%	12%	6%	7%	12%	100%

218 • Table 170

TREATY PROFILE OF SUDAN

	Partners (1)	Partner's World Total (2)	Dyads Absolutes (3)	Dyads Ratios Self (4)	Dyads Ratios Other (5)	Time 1946 1950 (6)	Time 1951 1955 (7)	Time 1956 1960 (8)	Time 1961 1965 (9)	Admin & Dipl (10)	Social Coop (11)	Econ Coop (12)	Aid (13)	Milit (14)	UN (15)	Spec Ag's (16)	Intl Court (17)	Arbitration (18)	Other (19)	Self-Registered (20)
	TOP THIRTY																			
1	USSR (Soviet Union)	1356	6	16%				2	4				1							
2	USA (United States)	2599	5	14%				2	3	1	1	3	4				1	1		
3	IBRD (World Bank)	452	4	11%	1%			2	2	1			4							
4	WHO (World Health)	187	2	5%	1%			1	1				2		2					
5	Germany, West	890	2	5%					2			1	1							
6	Germany, East	556	2	5%			1	1				1								
7	China People's Rep	766	2	5%				1	1		1	2								
8	UK Great Britain	981	1	3%				1		1	1					1	1	1		
9	United Arab Rep	232	1	3%					1											
10	Switzerland	426	1	3%							1					1	1	1		
11	Sweden	483	1	3%	1%			1			1					1	1	1		
12	UN Special Fund	113	1	3%				1					1		1					
13	United Nations	233	1	3%	1%			1	1				1		1					
14	UNICEF (Children)	122	1	3%	1%								1			1				
15	IDA (Devel Assoc)	82	1	3%																
16	Norway	461	1	3%				1			1									
17	Netherlands	548	1	3%							1							1		
18	Italy	755	1	3%					1	1	1				1	1				
19	Denmark	380	1	3%				1		1					1			2		
20	ICJ Option Clause	62	1	3%	2%			1												
21	Accept UN Charter	68	1	3%	1%			1												
22–30																				
31	All Others (0)																			
	GROUPS																			
32	African Group	968	1	3%																
33	Arab Group	937																		
34	Asian Group	1937																		
35	Commonwealth	1641	1	3%			1	1	1	1	1		1			1	1	1		
36	Communist Group	3310	10	27%				4	5		2	6								
37	Latin America	1674																		
38	Western Europe	5906	8	22%				4	4		5	1	2		1	3	1	5		
39	Intl Organs	1399	10	27%	1%			6	4				10		4	2	1	1	1	
	TOTALS																			
40	All Data	11752	37	100%			1	19	17	5	8	7	17		6	6	5	8	1	
41	UNTS Only		24																	
	COMPARISONS																			
42	Party Total					9%	3%	51%	46%	14%	22%	19%	46%	4%	25%	25%	21%	33%	4%	5%
43	Group Total					18%	24%	31%	36%	18%	27%	22%	29%		15%	20%	8%	15%	9%	100%
44	World Total					18%	23%	29%	29%	22%	25%	25%	20%	7%	8%	12%	6%	7%	12%	100%

Table 171

TREATY PROFILE OF SWEDEN

Partners (1)	Partner's World Total (2)	Dyads Abso- lutes (3)	Ratios Self (4)	Ratios Other (5)	Time 1946-1950 (6)	Time 1951-1955 (7)	Time 1956-1960 (8)	Time 1961-1965 (9)	Topics Admin & Dipl (10)	Topics Social Coop (11)	Topics Econ Coop (12)	Topics Aid (13)	Topics Milit (14)	Institutions UN (15)	Institutions Spec Ag's (16)	Institutions Intl Court (17)	Institutions Arbi- tration (18)	Other (19)	Self- Regis- tered (20)
TOP THIRTY																			
1 Norway	461	39	8%	8%	18	10	8	3	12	8	19				1	1	1	1	11
2 France	1033	24	5%	2%	12	8	3	1	4	4	16				1	2	1		8
3 UK Great Britain	981	23	5%	2%	6	6	7	4	6	5	11	1			6	1		7	2
4 Denmark	380	23	5%	6%	11	9	3		1	5	17							2	7
5 Finland	245	21	4%	9%	8	4	6	3	6	6	9				1	2		3	10
6 Austria	445	21	4%	5%	3	10	7	1	6	5	12				1		1	1	11
7 USA (United States)	2599	20	4%	1%	8	5	1	6	4	5	6	2	4	3	4	1		1	2
8 Germany, West	890	20	4%	2%	5	5	9	1	3	3	10		2		1	1	1		9
9 Netherlands	548	19	4%	3%	9	6	3	1	5	4	13				1			2	2
10 USSR (Soviet Union)	1356	17	4%	1%	10	4	1	2	2	6	8	1		1					3
11 Belgium	499	17	4%	3%	7	4	4	2	2	5	9							1	
12 Switzerland	426	16	3%	4%	5	5	3	3	3	5	11				1		1		6
13 Spain	437	15	3%	3%	6	4	2	3	1	3	12								1
14 Italy	755	15	3%	2%	7	4	3	1	1	3	11								3
15 Czechoslovakia	393	15	3%	4%	12	2	1		1	2	12								1
16 Greece	318	13	3%	4%	4	7	1	1	1	1	11				1	1	1	3	1
17 Poland	493	12	2%	2%	8	2	2		1	2	10				1			1	
18 Japan	443	12	2%	3%	2	7	3		2	2	7		1		1		1		1
19 Yugoslavia	525	11	2%	2%	6	3	2		1	2	8				1				1
20 Iceland	99	10	2%	10%	4	6			1	1	8				1	1	1		2
21 Hungary	290	8	2%	3%	5	2	1		1	1	7								
22 Turkey	298	7	1%	2%	5		2		1	1	4	1							
23 South Africa	120	6	1%	5%		4	1	1		3	3				1		1		1
24 Israel	232	6	1%	3%		1	3	2	3		3				2				
25 Ireland	103	6	1%	6%	3	1	2		1	2	3				1		1	1	3
26 India	299	6	1%	2%	3	2	1			1	5				1				1
27 China People's Rep	766	5	1%	1%		2	3		2		3		1						2
28 United Nations	233	4	1%	2%	3	1			2			1		1					
29 Portugal	131	4	1%	3%	1	1	2		2	1	3				1	1	2		
30 Pakistan	245	4	1%	2%				2			1	1							2
31 All Others (35)	4478	64	13%	1%	20	14	22	8	12	22	25	4	1	2	16	5	13	2	18
GROUPS																			
32 African Group	968	5	1%	1%		1	2	2		3	4	2			2	2	2		2
33 Arab Group	937	10	2%	1%	1	2	5	2		6	4				5	3	5		4
34 Asian Group	1937	22	5%	1%	7	6	8	1		8	12	2		1	7	3	5		6
35 Commonwealth	1641	39	8%	2%	11	13	9	6	9	9	19	2			10	1	1	7	4
36 Communist Group	3310	64	13%	2%	40	10	12	2	6	12	45	1			1				7
37 Latin America	1674	11	2%	1%	4	4	3		1	4	5				3		1	1	5
38 Western Europe	5906	274	57%	5%	110	90	56	18	45	58	168	1	1	1	13	7	9	14	75
39 Intl Organs	1399	6	1%			1	2	3	4			1	1	1		2	2	2	1
TOTALS																			
40 All Data	20521	483	100%		191	143	107	42	77	109	277	11	9	7	47	19	26	25	108
41 UNTS Only		271																	
COMPARISONS																			
42 Party Total					40%	30%	22%	9%	16%	23%	57%	2%	2%	3%	17%	7%	10%	9%	40%
43 Group Total					22%	25%	27%	26%	24%	26%	32%	10%	8%	4%	14%	6%	8%	17%	32%
44 World Total					18%	23%	29%	29%	22%	25%	25%	20%	7%	8%	12%	6%	7%	12%	100%

220 • Table 174

TREATY PROFILE OF SWITZERLAND

Partners (1)	Partner's World Total (2)	Dyads Absolutes (3)	Ratios Self (4)	Ratios Other (5)	Time 1946-1950 (6)	Time 1951-1955 (7)	Time 1956-1960 (8)	Time 1961-1965 (9)	Admin & Dipl (10)	Social Coop (11)	Econ Coop (12)	Aid (13)	Milit (14)	UN (15)	Spec Ag's (16)	Intl Court (17)	Arbitration (18)	Other (19)	Self-Registered (20)
TOP THIRTY																			
1 France	1033	50	12%	5%	10	8	16	16	24	14	10	1	1						
2 Italy	755	41	10%	5%	5	11	15	10	12	16	12	1			1	1	2	7	
3 Germany, West	890	33	8%	4%	2	17	8	6	9	11	13				1		1		
4 Austria	445	32	8%	7%	10	8	9	5	11	13	8				1				
5 Sweden	483	16	4%	3%	5	10	1			5	11				1		1		
6 USA (United States)	2599	15	4%	1%	6	4	2	3	2	2	7	3	1		3	2	1	5	
7 UK Great Britain	981	15	4%	2%	4	4	4	3	3	4	6	2			2	1	1	2	
8 Netherlands	548	15	4%	3%	2	8	2	5	3	5	7				2		2	1	
9 Norway	461	13	3%	3%	3	5	6	1	3	1	8		1		1			1	
10 Spain	437	11	3%	3%	2	1	4	4		6	5						1	1	
11 Denmark	380	10	2%	3%	3	3	3	1		4	6				1			1	
12 Belgium	499	10	2%	2%	3	1	5		5	2	2				1		1	2	
13 Yugoslavia	525	8	2%	2%	4	1	1	3		3	4	1	1			1			
14 Tunisia	97	6	1%	6%	3	1	5	4		1	2	1			1		1		
15 Liechtenstein	16	6	1%	38%			2	4	3	1	2				1				
16 Finland	245	6	1%	2%		2	4			1	5				1				
17 South Africa	120	5	1%	4%		3	2		3	3	2				1				
18 Poland	493	5	1%	1%	2			3		1	4								
19 Israel	232	5	1%	2%		2	2	1	2	2	1				1	1	1	1	
20 Ireland	103	5	1%	5%	3	1	1		1	2	2				1				
21 Czechoslovakia	393	5	1%	1%	2	1	1	1	1	2	3				1		2		
22 Canada	310	5	1%	2%	1		4		2	1	1	1							
23 USSR (Soviet Union)	1356	4	1%		4				1		3		1		2		1		
24 United Arab Rep	232	4	1%	2%	2	1	1			2	2								
25 United Nations	233	4	1%	2%	3			1	3							2			
26 Japan	443	4	1%	1%		2	2		1	1	2				1		1		
27 India	299	4	1%	1%	2		2		1	1	2				1		1		
28 Greece	318	4	1%	1%	2	1		1	1		3								
29 IBRD (World Bank)	452	3	1%	1%			1	1	1		1	2				2	1		
30 Portugal	131	3	1%	2%	1		1	1		2	1				1		2		
31 All Others (55)	5963	79	19%	1%	17	21	19	22	16	24	36	2	1	2	23	10	15	1	1
GROUPS																			
32 African Group	968	15	4%	2%	2	4	1	14	1	6	8	1			6	2	4		
33 Arab Group	937	18	4%	2%	4	4	5	7		9	8				9	1	7		
34 Asian Group	1937	17	4%	1%	4	4	7	2	3	7	7				6	1	1		
35 Commonwealth	1641	29	7%	2%	6	8	10	5	6	8	12	3			4	2	2	2	
36 Communist Group	3310	20	5%	1%	11	3	3	3	1	3	16				1		2	5	
37 Latin America	1674	16	4%	1%	3	6	6	1		3	11	1			3	1	2		
38 Western Europe	5906	260	61%	4%	53	78	79	50	71	87	96	3	1		14	4	9	14	1
39 Intl Organs	1399	17	4%	1%	8	4	3	2	14	1		2	3	1	1	7	5	1	
TOTALS																			
40 All Data	21472	426	100%		98	116	121	91	103	132	172	14	5	2	50	20	36	20	1
41 UNTS Only		160																	
COMPARISONS																			
42 Party Total					23%	27%	28%	21%	24%	31%	40%	3%	1%	1%	31%	13%	23%	13%	1%
43 Group Total					22%	25%	27%	26%	24%	26%	32%	10%	8%	4%	14%	6%	8%	17%	32%
44 World Total					18%	23%	29%	29%	22%	25%	25%	20%	7%	8%	12%	6%	7%	12%	100%

TREATY PROFILE OF SYRIA

Table 173

Partners (1)	Partner's World Total (2)	Dyads Absolutes (3)	Dyads Ratios Self (4)	Dyads Ratios Other (5)	Time 1946-1950 (6)	Time 1951-1955 (7)	Time 1956-1960 (8)	Time 1961-1965 (9)	Topics Admin & Dipl (10)	Topics Social Coop (11)	Topics Econ Coop (12)	Topics Aid (13)	Topics Milit (14)	Institutions UN (15)	Institutions Spec Ag's (16)	Institutions Intl Court (17)	Institutions Arbitration (18)	Institutions Other (19)	Self-Registered (20)
TOP THIRTY																			
1 Germany, East	556	11	13%	2%		2	3	6	1	4	5	1							
2 China People's Rep	766	10	12%	1%		2	3	5		4	5	1							
3 USSR (Soviet Union)	1356	9	11%	1%		2	4	3	3	3	2			1					1
4 UK Great Britain	981	4	5%	1%	1	2		1	1	2	1				2		1		1
5 Turkey	298	4	5%	1%	2	1	1			2	2								
6 USA (United States)	2599	3	4%		1	2				1		2			1	1			2
7 United Arab Rep	232	3	4%	1%		2		3	1	2			1						
8 Bulgaria	236	3	4%	1%				3		3									
9 Spain	437	2	2%			2			1	1									
10 WHO (World Health)	187	2	2%	1%		1		1	1	1	1	2		1	1				1
11 Poland	493	2	2%					2			1	1							
12 Pakistan	245	2	2%	1%		1			1										
13 Norway	461	2	2%		1		2		2	2									2
14 Jordan	65	2	2%	3%		2									1		1	1	
15 Italy	755	2	2%	1%		1	1			1	1				1			1	1
16 Greece	318	2	2%	1%	1	1				1	1	2			1				
17 Germany, West	890	2	2%	3%		1		2		1		1					1		1
18 Denmark	380	2	2%	1%		1		1		1	1								
19 Switzerland	426	1	1%			1		1	1		1								
20 Saudi Arabia	31	1	1%	3%									1						
21 UN Special Fund	113	1	1%	1%				1				1		1	1				
22 United Nations	233	1	1%					1	1					1					
23 UNICEF (Children)	122	1	1%	2%		1				1		1		1					
24 ILO (Labor Org)	59	1	1%	1%		1				1									
25 IDA (Devel Assoc)	82	1	1%	1%				1											
26 ICAO (Civil Aviat)	23	1	1%	4%				1											
27 Netherlands	548	1	1%		1					1									
28 Japan	443	1	1%		1													1	
29 Israel	232	1	1%		1								1						
30 Iraq	96	1	1%	1%				1			1								
31 All Others (5)	2064	5	6%		1	1	1	2	1	3	1			1					1
GROUPS																			
32 African Group	968	7	8%	1%		4		3	2	2	2		1		1		1	1	6
33 Arab Group	937	3	4%			2		1	2	1	1								1
34 Asian Group	1937	3	4%		1	2			1	2	1				2		1		1
35 Commonwealth	1641	4	5%	1%	1	2		1	1		1								2
36 Communist Group	3310	37	44%			6	11	20	4	17	12	4		1				1	
37 Latin America	1674																		
38 Western Europe	5906	20	24%	1%	5	7	4	4	1	11	5	3			6	1	2	2	3
39 Intl Organs	1399	8	10%			4		4	1			7		5	1	1	1		
TOTALS																			
40 All Data	15727	84	100%		9	26	15	34	11	33	22	16	2	7	11	2	5	4	14
41 UNTS Only		47																		
COMPARISONS																			
42 Party Total					11%	31%	18%	40%	13%	39%	26%	19%	2%	15%	23%	4%	11%	9%	30%
43 Group Total					9%	24%	31%	36%	18%	27%	22%	29%	4%	15%	20%	8%	15%	9%	5%
44 World Total					18%	23%	29%	29%	22%	25%	25%	20%	7%	8%	12%	6%	7%	12%	100%

222 • Table 174

TREATY PROFILE OF TAIWAN

Partners (1)	Partner's World Total (2)	Dyads Absolutes (3)	Ratios Self (4)	Ratios Other (5)	Time 1946 1950 (6)	Time 1951 1955 (7)	Time 1956 1960 (8)	Time 1961 1965 (9)	Topics Admin & Dipl (10)	Topics Social Coop (11)	Topics Econ Coop (12)	Topics Aid (13)	Topics Milit (14)	Institutions UN (15)	Institutions Spec Ag's (16)	Institutions Intl Court (17)	Institutions Arbitration (18)	Institutions Other (19)	Self-Registered (20)
TOP THIRTY																			
1 USA (United States)	2599	70	41%	3%	21	12	21	16	5	8	6	29	22	2	3	3	1	2	6
2 France	1033	12	7%	1%	7	4	1		2	5	4		1		3				3
3 Philippines	236	6	3%	3%	2		3	1	2	2	1			1					1
4 Japan	443	6	3%	1%		5	1		2	2	3		1						1
5 Italy	755	5	3%	1%	4		1			2	2		1		1				2
6 UK Great Britain	981	4	2%		4				2		2		1				1		1
7 Spain	437	4	2%			1	3		1	1	1						2		2
8 IDA (Devel Assoc)	82	4	2%	5%				4		2		4							
9 Ecuador	97	4	2%	4%	1		1	2	1		2								4
10 Thailand	132	3	2%	2%	1	1	1		1	2					1				1
11 WHO (World Health)	187	3	2%	2%		3				2		1		1	1				
12 UNICEF (Children)	122	3	2%	2%	2		1		2			1		2	1				
13 IBRD (World Bank)	452	3	2%	1%				3			1	3			1				
14 Portugal	131	3	2%	2%	3				1	1	2								1
15 Korea, South	80	3	2%	4%		1		2	1	1		1			1				1
16 Canada	310	3	2%	1%	3						2								1
17 Paraguay	75	2	1%	3%			2				1								2
18 Jordan	65	2	1%	3%			1	1	1	1		1			1				2
19 El Salvador	70	2	1%	3%				1	1										1
20 Brazil	195	2	1%	1%	1		1	1	1		1								
21 Australia	201	2	1%	1%		2				1	1				1				1
22 Uruguay	63	2	1%	2%				1		1						1			1
23 Turkey	298	1	1%										1						1
24 Switzerland	426	1	1%		1					1									1
25 Saudi Arabia	31	1	1%	3%	1				1							1	1		1
26 UN Special Fund	113	1	1%	1%			1					1		1	1				
27 United Nations	233	1	1%			1						1		1					
28 ILO (Labor Org)	59	1	1%	2%		1				1									
29 Peru	109	1	1%	1%				1			1								1
30 Panama	57	1	1%	2%			1			1									1
31 All Others (17)	2904	17	10%	1%	4	1	6	6	4	7	5		1	1	2	2	1	2	8
GROUPS																			
32 African Group	968	2	1%					2	1	1	2					1			2
33 Arab Group	937	6	3%	1%	1		4	1	2	2	2	1							3
34 Asian Group	1937	13	8%	1%	3	2	5	3	4	6	2	1	1		2				4
35 Commonwealth	1641	9	5%	1%	7	2				2	5				2		1		2
36 Communist Group	3310																		
37 Latin America	1674	18	10%	1%	3	1	3	11	3	8	7			1	1				17
38 Western Europe	5906	31	18%	1%	17	6	7	1	8	10	10		3		1	1	3		10
39 Intl Organs	1399	16	9%	1%	2	5	1	8	2	2		12		5	3		1		
TOTALS																			
40 All Data	12976	172	100%		55	33	42	42	26	41	35	43	27	9	12	6	6	2	45
41 UNTS Only		121																		
COMPARISONS																			
42 Party Total					32%	19%	24%	24%	15%	24%	20%	25%	16%	7%	10%	5%	5%	2%	37%
43 Group Total					16%	23%	31%	30%	21%	23%	20%	30%	7%	10%	15%	8%	8%	6%	16%
44 World Total					18%	23%	29%	29%	22%	25%	25%	20%	7%	8%	12%	6%	7%	12%	100%

Table 175 • 223

TREATY PROFILE OF TANZANIA

Partners (1)	Partner's World Total (2)	Dyads Absolutes (3)	Ratios Self (4)	Ratios Other (5)	Time 1946-1950 (6)	Time 1951-1955 (7)	Time 1956-1960 (8)	Time 1961-1965 (9)	Topics Admin & Dipl (10)	Topics Social Coop (11)	Topics Econ Coop (12)	Topics Aid (13)	Topics Milit (14)	Institutions UN (15)	Institutions Spec Ag's (16)	Institutions Intl Court (17)	Institutions Arbitration (18)	Institutions Other (19)	Self-Registered (20)
TOP THIRTY																			
1 China People's Rep	766	7	16%	1%				7	1	1	2	3							
2 Germany, West	890	5	11%	1%				5		1	2	2							
3 USA (United States)	2599	4	9%					4	1		1	2							
4 UK Great Britain	981	4	9%					4	3		1								
5 USSR (Soviet Union)	1356	3	7%	1%				3	1	1					1				
6 Germany, East	556	3	7%					3				2							
7 IDA (Devel Assoc)	82	2	4%	2%				2				2							
8 Israel	232	2	4%	1%				2	1			1							
9 Denmark	380	2	4%	1%				2	1					2					
10 Accept UN Charter	68	2	4%	3%				2	2		1			2					
11 Switzerland	426	1	2%					1	1										
12 WHO (World Health)	187	1	2%	1%				1				1		1	1	1	1		
13 UN Special Fund	113	1	2%	1%				1				1					2		
14 United Nations	233	1	2%					1						1					
15 UNICEF (Children)	122	1	2%	1%				1				1		1	1				
16 ILO (Labor Org)	59	1	2%	2%				1		1									
17 IBRD (World Bank)	452	1	2%					1				1							
18 Poland	493	1	2%					1				1							
19 Netherlands	548	1	2%					1				1							
20 Italy	755	1	2%					1											
21 France	1033	1	2%					1											
22																			
23																			
24																			
25																			
26																			
27																			
28																			
29																			
30																			
31 All Others (0)																			
GROUPS																			
32 African Group	968																		
33 Arab Group	937																		
34 Asian Group	1937																		
35 Commonwealth	1641	4	9%					4	3		1				1				
36 Communist Group	3310	14	31%					14	3	2	3	6							
37 Latin America	1674																		
38 Western Europe	5906	11	24%					11	2	2	3	4		2					
39 Intl Organs	1399	8	18%	1%				8	1			7		3	2	1	3	1	
TOTALS																			
40 All Data	12331	45	100%					45	13	4	8	20		7	3	1	3	1	
41 UNTS Only		25																		
COMPARISONS																			
42 Party Total					1%	5%	18%	100%	29%	9%	18%	44%	4%	28%	12%	4%	12%	4%	1%
43 Group Total					18%	23%	29%	75%	22%	21%	18%	35%	7%	19%	13%	10%	15%	4%	1%
44 World Total					18%	23%	29%	29%	22%	25%	25%	20%		8%	12%	6%	7%	12%	100%

224 • Table 176

TREATY PROFILE OF THAILAND

			Dyads			Time				Topics						Institutions			
Part-ners	Part-ner's World Total	Abso-lutes	Ratios Self	Other	1946 1950	1951 1955	1956 1960	1961 1965	Admin & Dipl	Social Coop	Econ Coop	Aid	Milit	UN	Spec Ag's	Intl Court	Arbi-tration	Other	Self-Regis-tered
(1)	(2)	(3)	(4)	(5)	(6)	(7)	(8)	(9)	(10)	(11)	(12)	(13)	(14)	(15)	(16)	(17)	(18)	(19)	(20)
TOP THIRTY																			
1 USA (United States)	2599	22	17%	1%	6	7	4	5	2	7	4	6	3	2	2			2	2
2 IBRD (World Bank)	452	14	11%	3%	3	1	2	8			6	14							
3 UK Great Britain	981	10	8%	1%	6	1	1	2	1	1	3	1	1		1	1		2	2
4 Germany, West	890	10	8%	1%			1	9		3	1	6			2		1		9
5 Japan	443	9	7%	2%		4	2	3		6	3				1			1	3
6 Netherlands	548	4	3%	1%	2	1	1		2	1			1	1		1		1	
7 Cambodia	55	4	3%	7%			4		3	1	1			3					1
8 Australia	201	4	3%	2%		1	3		1	2									
9 USSR (Soviet Union)	1356	3	2%				2	1	3										
10 WHO (World Health)	187	3	2%	2%	1	2			1	3		1							
11 United Nations	233	3	2%	1%	1	2			2	1					1				
12 Philippines	236	3	2%	1%	1	1	1		1	1	1								1
13 Norway	461	3	2%	1%	1		1	2	2	1					1				1
14 France	1033	3	2%		2	1			1		1	1	1	1	1	1	1		
15 Denmark	380	3	2%	1%	1	1	1		1	2								1	2
16 Taiwan	172	3	2%	2%			1	2	1										
17 Burma	102	3	2%	3%			2	1	3										3
18 Sweden	483	2	2%		1			1		1	1				1		1		
19 ILO (Labor Org)	59	2	2%	3%		1	1			1		1		2					1
20 ICAO (Civil Aviat)	23	2	2%	9%		1	1			1									
21 Laos	28	2	2%	7%		1		1	1	1	1								
22 Switzerland	426	1	1%				1								1		1		
23 UN Special Fund	113	1	1%	1%	1							1		1					
24 UNICEF (Children)	122	1	1%	1%			1					1		1					1
25 UNESCO (Educ/Cult)	19	1	1%	5%				1							1				
26 IAEA (Atom Energy)	44	1	1%	2%			1						1	1					
27 Pakistan	245	1	1%						1										
28 New Zealand	101	1	1%	1%			1			1	1						1		1
29 Luxembourg	136	1	1%	1%			1												1
30 Korea, South	80	1	1%	1%				1	1		1			1					
31 All Others (11)	2872	11	8%		3	2	4	2	6	3	2			1	3	3	3	1	3
GROUPS																			
32 African Group	968																		
33 Arab Group	937																		
34 Asian Group	1937	20	15%	1%	3	4	9	4	12	7	1			5	4	3	2	1	7
35 Commonwealth	1641	15	11%	1%	6	2	5	2	2	3	8	1	1		2			3	4
36 Communist Group	3310	3	2%		1		2		3										
37 Latin America	1674	1	1%					1			1								
38 Western Europe	5906	31	23%	1%	7	2	7	15	6	11	5	7		2	9	1	8		13
39 Intl Organs	1399	28	21%	2%	6	7	4	11	4	5		19	2	5	1	1		3	2
TOTALS																			
40 All Data	15080	132	100%		31	26	34	41	32	39	22	33	6	15	19	6	10	10	32
41 UNTS Only		123																	
COMPARISONS																			
42 Party Total					23%	20%	26%	31%	24%	30%	17%	25%	5%	12%	15%	5%	8%	8%	26%
43 Group Total					16%	23%	31%	30%	21%	23%	20%	30%	7%	10%	15%	8%	8%	6%	16%
44 World Total					18%	23%	29%	29%	22%	25%	25%	20%	7%	8%	12%	6%	7%	12%	100%

TREATY PROFILE OF TOGO

	Partners (1)	Partner's World Total (2)	Dyads Absolutes (3)	Ratios Self (4)	Ratios Other (5)	Time 1946-1950 (6)	Time 1951-1955 (7)	Time 1956-1960 (8)	Time 1961-1965 (9)	Topics Admin & Dipl (10)	Topics Social Coop (11)	Topics Econ Coop (12)	Topics Aid (13)	Topics Milit (14)	Institutions UN (15)	Institutions Spec Ag's (16)	Institutions Intl Court (17)	Institutions Arbitration (18)	Institutions Other (19)	Self-Registered (20)
	TOP THIRTY																			
1	France	1033	10	36%	1%				10	4	1	2	2	1						
2	USSR (Soviet Union)	1356	4	14%				1	3	1	1	2								
3	Germany, West	890	4	14%				2	2		1	3								
4	USA (United States)	2599	3	11%				1	2	1		1	2							
5	United Nations	233	2	7%	1%			1	1		1		1					1		
6	WHO (World Health)	187	1	4%	1%			1					1		1					
7	UN Special Fund	113	1	4%	1%				1	1			1		1					
8	UNICEF (Children)	122	1	4%	1%				1	1						1	1			
9	Israel	232	1	4%					1	1										
10	Accept UN Charter	68	1	4%	1%			1							1					
11-30																				
31	All Others (0)																			
	GROUPS																			
32	African Group	968																		
33	Arab Group	937																		
34	Asian Group	1937																		
35	Commonwealth	1641																		
36	Communist Group	3310	4	14%				1	3	1		3								
37	Latin America	1674																		
38	Western Europe	5906	14	50%				2	12	4	2	3	4			1	1	1		
39	Intl Organs	1399	5	18%				2	3	1	1		3	1	3	1	1	1	1	
	TOTALS																			
40	All Data	6833	28	100%				7	21	9	3	6	9	1	4	1	1	1	1	
41	UNTS Only		20																	
	COMPARISONS																			
42	Party Total					1%	5%	25%	75%	32%	11%	21%	32%	4%	20%	5%	5%	5%	4%	1%
43	Group Total						5%	18%	75%	22%	21%	18%	35%	4%	19%	13%	10%	15%		
44	World Total					18%	23%	29%	29%	22%	25%	25%	20%	7%	8%	12%	6%	7%	12%	100%

Table 177 • 225

228 • Table 180

TREATY PROFILE OF TUNISIA

Partners (1)	Partner's World Total (2)	Absolutes (3)	Dyads Ratios Self (4)	Dyads Ratios Other (5)	Time 1946 1950 (6)	Time 1951 1955 (7)	Time 1956 1960 (8)	Time 1961 1965 (9)	Admin & Dipl (10)	Social Coop (11)	Econ Coop (12)	Aid (13)	Milit (14)	UN (15)	Spec Ag's (16)	Intl Court (17)	Arbitration (18)	Other (19)	Self-Registered (20)
TOP THIRTY																			
1 France	1033	14	14%	1%		2	3	9	4	8	2								
2 USA (United States)	2599	11	11%				3	8	1	1		9				1	1		
3 USSR (Soviet Union)	1356	8	8%	1%			3	5	3		4	1							
4 Italy	755	7	7%	1%		1	2	4		3	2	2						5	
5 Switzerland	426	6	6%	1%			2	4		1	4	1			1		1		
6 Germany, West	890	6	6%	1%			1	5		1	2	3							
7 Belgium	499	5	55%	1%			1	4	1	1	1	2			1		1		
8 Netherlands	548	4	4%	1%				3		1	1					1	1		
9 Germany, East	556	4	4%	1%				4		2	3							2	
10 UK Great Britain	981	3	3%				1	2	1	1	2								
11 Norway	461	3	3%	1%			3		2			1			1	1	1		
12 Austria	445	3	3%	1%				3		1	1								
13 Sweden	483	2	2%				2			1	1				1				
14 WHO (World Health)	187	2	2%	1%			1	1										1	
15 IBRD (World Bank)	452	2	2%	1%				2			1	2					1		
16 Greece	318	2	2%				1	1			1	1							
17 Turkey	298	1	1%				1												
18 UN Special Fund	113	1	1%	1%			1					1		1	1	1	2		
19 United Nations	233	1	1%	5%			1												
20 UNESCO (Educ/Cult)	19	1	1%	1%				1											
21 IDA (Devel Assoc)	82	1	1%					1				1							
22 Poland	493	1	1%	2%				1		1					1				
23 Mali	54	1	1%	1%			1		1	1					1				
24 Luxembourg	136	1	1%				1												
25 Japan	443	1	1%					1		1	1				1		1		
26 Ghana	81	1	1%	1%			1												
27 Denmark	380	1	1%					1											
28 Czechoslovakia	393	1	1%				1				1								1
29 China People's Rep	766	1	1%					1						1					
30 Algeria	52	1	1%	2%				1	1										
31 All Others (1)	68	1	1%	1%				1											
GROUPS																			
32 African Group	968	2	2%					2		2					2		1		
33 Arab Group	937	1	1%					1		1					1				
34 Asian Group	1937																		
35 Commonwealth	1641	3	3%				1	2	1		2								
36 Communist Group	3310	15	15%				4	11	3	2	8	2						2	1
37 Latin America	1674																		
38 Western Europe	5906	55	57%	1%		3	19	33	8	20	16	11		1	6	2	5	6	
39 Intl Organs	1399	8	8%	1%			4	4	1			7			2	1	3		1
TOTALS																			
40 All Data	15600	97	100%			3	33	61	16	26	26	29		2	11	4	10	8	1
41 UNTS Only		49																		
COMPARISONS																			
42 Party Total					9%	3%	34%	63%	16%	27%	27%	30%	4%	4%	22%	8%	20%	16%	2%
43 Group Total					9%	24%	31%	36%	18%	27%	22%	29%	7%	15%	20%	8%	15%	9%	5%
44 World Total					18%	23%	29%	29%	22%	25%	25%	20%		8%	12%	6%	7%	12%	100%

TREATY PROFILE OF TURKEY

Table 181

Partners (1)	Partner's World Total (2)	Dyads Absolutes (3)	Dyads Ratios Self (4)	Dyads Ratios Other (5)	Time 1946-1950 (6)	Time 1951-1955 (7)	Time 1956-1960 (8)	Time 1961-1965 (9)	Topics Admin & Dipl (10)	Topics Social Coop (11)	Topics Econ Coop (12)	Topics Aid (13)	Topics Milit (14)	Institutions UN (15)	Institutions Spec Ag's (16)	Institutions Intl Court (17)	Institutions Arbitration (18)	Institutions Other (19)	Self-Registered (20)
TOP THIRTY																			
1 USA (United States)	2599	57	19%	2%	8	11	21	17	1	1	9	33	13	2	2	1		6	
2 Germany, West	890	24	8%	3%	4	7	7	6	4	6	10	4			1				
3 Italy	755	18	6%	2%	4	5	3	6	2	2	10	4			1	1		1	1
4 UK Great Britain	981	16	5%	2%	2	3	8	3	3	3	5	3	2		1	1	2	5	
5 Belgium	499	13	4%	3%	6	2	4	1	2	3	5	2			1			2	
6 Norway	461	11	4%	2%	3	1	5	2	3	2	6	2			1		1	1	2
7 France	1033	10	3%	1%	4	3	1	2	2	2	4	3			1				2
8 Yugoslavia	525	8	3%	2%	3	3	2		1	4	6				1			1	2
9 Netherlands	548	8	3%	1%	2	2	3	1	1	2	6	1			1			3	1
10 Iran	170	8	5%	5%	3	2	2	1	2	3	2								
11 Greece	318	8	3%	3%	4	4			1	4	3				1				
12 Sweden	483	8	2%	1%	5	1	2		2	2	4	1			1		1	5	
13 Pakistan	245	7	2%	3%	1	6			1	1					1	2		1	1
14 Finland	245	7	3%	3%	3	2	2		5	2									
15 Austria	445	7	2%	2%	1	2	2	2	3	1	6	2			1			1	
16 IDA (Devel Assoc)	82	6	2%	7%				6			1	6							
17 IBRD (World Bank)	452	6	2%	1%	3	2		1				6			1		2		
18 Spain	437	5	2%	1%	1	2	2		1		3								
19 Iraq	96	5	2%	5%	4	1			3	1								1	
20 USSR (Soviet Union)	1356	4	1%	1%		2		2	2	2			1	1			1		
21 Syria	84	4	1%	5%	2	1	1			1	2								
22 Lebanon	75	4	1%	5%	3	1			3	1					1				
23 Denmark	380	4	1%	1%	3		1				2	1			1		1		1
24 Canada	310	4	1%	1%	2	1	1		3		1		2			1	1		
25 Bulgaria	236	4	1%	2%	3			1			4								
26 Poland	493	3	1%	1%	2	1			1	1	3								
27 Israel	232	3	1%	1%	1	2			3	1									
28 India	299	3	1%	1%		3			2	1	1								
29 United Arab Rep	232	2	1%	1%	1	1			1	1		1					1	1	
30 Switzerland	426	2	1%	1%	1		1			1	1								
31 All Others (27)	3981	30	10%	1%	8	8	11	3	10	8	6	6		1	5	3	3		3
GROUPS																			
32 African Group	968																		
33 Arab Group	937	20	7%	2%	12	4	4		8	7	4		1	1	4		1	1	2
34 Asian Group	1937	23	8%	1%	5	11	6	1	8	10	5			3	3		1	1	1
35 Commonwealth	1641	22	7%	1%	4	4	11	3	8	3	6	3	2		1	1	2	5	
36 Communist Group	3310	14	5%	2%	7	5		2	2	3	9				1				1
37 Latin America	1674	3	1%	1%	1	1		1	1	2									
38 Western Europe	5906	126	42%	2%	41	31	34	20	22	26	58	20		1	9	1	3	13	8
39 Intl Organs	1399	19	6%	1%	4	5	1	9	1		1	17			2	2	3		
TOTALS																			
40 All Data	19368	298	100%		87	77	80	54	53	55	100	74	16	7	25	6	13	27	13
41 UNTS Only		147																	
COMPARISONS																			
42 Party Total					29%	26%	27%	18%	18%	18%	34%	25%	5%	5%	17%	4%	9%	18%	9%
43 Group Total					22%	25%	27%	26%	24%	26%	32%	10%	8%	4%	14%	6%	8%	17%	32%
44 World Total					18%	23%	29%	29%	22%	25%	25%	20%	7%	8%	12%	6%	7%	12%	100%

230 • Table 182

TREATY PROFILE OF UGANDA

Partners (1)	Partner's World Total (2)	Dyads Abso-lutes (3)	Ratios Self (4)	Ratios Other (5)	Time 1946 1950 (6)	Time 1951 1955 (7)	Time 1956 1960 (8)	Time 1961 1965 (9)	Topics Admin & Dipl (10)	Topics Social Coop (11)	Topics Econ Coop (12)	Topics Aid (13)	Topics Milit (14)	Institutions UN (15)	Institutions Spec Ag's (16)	Institutions Intl Court (17)	Institutions Arbi-tration (18)	Other (19)	Self-Registered (20)
TOP THIRTY																			
1 Germany, West	890	4	19%					4			1	2							
2 USSR (Soviet Union)	1356	3	14%					3	2	1	1								
3 USA (United States)	2599	2	10%					2	1			1							
4 UN Special Fund	113	2	10%	2%				2	1			1		1		1			
5 Norway	461	2	10%					2	1			1							
6 UK Great Britain	981	1	5%					1											
7 United Nations	233	1	5%					1		1									
8 IBRD (World Bank)	452	1	5%					1				1							
9 Israel	232	1	5%					1											
10 France	1033	1	5%					1											
11 China People's Rep	766	1	5%					1	1										
12 ICJ Option Clause	62	1	5%	2%				1	1							1			
13 Accept UN Charter	68	1	5%	1%				1						1					
31 All Others (0)																			
GROUPS																			
32 African Group	968																		
33 Arab Group	937																		
34 Asian Group	1937																		
35 Commonwealth	1641	1	5%					1	1										
36 Communist Group	3310	4	19%					4	2	1	1	1							
37 Latin America	1674																		
38 Western Europe	5906	7	33%					7	1	2	1	3							
39 Intl Organs	1399	4	19%					4	2			2		1		1			
TOTALS																			
40 All Data	9246	21	100%					21	8	3	2	8		2		3			
41 UNTS Only		11																	
COMPARISONS																			
42 Party Total					1%	5%	18%	100%	38%	14%	10%	38%	4%	18%	13%	27%	15%	4%	1%
43 Group Total					18%	23%	18%	75%	22%	21%	18%	35%	7%	19%	12%	10%	7%	12%	100%
44 World Total					18%	23%	29%	29%	22%	25%	25%	20%		8%	12%	6%			

TREATY PROFILE OF UK GREAT BRITAIN

Table 183

Part-ners (1)	Partner's World Total (2)	Dyads Abso-lutes (3)	Ratios Self (4)	Ratios Other (5)	Time 1946 1950 (6)	Time 1951 1955 (7)	Time 1956 1960 (8)	Time 1961 1965 (9)	Topics Admin & Dipl (10)	Topics Social Coop (11)	Topics Econ Coop (12)	Topics Aid (13)	Topics Milit (14)	Institutions UN (15)	Institutions Spec Ag's (16)	Institutions Intl Court (17)	Institutions Arbi-tration (18)	Other (19)	Self-Regis-tered (20)
TOP THIRTY																			
1 USA (United States)	2599	104	11%	4%	28	30	17	29	16	24	12	19	33	4	11	1		12	38
2 France	1033	49	5%	5%	21	11	5	12	15	17	12		5	1	5	4	1	9	43
3 Italy	755	40	4%	5%	14	13	8	5	12	10	12	1	5	5	2	1	1	6	34
4 Germany, West	890	33	3%	4%	1	7	16	9	9	5	7	1	11	1	5	3	3	17	33
5 Netherlands	548	31	3%	6%	15	6	5	5	7	7	9		8		1	1	1	5	15
6 Denmark	380	28	3%	7%	11	4	8	5	6	6	9	1	6		4		1	7	21
7 Belgium	499	28	3%	6%	11	11	4	2	9	4	5	2	8		2	2	1	7	13
8 Yugoslavia	525	26	3%	5%	6	6	5	9	3	8	9	4	2		1	2	1	11	26
9 Sweden	483	23	2%	5%	6	6	7	4	6	5	11	1			6	1			20
10 Greece	318	22	2%	7%	9	8	2	3	8	3	7		4		1		2	7	19
11 Japan	443	21	2%	5%		9	4	8	8	2	7	1	3		4	1		5	17
12 USSR (Soviet Union)	1356	20	2%	1%	3	1	7	9	5	10	4							1	12
13 Norway	461	20	2%	4%	8	4	4	4	8	4	5	1	2	1	4	1	3	6	16
14 United Arab Rep	232	18	2%	8%	7	8	1	2	5	2	8	1	2		2			2	16
15 Austria	445	18	2%	4%	3	8	5	2	4	3	8	1	2		3	1		7	17
16 Canada	310	17	2%	5%	6	1	7	3		6	5	1	5		4		2	2	10
17 Turkey	298	16	2%	5%	2	3	8	3	3	3	5	3	2		1	1	2	5	15
18 IBRD (World Bank)	452	16	2%	4%	3	3	5	8				16							
19 Portugal	131	16	12%	12%	3	9	1	3	5	3	4		2		2		1	8	15
20 Switzerland	426	15	2%	4%	4	4	2	5	3	4	6	2			2	2	1	5	14
21 Australia	201	15	2%	7%	3	1	4	7	2	10	3				2	1			6
22 Spain	437	14	1%	3%	4	3	5	2	3	2	8				1		1	2	10
23 UNICEF (Children)	122	14	1%	11%	8	6						14		12					1
24 Argentina	164	14	1%	9%	5	1	3	5		3	9		1		3			2	13
25 South Africa	120	13	1%	11%	7	1	3	2	1	1	10		1		3	1		1	9
26 Jordan	65	13	1%	20%	2	2	4	6	1		1	9	1	2	1	2			12
27 Israel	232	11	1%	5%	4	1	3	3	3	3	7				1				8
28 Finland	245	11	1%	4%	3	2	1	5	1	2	3	1	1	1	2		1		9
29 Cyprus	49	11	1%	22%			10	1	5	1	6	1			1			1	11
30 Thailand	132	10	1%	8%	6	1	1	2	7		3				1			2	7
31 All Others (84)	8157	294	30%	4%	82	65	66	81	90	64	88	20	32	12	48	14	24	22	220
GROUPS																			
32 African Group	968	39	4%	7%	1	5	13	20	19	7	7	2	4	1	6	1	2	4	33
33 Arab Group	937	68	7%	7%	13	29	11	15	16	13	21	11	7	5	10	6	8	7	58
34 Asian Group	1937	87	9%	4%	30	16	21	20	19	23	32	5	8		17	1	7	5	64
35 Commonwealth	1641	55	6%	3%	18	5	18	14	3	20	22	1	9		12	1	3	4	27
36 Communist Group	3310	50	5%	2%	20	6	14	10	9	16	19		5	3	2		1	2	38
37 Latin America	1674	64	7%	4%	25	13	8	18	15	11	26	5	7		10	1	3	5	59
38 Western Europe	5906	405	41%	7%	127	102	94	82	122	85	121	18	59	10	46	19	20	104	325
39 Intl Organs	1399	45	5%	3%	9	10	11	15	6	1		38		15	3	1	1	1	7
TOTALS																			
40 All Data	22508	981	100%		282	234	221	244	243	213	283	105	137	39	123	40	47	145	700
41 UNTS Only		946																	
COMPARISONS																			
42 Party Total					29%	24%	23%	25%	25%	22%	29%	11%	14%	4%	13%	4%	5%	15%	74%
43 Group Total					27%	25%	24%	24%	25%	24%	27%	10%	14%	4%	13%	4%	5%	12%	63%
44 World Total					18%	23%	29%	29%	22%	25%	25%	20%	7%	8%	12%	6%	7%	12%	100%

232 • Table 184

TREATY PROFILE OF UN HI COM REFUGEES

Part-ners	Part-ner's World Total	Dyads Abso-lutes	Ratios Self	Ratios Other	Time 1946-1950	Time 1951-1955	Time 1956-1960	Time 1961-1965	Topics Admin & Dipl	Topics Social Coop	Topics Econ Coop	Topics Aid	Topics Milit	Institutions UN	Institutions Spec Ag's	Institutions Intl Court	Institutions Arbi-tration	Institutions Other	Self-Regis-tered
(1)	(2)	(3)	(4)	(5)	(6)	(7)	(8)	(9)	(10)	(11)	(12)	(13)	(14)	(15)	(16)	(17)	(18)	(19)	(20)
TOP THIRTY																			
1 Sweden	483	1	100%				1		1					1		1	1	1	
2																			
3																			
4																			
5																			
6																			
7																			
8																			
9																			
10																			
11																			
12																			
13																			
14																			
15																			
16																			
17																			
18																			
19																			
20																			
21																			
22																			
23																			
24																			
25																			
26																			
27																			
28																			
29																			
30																			
31 All Others (0)																			
GROUPS																			
32 African Group	968																		
33 Arab Group	937																		
34 Asian Group	1937																		
35 Commonwealth	1641																		
36 Communist Group	3310																		
37 Latin America	1674																		
38 Western Europe	5906	1	100%				1		1								1	1	
39 Intl Organs	1399																			
TOTALS																			
40 All Data	483	1	100%				1		1					1					
41 UNTS Only		1																		
COMPARISONS																			
42 Party Total							100%		100%					100%		100%	100%	100%	
43 Group Total					12%	25%	23%	40%	19%	7%	1%	71%	1%	27%	11%	13%	15%	4%	74%
44 World Total					18%	23%	29%	29%	22%	25%	25%	20%	7%	8%	12%	6%	7%	12%	100%

Table 185 • 233

TREATY PROFILE OF UN RELIEF PALESTIN

Partners	Partner's World Total	Dyads Absolutes	Dyads Ratios Self	Dyads Ratios Other	Time 1946-1950	Time 1951-1955	Time 1956-1960	Time 1961-1965	Topics Admin & Dipl	Topics Social Coop	Topics Econ Coop	Topics Aid	Topics Milit	Institutions UN	Institutions Spec Ag's	Institutions Intl Court	Institutions Arbitration	Institutions Other	Self-Registered
(1)	(2)	(3)	(4)	(5)	(6)	(7)	(8)	(9)	(10)	(11)	(12)	(13)	(14)	(15)	(16)	(17)	(18)	(19)	(20)
TOP THIRTY																			
1 United Arab Rep	232	3	33%	1%	1	2			1			2		1				1	1
2 Jordan	65	2	22%	3%		2			1			1		1					
3 WHO (World Health)	187	1	11%	1%	1							1		1					
4 ILO (Labor Org)	59	1	11%	2%		1				1		1							
5 Lebanon	75	1	11%	1%		1						1							
6 Israel	232	1	11%				1												
7																			
8–30																			
31 All Others (0)																			
GROUPS																			
32 African Group	968																		
33 Arab Group	937	6	67%	1%	1	5			2			4		2				1	
34 Asian Group	1937																		
35 Commonwealth	1641																		
36 Communist Group	3310																		
37 Latin America	1674																		
38 Western Europe	5906																		
39 Intl Organs	1399	2	22%		1	1				1		1		2					
TOTALS																			
40 All Data	850	9	100%		2	6	1		2	1		6		4				1	
41 UNTS Only		9																		
COMPARISONS																			
42 Party Total					22%	67%	11%		22%	11%		67%		44%	11%	13%	15%	11%	
43 Group Total					12%	25%	23%	40%	19%	7%	1%	71%	1%	27%	11%	6%	7%	4%	74%
44 World Total					18%	23%	29%	29%	22%	25%	25%	20%	7%	8%	12%	6%	7%	12%	100%

234 • Table 186

TREATY PROFILE OF UN SPECIAL FUND

	Partners (1)	Partner's World Total (2)	Dyads Absolutes (3)	Ratios Self (4)	Ratios Other (5)	Time 1946-1950 (6)	Time 1951-1955 (7)	Time 1956-1960 (8)	Time 1961-1965 (9)	Topics Admin & Dipl (10)	Topics Social Coop (11)	Topics Econ Coop (12)	Topics Aid (13)	Topics Milit (14)	Institutions UN (15)	Institutions Spec Ag's (16)	Institutions Intl Court (17)	Institutions Arbitration (18)	Other (19)	Self-Registered (20)
	TOP THIRTY																			
1	Zambia	9	2	2%	22%				2				1		1		1	1		
2	Vietnam, South	106	2	2%	2%			2		1			2		1	1	1	1		
3	Uganda	21	2	2%	10%				2	1			1		1	1	1	1		
4	Netherlands	548	2	2%	1%			1	1				2		2	2	2	1		
5	Iran	170	2	2%	1%			2					2		1	1	1	1		
6	Yugoslavia	525	1	1%				1					1		1		1	1		
7	Yemen	35	1	1%	3%				1				1		1	1	1	1		
8	Western Samoa	10	1	1%	10%				1				1		1	1	1	1		
9	Venezuela	47	1	1%	2%				1				1		1	1	1	1		
10	Uruguay	63	1	1%	2%				1				1		1	1	1	1		
11	Upper Volta	15	1	1%	7%				1				1		1	1	1	1		
12	UK Great Britain	981	1	1%					1				1		1	1		1		
13	United Arab Rep	232	1	1%				1					1		1	1		1		
14	Turkey	298	1	1%				1					1		1	1	2	1		
15	Tunisia	97	1	1%	1%			1					1		1	1	1	1		
16	Trinidad/Tobago	11	1	1%	9%				1				1		1	1	1	1		
17	Togo	28	1	1%	4%				1				1		1	1	1	1		
18	Thailand	132	1	1%	1%			1					1		1	1		1		
19	Tanzania	45	1	1%	2%				1				1		1	1	1	1		
20	Syria	84	1	1%	1%				1				1		1	1	1	1		
21	Sudan	37	1	1%	3%			1					1		1	1	1	1		
22	Spain	437	1	1%					1				1		1	1	1	1		
23	Somalia	37	1	1%	3%				1				1		1	1		1		
24	Singapore	3	1	1%	33%				1	1					1	1				
25	Sierra Leone	27	1	1%	4%				1				1		1	1	1	1		
26	Senegal	40	1	1%	3%				1				1		1	1	1	1		
27	Saudi Arabia	31	1	1%	3%				1				1		1					
28	WMO (Meteorology)	6	1	1%	17%			1		1					1	1				
29	WHO (World Health)	187	1	1%	1%				1	1					1					
30	UNESCO (Educ/Cult)	19	1	1%	5%	1				1					1					
31	All Others (78)	8635	78	69%	1%			37	41	9	1		68		66	54	65	37	3	1
	GROUPS																			
32	African Group	968	32	28%	3%			5	27	4			28		22	16	26	14	1	1
33	Arab Group	937	13	12%	1%			9	4				13		12	10	12	6		
34	Asian Group	1937	20	18%	1%			13	7	1	1		19		15	14	15	8	1	
35	Commonwealth	1641	3	3%				1	2				2		3	2	3	3		
36	Communist Group	3310	2	2%				1	1				1		2	2	2	2		
37	Latin America	1674	22	19%	1%			10	12	1			22		19	15	21	12	1	
38	Western Europe	5906	10	9%				5	5				9		9	8	9	4		
39	Intl Organs	1399	8	7%	1%		1	6	1	8					8	3				
	TOTALS																			
40	All Data	12916	113	100%			1	52	60	15	1		97	1	93	73	91	52	3	1
41	UNTS Only		111																		
	COMPARISONS																			
42	Party Total					12%	1%	46%	53%	13%	1%	1%	86%	1%	84%	66%	82%	47%	3%	1%
43	Group Total					18%	25%	23%	40%	19%	7%	1%	71%	7%	27%	11%	13%	15%	4%	74%
44	World Total					18%	23%	29%	29%	22%	25%	25%	20%		8%	12%	6%	7%	12%	100%

Table 187

TREATY PROFILE OF UNESCO (EDUC/CULT)

Partners (1)	Partner's World Total (2)	Dyads Absolutes (3)	Ratios Self (4)	Ratios Other (5)	Time 1946-1950 (6)	Time 1951-1955 (7)	Time 1956-1960 (8)	Time 1961-1965 (9)	Topics Admin & Dipl (10)	Topics Social Coop (11)	Topics Econ Coop (12)	Topics Aid (13)	Topics Milit (14)	Institutions UN (15)	Institutions Spec Ag's (16)	Institutions Intl Court (17)	Institutions Arbitration (18)	Institutions Other (19)	Self-Registered (20)
TOP THIRTY																			
1 USA (United States)	2599	2	11%					2	1	1				1					
2 United Nations	233	2	11%	1%	1	1			2					2		1			
3 FAO (Food Agri)	19	2	11%	11%	2				2					1				1	1
4 France	1033	2	11%			2		1	2							1			1
5 Yugoslavia	525	1	5%				1		1										
6 UK Great Britain	981	1	5%				1					1							
7 United Arab Rep	232	1	5%	1%			1			1		1							1
8 Tunisia	97	1	5%	1%				1	1										
9 Thailand	132	1	5%	1%				1	1										
10 WHO (World Health)	187	1	5%	1%	1				1					1				1	
11 UN Special Fund	113	1	5%	1%		1			1					1					
12 IAEA (Atom Energy)	44	1	5%	2%			1	1	1	1				1					
13 Morocco	94	1	5%	1%					1			1							
14 Austria	445	1	5%																
15 Afghanistan	83	1	5%	1%	1					1									
31 All Others (0)																			
GROUPS																			
32 African Group	968	3	16%		1			2				2							2
33 Arab Group	937	2	11%				1	1	1			1							
34 Asian Group	1937	1	5%						1										
35 Commonwealth	1641																		
36 Communist Group	3310																		
37 Latin America	1674																		
38 Western Europe	5906	3	16%			2		1	3	1				1		1			1
39 Intl Organs	1399	7	37%	1%	4	2	1		7	1				6		1		2	1
TOTALS																			
40 All Data	6817	19	100%		5	4	3	7	13	3		3		7		2		2	4
41 UNTS Only		17	100%																
COMPARISONS																			
42 Party Total					26%	21%	16%	37%	68%	16%	16%	16%	1%	41%		12%	15%	12%	24%
43 Group Total					12%	25%	23%	40%	19%	7%	1%	71%	1%	27%	11%	13%	15%	4%	74%
44 World Total					18%	23%	29%	29%	22%	25%	25%	20%	7%	8%	12%	6%	7%	12%	100%

236 • Table 188

TREATY PROFILE OF UNICEF (CHILDREN)

	Partners (1)	Partner's World Total (2)	Dyads Absolutes (3)	Ratios Self (4)	Ratios Other (5)	Time 1946-1950 (6)	Time 1951-1955 (7)	Time 1956-1960 (8)	Time 1961-1965 (9)	Topics Admin & Dipl (10)	Topics Social Coop (11)	Topics Econ Coop (12)	Topics Aid (13)	Topics Milit (14)	Institutions UN (15)	Institutions Spec Ag's (16)	Institutions Intl Court (17)	Institutions Arbitration (18)	Institutions Other (19)	Self-Registered (20)
	TOP THIRTY																			
1	UK Great Britain	981	14	11%	1%	8	6						14		12					
2	Iran	170	3	2%	2%		1		2	1			2		2					
3	Taiwan	172	3	2%	2%	2			1	2			1		2	1				
4	Poland	493	2	2%	7%	1			1				2		1					
5	Laos	28	2	2%			1	1				1	1		1					
6	Jordan	65	2	2%	3%		1	1					2		1					
7	Italy	755	2	2%		1	1			1			1		2					
8	Iraq	96	2	2%	2%		1		1	1			1		2					
9	Indonesia	126	2	2%	2%	1	1			2			1		1					
10	Guatemala	50	2	2%	4%	1	1						2		1					
11	Ethiopia	98	2	2%	2%	1	1			1			1		1					
12	Chile	119	2	2%	2%	1	1			1			1		1					
13	Cambodia	55	2	2%	4%			2					2		1					
14	Yugoslavia	525	1	1%	3%	1							1		1					
15	Yemen	35	1	1%	1%		1						1		1					
16	Vietnam, South	106	1	1%	2%			1					1		1					
17	Uruguay	63	1	1%	7%			1		1										
18	Upper Volta	15	1	1%					1				1		1					
19	United Arab Rep	232	1	1%		1							1		1					
20	Turkey	298	1	1%	9%		1						1							
21	Trinidad/Tobago	11	1	1%	4%				1						1					
22	Togo	28	1	1%					1	1					1					
23	Thailand	132	1	1%	1%	1				1			1		1					
24	Tanzania	45	1	1%	2%				1				1		1					
25	Syria	84	1	1%	1%		1								1					
26	Sudan	37	1	1%	3%			1					1		1					
27	Spain	437	1	1%			1						1		1					
28	Somalia	37	1	1%	3%				1				1		1					
29	Sierra Leone	27	1	1%	4%				1				1		1					
30	Senegal	40	1	1%	3%				1	1					1					
31	All Others (65)	8872	65	53%	1%	27	10	8	20	24	2		39		57	1			1	
	GROUPS																			
32	African Group	968	25	20%	3%	11	2	4	19	8			17		18					
33	Arab Group	937	13	11%	1%	8	5	4	4	1			12		12					
34	Asian Group	1937	23	19%	1%	11	4	4	4	12		1	10		18	1				
35	Commonwealth	1641	15	12%	1%	8	7						15		13					
36	Communist Group	3310	8	7%		6			2	5			3		6					
37	Latin America	1674	23	19%	1%	12	5	3	3	7	1		15		20					
38	Western Europe	5906	12	10%		5	4	1	2	5			6		10	1				
39	Intl Organs	1399																		
	TOTALS																			
40	All Data	14232	122	100%		44	28	16	34	38	2	1	81		100	2				
41	UNTS Only		121																	
	COMPARISONS																			
42	Party Total					36%	23%	13%	28%	31%	2%	1%	66%	1%	83%	2%		15%	4%	74%
43	Group Total					12%	25%	23%	40%	19%	7%	1%	71%	7%	27%	11%	13%	7%		100%
44	World Total					18%	23%	29%	29%	22%	25%	25%	20%		8%	12%	6%		12%	

Table 189 • 237

TREATY PROFILE OF UNITED ARAB REP

Partners (1)	Partner's World Total (2)	Dyads Absolutes (3)	Ratios Self (4)	Ratios Other (5)	Time 1946-1950 (6)	Time 1951-1955 (7)	Time 1956-1960 (8)	Time 1961-1965 (9)	Topics Admin & Dipl (10)	Topics Social Coop (11)	Topics Econ Coop (12)	Topics Aid (13)	Topics Milit (14)	Institutions UN (15)	Institutions Spec Ag's (16)	Institutions Intl Court (17)	Institutions Arbitration (18)	Institutions Other (19)	Self-Registered (20)
TOP THIRTY																			
1 USA (United States)	2599	33	14%	1%	5	12	8	8	1	11	3	16	2	1	6	1	1	4	1
2 USSR (Soviet Union)	1356	27	12%	2%	1	6	15	5	3	6	11	7						1	
3 China People's Rep	766	21	9%	3%		2	9	10		5	14	2							2
4 UK Great Britain	981	18	8%	2%	7	8	1	2	5	2	8	1	2		2		1	2	
5 Germany, East	556	15	6%	3%		2	9	4	3	4	5	3							
6 Italy	755	12	5%	2%	1	1	6	4	2	2	6	1	1		1			2	
7 Germany, West	890	7	3%	1%		2	5			2	4		1				1		
8 United Nations	233	6	3%	3%			3	3	3			2	1		4	1	3	2	
9 Netherlands	548	6	3%	1%	1	2	2	1		3	3				1		1		
10 Greece	318	5	2%	2%	2	2	1			2	2		1		1	1	1	2	
11 Czechoslovakia	393	5	2%	1%			4	1		3	1	1			2		1		
12 Switzerland	426	4	2%	1%	2	1	1		1	2	2				2		1		
13 Pakistan	245	4	2%	2%		4				3					1		1		
14 Belgium	499	4	2%	1%	3		1		1	3	2			1	1		1	1	
15 Syria	84	3	1%	4%		2		1		2			1		1				
16 Sweden	483	3	1%	1%	1		2			1	2					1			
17 WHO (World Health)	187	3	1%	2%	1	1		1	2			1		3			3		1
18 UN Relief Palestin	9	3	1%	33%	1	2			1			2		1					
19 Poland	493	3	1%	1%			2	1		2	1				1				
20 Japan	443	3	1%	1%			1	2			1					1	1		
21 France	1033	3	1%	1%	1	4	1	1	1	1	1		1		1		3	1	
22 Denmark	380	3	1%	1%	1	7	1	2	2	5	1				4	1	1		
23 Turkey	298	3	1%	1%	7	10	1	1	5	7			1		3				
24 ICAO (Civil Aviat)	23	2	1%	9%	1	10	42	22	7	3	9	14	2	1	3		1	2	
25 IAEA (Atom Energy)	44	2	1%	5%			1	3		23	31			2	3	2		1	
26 Romania	251	2	1%	1%			2			1	3								
27 Philippines	236	2	1%	1%		1		1	1	2									
28 Norway	461	2	1%	1%	1			1		1	1				1				
29 Mexico	138	2	1%	1%			1	1		1	1								
30 Jordan	65	2	1%	3%	1	1		1		1	1				1		1		
31 All Others (21)	4463	25	11%	1%	2	8	9	6	4	11	6	3	1	5	8	3	5	3	2
GROUPS																			
32 African Group	968	1	3%	1%	1	4	1	1	1	1	1		1		1	1	1	1	1
33 Arab Group	937	8	3%	1%	1	4	2	1	2	5	1		1		4		3	3	
34 Asian Group	1937	10	4%	1%		7	1	2	2	7		1		1	3		1	1	
35 Commonwealth	1641	20	9%	1%	7	10	1	2	5	3	9	1			3				
36 Communist Group	3310	75	32%	2%	1	10	42	22	7	23	31	14	2	1	3		1	2	2
37 Latin America	1674	4	2%				1	3		1	3							1	
38 Western Europe	5906	54	23%	1%	14	10	20	10	3	20	27	1	3		11	1	5	5	1
39 Intl Organs	1399	20	9%	1%	2	6	6	6	7	1		11	1	8	5	5	8	3	
TOTALS																			
40 All Data	19656	232	100%		32	60	85	55	28	75	76	43	10	13	37	11	23	18	6
41 UNTS Only		145																	
COMPARISONS																			
42 Party Total					14%	26%	37%	24%	12%	32%	33%	19%	4%	9%	26%	8%	16%	12%	4%
43 Group Total			100%		9%	24%	31%	36%	18%	27%	22%	29%	4%	15%	20%	8%	15%	9%	5%
44 World Total					18%	23%	29%	29%	22%	25%	25%	20%	7%	8%	12%	6%	7%	12%	100%

TREATY PROFILE OF UNITED NATIONS

Table 190

	Partners (1)	Partner's World Total (2)	Dyads Absolutes (3)	Ratios Self (4)	Ratios Other (5)	Time 1946-1950 (6)	Time 1951-1955 (7)	Time 1956-1960 (8)	Time 1961-1965 (9)	Topics Admin & Dipl (10)	Topics Social Coop (11)	Topics Econ Coop (12)	Topics Aid (13)	Topics Milit (14)	Institutions UN (15)	Institutions Spec Ag's (16)	Institutions Intl Court (17)	Institutions Arbitration (18)	Institutions Other (19)	Self-Registered (20)
	TOP THIRTY																			
1	Japan	443	9	4%	2%		5	1	3	5	1		1	2		1	1		1	5
2	League of Nations	9	8	3%	89%	8				8						3		1		8
3	India	299	7	3%	2%		3	1	3	3	2		4	1			1			7
4	United Arab Rep	232	6	3%	3%			3	3	3			2	1		4		3	2	6
5	USA (United States)	2599	5	2%		3	1		1	2	1		2						2	5
6	Pakistan	245	5	2%	2%	1	2	1	1	1	1		3							5
7	Lebanon	75	5	2%	7%			4	1	2	1			1		1	1	1		5
8	Yugoslavia	525	4	2%	1%		2	1	1	2	1		2	1				1		4
9	Switzerland	426	4	2%	1%	3			1	3							1			3
10	Sweden	483	4	2%	1%			1	2	2	1		1	1			2			4
11	ILO (Labor Org)	59	4	2%	7%	4				4							1			4
12	Mexico	138	4	3%	3%		1	1	2	3	1				1					4
13	Greece	318	4	2%	1%	1	1		2	1	1		2			1		2	1	4
14	Ethiopia	98	4	2%	4%		1	2	1	3			3			1				4
15	Congo (Zaire)	29	4	2%	14%			1	3	1	1		2	1		1			2	4
16	UK Great Britain	981	3	1%		1			2	2	1									3
17	Thailand	132	3	1%	2%	1	2			1	1		1				1			3
18	WHO (World Health)	187	3	1%	2%	3				3						2	1	1		3
19	IMCO (Maritime Org)	5	3	1%	60%			2	1	3					1					3
20	IBRD (World Bank)	452	3	1%	1%	1		1	1	3						2				3
21	Jordan	65	3	1%	5%				3	1			2			4		1		3
22	Italy	755	3	1%			1		2	2	1					2				3
23	Cyprus	49	3	1%	6%				3	2			1				1	3	1	3
24	Belgium	499	3	1%	1%				3	2		2		1						3
25	Austria	445	3	1%	1%				3	3						2				3
26	South Pacific Com	2	2	1%	100%				2											2
27	Vietnam, South	106	2	1%	2%		1	1		1			2					2		2
28	Venezuela	47	2	1%	4%		1	1		1			1							2
29	Togo	28	2	1%	7%			1	1		1		1					1		2
30	Saudi Arabia	31	2	1%	6%				2	1										2
31	All Others (88)	9845	116	50%	1%	15	27	26	48	49	11		50	6	7	8	14	69	3	116
	GROUPS																			
32	African Group	968	30	13%	3%		2	6	22	9	1		19	1	2	3	2	26	2	30
33	Arab Group	937	25	11%	3%		2	12	11	10	1		12	2		9		15	2	25
34	Asian Group	1937	37	16%	2%	2	14	11	10	8	5		22	1		1	4	17	3	37
35	Commonwealth	1641	7	3%		2		1	4	2	4			1		1	1	1		7
36	Communist Group	3310	4	2%		1			3	3	1									4
37	Latin America	1674	28	12%	2%		13	6	9	10	2		15	1		3	1	15	2	28
38	Western Europe	5906	38	16%	1%	8	5	5	20	18	7	2	6	5		4	7	9	1	37
39	Intl Organs	1399	43	18%	3%	25	4	7	7	40	1		2		7	10	8	2	2	43
	TOTALS																			
40	All Data	19607	233	100%		41	49	50	93	109	24	2	83	15	9	32	25	88	13	228
41	UNTS Only		228																	228
	COMPARISONS																			
42	Party Total					18%	21%	21%	40%	47%	10%	1%	36%	6%	4%	14%	11%	39%	6%	100%
43	Group Total					12%	25%	23%	40%	19%	7%	1%	71%	1%	27%	11%	13%	15%	4%	74%
44	World Total					18%	23%	29%	29%	22%	25%	25%	20%	7%	8%	12%	6%	7%	12%	100%

TREATY PROFILE OF UNRRA (RELIEF)

Table 191 • 239

Partners (1)	Partner's World Total (2)	Dyads Absolutes (3)	Dyads Ratios Self (4)	Dyads Ratios Other (5)	Time 1946 1950 (6)	Time 1951 1955 (7)	Time 1956 1960 (8)	Time 1961 1965 (9)	Topics Admin & Dipl (10)	Topics Social Coop (11)	Topics Econ Coop (12)	Topics Aid (13)	Topics Milit (14)	Institutions UN (15)	Institutions Spec Ag's (16)	Institutions Intl Court (17)	Institutions Arbitration (18)	Institutions Other (19)	Self-Registered (20)
TOP THIRTY																			
1 United Nations	233	1	50%		1				1						1				
2 Austria	445	1	50%		1							1							
3																			
4																			
5																			
6																			
7																			
8																			
9																			
10																			
11																			
12																			
13																			
14																			
15																			
16																			
17																			
18																			
19																			
20																			
21																			
22																			
23																			
24																			
25																			
26																			
27																			
28																			
29																			
30																			
31 All Others (0)																			
GROUPS																			
32 African Group	968																		
33 Arab Group	937																		
34 Asian Group	1937																		
35 Commonwealth	1641																		
36 Communist Group	3310																		
37 Latin America	1674	1	50%		1														
38 Western Europe	5906	1	50%		1							1					1		
39 Intl Organs	1399								1										
TOTALS																			
40 All Data	678	2	100%		2				1			1					1		
41 UNTS Only		1																	
COMPARISONS																			
42 Party Total					100%	25%	23%	40%	50%	7%	1%	50%	1%	27%	100%	13%	15%	4%	74%
43 Group Total					12%	25%	23%	29%	19%	7%	1%	71%	1%	27%	11%	13%	15%	4%	74%
44 World Total					18%	23%	29%	29%	22%	25%	25%	20%	7%	8%	12%	6%	7%	12%	100%

240 • Table 192

TREATY PROFILE OF UNTAB (TECH ASSIS)

	Partners (1)	Partner's World Total (2)	Dyads Absolutes (3)	Ratios Self (4)	Ratios Other (5)	Time 1946-1950 (6)	Time 1951-1955 (7)	Time 1956-1960 (8)	Time 1961-1965 (9)	Topics Admin & Dipl (10)	Topics Social Coop (11)	Topics Econ Coop (12)	Topics Aid (13)	Topics Milit (14)	Institutions UN (15)	Institutions Spec Ag's (16)	Institutions Intl Court (17)	Institutions Arbitration (18)	Institutions Other (19)	Self-Registered (20)
	TOP THIRTY																			
1	Philippines	236	10	100%	4%		8	2					10							
2																				
3																				
4																				
5																				
6																				
7																				
8																				
9																				
10																				
11																				
12																				
13																				
14																				
15																				
16																				
17																				
18																				
19																				
20																				
21																				
22																				
23																				
24																				
25																				
26																				
27																				
28																				
29																				
30																				
31	All Others (0)																			
	GROUPS																			
32	African Group	968																		
33	Arab Group	937																		
34	Asian Group	1937	10	100%	1%		8	2					10							
35	Commonwealth	1641																		
36	Communist Group	3310																		
37	Latin America	1674																		
38	Western Europe	5906																		
39	Intl Organs	1399																		
	TOTALS																			
40	All Data	236	10	100%			8	2					10							
41	UNTS Only		0																	
	COMPARISONS																			
42	Party Total					12%	80%	20%	40%	19%	7%	1%	100%	1%	27%	11%	13%	15%	4%	74%
43	Group Total					18%	25%	23%	29%	22%	25%	25%	71%	7%	8%	12%	6%	7%	12%	100%
44	World Total						23%	29%				20%								

Table 193 • 241

TREATY PROFILE OF UPPER VOLTA

Partners (1)	Partner's World Total (2)	Dyads Absolutes (3)	Ratios Self (4)	Ratios Other (5)	Time 1946-1950 (6)	Time 1951-1955 (7)	Time 1956-1960 (8)	Time 1961-1965 (9)	Admin & Dipl (10)	Social Coop (11)	Econ Coop (12)	Aid (13)	Milit (14)	UN (15)	Spec Ag's (16)	Intl Court (17)	Arbitration (18)	Other (19)	Self-Registered (20)
TOP THIRTY																			
1 France	1033	5	33%				1	4	2		2								
2 USA (United States)	2599	2	13%					2	2	1	1	1							
3 Germany, West	890	2	13%					2			1	1							
4 WHO (World Health)	187	1	7%	1%			1							1					
5 UN Special Fund	113	1	7%	1%				1	1			1				1			
6 United Nations	233	1	7%					1				1							
7 UNICEF (Children)	122	1	7%	1%			1					1							
8 Israel	232	1	7%					1									2		
9 Accept UN Charter	68	1	7%	1%			1		1					1					
10																			
11																			
12																			
13																			
14																			
15																			
16																			
17																			
18																			
19																			
20																			
21																			
22																			
23																			
24																			
25																			
26																			
27																			
28																			
29																			
30																			
31 All Others (0)																			
GROUPS																			
32 African Group	968																		
33 Arab Group	937																		
34 Asian Group	1937																		
35 Commonwealth	1641																		
36 Communist Group	3310																		
37 Latin America	1674																		
38 Western Europe	5906	7	47%				1	6	2	1	3	1							
39 Intl Organ.	1399	4	27%				2	2	1			3		1		1	2		
TOTALS																			
40 All Data	5477	15	100%				4	11	4	1	4	6		2		2	2		
41 UNTS Only		8																	
COMPARISONS																			
42 Party Total					1%	5%	27%	73%	27%	7%	27%	40%	4%	25%	13%	25%	25%	4%	1%
43 Group Total					18%	23%	18%	75%	22%	21%	18%	35%	7%	19%	12%	10%	15%	12%	
44 World Total					18%	23%	29%	29%	22%	25%	25%	20%	7%	8%	12%	6%	7%	12%	100%

TREATY PROFILE OF UPU (POSTAL UNION)

Table 194

	Partners (1)	Partner's World Total (2)	Dyads Abso-lutes (3)	Ratios Self (4)	Ratios Other (5)	Time 1946 1950 (6)	Time 1951 1955 (7)	Time 1956 1960 (8)	Time 1961 1965 (9)	Topics Admin & Dipl (10)	Topics Social Coop (11)	Topics Econ Coop (12)	Topics Aid (13)	Topics Milit (14)	Institutions UN (15)	Institutions Spec Ag's (16)	Institutions Intl Court (17)	Institutions Arbi-tration (18)	Institutions Other (19)	Self-Regis-tered (20)
	TOP THIRTY																			
1	Switzerland	426	1	50%		1				1										
2	United Nations	233	1	50%		1				1										
3																				
4																				
5																				
6																				
7																				
8																				
9																				
10																				
11																				
12																				
13																				
14																				
15																				
16																				
17																				
18																				
19																				
20																				
21																				
22																				
23																				
24																				
25																				
26																				
27																				
28																				
29																				
30																				
31	All Others (0)																			
	GROUPS																			
32	African Group	968																		
33	Arab Group	937																		
34	Asian Group	1937																		
35	Commonwealth	1641																		
36	Communist Group	3310																		
37	Latin America	1674																		
38	Western Europe	5906	1	50%		1				1										
39	Intl Organs	1399	1	50%		1				1										
	TOTALS																			
40	All Data	659	2	100%		2				2										
41	UNTS Only		1																	
	COMPARISONS																			
42	Party Total					100%				100%										
43	Group Total					12%	25%	23%	40%	19%	7%	1%	71%	1%	27%	11%	13%	15%	4%	74%
44	World Total					18%	23%	29%	29%	22%	25%	25%	20%	7%	8%	12%	6%	7%	12%	100%

Table 195 • 243

TREATY PROFILE OF URUGUAY

	Partners	Partner's World Total	Dyads Abso-lutes	Dyads Ratios Self	Dyads Ratios Other	Time 1946-1950	Time 1951-1955	Time 1956-1960	Time 1961-1965	Topics Admin & Dipl	Topics Social Coop	Topics Econ Coop	Topics Aid	Topics Milit	Institutions UN	Institutions Spec Ag's	Institutions Intl Court	Institutions Arbitration	Institutions Other	Self-Registered
	(1)	(2)	(3)	(4)	(5)	(6)	(7)	(8)	(9)	(10)	(11)	(12)	(13)	(14)	(15)	(16)	(17)	(18)	(19)	(20)
	TOP THIRTY																			
1	USA (United States)	2599	17	27%	1%	4	5	4	4	2	7	1	5	2	1	1			1	1
2	Spain	437	7	11%	2%		5	2				7								
3	IBRD (World Bank)	452	6	10%	1%	1	1	2	2				6					1		
4	Argentina	164	5	8%	3%	1		2	2	2	1	1	1			1				
5	USSR (Soviet Union)	1356	3	5%	1%		1	2				3								
6	Norway	461	3	5%			2	1	1	2	1					1				
7	Germany, West	890	3	5%	1%		2	1				2								
8	Denmark	380	3	5%			2			2		3								
9	UK Great Britain	981	2	3%		2						2								
10	Sweden	483	2	3%		1	1				1	1								
11	WHO (World Health)	187	1	2%	1%		1						1		1	1				
12	UN Special Fund	113	1	2%	1%				1				1					1		
13	United Nations	233	1	2%				1		1							1			
14	UNICEF (Children)	122	1	2%	1%				1				1							
15	ILO (Labor Org)	59	1	2%	2%		1		1		1									
16	IAEA (Atom Energy)	44	1	2%	2%				1	1										
17	Netherlands	548	1	2%		1					1									
18	Italy	755	1	2%		1					1	1								
19	Israel	232	1	2%				1												
20	France	1033	1	2%			1				1									
21	Taiwan	172	1	2%	1%				1											
22	Austria	445	1	2%					1	1										
31	All Others (0)																			
	GROUPS																			
32	African Group	968																		
33	Arab Group	937																		
34	Asian Group	1937	1	2%					1		1									
35	Commonwealth	1641	2	3%		2		2				2								
36	Communist Group	3310	3	5%			1	2	2			3								
37	Latin America	1674	5	8%		1		2	2	2	1	1	1							
38	Western Europe	5906	22	35%		3	12	5	2	3	4	15				2	2	3		
39	Intl Organs	1399	12	19%	1%	1	4	3	4	1			11		1	1				
	TOTALS																			
40	All Data	12146	63	100%		11	23	16	13	8	14	22	17	2	2	4	2	3	1	1
41	UNTS Only		43																	
	COMPARISONS																			
42	Party Total					17%	37%	25%	21%	13%	22%	35%	27%	3%	5%	9%	5%	7%	2%	2%
43	Group Total					18%	27%	24%	31%	16%	25%	18%	31%	9%	7%	10%	5%	6%	7%	6%
44	World Total					18%	23%	29%	29%	22%	25%	25%	20%	7%	8%	12%	6%	7%	12%	100%

TREATY PROFILE OF USA (UNITED STATES)

Partners	Partner's World Total	Dyads Abso-lutes	Ratios Self	Ratios Other	Time 1946-1950	Time 1951-1955	Time 1956-1960	Time 1961-1965	Topics Admin & Dipl	Topics Social Coop	Topics Econ Coop	Topics Aid	Topics Milit	Institutions UN	Institutions Spec Ag's	Institutions Intl Court	Institutions Arbi-tration	Institutions Other	Self-Registered
(1)	(2)	(3)	(4)	(5)	(6)	(7)	(8)	(9)	(10)	(11)	(12)	(13)	(14)	(15)	(16)	(17)	(18)	(19)	(20)
TOP THIRTY																			
1 Canada	310	113	4%	36%	30	29	23	31	31	35	15	2	30	1	5	1		25	104
2 UK Great Britain	981	104	4%	11%	28	30	17	29	16	24	12	19	33	4	11	1		12	66
3 Philippines	236	94	4%	40%	40	11	15	28	21	19	13	17	24	4	3			3	60
4 Japan	443	84	3%	19%	1	36	23	24	16	9	14	25	20	4	8	1	1	7	65
5 France	1033	79	3%	8%	40	14	19	6	8	12	17	14	28	5	9	2		6	78
6 Taiwan	172	70	3%	41%	21	12	21	16	5	8	6	29	22	2	3	3	1	2	45
7 Germany, West	890	67	3%	8%	1	34	24	8	11	13	11	8	24	3	6	2	1	16	66
8 Italy	755	63	2%	8%	17	22	14	10	9	7	7	21	19	4	5	3		8	58
9 Turkey	298	57	2%	19%	8	11	21	17	1	1	9	33	13	2	2	1		6	39
10 Yugoslavia	525	56	2%	11%	9	17	11	19	6	3	5	34	8	1	1			1	56
11 Greece	318	52	2%	16%	18	15	11	8	3	6	10	18	15	2	6	2		6	43
12 Brazil	195	52	2%	27%	16	14	7	15	3	13	5	20	11	2	2			8	52
13 Peru	109	47	2%	43%	10	12	15	10	2	11	3	19	12	1	6			3	47
14 Netherlands	548	47	2%	9%	17	18	8	4	7	3	11	9	17	6	3	3	1	10	25
15 Mexico	138	47	2%	34%	13	13	10	11	7	25	4	10	1		5	1	1	7	47
16 Colombia	112	44	2%	39%	8	13	10	13	2	12	6	17	7	2	2		1		44
17 Korea, South	80	43	2%	54%	10	8	15	10	2	7	3	17	12	9	2	5	1	2	43
18 Chile	119	43	2%	36%	6	18	13	6	4	8	8	21	7	1	7	1	1	2	43
19 Israel	232	40	2%	17%	3	17	6	14	5	7	4	21	3		2	1		1	31
20 India	299	40	2%	13%	7	7	11	15	2	9	5	18	6	2	5	1	1	2	40
21 Ecuador	97	40	2%	41%	10	10	11	9	3	10	1	17	9	1	1	1	1	3	40
22 Pakistan	245	37	1%	15%	4	14	12	7	4	5	4	16	8	2	5	1	1		31
23 Belgium	499	36	1%	7%	12	13	4	7	6	5	10	3	12	2	2	2	1		21
24 Spain	437	34	1%	8%	4	9	13	8	3	9	4	11	7	1	3	1		7	33
25 Panama	57	34	1%	60%	12	11	6	5	10	11	2	9	2		1			1	34
26 Bolivia	58	34	1%	59%	8	8	5	13		8	2	17	7	2	5		1	3	34
27 Australia	201	34	1%	17%	6	7	10	11	4	12	6	2	9	1	1	1		3	25
28 USSR (Soviet Union)	1356	33	1%	2%	8	7	10	8	13	13	1	2	4	2	5	1			14
29 United Arab Rep	232	33	1%	14%	5	12	8	8	1	11	3	16	2	1	4	1	1	4	33
30 Denmark	380	33	1%	9%	9	14	7	3	3	9	7	3	11		6	2		8	25
31 All Others (99)	9216	1009	39%	11%	194	287	219	309	115	172	138	404	180	64	77	40	22	76	966
GROUPS																			
32 African Group	968	140	5%	14%	7	25	15	93	13	18	24	69	16	13	4	9	4	11	140
33 Arab Group	937	149	6%	16%	9	69	35	36	8	25	5	97	14	10	11	4	3	9	148
34 Asian Group	1937	439	17%	23%	105	92	122	120	52	75	45	174	93	29	27	15	5	16	361
35 Commonwealth	1641	281	11%	17%	76	71	58	76	57	77	39	29	79	8	27	3	1	42	219
36 Communist Group	3310	70	3%	2%	22	8	20	20	22	21	7	11	9	2	6			1	50
37 Latin America	1674	627	24%	37%	145	200	135	147	60	162	57	221	127	16	29	11	12	45	623
38 Western Europe	5906	686	26%	12%	194	203	169	120	76	97	138	181	194	41	81	30	9	98	598
39 Intl Organs	1399	26	1%	2%	3	5	5	13	8	3	4	11		3	5	1	2	2	17
TOTALS																			
40 All Data	20571	2599	100%		575	743	599	682	324	497	342	873	563	127	208	76	38	233	2308
41 UNTS Only		2490																	
COMPARISONS																			
42 Party Total					22%	29%	23%	26%	12%	19%	13%	34%	22%	5%	8%	3%	2%	9%	93%
43 Group Total					18%	23%	29%	29%	22%	25%	25%	20%	7%	8%	12%	6%	7%	12%	
44 World Total																			100%

Table 197 • 245

TREATY PROFILE OF USSR (SOVIET UNION)

	Partners	Partner's World Total	Dyads Absolutes	Dyads Ratios Self	Dyads Ratios Other	Time 1946-1950	Time 1951-1955	Time 1956-1960	Time 1961-1965	Topics Admin & Dipl	Topics Social Coop	Topics Econ Coop	Topics Aid	Topics Milit	Institutions UN	Institutions Spec Ag's	Institutions Intl Court	Institutions Arbitration	Other	Self-Registered
	(1)	(2)	(3)	(4)	(5)	(6)	(7)	(8)	(9)	(10)	(11)	(12)	(13)	(14)	(15)	(16)	(17)	(18)	(19)	(20)
	TOP THIRTY																			
1	China People's Rep	766	108	8%	14%	27	35	32	14	29	36	21	18	4	1				2	11
2	Poland	493	84	6%	17%	21	9	36	18	22	20	14	24	4	1				8	6
3	Romania	251	75	6%	30%	26	13	31	5	24	15	18	14	4					2	8
4	Germany, East	556	75	6%	13%	7	23	32	13	19	22	15	12	7	1				3	10
5	Mongolia	119	61	4%	51%	9	15	32	5	14	16	7	23	1					1	6
6	Hungary	290	60	4%	21%	21	7	24	8	15	13	14	9	6					3	7
7	Czechoslovakia	393	48	4%	12%	14	4	23	7	9	10	16	10					1		7
8	Bulgaria	236	48	4%	20%	12	4	26	6	6	13	12	18	2					1	8
9	Finland	245	43	3%	18%	20	6	10	7	19	7	10	4	3					4	10
10	Yugoslavia	525	40	3%	8%	11	13	14	2	8	13	13	5	1	1				2	7
11	Korea, North	99	38	3%	38%	4	8	22	4	7	9	8	13	1				1	1	7
12	USA (United States)	2599	33	2%	1%	8	7	10	8	13	13	1	2	4		4				3
13	Norway	461	30	2%	7%	9	2	12	7	16	6	7		1					5	2
14	India	299	29	2%	10%	1	5	17	6	5	5	7	12						1	3
15	Albania	125	28	2%	22%	5	4	18	1	4	6	9	9						1	5
16	United Arab Rep	232	27	2%	12%	1	6	15	5	3	6	11	7						1	5
17	Vietnam, North	81	26	2%	32%	1	5	16	4	2	5	7	12							3
18	Iran	170	25	2%	15%	3	6	12	4	13	3	8	1					1		2
19	Indonesia	126	25	2%	20%	2	1	14	8	4	5	4	11						2	2
20	Cuba	111	25	2%	23%			11	14	3	6	8	8	1					1	5
21	Afghanistan	83	24	2%	29%	3	3	14	4	5	6	3	10						1	3
22	UK Great Britain	981	20	1%	2%	3	1	7	9	5	10	4	1							2
23	Italy	755	19	1%	3%	6		9	4	6	2	10		1	1				1	4
24	Japan	443	18	1%	4%	1		15	2	8	3	7								2
25	Austria	445	18	1%	4%	1	12	5		7	4	5	1	1						5
26	Sweden	483	17	1%	4%		2	4	1	2	6	8	1							1
27	Ghana	81	17	1%	21%			5	12	3	5	9	3							5
28	France	1033	16	1%	2%	1	3	9	3		2	11								3
29	Denmark	380	16	1%	4%	5	3	6	2	5	4	7								2
30	Guinea	75	14	1%	19%			10	4	2	2	2	8							2
31	All Others (54)	6531	249	18%	4%	19	24	105	101	76	33	92	47	1	2	2			5	53
	GROUPS																			
32	African Group	968	87	6%	9%	1	11	29	58	25	13	28	21	1					2	24
33	Arab Group	937	82	6%	9%	1	16	46	24	18	12	30	21	1	2				1	19
34	Asian Group	1937	152	11%	8%	12	16	85	39	38	24	37	52						6	17
35	Commonwealth	1641	31	2%	2%	5	2	12	12	10	12	8	1			1				4
36	Communist Group	3310	651	48%	20%	147	127	292	85	151	168	141	162	29	3			3	23	78
37	Latin America	1674	43	3%	3%	1	4	16	22	7	7	18	11						2	8
38	Western Europe	5906	211	16%	4%	63	38	76	34	70	44	84	7	6	1	1		1	10	35
39	Intl Organs	1399	2					1	1	1			1							
	TOTALS																			
40	All Data	19467	1356	100%		251	221	596	288	354	309	368	283	42	7	6		4	46	197
41	UNTS Only		305																	
	COMPARISONS																			
42	Party Total					19%	16%	44%	21%	26%	23%	27%	21%	3%	2%	2%		1%	15%	65%
43	Group Total					16%	17%	38%	29%	20%	32%	32%	13%	2%	4%	4%	.	3%	17%	33%
44	World Total					18%	23%	29%	29%	22%	25%	25%	20%	7%	8%	12%	6%	7%	12%	100%

246 • Table 198

TREATY PROFILE OF VATICAN/HOLY SEE

Partners	Partner's World Total	Dyads Absolutes	Dyads Ratios Self	Dyads Ratios Other	Time 1946-1950	Time 1951-1955	Time 1956-1960	Time 1961-1965	Admin & Dipl	Social Coop	Econ Coop	Aid	Milit	UN	Spec Ag's	Intl Court	Arbitration	Other	Self-Registered
(1)	(2)	(3)	(4)	(5)	(6)	(7)	(8)	(9)	(10)	(11)	(12)	(13)	(14)	(15)	(16)	(17)	(18)	(19)	(20)
TOP THIRTY																			
1 Italy	755	6	38%	1%	3	2			3	1	2								
2 Spain	437	5	31%	1%	2	1		1	3	2									
3 Austria	445	4	25%	1%		1	1	1	2	1	1								
4 Philippines	236	1	6%				2	2					1						
5																			
6																			
7																			
8																			
9																			
10																			
11																			
12																			
13																			
14																			
15																			
16																			
17																			
18																			
19																			
20																			
21																			
22																			
23																			
24																			
25																			
26																			
27																			
28																			
29																			
30																			
31 All Others (0)																			
GROUPS																			
32 African Group	968																		
33 Arab Group	937																		
34 Asian Group	1937	1	6%			1							1						
35 Commonwealth	1641																		
36 Communist Group	3310																		
37 Latin America	1674																		
38 Western Europe	5906	15	94%		5	3	3	4	8	4	3								
39 Intl Organs	1399																		
TOTALS																			
40 All Data	1873	16	100%		5	4	3	4	8	4	3		1						
41 UNTS Only		2																		
COMPARISONS																			
42 Party Total					31%	25%	19%	25%	50%	25%	19%		6%	4%	14%	6%	8%	17%	
43 Group Total					22%	25%	27%	26%	24%	26%	32%	10%	8%	8%	12%	6%	7%	17%	32%
44 World Total					18%	23%	29%	29%	22%	25%	25%	20%	7%	8%	12%	6%	7%	12%	100%

Table 199 • 247

TREATY PROFILE OF VENEZUELA

Partners (1)	Partner's World Total (2)	Dyads Absolutes (3)	Ratios Self (4)	Ratios Other (5)	Time 1946-1950 (6)	Time 1951-1955 (7)	Time 1956-1960 (8)	Time 1961-1965 (9)	Admin & Dipl (10)	Social Coop (11)	Econ Coop (12)	Aid (13)	Milit (14)	UN (15)	Spec Ag's (16)	Intl Court (17)	Arbitration (18)	Other (19)	Self-Registered (20)
TOP THIRTY																			
1 USA (United States)	2599	21	45%	1%	6	7	5	3	2	5	2	7	5		2	1	1		
2 IBRD (World Bank)	452	5	11%	1%				5				5							
3 Canada	310	3	6%	1%	1		1	1	1	1	1								
4 United Nations	233	2	4%	1%		1	1		1	1		1							
5 Norway	461	2	4%				2		1	1	1								
6 Netherlands	548	2	4%			1	1		1	1									
7 UK Great Britain	981	1	2%			1			1		1								
8 Switzerland	426	1	2%				1												
9 Sweden	483	1	2%						1										
10 WHO (World Health)	187	1	2%	1%	1											1			
11 UN Special Fund	113	1	2%	1%				1				1		1					
12 ILO (Labor Org)	59	1	2%	2%		1				1				1	1				
13 Portugal	131	1	2%	1%	1														
14 Mexico	138	1	2%	1%			1			1									
15 Italy	755	1	2%		1					1									
16 France	1033	1	2%		1			1	1		1								
17 Brazil	195	1	2%	1%															
18 Belgium	499	1	2%																
19																			
20-30																			
31 All Others (0)																			
GROUPS																			
32 African Group	968																		
33 Arab Group	937																		
34 Asian Group	1937																		
35 Commonwealth	1641	4	9%		1		2	1	2	1	1								
36 Communist Group	3310																		
37 Latin America	1674	2	4%		2				1	1									
38 Western Europe	5906	10	21%		1	2	5	2	3	4	3								
39 Intl Organs	1399	10	21%	1%	1	2	1	6	1			9		2	1	1			
TOTALS																			
40 All Data	9603	47	100%		11	11	13	12	9	11	6	16	5	2	3	2	1		
41 UNTS Only		41																		
COMPARISONS																			
42 Party Total					23%	23%	28%	26%	19%	23%	13%	34%	11%	5%	7%	5%	2%	7%	
43 Group Total					18%	27%	24%	31%	16%	25%	18%	31%	9%	7%	10%	5%	6%	7%	6%
44 World Total					18%	23%	29%	29%	22%	25%	25%	20%	7%	8%	12%	6%	7%	12%	100%

TREATY PROFILE OF VIETNAM, NORTH

Table 200

	Partners (1)	Partner's World Total (2)	Dyads Absolutes (3)	Ratios Self (4)	Ratios Other (5)	Time 1946-1950 (6)	Time 1951-1955 (7)	Time 1956-1960 (8)	Time 1961-1965 (9)	Admin & Dipl (10)	Social Coop (11)	Econ Coop (12)	Aid (13)	Milit (14)	UN (15)	Spec Ag's (16)	Intl Court (17)	Arbitration (18)	Other (19)	Self-Registered (20)
	TOP THIRTY																			
1	China People's Rep	766	38	47%	5%		9	14	15	1	20	13	4							
2	USSR (Soviet Union)	1356	26	32%	2%		5	16	4	2	5	7	12					1		
3	Germany, East	556	10	12%	2%			8	2	1	4	4	1						1	
4	Poland	493	4	5%	1%			4			4								1	
5	Romania	251	2	2%	1%			2			2									
6	Czechoslovakia	393	1	1%		1			1	1										
7																				
8–29																				
30																				
31	All Others (0)																			
	GROUPS																			
32	African Group	968																		
33	Arab Group	937																		
34	Asian Group	1937																		
35	Commonwealth	1641																		
36	Communist Group	3310	81	100%	2%	1	14	44	22	5	35	24	17					1	2	
37	Latin America	1674																		
38	Western Europe	5906																		
39	Intl Organs	1399																		
	TOTALS																			
40	All Data	3815	81	100%		1	14	44	22	5	35	24	17					1	2	
41	UNTS Only		7																	
	COMPARISONS																			
42	Party Total					1%	17%	54%	27%	6%	43%	30%	21%	2%	4%	4%		14%	29%	
43	Group Total					16%	17%	38%	29%	20%	32%	32%	13%	7%	8%	12%	6%	3%	17%	33%
44	World Total					18%	23%	29%	29%	22%	25%	25%	20%					7%	12%	100%

Table 201 • 249

TREATY PROFILE OF VIETNAM, SOUTH

Part-ners (1)	Partner's World Total (2)	Dyads Abso-lutes (3)	Ratios Self (4)	Ratios Other (5)	Time 1946-1950 (6)	Time 1951-1955 (7)	Time 1956-1960 (8)	Time 1961-1965 (9)	Topics Admin & Dipl (10)	Topics Social Coop (11)	Topics Econ Coop (12)	Topics Aid (13)	Topics Milit (14)	Institutions UN (15)	Institutions Spec Ag's (16)	Institutions Intl Court (17)	Institutions Arbi-tration (18)	Institutions Other (19)	Self-Regis-tered (20)
TOP THIRTY																			
1 France	1033	38	36%	4%	4	19	9	6	11	14	6	2	5						
2 USA (United States)	2599	28	26%	1%		9	6	13	4	2	3	16	3		2	2			
3 Japan	443	5	5%	1%		1	3	1	2		1	2	1			1			
4 Germany, West	890	5	5%	1%		1	1	3	2	1		3							
5 Laos	28	3	3%	11%		1	2		1		1								
6 UK Great Britain	981	2	2%			1		1			1								
7 WHO (World Health)	187	2	2%	1%		1	1			1		1		1	1	1			
8 UN Special Fund	113	2	2%	2%			2					2		1	1				
9 United Nations	233	2	2%	1%			1		1			1							
10 Netherlands	548	2	2%			1					2								
11 Korea, South	80	2	2%	3%		2					1							2	
12 Canada	310	2	2%	1%			1	2				2	1						
13 Cambodia	55	2	2%	4%		2		1		1	1								
14 Australia	201	2	2%	1%		2			2										
15 UNICEF (Children)	122	1	1%	1%		1						1		1	1				
16 ILO (Labor Org)	59	1	1%	2%		1		1			1	1							
17 FAO (Food Agri)	19	1	1%	5%		1													
18 Philippines	236	1	1%				1		1										
19 Italy	755	1	1%			1					1								
20 Israel	232	1	1%	1%				1			1								
21 Ireland	103	1	1%			1											1		
22 Belgium	499	1	1%			1													
23 ICJ Option Clause	62	1	1%	2%		1			1							1			

GROUPS																			
32 African Group	968																		
33 Arab Group	937																		
34 Asian Group	1937	8	8%			3	3	2	3	2	2								
35 Commonwealth	1641	6	6%			3	1	2	3		1	2	1						
36 Communist Group	3310																		
37 Latin America	1674																		
38 Western Europe	5906	48	45%	1%	4	24	10	10	11	15	12	5	5	4	1	2	2		
39 Intl Organs	1399	9	8%	1%		5	4	1	1	1		7							

TOTALS																			
40 All Data	9788	106	100%		4	46	27	29	25	20	19	32	10	4	3	6	2	1	
41 UNTS Only		40																	

COMPARISONS																			
42 Party Total					4%	43%	25%	27%	24%	19%	18%	30%	9%	10%	8%	15%	5%	3%	16%
43 Group Total					16%	23%	31%	30%	21%	23%	20%	30%	7%	10%	15%	8%	8%	6%	100%
44 World Total					18%	23%	29%	29%	22%	25%	25%	20%	7%	8%	12%	6%	7%	12%	

TREATY PROFILE OF WESTERN SAMOA

Partners (1)	Partner's World Total (2)	Dyads Absolutes (3)	Dyads Ratios Self (4)	Dyads Ratios Other (5)	Time 1946-1950 (6)	Time 1951-1955 (7)	Time 1956-1960 (8)	Time 1961-1965 (9)	Admin & Dipl (10)	Social Coop (11)	Econ Coop (12)	Aid (13)	Milit (14)	UN (15)	Spec Ag's (16)	Intl Court (17)	Arbitration (18)	Other (19)	Self-Registered (20)
TOP THIRTY																			
1 New Zealand	101	5	50%	5%				5	2	2		1							
2 USSR (Soviet Union)	1356	1	10%					1	1	1									1
3 USA (United States)	2599	1	10%					1											
4 WHO (World Health)	187	1	10%	1%				1				1			1	1	1		
5 UN Special Fund	113	1	10%	1%				1				1							
6 United Nations	233	1	10%					1				1		1			2		
7																			
8																			
9																			
10																			
11																			
12																			
13																			
14																			
15																			
16																			
17																			
18																			
19																			
20																			
21																			
22																			
23																			
24																			
25																			
26																			
27																			
28																			
29																			
30																			
31 All Others (0)																			
GROUPS																			
32 African Group	968																		
33 Arab Group	937																		
34 Asian Group	1937																		
35 Commonwealth	1641	5	50%					5	2	2		1							
36 Communist Group	3310	1	10%					1	1										
37 Latin America	1674																		
38 Western Europe	5906																		
39 Intl Organs	1399	3	30%					3				3		1	1	1	3		
TOTALS																			
40 All Data	4589	10	100%					10	3	3		4		1	1	1	3		1
41 UNTS Only		9																		
COMPARISONS																			
42 Party Total					16%	23%	31%	100%	30%	30%		40%		11%	11%	11%	33%		11%
43 Group Total					18%	23%	29%	30%	21%	23%	20%	30%	7%	10%	15%	8%	8%	6%	16%
44 World Total					18%	23%	29%	29%	22%	25%	25%	20%	7%	8%	12%	6%	7%	12%	100%

TREATY PROFILE OF WEU (WEST EUROPE)

Table 203 • 251

	Partners (1)	Partner's World Total (2)	Dyads Absolutes (3)	Ratios Self (4)	Ratios Other (5)	Time 1946-1950 (6)	Time 1951-1955 (7)	Time 1956-1960 (8)	Time 1961-1965 (9)	Topics Admin & Dipl (10)	Topics Social Coop (11)	Topics Econ Coop (12)	Topics Aid (13)	Topics Milit (14)	Institutions UN (15)	Institutions Spec Ag's (16)	Institutions Intl Court (17)	Institutions Arbitration (18)	Institutions Other (19)	Self-Registered (20)
	TOP THIRTY																			
1	France	1033	1	100%				1			1									
2-30																				
31	All Others (0)																			
	GROUPS																			
32	African Group	968																		
33	Arab Group	937																		
34	Asian Group	1937																		
35	Commonwealth	1641																		
36	Communist Group	3310																		
37	Latin America	1674																		
38	Western Europe	5906	1	100%				1			1									
39	Intl Organs	1399																		
	TOTALS																			
40	All Data	1033	1	100%																
41	UNTS Only		0																		
	COMPARISONS																			
42	Party Total							100%			100%									
43	Group Total					12%	25%	23%	40%	19%	7%	1%	71%	1%	27%	11%	13%	15%	4%	74%
44	World Total					18%	23%	29%	29%	22%	25%	25%	20%	7%	8%	12%	6%	7%	12%	100%

252 • Table 204

TREATY PROFILE OF WHO (WORLD HEALTH)

	Partners	Partner's World Total	Dyads Absolutes	Dyads Ratios Self	Dyads Ratios Other	Time 1946-1950	Time 1951-1955	Time 1956-1960	Time 1961-1965	Topics Admin & Dipl	Topics Social Coop	Topics Econ Coop	Topics Aid	Topics Milit	Institutions UN	Institutions Spec Ag's	Institutions Intl Court	Institutions Arbitration	Institutions Other	Self-Registered
(1)		(2)	(3)	(4)	(5)	(6)	(7)	(8)	(9)	(10)	(11)	(12)	(13)	(14)	(15)	(16)	(17)	(18)	(19)	(20)
	TOP THIRTY																			
1	India	299	15	8%	5%	1	14				6		8		7		5	4	1	14
2	Burma	102	9	5%	9%		8	1			7		2		2	2	3	2	1	9
3	Denmark	380	6	3%	2%		5	1		1	5				3		1			5
4	Ceylon (Sri Lanka)	123	5	3%	4%	1	3	1		1	2		3		1					5
5	Philippines	236	4	2%	2%	1	3						3			2	2			2
6	Jordan	65	4	2%	6%			1		1			4		1		1			4
7	Ethiopia	98	4	2%	4%		1	1	2				3		3	2		1		4
8	Chile	119	4	2%	3%		4			1	3		1		3		1	3		4
9	United Arab Rep	232	3	2%	1%	1	1	1		2					3	2				2
10	Thailand	132	3	2%	2%	1	2				3									3
11	United Nations	233	3	2%	1%	3				3							1		1	
12	Pakistan	245	3	2%	1%		2	1		1	1		2		2	2				3
13	Mexico	138	3	2%	2%		3						2		3					3
14	Lebanon	75	3	2%	4%		2	1			1		2		2	1		1		3
15	Guatemala	50	3	2%	6%	1		1	1	1	3				3					3
16	France	1033	3	2%			3						2				2		1	3
17	Costa Rica	51	3	2%	6%		3				3		2		1	1	1	1	2	3
18	Colombia	112	3	2%	3%		3			1	1				1	1			1	3
19	Taiwan	172	3	2%	2%		3				2		1		1					3
20	Vietnam, South	106	2	1%	2%		1	1			1		1		1		1			1
21	Tunisia	97	2	1%	2%			1	1	1			2		1					2
22	Syria	84	2	1%	2%		1		1				2							2
23	Sudan	37	2	1%	5%			1	1				2		2					2
24	Somalia	37	2	1%	5%				2	1			1					2		2
25	Sierra Leone	27	2	1%	7%				2	1								2		2
26	Saudi Arabia	31	2	1%	6%			1					2		2					2
27	Rwanda	14	2	1%	14%				2				2							2
28	Peru	109	2	1%	2%	2					1		1		1	1	1		1	2
29	Nicaragua	50	2	1%	4%	1	1				1		1		2	1	1	1	1	2
30	Malawi	11	2	1%	18%				2				2							2
31	All Others (68)	7934	81	43%	1%	13	28	14	26	7	11		63		40	4	13	6	4	76
	GROUPS																			
32	African Group	968	33	18%	3%	1	2	6	25	4			29		14	2	1	7		33
33	Arab Group	937	26	14%	3%	1	10	7	8	3	1		22		16	2	3	4		25
34	Asian Group	1937	58	31%	3%	5	42	9	2	3	22		33		19	4	13	6	2	53
35	Commonwealth	1641	1	1%			1						1		1					
36	Communist Group	3310	2	1%					2				2							2
37	Latin America	1674	37	20%	2%	8	27		2	3	21		16		16	10	8	3	9	37
38	Western Europe	5906	16	9%		3	12	1			5		8		8	1	5	2	1	15
39	Intl Organs	1399	10	5%	1%	8		2		8	2				5	2	1	1	1	4
	TOTALS																			
40	All Data	12432	187	100%		25	97	26	39	21	51		115		82	19	31	23	13	173
41	UNTS Only		183											1%					1%	
	COMPARISONS																			
42	Party Total					13%	52%	14%	21%	11%	27%	1%	61%		45%	10%	17%	13%	7%	95%
43	Group Total					12%	25%	23%	40%	19%	7%	1%	71%	1%	27%	11%	13%	15%	4%	74%
44	World Total					18%	23%	29%	29%	22%	25%	25%	20%	7%	8%	12%	6%	7%	12%	100%

Table 205 • 253

TREATY PROFILE OF WMO (METEOROLOGY)

Partners (1)	Partner's World Total (2)	Dyads Absolutes (3)	Ratios Self (4)	Ratios Other (5)	Time 1946-1950 (6)	Time 1951-1955 (7)	Time 1956-1960 (8)	Time 1961-1965 (9)	Topics Admin & Dipl (10)	Topics Social Coop (11)	Topics Econ Coop (12)	Topics Aid (13)	Topics Milit (14)	Institutions UN (15)	Institutions Spec Ag's (16)	Institutions Intl Court (17)	Institutions Arbitration (18)	Institutions Other (19)	Self-Registered (20)
TOP THIRTY																			
1 United Nations	233	2	33%	1%		2			2					1		1			
2 UK Great Britain	981	1	17%			1		1				1					1		
3 Switzerland	426	1	17%	1%			1		1					1	1				1
4 UN Special Fund	113	1	17%	1%			1		1					1					
5 IAEA (Atom Energy)	44	1	17%	2%					1					1					1
6																			
7																			
8																			
9																			
10																			
11																			
12																			
13																			
14																			
15																			
16																			
17																			
18																			
19																			
20																			
21																			
22																			
23																			
24																			
25																			
26																			
27																			
28																			
29																			
30																			
31 All Others (0)																			
GROUPS																			
32 African Group	968																		
33 Arab Group	937																		
34 Asian Group	1937																		
35 Commonwealth	1641	1	17%					1				1							
36 Communist Group	3310																		
37 Latin America	1674																		
38 Western Europe	5906	1	17%			1			1					1		1	1	1	1
39 Intl Organs	1399	4	67%			2	2		4					3	1	1			1
TOTALS																			
40 All Data	1797	6	100%			3	2	1	5			1		4	1	2	1		2
41 UNTS Only		6																		
COMPARISONS																			
42 Party Total					12%	50%	33%	17%	83%			17%		67%	17%	33%	17%		33%
43 Group Total					18%	25%	23%	40%	19%	7%	1%	71%	1%	27%	11%	13%	15%	4%	74%
44 World Total					18%	23%	29%	29%	22%	25%	25%	20%	7%	8%	12%	6%	7%	12%	100%

254 • Table 206

TREATY PROFILE OF YEMEN

Partners (1)	Partner's World Total (2)	Dyads Absolutes (3)	Dyads Ratios Self (4)	Dyads Ratios Other (5)	Time 1946 1950 (6)	Time 1951 1955 (7)	Time 1956 1960 (8)	Time 1961 1965 (9)	Topics Admin & Dipl (10)	Topics Social Coop (11)	Topics Econ Coop (12)	Topics Aid (13)	Topics Milit (14)	Institutions UN (15)	Institutions Spec Ag's (16)	Institutions Intl Court (17)	Institutions Arbitration (18)	Institutions Other (19)	Self-Registered (20)
TOP THIRTY																			
1 USSR (Soviet Union)	1356	10	29%	1%		1	5	4	3		3	4		1					
2 China People's Rep	766	7	20%	1%			3	4	2	3	1	1							
3 USA (United States)	2599	2	6%		1		1		1		1	1							
4 Italy	755	2	6%				1	1	1		1								
5 Bulgaria	236	2	6%	1%			1	2	1	1									
6 UK Great Britain	981	1	3%			1			1					1				1	
7 Turkey	298	1	3%			1			1										
8 Spain	437	1	3%			1			1										
9 WHO (World Health)	187	1	3%	1%			1					1		1					
10 UN Special Fund	113	1	3%	1%				1				1							
11 United Nations	233	1	3%			1			1					1					
12 UNICEF (Children)	122	1	3%	1%				1	1					1					
13 Japan	443	1	3%					1											
14 Hungary	290	1	3%				1		1										
15 Germany, West	890	1	3%					1	1										
16 Germany, East	556	1	3%			1		1	1										
17 Accept UN Charter	68	1	3%	1%	1									1					
18																			
19																			
20																			
21																			
22																			
23																			
24																			
25																			
26																			
27																			
28																			
29																			
30																			
31 All Others (0)																			
GROUPS																			
32 African Group	968																		
33 Arab Group	937																		
34 Asian Group	1937																		
35 Commonwealth	1641	1	3%			1			1					1					
36 Communist Group	3310	21	60%	1%		1	8	12	8	4	4	5		1				1	
37 Latin America	1674																		
38 Western Europe	5906	5	14%			3	1	1	4		1					1			
39 Intl Organs	1399	4	11%			1	1	2		4		4		2		1			
TOTALS																			
40 All Data	10330	35	100%		2	7	11	15	15	4	6	10		5		1		1	
41 UNTS Only		14																	
COMPARISONS																			
42 Party Total					6%	20%	31%	43%	43%	11%	17%	29%	4%	36%	20%	7%	15%	7%	5%
43 Group Total					9%	24%	31%	36%	18%	27%	22%	29%	7%	15%	12%	8%	7%	9%	5%
44 World Total					18%	23%	29%	29%	22%	25%	25%	20%		8%	12%	6%		12%	100%

Table 207 • 255

TREATY PROFILE OF YUGOSLAVIA

	Partners (1)	Partner's World Total (2)	Dyads Absolutes (3)	Ratios Self (4)	Ratios Other (5)	Time 1946-1950 (6)	Time 1951-1955 (7)	Time 1956-1960 (8)	Time 1961-1965 (9)	Topics Admin & Dipl (10)	Topics Social Coop (11)	Topics Econ Coop (12)	Topics Aid (13)	Topics Milit (14)	Institutions UN (15)	Institutions Spec Ag's (16)	Institutions Intl Court (17)	Institutions Arbitration (18)	Institutions Other (19)	Self-Registered (20)
	TOP THIRTY																			
1	USA (United States)	2599	56	11%	2%	9	17	11	19	6	3	5	34	8	1	3			1	
2	USSR (Soviet Union)	1356	40	8%	3%	11	13	14	2	8	13	13	5	1					2	9
3	Italy	755	38	7%	5%	11	6	13	8	16	8	9		5		1		1	6	10
4	Austria	445	31	6%	7%		10	7	14	20	9	2			2	1	1	1	3	6
5	Albania	125	30	6%	24%	23		7		3	9	7							9	30
6	Poland	493	28	5%	6%	12	2	12	2	3	12	10	11	1	1	1		1	7	10
7	UK Great Britain	981	26	5%	3%	6	6	5	9	3	8	9	2	2		1	2			
8	Czechoslovakia	393	25	5%	6%	12		7	6	3	9	9	4	1	1	1		1	8	15
9	Bulgaria	236	25	5%	11%		9	15		6	13	4			1				9	25
10	Hungary	290	24	5%	8%	1		5	6	8	7	7	1	5		1		4	7	13
11	China People's Rep	766	21	4%	3%	13		16	5	3	8	10			1					
12	Greece	318	18	3%	6%		3	13	2	8	7	3				1	1	2	8	12
13	Romania	251	17	3%	7%	7		6	4	5	9	2	1			1		2	5	8
14	Germany, West	890	16	3%	2%		5	9	2	4	3	8	1					1		
15	Germany, East	556	16	3%	3%			5	11	4	6	6				1	1			
16	Sweden	483	11	2%	2%	6	3	2		1	2	8				1	1	1	1	
17	Norway	461	9	2%	2%	2	2	3	2	1	5	6					1			
18	France	1033	9	2%	1%	2	1	2	5		2	4				1	1	1	1	
19	Turkey	298	8	2%	3%	3	3	2			5	6							1	
20	Switzerland	426	8	2%	2%	3	1	1	3	8	3	4	1			1		1	1	1
21	IBRD (World Bank)	452	8	2%	2%	1	2		5	5			8			1				5
22	Netherlands	548	6	1%	1%	1		3	2	4		3								
23	Burma	102	5	1%	5%		2	3				2	3						1	
24	United Nations	233	4	1%	2%		2	1	1	1	2		2	1	1		1	1		
25	IAEA (Atom Energy)	44	4	1%	9%				4				2				2			
26	Israel	232	4	1%	2%		1	2	1		2	3					1		1	2
27	Denmark	380	4	1%	1%	1	1	1	1	1	1	1	1			1	1		1	1
28	Australia	201	4	1%	2%	2	1	1		2	1	1								
29	Mexico	138	3	1%	2%	1		1	1	1	1	2								
30	Belgium	499	3	1%	1%		1	1	1		3								3	
31	All Others (19)	3001	24	5%	1%	2	9	7	6	2	5	10	5	2	6	2	2	5	1	6
	GROUPS																			
32	African Group	968	2		1%		1	1			2	1	1		1					2
33	Arab Group	937	2		1%		2				2				1					
34	Asian Group	1937	11	2%	2%		5	5	1		9	6	3			2		2	2	8
35	Commonwealth	1641	33	6%	2%	9	8	7	9	4	9	11	5	4	1	2	2	1		
36	Communist Group	3310	226	43%	7%	79	24	87	36	44	86	68	20	8	3	1		7	47	110
37	Latin America	1674	5	1%		1		1	3		1	4								1
38	Western Europe	5906	163	31%	3%	29	36	57	41	53	48	55	2	5	2	11	7	11	23	30
39	Intl Organs	1399	21	4%	2%	2	6	2	11	2	2		16	1	4	1	4	4		
	TOTALS																			
40	All Data	18985	525	100%		129	100	174	122	111	153	154	81	26	13	18	14	26	74	153
41	UNTS Only		356																	
	COMPARISONS																			
42	Party Total					25%	19%	33%	23%	21%	29%	29%	15%	5%	4%	5%	5%	7%	21%	43%
43	Group Total					18%	23%	29%	29%	22%	25%	25%	20%	7%	8%	12%	6%	7%	12%	100%
44	World Total																			

256 • Table 208

TREATY PROFILE OF ZAMBIA

	Partners	Partner's World Total	Dyads Abso-lutes	Ratios Self	Ratios Other	Time 1946-1950	Time 1951-1955	Time 1956-1960	Time 1961-1965	Topics Admin & Dipl	Topics Social Coop	Topics Econ Coop	Topics Aid	Topics Milit	Institutions UN	Institutions Spec Ag's	Institutions Intl Court	Institutions Arbi-tration	Institutions Other	Self-Regis-tered
	(1)	(2)	(3)	(4)	(5)	(6)	(7)	(8)	(9)	(10)	(11)	(12)	(13)	(14)	(15)	(16)	(17)	(18)	(19)	(20)
	TOP THIRTY																			
1	UN Special Fund	113	2	22%	2%				2	1			1		1		1	1		
2	UK Great Britain	981	1	11%					1	1										1
3	United Nations	233	1	11%					1	1					1					
4	Norway	461	1	11%					1											
5	Netherlands	548	1	11%					1		1	1								
6	Japan	443	1	11%					1			1	1							
7	Denmark	380	1	11%					1											
8	Accept UN Charter	68	1	11%	1%					1					1					
9																				
10																				
11																				
12																				
13																				
14																				
15																				
16																				
17																				
18																				
19																				
20																				
21																				
22																				
23																				
24																				
25																				
26																				
27																				
28																				
29																				
30																				
31	All Others (0)																			
	GROUPS																			
32	African Group	968																		
33	Arab Group	937																		
34	Asian Group	1937																		
35	Commonwealth	1641	1	11%					1											1
36	Communist Group	3310																		
37	Latin America	1674																		
38	Western Europe	5906	3	33%					3		1	1	1		2		1	1		
39	Intl Organs	1399	3	33%					3	2										
	TOTALS																			
40	All Data	3227	9	100%					9	3	2	2	2		3		1	1		1
41	UNTS Only		7																	
	COMPARISONS																			
42	Party Total					1%	5%	18%	100%	33%	22%	22%	22%		43%		14%	14%		14%
43	Group Total					1%	23%	29%	75%	22%	21%	18%	35%	4%	19%	13%	10%	15%	4%	1%
44	World Total					18%	29%	29%	29%	22%	25%	25%	20%	7%	8%	12%	6%	7%	12%	100%

Designed by Jack Swartz
Composed by Camera-ready Composition
Printed and bound by Halliday Lithograph Corporation
in the United States of America

FEB 17 1977